T0356263

Get the eBook FREE!

(PDF, ePub, Kindle, and liveBook all included)

We believe that once you buy a book from us, you should be able to read it in any format we have available. To get electronic versions of this book at no additional cost to you, purchase and then register this book at the Manning website.

Go to https://www.manning.com/freebook and follow the instructions to complete your pBook registration.

That's it!
Thanks from Manning!

The Well-Grounded Data Analyst

SOLVE MESSY DATA PROBLEMS LIKE A PRO

DAVID ASBOTH

FOREWORD BY REUVEN M LERNER

MANNING

SHELTER ISLAND

Manning Publications Co.
20 Baldwin Road
PO Box 761
Shelter Island, NY 11964

Development editor:	Sarah G Harter
Technical editor:	Brent J Broadnax
Review editor:	Kishor Rit
Production editor:	Kathy Rossland
Copy editor:	Lana Todorovic-Arndt
Proofreader:	Katie Tennant
Technical proofreader:	Andrew R Freed
Typesetter:	Dennis Dalinnik
Cover designer:	Marija Tudor

ISBN: 9781633437531
Printed in the United States of America

To my wife, Barbara, who has always believed in me

brief contents

contents

foreword

In the modern world, data is everywhere. Applications run by governments and companies collect data about the world and about our actions. We walk around with smartphones, which constantly collect data about our movements, purchases, and preferences, and then share that information with a wide variety of companies.

The good news is that this data makes it easier than ever to ask interesting questions about the world, ourselves, and our customers, and to get coherent answers. The bad news is that you need to find the data that will allow you to solve the problem, which isn't trivial. You then need to clean that data and modify it to suit your purposes. Only when you have wrestled the data into submission can you finally start to perform analysis. And then, when you finally have answered your questions, you have to decide how to present your analysis to others.

In other words, analyzing data involves much more than just analyzing it. Most of your time in a data project will be spent searching, retrieving, cleaning, editing, and producing reports. Each of these steps, in and of itself, can be quite frustrating, and they require practice and understanding.

But for a beginner, it's worse than that because it's not clear where to start. Even if you have lots of experience with Python and `pandas`, that doesn't mean you know how to solve problems—much as knowing how to use a hammer and screwdriver doesn't necessarily make you qualified to take on a carpentry project.

That's where this book, *The Well-Grounded Data Analyst*, comes in. David Asboth gives you a clear set of steps to follow when you want to solve a problem. Follow these steps, and you'll know what questions to ask at each stage of a project, what inputs you'll need, and what outputs you'll be creating.

For example, David tells you to start a project by understanding it, and then by starting from the end—that is, thinking about what answers you're trying to find and who those answers are meant for. These might seem obvious to someone experienced in data analysis problems, but as I've repeatedly seen in my pandas courses, it's all too easy to forget or ignore them.

This book goes far beyond just laying out the steps: it walks you through a number of projects, each of which presents its own obstacles and problems that you'll need to overcome. David guides you through the solutions, not only explaining how to solve them, but what pitfalls you might encounter and what tradeoffs are involved with different approaches.

Every project in the book uses real-world data, which is always problematic and dirty. As you work through the examples, you'll learn how to handle such problems—including how to decide what's worth keeping, as opposed to throwing away.

No analysis project ever truly ends. It's thus appropriate that the final step of David's strategy is *iterate*. Once you've gotten an answer to your question, don't spend too much time congratulating yourself. Instead, see where the flaws are in what you just did, and see if you can do even better.

If you feel nervous when starting to solve an actual data analysis problem, even (or especially) after learning the basics of Python and pandas, then this book should boost your confidence. That confidence will go a long way toward helping you analyze your own problems and projects.

— REUVEN M LERNER
Owner, LernerPython.com
Author, *Python Workout* and *Pandas Workout*

preface

When I graduated from data education and started working as a data scientist, I was shocked at how different the job was from what I expected based on my studies. Data was harder to come by than I imagined. There weren't clean datasets just sitting around waiting for me to analyze them. When I did get my hands on some data, it was undocumented and full of problems. I soon found out I wasn't the only one who had this experience, so when I started teaching data science alongside my day job, I wanted to bridge this gap between the classroom and the real world.

I've been teaching data topics for a number of years now, and the single most frequently asked question I get after a course is, what should I learn next? Based on my own experiences, I usually give a standard answer: solve real problems and learn by doing. I've given this answer so many times now that I wanted to write it down somewhere. This book is my extended answer.

To improve as an analyst, you need two things: get better at the process of analyzing data, regardless of what tools you use, and be immersed in a business environment where your work directly affects your surroundings. The market is saturated with introductory material. "Introduction to data science/analysis" books and courses are everywhere. What has always struck me was the lack of follow-up resources. What about intermediate or advanced data science? Everything that's out there is exclusively about tools and algorithms. That's great, but there is more to data science than the technical details. In fact, the technical details change, whereas the job of an analyst fundamentally does not.

Analysts need to be problem solvers. People have questions that can be answered with data; analysts answer them and, in doing so, have to solve technical and organizational problems. At a high level, problem solving is the skill that analysts need to hone most after initial training. The best way to do that is to actually solve problems. But what problems? And with what projects? With this book, I want aspiring analysts to continue learning, while creating a portfolio of projects to show off their advanced skills.

When choosing the projects, I was careful to focus on topics that don't normally make it into an introductory syllabus but come up often in the real world. I also chose real-world datasets and made little or no modifications so the problems would be as true to life as possible. I hope you enjoy solving these problems as much as I enjoyed creating them.

acknowledgments

This book took approximately twice as long to write as I thought it would, and it would not exist without the help of many individuals.

Most importantly, I thank my wife, Barbara, for supporting me from the moment I decided on a whim to write a book. I'm sorry in advance if I decide to write any more.

I'm grateful to everyone at Manning who made this book a reality. First, I thank Mike Stephens for immediately believing in the book and always making it better, mostly by making me remove words that didn't need to be there. A huge thanks goes to my development editor, Sarah G Harter, for her continued support and encouragement. I'm sorry there was no precedent in the Manning guides for all the things I decided to do in the book. And I thank everyone else at Manning who was involved in the production and promotion of the book.

Thanks also go to all the reviewers for taking the time to provide feedback on the book. I took everything on board, and the book is better for all your suggestions: Amarjit Bhandal, Alexander Klyanchin, Amílcar de Abreu Netto, Andrew R Freed, Arun Lakhera, Bijith Komalan, Carlos Aya-Moreno, Carlos Pavia, Deborah Mesquita, Dirk Gomez, Ed Lo, Esref Durna, Gaël Penessot, George E Carter, Giampiero Granatella, Gregorio Piccoli, Hilde Van Gysel, Igor Vieira, James Nyika, Johnny Hopkins, Juan Delgado, Louis Luangkesorn, Maxim Volgin, Murugan Lakshmanan, Nick Radcliffe, Oliver Korten, Randy Au, Rene Perrin, Rui Liu, Sriram Macharla, Sumit Bhattacharyya, Walter Alexander Mata López, and Weronika Burman.

Thank you, my technical editor, Brent J Broadnax, for your early contributions as the manuscript took shape. Brent graduated with an MBA in Marketing and Information

Systems and currently works as a data engineer for a wide range of clients across tele-communications, home services, and finance industries.

Thank you, Andrew Freed, technical proofreader, for your dedication and meticulous attention to detail. Special thanks go to Reuven Lerner for your thoughts and for writing the foreword; as an admirer of your work, I'm truly honored.

Thanks also are due Shaun McGirr for hiring me for my first data role. Everything I learned about the reality of data science was through our work together. We're probably overdue for recording some more podcast episodes.

Finally, I thank you, the reader. I hope you find the book valuable, and I'd be interested to hear how you solved its problems in your own unique way.

about this book

The Well-Grounded Data Analyst was written to help you improve your data analysis skills by solving real-world problems. It presents eight scenarios you would encounter as an analyst, each of them on a topic that is prevalent in industry but often missing from data education. It also provides a framework that can be used to solve any analysis problem, mostly by helping you define the problem properly before you start.

Who should read this book

The book is for junior or aspiring analysts who are looking to build on their foundational data analysis skills and want exposure to real-world problems. Readers should have at least six months of experience with data analysis and be familiar with problem framing, data cleaning, analysis, and visualization. Even seasoned analysts would benefit from solving the problems in the book because we never stop learning.

How this book is organized: A road map

The book contains eight data analysis projects to attempt, spread across 13 chapters. Each chapter, starting from chapter 2, describes a project, explains the available data, provides a step-by-step breakdown of how you might approach the project, and offers an example solution in Python:

- Chapter 1 introduces a results-oriented framework you can apply to any data problem. It also walks through an example of applying it to a real-world scenario.

- Chapter 2 contains the first project. In it, the task is to retrieve information from free text address data. The chapter includes a detailed application of the results-oriented process to the specific problem.

- Chapter 3 is about data modeling. In the project, customer information needs to be retrieved and deduplicated from raw transaction data.

- Chapter 4 is about defining metrics. The project requires you to define what it means for a product to be a best performer and analyze the data accordingly.

- Chapter 5 deals with unusual data sources. The project task is to analyze the changes in the film industry during and after the COVID-19 lockdowns. To do this, you need to retrieve data from a collection of PDF files.

- Chapter 6 introduces a project about handling categorical data. Your task is to analyze a developer survey to understand attitudes toward and uses of AI tools. The example solution in this chapter focuses on exploring the data and answering some initial questions.

- Chapter 7 continues the project from the previous chapter. In the example solution, we apply more advanced methods to working with categorical data to better understand the survey results.

- Chapter 8 introduces the next project, which is working with time series data. The task is to explore traffic data to understand where cycling infrastructure could be improved. The example solution in this chapter contains an exploration and initial analysis of the data.

- Chapter 9 continues the time series project from the previous chapter by applying more advanced methods, including forecasting traffic numbers into the future. The results of the project are also discussed.

- Chapter 10 introduces a new project, which is about creating rapid proofs of concept to test the viability of an idea given the available data. In this chapter's example solution, the data is explored, analyzed, and exported to be used in the next chapter.

- Chapter 11 contains the build of the example proof of concept which we prepared in chapter 10. The design and build of this application are described in detail.

- Chapter 12 introduces the final project that is about taking over someone else's analysis. Your task is to review another analyst's work and create the next version of the analysis. The topic is customer segmentation, specifically, analyzing mobile phone events to find distinct customer behaviors.

- Chapter 13 contains the second part of the example solution for the final project. It walks through how the mobile event data can be used to create distinct customer segments and how those would be presented to stakeholders.

The best way to read the book is to start with chapter 1 to understand the framework and then read chapter 2 to get a feel for how the project chapters are structured. For example, before reading any of the example solutions, I strongly advise that you attempt the project yourself. After chapter 2, I suggest choosing one of the projects that interests you. The eight projects are introduced in chapters 2 through 6, 8, 10, and 12. They do not need to be completed in order.

About the code

This book contains many examples of source code in line with normal text. In these cases, source code is formatted in a `fixed-width font like this` to separate it from ordinary text.

In many cases, the original source code has been reformatted; we've added line breaks and reworked indentation to accommodate the available page space in the book. In some cases, even this was not enough, and listings include line-continuation markers (➥). Code annotations accompany many of the code snippets, highlighting important concepts.

Every chapter from chapter 2 onwards contains supplementary materials. The main repository for all the materials can be found at https://davidasboth.com/book-code. The repository is organized into one folder per chapter. Each folder contains

- The data file(s) required to attempt the project yourself
- Additional files, such as data dictionaries, to lend more context to the problem
- Example solutions in the form of Jupyter notebook files

The projects can be attempted with any data analysis tool, so software and hardware requirements will vary. The example solutions are in Python, and if you want to run the code, see the appendix for details on setting up a Python environment that mimics the one I used for the solutions.

You can get executable snippets of code from the liveBook (online) version of this book at https://livebook.manning.com/book/the-well-grounded-data-analyst. The complete code for the examples in the book is also available for download from the Manning website at https://www.manning.com/books/the-well-grounded-data-analyst.

liveBook discussion forum

Purchase of *The Well-Grounded Data Analyst* includes free access to liveBook, Manning's online reading platform. Using liveBook's exclusive discussion features, you can attach comments to the book globally or to specific sections or paragraphs. It's a snap to make notes for yourself, ask and answer technical questions, and receive help from the author and other users. To access the forum, go to https://livebook.manning.com/book/the-well-grounded-data-analyst/discussion. You can also learn more about Manning's forums and the rules of conduct at https://livebook.manning.com/discussion.

Manning's commitment to our readers is to provide a venue where a meaningful dialogue between individual readers and between readers and the author can take place. It is not a commitment to any specific amount of participation on the part of the author, whose contribution to the forum remains voluntary (and unpaid). We suggest you try asking the author some challenging questions lest his interest stray! The forum and the archives of previous discussions will be accessible from the publisher's website as long as the book is in print.

about the author

 **DAVID ASBOTH** is a "data generalist." Currently, he works as a freelance data consultant and educator with an M.S. in Data Science, and has a background in software and web development in various industries. His previous roles include a range of data science, software development, and software architecting jobs, and his latest interest is figuring out what skills the analysts of the future actually need to succeed. Beyond having over a decade's worth of technical experience in multiple industries, David cohosts the *Half Stack Data Science* podcast about data science in the real world, has spoken at multiple conferences, including the Data Science Festival in London, and has taught a variety of data science courses to enterprise students, including large banks and consultancies. David has taught hundreds of students introductory data science over the years and wanted to write a book about what he thinks students like those could benefit from after learning the basics.

about the cover illustration

The figure on the cover of *The Well-Grounded Data Analyst* is "Hongrois," or "Hungarian," taken from a collection by Jacques Grasset de Saint-Sauveur, published in 1788. Each illustration is finely drawn and colored by hand.

In those days, it was easy to identify where people lived and what their trade or station in life was just by their dress. Manning celebrates the inventiveness and initiative of the computer business with book covers based on the rich diversity of regional culture centuries ago, brought back to life by pictures from collections such as this one.

Bridging the gap between data science training and the real world

This chapter covers

- Approaching data analysis using a results-driven process
- Important data science concepts using true-to-life projects
- Focusing on pragmatic solutions when analyzing data and learning new skills

Does the following scenario sound familiar? You've just received a data request from a department in your organization, and you have no idea how to handle it or perhaps even exactly what you've been asked to do. Outside the structured experience of your initial training, the real world is messy and uncertain. You may be wondering

- How do you use your existing skills to complete projects for demanding stakeholders?
- How do you keep learning now that the structured training environment is no longer there?
- How can you apply your general skills to domain-specific tasks?
- What do you need to learn next?

Any senior data scientist will tell you that the answer to all these questions is "experience." By completing the eight projects in this book, you will accelerate the process of getting the experience you need to succeed as a data analyst.

You will hone your existing skills and learn new ones by completing projects similar to those you may encounter in the real world. As you go, you will do most of the work, but ideas will be provided to get you started. To augment the specific skills, I also lay out an approach to make you a better analyst by focusing on pragmatic results. Along the way, you'll follow a process to make it easier to learn new skills efficiently and to get the most value out of each new challenge you face.

1.1   *The data analyst's toolkit*

There are certain fundamental skills analysts learn at the start of their journeys and bring to their roles. These are the ability to

- Read in (load) a dataset from a variety of sources
- Join datasets together
- Manipulate columns by creating, deleting, renaming, and transforming them
- Perform basic statistical analysis, such as calculating averages
- Explore your data using visualizations such as bar charts, line charts, or scatter plots
- Present your findings by creating appropriate visualizations or designing dashboards

Which tool you find comfortable using for these tasks does not matter. Appropriate tools include

- Microsoft Excel (or equivalent)
- Business intelligence (BI) tools, such as Tableau or Power BI
- Database query languages such as SQL, although these typically don't have visualization capabilities
- Programming languages with data analysis capabilities, such as Python or R

The example solutions to the projects are provided in Python, but the focus will be on problem solving, not the specifics of the Python programming language.

Completing the projects will build on your foundational skill set by adding skills specific to real-world use cases, which include data modeling, working with categorical data, extracting data from unusual sources, and rapid prototyping. In each case, I will highlight the exact kind of functionality required to solve the problem so that you can find the appropriate way to do that with your preferred tool. Some of the projects use machine learning models, but in-depth discussions about machine learning are beyond the scope of our projects.

The projects will also let you hone more "meta-skills," which are vital for any data analysis project. These skills are the ability to

- Take a human question, one that is vague and contains no technical jargon, and translate it into one that can be answered with data
- Evaluate the available data and determine whether it's suitable for answering the question
- Know how to pivot your analysis and change your analytical question if it cannot be answered with the available data
- Communicate your results to someone with no knowledge, or even interest, in the technical details

NOTE The practice projects focus on building technical and problem-solving skills, but there are other professional skills needed for a good data analyst. If you want a deeper dive into these, I recommend *Build a Career in Data Science* by Robinson and Nolis (Manning, 2020).

The future of data analysis also includes artificial intelligence (AI) tools, such as ChatGPT and similar large language models. AI tools cannot replace your ability to think critically, communicate with stakeholders, or work within the constraints of your business environment; however, AI tools can accelerate your work by helping you automate the more mechanical aspects of a project. I will highlight instances where such a tool could help solve a part of your problem. For example, if you don't know how to read data from a PDF file, an AI model will be able to tell you how to access this functionality in your preferred tool and give you code snippets to use. This means that you can solve that particular subproblem faster, which will make you more productive.

A note on terminology

I use the terms "data science" and "data analysis" interchangeably. First and foremost, data scientists need to be good analysts, so I prefer to use the phrase "analysis" instead of "data science" to describe the discipline and "analyst" instead of "data scientist" when describing the practitioner. When I use "data science," I just mean "the process of analyzing data."

I also refer to the "real world" a lot. The reason for this is to emphasize the disconnect between what you learn in a classroom versus what an analyst job looks like in practice. This disconnect doesn't mean classrooms are bad; there are simply multiple, not necessarily technical, hurdles to overcome that cannot be taught in a classroom. My focus is on preparing junior analysts for their jobs by teaching them all the things they couldn't have learned in their formal training. When I say, "real world," I mean "outside a learning environment."

Similarly, the word "stakeholder" is also a loaded term. I will use it to mean your boss, an internal client, or an external customer. They are the originators of the requests that generate the work you do. A stakeholder is anyone who is the target audience of your analysis and will be directly affected by your work.

1.2   *A results-driven approach*

On the job, your success depends far more on the results you deliver than the skills and knowledge you bring to a task. Being results oriented means your focus is always on problem solving. You should arrive at a first draft solution as soon as possible—something I like to call the *minimum viable answer*. This is what you present to your stakeholders and what is used as the basis for future iterations. Applying this thinking streamlines your work and delivers immediate value. You spend time learning something that will be immediately applicable, getting a higher return on the time you invest. With this results-focused approach, you do not need to be an expert in everything up front; instead, by completing each project, you will add new, specific skills to your toolbox and learn a method for approaching new tasks efficiently as you go. The results-driven approach I present means practicing learning by doing and working in a results-focused way.

Let's look at this approach through the lens of a classic example from industry. Suppose you work for a car dealership and need to answer the seemingly simple question, "How many cars did we sell yesterday?" for your manager. In an ideal world, this is a simple business intelligence question that requires nothing more than filtering a sales table down to just cars sold yesterday and providing an answer. The reality is that we need to think deeper about the problem, starting with defining the terms before we begin.

A results-driven analytical method to solve such a problem looks like this:

1 *Understand the problem*—This includes definitions of individual words/concepts.
2 *Start at the end*—What is a minimum viable answer that could spark further conversation?
3 *Identify additional resources*—These can be data, people, or access permissions you need to get this minimum viable answer.
4 *Obtain the data you will need to get your minimum viable answer*—Does this data even exist?
5 *Do the work to get your minimum viable answer*—Ideally, this step shouldn't take more than a few days so you can iterate quickly.
6 *Present the minimum viable answer to a stakeholder*—This could be anything from a casual conversation to a presentation to an audience.
7 *Iterate if necessary*—If the work is valuable, stakeholders will ask you to pursue it further.

Figure 1.1 is a visual representation of this process. Notice the arrows going back from step 7: they highlight the nonlinearity of the process. Depending on how step 6 goes, you might need to go back to an earlier step, even as far back as the very beginning.

The icons in figure 1.1 will be used throughout the book when discussing how this approach can be applied to specific projects. To apply this process to our car example, we start with step 1, "Understand the problem."

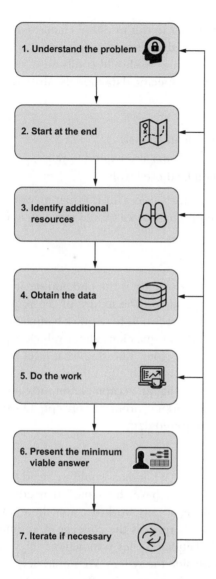

**Figure 1.1   The results-driven
process visualized**

1.2.1   *Understand the problem*

What do we mean by "car"? When I worked in the automotive industry, every time a
question about vehicles came up, we would have to clarify whether that included vans
or other vehicles that weren't quite cars. Sometimes vans were relevant, sometimes
they weren't. Then, what do we mean by "yesterday"? Often, several dates could be
associated with a sale event: the day the customer bought an item in a store, the day
we invoiced a customer for an item, the day the customer paid, or even the date a sale-
related dispute was resolved. So, when we ask about "yesterday," we need to know
which date column to use. Even the word "sell" can be ambiguous. What if a customer

returns an item later? Does that mean the answer to this question changes over time? We might explicitly decide that what happened in the past isn't fixed, which will make our analyses more complicated. Incidentally, we should codify answers to these kinds of questions and record them in business-specific data models. More on this in chapter 3.

The output of this step should be

- A clear question that can be tackled with an analysis
- A defined scope (e.g., does the analysis of cars also extend to vans?)
- Clearly defined terminology agreed on by those involved

These items should be documented as part of the project for transparency and reproducibility. Once we have understood the requirements, we should move on to envisaging a solution.

1.2.2 Start at the end

Assuming we have agreed on terminology, we can start at the end and decide what a minimum viable answer looks like. This depends on the nature of the request and what our stakeholders want to do with the information. If it's a quick ballpark estimate they need, we can sidestep some of those difficult questions about vehicle types and dates unless we have a good data model to pull from. Knowing what level of answer our stakeholder expects is crucial to deciding how much effort the request warrants.

The output of this step is a clear picture of what an acceptable solution looks like. Is it a document, a presentation, or even a working proof of concept? Once this is understood, the next step is to identify the required data.

1.2.3 Identify additional resources

Even for simple requests, it is important to ask, "What data would we need to answer this question?" immediately followed by "Do we have this data?" It is advisable to research the available data before committing to any work because there are cases where we just don't have a dataset that directly records the concept we're interested in. For example, in an online auction marketplace, sales transactions might not be recorded directly as they could take place outside the system. We would need to know where a record is made if a sale is agreed over the phone after the auction takes place.

The output should be a list of what the appropriate data might look like to answer the question. This should include possible datasets already available to the organization and external datasets that will need to be obtained.

1.2.4 Obtain the data

Now, we need to obtain the relevant data, either by extracting it from somewhere or by creating it. If our online auction marketplace is only used for listing and bidding, we might have to make do with inferring when something was sold by seeing when it stopped being listed. This is a dataset we would need to create from the raw listing data. In this case, we would have to stop at step 3 and regroup to figure out whether creating such an inferred sales dataset is worth the effort. This will depend on the minimum viable answer we defined in step 2.

The output should be a tangible dataset or extract, which we can use to get to our minimum viable answer. If the data is only an extract, it should be representative of the larger data.

1.2.5   *Do the work*

You will notice that step 5 just says "Do the work." This is intentionally broad and vague. Step 5 might encompass the entirety of other data analysis workflows you may have encountered. Steps 1–4 ensure that the doing part will have a higher ROI. By this point, you've given the problem enough thought that you're not just aimlessly jumping into writing code, which is certainly a temptation when your skills are fresh and you're eager to deliver. I encourage you to spend time on steps 1–4, perhaps even more than you instinctively would.

In the car example, during this phase, you might find that the sale date of a vehicle changes over time based on events such as a customer waiting for a finance agreement to come through, or previously undisclosed faults were subsequently noticed, and the customer raised a complaint. You as the analyst should not be making the decision alone about which possible date constitutes the actual sale date. Here, you would go all the way back to step 1 to have a conversation with your stakeholders before continuing your analysis.

Whatever happens in the analysis, documenting your specific choices and assumptions is critical for transparency and reproducibility. In the example solutions presented for each project, I have documented the specific choices I made and where another analyst's path might have diverged had they made different decisions.

The output here is whatever was decided in step 2, "Start at the end." This artifact should be recorded as part of the project and be reproducible by other analysts. Chapters 12 and 13 present a project where we do just that.

1.2.6   *Present the minimum viable answer*

A key component of the results-driven approach is presenting results earlier than we might be inclined to. We are looking for a satisfactory solution, so we should be discussing preliminary results as early as possible to allow iteration. Data teams have failed in the past when they siloed themselves away from the rest of the business, only to emerge months later with work that no one asked for and has no tangible business value.

Is anyone using your work?

I once sat through an interesting presentation at a conference where the data science team had built a complicated sales forecasting model. The presentation was purely technical and told the story of how they arrived at their hierarchical Bayesian approach.

(continued)

In the Q&A portion, I asked the difficult question: "Does anyone use your forecasts, and if so, what for?" The data scientists sheepishly admitted that they're still working on convincing the business that their forecasts are worthwhile. I suspect a lot of needless work could have been avoided had they engaged in that conversation sooner.

The output of this step is minutes of a meeting with, or presentation to, our stakeholders. The outcomes should also be recorded as part of the project. Was further work requested? If so, what?

1.2.7 Iterate if necessary

Finally, you will almost always end up iterating your first answer. It is an important step to include in any data analysis framework because it highlights the inherent uncertainty of the job. You will never have all the answers up front, including an answer to the question "How long will this analysis take?" and that's fine. Accept that a first draft will be necessary to reach a satisfying solution, and the sooner that first draft exists, the better. The added benefit of this iterative approach is that you become better at estimating how long your work will take because you only ever have to estimate one iteration rather than the entire project.

Using a results-driven approach, you will develop an intuition for how to make analytical decisions that help focus on providing a pragmatic solution rather than an unnecessarily deep answer up front. Of course, you will need to learn new tools along the way. Sometimes, these tools will only be used for the analysis you have in front of you. The next analysis may need different tools. That's okay—tools come and go, but the knowledge and concepts you learn will remain the same, and these are what make a good analyst.

It is important to note that this approach is not a substitute for going deep when necessary. I'm not encouraging anyone to learn to take shortcuts. However, a key skill in analytics is identifying the highest ROI on your time, which often means adopting a breadth-first rather than depth-first approach.

1.3 Project structure

The projects are designed to represent common problems faced by analysts in industry. Each project is designed to be approachable with fundamental analyst skills and not take too long. There are a lot of factors at play: your level of experience with your tools, your familiarity with the topics at hand, the speed at which you learn new concepts, and so on, but generally, the first iteration of your solution to each project should take somewhere between 2 hours and two days. That's a broad range, but even a two-day "sprint" to deliver something you can discuss with a stakeholder would be considered a quick turnaround time.

The projects not only reflect common industry problems but are also designed to bridge specific skill gaps between initial training and the real world. Table 1.1 is an overview of these projects.

Table 1.1 A summary of the eight projects in the book

Project	Data analysis skill(s)	Chapter(s)
Analyzing customer retail spend in different geographic areas	Extracting structured data from free text	2
Extracting unique customer records from e-commerce transactions	Data modeling	3
Defining and finding best-performing products on an e-commerce store	Defining metrics	4
Analyzing the effects of the coronavirus pandemic on the film industry	Extracting data from PDFs	5
Investigating developer attitudes toward AI tools from a survey	Handling categorical data	6, 7
Identifying potential improvements to cycling infrastructure	Working with time series data	8, 9
Building a proof-of-concept application to explore the Welsh property market	Rapid prototyping	10, 11
Continuing another analyst's work and creating customer segments using mobile phone activity	Iterating on someone else's work Customer segmentation, clustering	12, 13

Each project is structured in the following way:

- It starts with a high-level description and the data. Beyond that, you're on your own. This section is sufficient to read if you either feel more comfortable formulating an action plan based on a somewhat vague analytical question or want to practice that skill explicitly.
- What follows is a more detailed step-by-step breakdown of how you might go about attempting a solution. There will be no code snippets here, but if the high-level description has you stuck on where to start, this section should help kick-start your solution attempt.
- Finally, I will always include an example solution. There will be discussions on how you might go about attempting to solve the problem, what assumptions you'll have to make, how you might change your analytical question given the constraints of the data, and what an acceptable result will look like. In the example solution, I'll have made some specific assumptions and decisions that may differ from yours. That's to be expected. The goal is not that you arrive at my solution—my solution won't be *the* solution. In fact, I'll highlight places

where the analysis may have diverged. The goal is to practice going from problem definition to a minimum viable answer.

Consider this collection of realistic analysis projects as a practice companion to help you get used to diving into something without knowing the answers or even the required tools up front. When learning through practice projects, you will

- Have an end goal in mind and work toward it.
- Learn the skills necessary to get an answer rather than learning skills with no real end goal in mind.
- Learn breadth-first, not depth-first.

Approaching projects using the results-driven method will prepare you to apply these methods to any project. These projects should inspire you to continue analyzing data and use the "solve a problem" framework for learning, all while accumulating new skills and building a handy portfolio to show to prospective employers.

Let's get started! The next step is to take on your first project, an analysis of some customer demographics for a hypothetical UK-based retailer. I hope you enjoy the journey!

Summary

- Expect a gap between your formal data science training and the real world.
- Being pragmatic and results driven helps navigate the inherent uncertainty in data analysis.
- Practicing this results-driven approach through real-world examples will help you
  - Focus on problem-solving
  - Get better at identifying additional considerations
  - Develop an intuition for how to make analytical decisions to provide a pragmatic solution to stakeholder questions sooner
  - Create a real-world project portfolio to make yourself stand out as a candidate

Encoding geographies

This chapter covers

- How to use the results-driven approach to tackle a real problem
- Making analytical decisions in the face of uncertainty

Now that you have been introduced to the results-driven approach, let's apply it to a real data science task. We will tackle a real-world problem and apply the results-driven method to it. It is a template for approaching the other projects and any other project you encounter in the future.

All the projects and data are available at https://davidasboth.com/book-code for you to attempt them yourself. There, you will find both the dataset for the project and the same example solution presented in the chapter in the form of a Jupyter notebook.

For this chapter's project, let's examine an example task that analysts encounter, which at first glance might seem simple enough—encoding geography.

A note on Jupyter notebooks

Jupyter is a development environment that allows the mixing of code and accompanying text in the form of notebooks. Notebook files let you read the text and run the code directly within the document. They are popular for education and data analysis.

The notebooks accompanying the book collect the code snippets from each chapter into a single document where the code is also runnable. Sites such as GitHub even let you view the notebooks in the browser without requiring Jupyter to be installed. See the appendix for instructions on how to install Python to run the code yourself.

2.1   *Project 1: Identifying customer geographies*

Let's look at the project in which we will extract location information from free text to better understand our customer base. As an analyst for ProWidget Systems, a UK-based B2B (business-to-business) retailer, you've been asked to report on spending volumes for London-based customers versus those based in the rest of the United Kingdom. The board has supplied a high-level data extract containing all customers' addresses and their total spending to date. They want to know

- Which UK cities are currently underserved
- Whether their customers are primarily London based

If this were a sanitized tutorial, your data would likely have a column called `city`, and your task would be more about the technical steps required to group the data by city and summarize it using an appropriate metric. Perhaps you would take the total spending from all London-based customers and compare it against the same figure from other major cities in the United Kingdom or all data where the `city` column is not London. Perhaps you would choose to show the distribution instead to get a more detailed picture of the difference. Either way, your choice is more about the specific *technical* steps required to get an answer.

Compare this to answering the same question as an analyst in a real business. For instance, in this project, the available data is not organized cleanly enough to have a `city` column: we only have a single `customer address` column, which may or may not contain the city somewhere within it. The address data for this project comes from Companies House, an executive agency sponsored by the UK government's Department for Business and Trade. The original public data, which I modified for this exercise, is available at https://mng.bz/mGxr.

Before doing any analysis, we need to decide how to identify what city an address relates to. We will follow the results-driven process laid out in chapter 1 to do this and get an answer for our stakeholders.

> **Real business case: Finding new leads with address data**
>
> As a data scientist, one data-driven tool I built was a map of all our customers combined with a list of all companies in the United Kingdom that were in a relevant industry to be our potential customers. The sales team used this map to identify prospective customers in the local area whenever they went to visit an existing customer.
>
> The project involved combining our own customer data with the government's official public list of companies, and the bulk of the work was sanitizing address data in both lists so they could be compared, which is why that is the topic of this chapter.

2.1.1 Data dictionary

The first step in understanding what's in a dataset is to read the data dictionary or ask for one if it wasn't provided. You may ultimately need to write one yourself. One of the ways the real world differs from this book's projects is that I provide well-documented data dictionaries. Don't get used to it! Table 2.1 shows the data dictionary for the supplied data, and figure 2.1 shows a snapshot of the first few rows.

Table 2.1 Data dictionary for the customer address dataset

Column	Definition
company_id	A unique identifier for each customer company in the dataset
address	A single field to store the customer address
total_spend	The total amount this customer has spent to date (in GBP)

	company_id	address	total_spend
0	1	APARTMENT 2,\n52 BEDFORD ROAD,\nLONDON,\nENGLA...	5700
1	2	107 SHERINGHAM AVENUE,\nLONDON,\nN14 4UJ	4700
2	3	43 SUNNINGDALE,\nYATE,\nBRISTOL,\nENGLAND,\nBS...	5900
3	4	HAWESWATER HOUSE,\nLINGLEY MERE BUSINESS PARK,...	7200
4	5	AMBERFIELD BARN HOUSE AMBER LANE,\nCHART SUTTO...	4600

Figure 2.1 A snapshot of the first few rows of customer address data

Now that we have our problem statement and have seen the available data, it is time to start our results-driven process to arrive at a solution.

2.2   *An example solution: Finding London*

In this section, I will dive into an example solution, focusing on the steps of the results-driven approach, as well as the details of solving the problem. You may wish to attempt this problem yourself before going further or use this chapter to get a feel for the structure of the rest of the projects. As for most solutions I provide, the code itself will be written in Python, primarily using the `pandas` library. While code snippets will be used to explain the example solution, I will focus discussions on the conceptual solution and less on the code specifics. The solution will have three parts: setting up the problem statement and the data, creating the first iteration of a solution, and reviewing the work and deciding on further steps.

2.2.1   *Setting ourselves up for success*

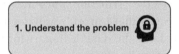

The first step is to ensure we understand the problem. In this case, we know we need to use our customer address data to calculate the total spending by city across the United Kingdom and come up with an answer for how London customers compare with the rest of the country. If we encountered multiple metrics in the data, such as the number of transactions a customer has made or how long they have been a customer, we would need to clarify the purpose of the question with our stakeholders so that we know which metrics to focus on.

In this case, the data provided does not contain this ambiguity; it is clear we are focusing on spending patterns across two predefined geographic areas. However, had our stakeholders asked us about which areas are underserved in general, we would also seek to understand whether we should look at data at a city level or a different level of granularity.

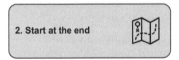

The crucial step in any analysis is to think of where we are going. What form will a minimum viable answer take? In this example, our stakeholders have two questions:

- *Are different cities underserved?* This requires us to calculate total customer spending by city and find cities with the lowest customer spending.
- *How does London compare to the rest of the United Kingdom?* This can then be answered from the output of the first answer.

For a minimum viable answer to exist, we need to add a `city` column to our data, which we will extract from the address. This will allow us to have a breakdown of spending by city, meaning we could take the row for London and compare it against the rest of the table. As for the final output, a table or a bar chart will suffice for both cases. It may seem obvious, but knowing the exact format of our output will guide us toward a relevant solution, which is a table containing one row per city and an associated total spending figure.

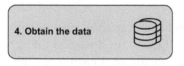

3. Identify additional resources

To tackle any analytical question, we need to know what data is required to answer it. To get city-level customer figures, we need data on which city each customer belongs to. This requires that each customer record has a `city` column, or at least some sort of address data, against it. We know in this case that an address field has been provided, so we have sufficient data to attempt the problem, even if we are unsure at this stage whether we can get a satisfactory answer. In this step, we also decide on additional data sources we might need. In this case, it might be to enhance the accuracy of our address data. Our first iteration should usually focus on the data we already have, and additional data sources can be considered in future iterations.

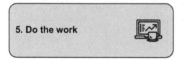

4. Obtain the data

The step of acquiring data should not be underestimated. Entire data science initiatives have failed because the data science team never received any usable data to analyze. The obstacles to obtaining data are not technical but organizational, and it is one aspect of the real world we won't simulate. Throughout the projects, you will not need to find any data yourself; it will be provided. It will not always be easy to clean, but you will not spend any time emailing someone in your organization and hoping for their goodwill to send you a data extract!

2.2.2   Creating the first iteration of a solution

5. Do the work

By this point, we have established the problem statement and obtained all necessary data. It is now time to explore the dataset before extracting the city component of each address and summarizing customer spending data by city. Let's start by importing the necessary libraries and reading in the data:

```
import pandas as pd
customers = pd.read_csv("./data/addresses.csv")
print(customers.shape)
```

The output is (100000, 3), meaning we have a total of 100,000 rows of data and the three columns we saw in the data dictionary. Before extracting any city data, we should check for missing values.

INVESTIGATING MISSING VALUES

Depending on your tool of choice, attempting to extract data from empty addresses may yield errors. The output of the following code snippet is shown in figure 2.2:

```
customers.isnull().sum()
```

```
company_id      0
address       968
total_spend     0      Figure 2.2  A table showing the number
dtype: int64           of missing values per column
```

We can see there are 968 missing addresses, which is just under 1% of our rows. Since we have no way of knowing the addresses of those missing customers just from the data provided, we can safely drop these rows:

```
customers = customers.dropna(subset=["address"])
```

What percentage of rows is acceptable to drop will depend on the context, but losing 1% due to missing key information is fine. If, say, 10% of our customers had missing addresses, we might want to examine why.

However, this is a point where analyses might diverge. The missing address data could either be kept and categorized simply as "Other" or, if we had more customer-related data, we may choose to spend the time looking up a customer's address elsewhere to get a more complete dataset.

There are many places in an analysis where there is no definitive right decision, only different decisions based on different assumptions. Because of this, your analysis will diverge from mine at various points. Figure 2.3 illustrates this branching of possible paths in a diagram, which I will use heavily to reiterate this point.

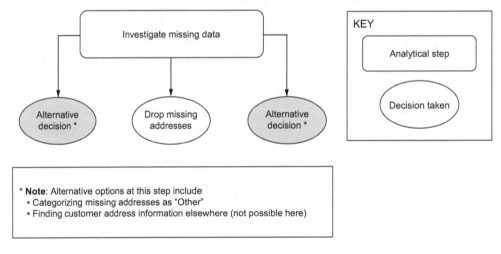

Figure 2.3   The first step of the analysis and its alternative paths visualized

There are two types of shapes: steps and decisions. Steps represent sequential tasks to be undertaken in the analysis. These come from the original action plan but may also be informed by what we find in the data. Decisions represent places where the analysis might diverge, depending on the assumptions and choices made. Your analysis will not necessarily contain the same steps or the same decisions as mine.

While we are exploring our columns, we should also check if our `total_spend` column contains any strange values, such as negatives. The output of the following code snippet is shown in figure 2.4:

```
customers["total_spend"].describe()
```

```
count    99032.000000
mean      4951.673197
std       1500.642398
min          0.000000
25%       3900.000000
50%       5000.000000
75%       6000.000000
max      11700.000000
Name: total_spend, dtype: float64
```

Figure 2.4   Summary statistics of the `total_spend` column

As the figure shows, the values range from 0 to just under £12,000 with no negative values. Now that we have seen our data, we need to decide on an approach to extract the information about cities. Let's think back to our two stakeholder questions: "Are different cities underserved?" and "How does London compare to the rest of the United Kingdom?" The second question is a subset of the first. That is, once you have a dataset of customer spending by city, it is easy to compare London against other cities. To solve one question means solving the other, so if we start by focusing on identifying addresses in London first, we can find the nuances and edge cases of how addresses are represented.

EXTRACTING CITY COLUMN FROM ADDRESSES

Before deciding on a method, we should look at some sample addresses. The following code prints the first five addresses, the output of which is shown in figure 2.5:

```
for address in customers["address"].head():
    print(address, "\n")
```

We can already notice some patterns, as well as some potential pitfalls. From our limited sample, it appears that addresses end with the postcode, but sometimes London addresses contain a line for England, and sometimes they don't. This means we cannot rely on looking at a specific row of an address to give us the city, which is useful information.

What about looking for the string "London" to identify customers in London? Would that be sufficient? Probably not. You would end up including people who live on "London Road" in other towns, for a start. Examining the data, we can see that address lines are separated by a comma and a new line character, so looking for

```
APARTMENT 2,
52 BEDFORD ROAD,
LONDON,
ENGLAND,
SW4 7HJ

107 SHERINGHAM AVENUE,
LONDON,
N14 4UJ

43 SUNNINGDALE,
YATE,
BRISTOL,
ENGLAND,
BS37 4HZ

HAWESWATER HOUSE,
LINGLEY MERE BUSINESS PARK,
LINGLEY GREEN AVENUE,
GREAT SANKEY, WARRINGTON,
WA5 3LP

AMBERFIELD BARN HOUSE AMBER LANE,
CHART SUTTON,
MAIDSTONE,
ENGLAND,
ME17 3SF
```

Figure 2.5   Five sample addresses

"LONDON," could alleviate this particular problem. Note the extra comma in the search string. Our rule could simply be the following: if one of the rows of an address is "London," then that address is a London one. In our sample, all addresses were uppercase, but we should not assume this will be the case for all 100,000 rows, so we should ensure they are all uppercase ourselves. To compare our cleaned address data with the original, we will create a new column to store the cleaned version. It is usually a good idea to keep data in its raw form somewhere to reference as needed:

```
customers["address_clean"] = customers["address"].str.upper()
```

Now that we have ensured that the casing is consistent, we can investigate the difference between looking for "LONDON" and "LONDON,":

```
len(customers[customers["address_clean"].str.contains("LONDON")])
len(customers[customers["address_clean"].str.contains("LONDON,")])
```

The output of these lines of code is 21,768 and 20,831, respectively, which means nearly 1,000 rows are no longer selected when we add the commas. Those are the addresses that contain the word London, but we assume are not, in fact, in the city of London (e.g., addresses on London Road). We have already seen from our sample addresses that we cannot rely on the position of a row to decide where the city component is. However, there may only be a finite number of address structures. Let's look at how many addresses consist of how many rows. The output of this code is shown in figure 2.6:

```
customers["address_lines"] = (
    customers["address_clean"]
    .str.split(",\n")
    .apply(len)
)
customers["address_lines"].value_counts().sort_index()
```

Splits an address into a list of substrings (i.e., separate the rows)

Counts the length of each list (i.e., the number of rows in the address)

Now counts how many addresses are made of how many rows

```
1       6
2      52
3    3284
4   35850
5   45931
6   13909
Name: address_lines, dtype: int64
```

Figure 2.6   Distribution of address lengths

We can observe that some addresses consist of only one or two lines, and some have as many as six. In theory, if every three-line, four-line, five-line, and so forth address is consistent, we could come up with a rule to extract the city slightly differently from each. We should also examine some of these shorter addresses to see what they look like. The output of this code is shown in figures 2.7 and 2.8, respectively:

```
print(customers.loc[customers["address_lines"] == 1, "address_clean"])
print((
    customers[customers["address_lines"] == 2]
    .sample(5, random_state=42)
    ["address_clean"])
)
```

Looks at five random rows that have only two lines of address. The random_state parameter ensures we get the same results each time for reproducibility.

```
17789                    FALKIRK
31897                 HADDINGTON
61750          CREAG BHAITHEACHAIN
75330                   NEWMILNS
78045     REDCLOAK FARM, STONEHAVEN
90897      REFER TO PARENT REGISTRY
Name: address_clean, dtype: object
```

Figure 2.7   All the one-line addresses in our data

```
39443                                              FORFAR,\nANGUS
80846                                   12 HOPE STREET,\nEDINBURGH
95979       BRANCH REGISTRATION,\nREFER TO PARENT REGISTRY
23563       BRANCH REGISTRATION,\nREFER TO PARENT REGISTRY
81155                                    PO BOX 2230,\nGLASGOW
Name: address_clean, dtype: object
```

Figure 2.8   A sample of five rows of two-line address data

These figures show the variability of our data. Some rows are simply a city, Falkirk; there are entirely missing addresses referring us to a parent registry; and we also have PO Box addresses. It is unlikely we can come up with a rule to extract cities purely based on their position in the lines of an address without writing a lot of bespoke code.

Let's remind ourselves of our goal: our immediate task is to create a `city` column, and we now have to decide how to proceed. One option is to take our London-finding example and extend it by explicitly looking for city names in the `address` column. This would require a comprehensive list of cities in the United Kingdom, which is not an impossible task. Such lists exist—for example, the list available at https://mng.bz/5gKB is provided by the UK government. In this case, we would still need to decide what to do with addresses that fall outside of these cities. Do we simply label them "Other"? For a first iteration, this may suffice, as the question was specifically asking about cities, not towns or villages.

Another option is to use the postcode component of each address and look it up against a national postcode database, which we would have to obtain and ensure we are allowed to use. This might be a more accurate method but would require additional work, such as identifying the postcode component of each address in the first place.

In general, we should err on the side of less effort for our first iteration, so we will attempt to use the list of cities in the UK provided by the UK government. The web page consists of a bulleted list of cities for each country of the United Kingdom, an extract of which is shown in figure 2.9.

There are multiple ways to extract these into a code-friendly form. The simplest one is to copy and paste the bullet points from the website directly into Excel, so each city is on a separate line, and then import and clean the data in our code. The quickest option isn't always to write code! However, for full reproducibility, you may want to automate that step. Obtaining this data manually will suit us here since we don't expect the list of UK cities to change very often. This raw data is provided in the

Guidance

List of cities (HTML)

Published 29 August 2022

List of cities (* indicates the city has also been awarded a Lord Mayoralty or Lord Provostship)[footnote 1]

United Kingdom

England

- Bath
- Birmingham*
- Bradford*
- Brighton & Hove
- Bristol*
- Cambridge
- Canterbury*
- Carlisle
- Chelmsford
- Chester*
- Chichester
- Colchester
- Coventry*
- Derby
- Doncaster
- Durham
- Ely

Figure 2.9   An extract of the UK government's web page listing all the cities in the United Kingdom

accompanying materials as a separate file called `cities.csv`. The first few rows of this data are shown in figure 2.10:

```
cities = pd.read_csv("./data/cities.csv", header=None, names=["city"])
cities.head()
```

	city
0	England
1	Bath
2	Birmingham*
3	Bradford*
4	Brighton & Hove

Figure 2.10   The first few rows of city data

There are clearly some aspects of this data to clean before using it as a definitive list of cities. First, the country headings were included as rows in the data, so the values `England`, `Scotland`, `Wales`, and `Northern Ireland` need to be removed. Then, the trailing asterisk * character also needs to be trimmed, and the remaining city names should be uppercased to match our address data. Figure 2.11 shows a sample of our final, cleaned city list:

```
countries_to_remove = ["England", "Scotland", "Wales", "Northern Ireland"]

print(len(cities))
cities_to_remove = cities[cities["city"].isin(countries_to_remove)].index
cities = cities.drop(index=cities_to_remove)
print(len(cities))

cities["city"] = cities["city"].str.replace("*", "", regex=False)

cities["city"] = cities["city"].str.upper()
cities.head()
```

	city
1	BATH
2	BIRMINGHAM
3	BRADFORD
4	BRIGHTON & HOVE
5	BRISTOL

Figure 2.11   A sample of our cleaned, definitive city list

Now that we have our definitive list of cities, we can use it to create the `city` column. Figure 2.12 shows the work we have done so far and the alternatives in our most recent step.

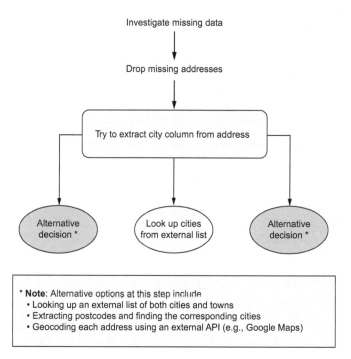

Figure 2.12   Diagram of the analysis so far after two main steps

CREATING A CITY COLUMN

We can use our city list to tag an address with a particular city if that city name and an additional comma are found somewhere in the address. Using figure 2.11 as an example, we will assume that an address that contains the substring `"BATH,"` is an address in the city of Bath, so the value in the `city` column will be `"BATH"`. Anything where this newly created `city` column doesn't have a value, where none of the city names was found in the address, will be categorized as `"OTHER"`. The following code achieves this, and figure 2.13 shows the latest state of our data:

```
for city in cities["city"].values:
    customers.loc[customers["address_clean"].str.contains(f"\n{city},"),
 "city"] = city

customers["city"] = customers["city"].fillna("OTHER")

customers.head()
```

	company_id	address	total_spend
0	1	APARTMENT 2,\n52 BEDFORD ROAD,\nLONDON,\nENGLA...	5700
1	2	107 SHERINGHAM AVENUE, \nLONDON,\nN14 4UJ	4700
2	3	43 SUNNINGDALE,\nYATE, \nBRISTOL,\nENGLAND,\nBS...	5900
3	4	HAWESWATER HOUSE,\nLINGLEY MERE BUSINESS PARK,...	7200
4	5	AMBERFIELD BARN HOUSE AMBER LANE,\nCHART SUTTO...	4600

(continued)	address_clean	address_lines	city
	APARTMENT 2,\n52 BEDFORD ROAD,\nLONDON,\nENGLA...	5	LONDON
	107 SHERINGHAM AVENUE, \nLONDON,\nN14 4UJ	3	LONDON
	43 SUNNINGDALE,\nYATE, \nBRISTOL,\nENGLAND,\nBS...	5	BRISTOL
	HAWESWATER HOUSE,\nLINGLEY MERE BUSINESS PARK,...	5	OTHER
	AMBERFIELD BARN HOUSE AMBER LANE,\nCHART SUTTO...	5	OTHER

Figure 2.13   An extract of the data with a newly added `city` column

Now that we have our new `city` column, we need to explore it to see which cities our customers are in and what proportion of our customers we weren't able to allocate to a city based on their address.

EXPLORING THE NEW CITY COLUMN

Based on figure 2.13, it looks like we have correctly categorized the London and Bristol addresses from the first five rows, and put the rest in the "Other" category. We can now do our first piece of analysis by counting how many customers appear in each city, according to our categorization. Let's look at the top 20, which are shown in figure 2.14:

```
customers["city"].value_counts().head(20)
```

Over half of our data is in the "Other" category, which means half of our customer base is established outside of major cities. This is an important insight to communicate

```
OTHER             54458
LONDON            20762
MANCHESTER         1902
BIRMINGHAM         1866
GLASGOW            1273
BRISTOL            1150
LEEDS              1040
EDINBURGH          1038
LEICESTER           905
NOTTINGHAM          838
LIVERPOOL           838
CARDIFF             797
SHEFFIELD           706
COVENTRY            553
MILTON KEYNES       493
SOUTHAMPTON         477
NORWICH             449
BRADFORD            417
BELFAST             416
PRESTON             406
Name: city, dtype: int64
```

Figure 2.14 The top 20 cities by number of customers

to our stakeholders. Let's look at some addresses from this category, as shown in figure 2.15:

```
sample_other = customers[customers["city"] == "OTHER"]
    .sample(5, random_state=42)
for address in sample_other["address_clean"].values:
    print(address, "\n")
```

Some of these addresses relate to towns, but there is an address in Twickenham, which is a suburban district in London. While the address did not contain the word "London," that customer should be categorized as being London based. We can already see some of the shortfalls of our chosen approach. At this point, we note them down and may consider tackling them in a future iteration.

> **NOTE** Unless you have knowledge of UK geography, you may miss these instances of London addresses without the word "London" in them. This highlights how important domain knowledge is for an analyst and why you should work closely with domain experts.

One sanity check at this point is to see how many unique cities are in the government data and our tagged address data. Depending on the business, we might assume that we have at least one customer in every major UK city, and we can verify this. A Python trick is to create a unique set of the government's city list and the list of unique cities in our new `city` column and subtract one set from the other. This will give us the

```
82 CROSSE COURTS,
BASILDON,
ENGLAND,
SS15 5JE

70 NORMAN CRESCENT,
PINNER,
ENGLAND,
HA5 3QL

23 STATION ROAD,
GERRARDS CROSS,
BUCKINGHAMSHIRE,
ENGLAND,
SL9 8ES

5 STEWARTS PARK AVENUE,
MARTON,
MIDDLESBROUGH,
CLEVELAND,
UNITED KINGDOM,
TS4 3FD

FIRST FLOOR,
6 YORK STREET,
TWICKENHAM,
ENGLAND,
TW1 3LD
```

Figure 2.15   A sample of addresses whose city is categorized as "Other"

difference between the lists, that is, cities that appear in the government list but not in our address data:

```
set(cities["city"]) - set(customers["city"])
```

> Subtracting sets in Python means finding items in one list that aren't in another.

The output of this code is the string { 'KINGSTON-UPON-HULL' }, which tells us that the city Kingston-upon-Hull is not in the city column of our customer address data. This either means we have no customers there, which is not impossible given its population is only around 250,000, or there is something else going on. The city is usually abbreviated to just "Hull," which again is a case of applying specific domain knowledge to the problem, so let's look for that in our address data:

```
customers[customers["address_clean"].str.contains("\nHULL,")]
```

The output of this code tells us there are 284 relevant records. We can manually update our city column to fix this problem:

```
customers.loc[customers["address_clean"].str.contains("\nHULL,"),
    "city"] = "HULL"
```

Let's again review our analysis so far. The work we have done and the alternative steps are shown in figure 2.16.

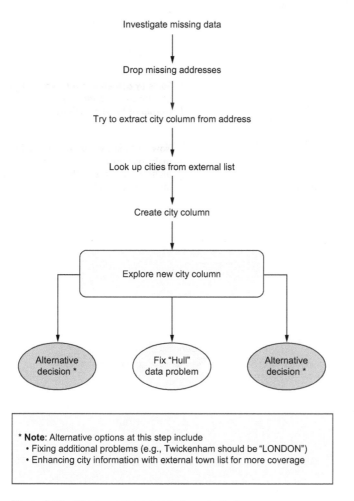

Figure 2.16   The current progress of our analysis

We can now finally take a look at spending figures by city using the newly created `city` column.

ANALYZING SPENDING BY CITY

The hard work was getting the data into the correct format; the analysis itself is a simple grouping and aggregation. The output chart is shown in figure 2.17:

```
from matplotlib.ticker import FuncFormatter
import matplotlib.pyplot as plt
```

```
def millions(x, pos):
    return '£%1.1fM' % (x * 1e-6)
```
◁──┐ **Defines a function to**
    │ **show figures in millions**

```
formatter = FuncFormatter(millions)

fig, axis = plt.subplots()

top_20_spend = (
    customers
    .groupby("city")
    ["total_spend"].sum()
    .sort_values(ascending=False)
    .head(20)
    .sort_values(ascending=True)
)
```
┌─ **Sorts by descending total spending to**
│ **get the top 20 highest spenders**
◁─ **(required for the analysis)**

┌─ **Now sorts in the opposite direction to**
│ **make our horizontal bar chart have the**
◁ **highest numbers at the top (required**
   for the Python plot)

```
top_20_spend.plot.barh(ax=axis)

axis.xaxis.set_major_formatter(formatter)
axis.set(
    title="Total customer spend by city",
    xlabel="Total spend"
)

plt.show()
```

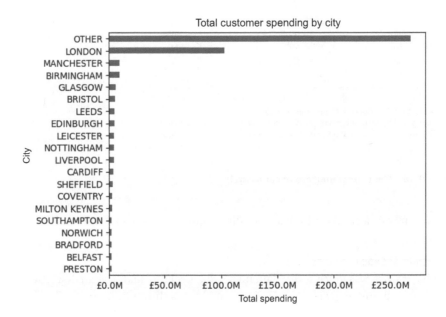

Figure 2.17   Total customer spending by city

It is clear that the "Other" category dominates. As we have seen before, our customers are just as likely to be based outside of a major city. This is partly down to how cities are defined in the United Kingdom. There are only 76 that are officially called "cities," but there are many "towns" with significant populations. This distinction between towns and cities partly explains why the "Other" category is so large.

Another observation is that London does indeed come out as the top city in terms of customer spending, as well as the number of customers. The next largest cities in terms of spending, Manchester and Birmingham, are also the next largest by population. The top cities in both this chart and our customer volume calculation in figure 2.14 generally correspond to the top cities by population. Leeds is perhaps lower than you would expect based on its population, but there is no reason customer spending figures should correlate perfectly with population.

Our final inquiry is to compare London against the rest of the United Kingdom. We can take this to mean either "all of the United Kingdom that isn't London" or "all major cities except London." We should calculate both figures and decide how to report our findings:

```
print("Total spend for all customers:")
print(customers["total_spend"].sum())

print("Total spend for London customers:")
print(customers.loc[customers["city"] == "LONDON", "total_spend"].sum())

print("Total spend outside London:")
print(customers.loc[customers["city"] != "LONDON", "total_spend"].sum())

print("Total spend outside London (excluding OTHER):")
print(customers.loc[customers["city"].isin(["LONDON", "OTHER"]) == False,
➡ "total_spend"].sum())
```

The output of this code tells us the total spending across our customers was £490M. This breaks down into £103M for London customers and £387M for the rest of the United Kingdom. If we look at all major cities outside London, the total is £119M. That is, if we compare London to other cities, we can see that our London customers generate nearly as much revenue as all other major cities combined. It does appear that our customer base is London-centric.

This gets us our minimum viable answer, except we haven't fully answered the question of whether certain cities are underserved. Figure 2.17 shows us that the largest cities produce the highest amount of customer spend. To understand whether a city is being underserved, we would need to know more about what we would base that on. This would require a conversation with our stakeholders to understand whether they are missing any cities they expected to see among the highest-spending ones shown in figure 2.17. Before we move on, let's review all the steps we took in this analysis (figure 2.18).

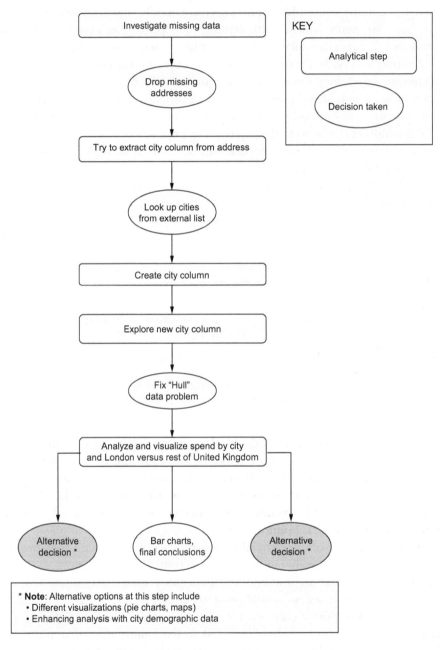

Figure 2.18   The final analysis steps visualized

At the end of this process, we have our minimum viable answer, and we're ready to bring it to our stakeholders.

2.2.3 Review and future steps

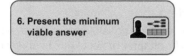

After cleaning our data and extracting city information, we have arrived at an answer to our analytical questions. Our customers spend the most in bigger cities since there are generally more customers in larger cities, and London generates nearly as much income as all the other cities combined. This insight, coupled with the table in figure 2.14 and the chart from figure 2.17, would fit on one or two slides to present to our stakeholders.

When presenting, we should be clear about the caveats of our analysis; namely, that not all addresses are in a format that allows us to extract the city correctly, at least with the method we have chosen. Another caveat is we have used the government's list of cities, which excludes larger towns that our stakeholders may be interested in. We would make it clear to our stakeholders that further work is possible to make our city-level figures more accurate. However, we would need to understand the business value of spending more time arriving at a more accurate figure when it might not change the overall result.

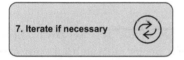

After presenting our results, our stakeholders may want us to continue the analysis and get a more comprehensive answer. What could we do to improve our solution? Perhaps, as we have discussed, we could identify the city or town an address refers to by identifying the postcode. Well, for that, we need a comprehensive list of UK postcodes, the assumption that all values in the "customer address" field contain postcodes, and the assumption that we can find the postcode every time. Another option is to expand our current city list to include towns above a certain population. However, this would not solve the problem where sometimes the name of the city or town is not in the address.

Another option is to send these addresses to a third-party geocoding system, such as the Google Maps API, which would find the best match for an address we provide, and the resulting data would contain a field for the town/city that we could use. However, this particular option raises privacy concerns. Do we want to send all our customers' addresses to a third party? Are we even allowed to do that?

Finally, we could augment our data with population statistics or even demographic information about each city or town. This could help us understand whether there are cities where customers are spending less than expected based on their city's population and are, therefore, being underserved. This was one of our stakeholders' initial concerns, and this would be one way to address it further.

You can start to see how many additional considerations are involved in solving a real business problem. This is why it is vital to arrive at a viable solution as soon as possible so that these additional possibilities are only considered if there is tangible business value in doing so. The value of any further work should be decided in collaboration with key stakeholders.

Activity: Further project ideas with this data

In each project chapter, I encourage you to think of other possible research questions to answer with this data, unrelated to the specific chapter project. This is an exercise to help you make your solution really your own and let it stand out in a portfolio. Here are some ideas to get you started:

- What do customer spending figures look like at different levels of granularity? You would need to either dig down into subcity levels, such as boroughs, or figure out how to group addresses that belong to the same geographic region (e.g., South West England).
- Can you identify business addresses and consider comparing customers with private addresses versus those with business addresses?
- Augment your geographic analysis with population figures or other demographics. Are there any patterns, such as a relationship between the wealth of an area and the amount of customer spend? You could also calculate "spending per capita" for each city and see if that varies across the country.

2.3   How to use the rest of the book

This chapter introduced both a specific example of the results-driven approach in practice and the format of all the projects. Each project throughout your career will require you to

- Ensure you understand the problem
- Think about the end goal you are working toward
- Consider whether you have the right data
- Identify the caveats you would need to flag when presenting your findings
- Document what further work is possible once you have arrived at a minimum viable answer

Each of this book's projects addresses a different topic you will encounter in real-world analytical projects, and they will all follow the same flow as the one in this chapter.

Summary

- Using a results-driven approach helps focus on the specific problem you are solving.
- Part of the results-driven approach is to ensure you understand the problem before starting the analysis.
- Envisioning the end result at the start creates a goal to work toward.

- There are multiple possible approaches to extracting the city part of a free-type address, each with its pros and cons.
- Analyses will diverge depending on the choices and assumptions made; therefore, it is possible to get different, but still correct, results.
- Even seemingly smaller tasks, such as extracting city information from address data, benefit from a results-driven approach by helping focus on a valuable outcome.

Data modeling 3

This chapter covers
- Modeling data as a fundamental analytical activity
- How to define business entities from raw data
- How to structure a data model to best suit the analytical question

As an analyst, you will find yourself applying the same logic to raw data over and over again. For example, every time you calculate revenue, you might need to remember to remove internal money transfers between departments. Or when you look at customer spending, you might need to exclude a certain customer because they operate differently. Whenever these business rules need to be applied constantly to ensure data is accurate, it is a good opportunity to build a *data model*.

A data model is a dataset created from raw data that has been cleaned, with specific business rules built into it. Creating reusable data models will save you time and maintenance headaches in the future. Data modeling also forces you to think deeply about your or your stakeholder's question, which leads to a more valuable answer.

Real business case: Customer deduplication

Once, when working in industry, I spent months on a customer deduplication project. We wanted to track the number of customers over time, but our customers were spread across multiple databases. Deduplicating them was not a trivial task, especially because, in some databases, customers appeared as company names, such as "South West Motors," and in others, they were recorded as individuals, such as "John Smith," with no information about the company they worked for.

In the end, our solution involved text similarity algorithms to find instances where "South West Motors" from one database existed as "South West Motors Limited" in another. We also used graph theory to link customers together across our company network. These are advanced algorithms for the seemingly simple task of counting customers. Entity resolution problems are everywhere, which is why this chapter explores the topic and lets you practice on a real problem.

In this chapter, we will review the fundamentals and importance of data modeling and practice converting raw data into a reusable data model using a real-world project.

3.1 The importance of data modeling

Data modeling is a foundational step in the analytical workflow. It is the process of taking raw data, mapping it to business-specific entities, and creating new data models. We can think of it as converting data in its raw state to a more useful form, which we can call information. Data analysis is then the process of converting this information into insight. The intermediate step is required because, in its raw form, data is often not ready for analysis. Figure 3.1 shows where data modeling fits into both the abstract and concrete versions of a data science workflow.

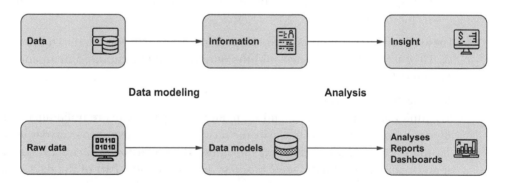

Figure 3.1 Data modeling and analysis as mapped to the data science process

Your data models should encode any business logic required to transform the raw data to be suitable for analysis. If you always need to remember to filter out certain rows from your raw data, you should have an intermediate data model where that filter has already been applied. What does a "lapsed customer" mean for your business? Is it someone who hasn't purchased anything for a certain time? Or perhaps someone who hasn't even logged in to your platform for a while? Whatever that definition, it should be encoded in a data model.

Creating data models increases transparency because there is a single place to look for how a customer, a vehicle, or a purchase event is defined. All other analyses should be done using these intermediate models, not the raw data. Another benefit is that this kind of cleaner data model could be exposed to data-savvy stakeholders to work with directly, thus enabling self-service. Business intelligence tools such as Tableau and Power BI allow power users to create their own reports. If that is done using centralized data models, analytical mistakes are less likely.

As analysts, we should be looking out for opportunities to standardize business logic by encoding it in data models. These don't have to be technically complex since they can simply be additional tables in our database. Let's look at some tasks involved in data modeling, which we will then practice in the project.

3.1.1 *Common data modeling tasks*

Data modeling usually involves some combination of

- Repetitive data cleaning tasks, such as fixing date formats or converting text columns into their numeric equivalents.
- Defining business entities, concepts, and activities.
- Deduplicating the source data.
- Restructuring the raw data to be in a format more useful to the analytical questions it is designed to answer. This might involve making a choice between wide or long data, which we will discuss later in this section.
- Zooming in or out, altering the level of granularity for different analytical questions.

These are all tasks you do not want to perform every time you need to do some analysis. They should be done once, and the output should be captured in an appropriate data model.

AGREEING ON TERMINOLOGY

As a junior analyst, you might end up in an industry that you are unfamiliar with. It is important to ask questions to clarify the terminology because even everyday terms like "customer" might have ambiguous meanings. Does a customer mean a single person or an organization? What if your business deals with both? Part of the data modeling process is defining these terms so that they can be encoded in a data table.

> **NOTE** When it comes to definitions, you cannot work in a vacuum; decisions about what concepts mean concretely need to be made in collaboration with your stakeholders.

HANDLING DUPLICATION

The data you will work with will inevitably contain some duplication, which might be in the form of duplicated rows of data or duplicate records across multiple systems. If you worked in the automotive industry, you could spend a nontrivial amount of time figuring out whether "John Smith Motors" in one database is the same customer as "JS Motors" in another. Time invested in reconciling this at the data modeling stage is time well spent.

Another important data modeling task is deciding the structure of your data, such as whether the data should be stored in a wide or a long format.

WIDE VS. LONG DATA

In many cases, your data will consist of one row per entity, such as a customer. Each row represents a customer, and each column represents a property or attribute of that customer, such as their name, age, department, and so forth. This is called a *wide* format because as the number of measurements grows, the data gains additional columns.

In contrast, *long* data is when one row represents a single measurement of an entity. This means an entity, such as a customer, will require multiple rows. When a new measurement about the entities is added, the data gains additional rows.

Let's take a concrete example. Suppose you are working for a sports analytics company and want to analyze the factors that go into sports teams that win major competitions. Table 3.1 shows the dataset of football results that you have.

Table 3.1   Football results in a wide format

Match ID	Date	Competition	Round	Home team	Away team	Home goals	Away goals
1	2014-07-04	World Cup 2014	Quarter-final	France	Germany	0	1
2	2014-07-04	World Cup 2014	Quarter-final	Brazil	Colombia	2	1
3	2014-07-05	World Cup 2014	Quarter-final	Argentina	Belgium	1	0

This is wide data because each row represents an entity, in this case, a match. With some enhancement (for instance, adding a "Winner" column), this dataset would allow easy analysis of questions such as "Which country has won the most games at a World Cup?"

However, what if someone asked, "Which country participated in the most World Cup games?" This is trickier because the level of granularity of each row is one row per match, so we would have to consider both the "Home team" and "Away team" columns. What we would need to answer this second question more easily is one row per *participant*. We could consider creating a long-format version of the data that would look more like table 3.2.

Table 3.2 The same football results in a long format, one row per match participant

Match ID	Date	Competition	Round	Team	Home or away?	Goals scored
1	2014-07-04	World Cup 2014	Quarter-final	France	Home	0
1	2014-07-04	World Cup 2014	Quarter-final	Germany	Away	1
2	2014-07-04	World Cup 2014	Quarter-final	Brazil	Home	2
2	2014-07-04	World Cup 2014	Quarter-final	Colombia	Away	1
3	2014-07-05	World Cup 2014	Quarter-final	Argentina	Home	1
3	2014-07-05	World Cup 2014	Quarter-final	Belgium	Away	0

This is now long data because rows don't represent unique entities. The table encodes the same information, but each match is duplicated on purpose. From this table, it is easier to focus only on the "Team" column to find the team with the most World Cup matches. The downside of this format is that we cannot simply count the number of rows to find statistics such as the number of games played at a World Cup because we would be double counting.

Neither a wide nor a long format is better than the other; the choice between them depends on the question you are trying to answer using the data. Assessing what format is best suited to your analytical question is the essence of data modeling.

IDENTIFYING THE RIGHT LEVEL OF GRANULARITY

Just like the football example, you will encounter datasets that have the wrong level of granularity for your analysis. US election result data might be at an individual county level, but you might have analytical questions about individual candidates. Having a candidate-level data model would help answer candidate-specific questions much faster. The information is the same; it is just stored in a format that is more appropriate for your analytical questions.

When beginning this project, start by asking, "What should the structure of the final data model be?" Working toward that goal (in a results-focused way!) will guide the concrete steps you will need to take.

3.2   *Project 2: Who are your customers?*

Let's look at our project, in which we will extract a customer database from a series of retail transactions. We will look at the problem statement, which is what our stakeholders want to achieve in their own words. I provide an overview of the available data and discuss some of the technical specifics of the example solution. Reading section 3.2 is sufficient to get started, but you may find section 3.3 helpful to see how the results-driven approach would be applied in this scenario.

The data is available at https://davidasboth.com/book-code. You will find the datasets with which you can attempt the project, as well as the example solution in the form of a Jupyter notebook.

3.2.1   Problem statement

In this example, you have been hired by Ebuy Emporium, a new e-commerce startup. They have been up and running for a month and have had unexpected success. They are starting to have an active interest in their customer base. Who are their customers? What do they buy? What drives their purchasing behavior? However, before they do any serious analysis, they need to be able to count their customers, which happens to be more difficult than anticipated. One problem is there are multiple sources of customer data, which are

- The e-commerce platform's customer database, where customer details are recorded when they sign up for an account online. This is where most of the customer details should be found.
- The in-house CRM (customer relationship management) system, where customer details are recorded when they make a purchase over the phone or are otherwise onboarded as customers (except because of purchasing online with a registered account).
- The raw transaction data, which we will hereafter refer to as "purchases" or "sales," and which also contains purchases made "as a guest," meaning customer records are not explicitly created at the time of purchase.

NOTE Original transaction data courtesy of REES46 (https://mng.bz/6eZo), enhanced with fictitious customer data from a European Union Collaboration in Research and Methodology (CROS) training program on record linkage (https://mng.bz/oKad). Thank you to the dataset owners for providing permission to repurpose the original source data.

Another problem is that the existing data sources may not be mutually exclusive—there might be overlaps across them all. There is almost certainly some duplication, either because the same customer had their details entered into multiple systems or because they have made purchases both as a guest and with a registered account. Duplicate accounts may not contain exactly the same information; there may be typos or misspellings. These complications are why the startup needs the help of an analyst to answer their question: "Who are our customers?"

3.2.2   Data dictionary

Tables 3.3 and 3.4 show the data dictionaries for the three data sources, and figures 3.2 and 3.3 show sample data.

Table 3.3   Data dictionary for the "purchases" dataset

Column	Definition
event_time	The exact date and time the purchase occurred.
product_id	The unique identifier of the purchased product.

Table 3.3   Data dictionary for the "purchases" dataset *(continued)*

Column	Definition
category_id	The unique identifier of the purchased product's specific category.
category_code	A broad category for the purchased product. In a hierarchy, category codes contain multiple category IDs, and one `category_id` should only be linked to one `category_code`.
brand	The purchased item's brand (if applicable).
price	The price the item was bought for (in USD).
session_id	A unique identifier for a purchase session. If multiple items are purchased in a transaction, each item will have a row in the table, and the rows will share a `session_id`.
customer_id	The unique identifier of the customer if they purchased using a registered account. For guest purchases, this value will be missing.
guest_first_name	The first name that was supplied if a purchase was made as a guest. For purchases made using registered accounts, this value will be missing.
guest_surname	The surname that was supplied if a purchase was made as a guest. For purchases made using registered accounts, this value will be missing.
guest_postcode	The postcode that was supplied if a purchase was made as a guest. For purchases made using registered accounts, this value will be missing.

	event_time	product_id	category_id	category_code	brand
0	2022-10-01 02:26:08+00:00	32701106	2055156924466332447	NaN	shimano
1	2022-10-01 02:28:32+00:00	9400066	2053013566067311601	NaN	jaguar
2	2022-10-01 02:31:01+00:00	1004238	2053013555631882655	electronics.smartphone	apple
3	2022-10-01 02:33:31+00:00	11300059	2053013555531219353	electronics.telephone	texet
4	2022-10-01 02:40:18+00:00	17300751	2053013553853497655	NaN	versace

(continued)

	price	session_id	customer_id	guest_first_name	guest_surname	guest_postcode
0	95.21	64c68405-7002-4ce0-9604-a4c2e1f7384b	NaN	MICHAEL	MASON	RG497ZQ
1	164.20	3b7d6741-3c82-4c75-8015-6f54b52612e0	7466.0	NaN	NaN	NaN
2	1206.40	38c6d3f7-6c32-4fed-bca6-ef98e1746386	NaN	COLE	WILKINSON	SW75TQ
3	17.48	3398c966-7846-4186-89be-323daad735b9	NaN	MOHAMMED	RICHARDS	RG150RE

Figure 3.2   A snapshot of the purchases dataset

Table 3.4   Data dictionary for the CRM and customers datasets, which share an identical structure

Column	Definition
customer_id	The unique identifier of the customer in this system
first_name	The customer's first name
surname	The customer's surname
postcode	The customer's postal code
age	The customer's age, in years

	customer_id	first_name	surname	postcode	age
0	29223	Holly	Rogers	LS475RT	12
1	27826	Daniel	Owen	M902XX	5
2	7432	Eleanor	Russell	HR904ZA	34
3	2569	Paige	Roberts	DE732EP	61
4	9195	Matilda	Young	LS670FU	78

Figure 3.3   A snapshot of the customer data

NOTE It is important to remember that the data dictionary refers to the assumptions about what data is present in each column. It is good practice to verify some of these assumptions as part of the exploratory data analysis phase. For example, do the customer IDs provided in the purchase data always match a record in one of the customer databases?

In this case, the data dictionaries are self-explanatory, but the first step in working with a new dataset should always be making sure we've read any relevant documentation.

3.2.3   Desired outcomes

The output of this project should be a single dataset representing your customer data model—your best estimate of the entire customer base the startup currently has. Data will come from the three sources provided, and you will need to consolidate and deduplicate accordingly. You will need to decide on the structure of the data model based on the columns available in the datasets. This data model should be structured so that all the logic to define customers is already in place, and answering the question "How many customers do we have?" should be done as simply as counting the rows.

There is no single right solution you're aiming for and no ground truth to check your answers against. This is partly because analysis contains so much ambiguity that different analysts will make different assumptions and arrive at different conclusions, and partly because tasks like this never have answers to check against in the real world. Part of being a good analyst is embracing constant uncertainty and ambiguity and being comfortable with an answer that may never be a complete one. The important thing is being able to provide an answer your stakeholders can use.

3.2.4   *Required tools*

Although the projects are technology agnostic, for this example solution, I use the Python library `pandas` to manipulate the datasets and `numpy` for numerical functions. I also introduce the `recordlinkage` library used for entity resolution. I keep the code snippets to a minimum and focus on the conceptual solution, but the full solution is presented as a Jupyter notebook. This is a tool for presenting code, data, and text in a single document, making it easy to share your findings, as well as the underlying methods. You can attempt this exercise with any number of tools as long as they satisfy the following criteria, that is, they are able to

- Load a dataset of tens of thousands of rows from a CSV file
- Create new columns and manipulate existing ones
- Join datasets together
- Perform basic analysis tasks such as sorting, grouping, and reshaping data

3.3   *Planning our approach to customer data modeling*

Let's use the results-driven approach to break the problem down into its logical components. This will give us a deeper understanding of our problem before we start working on it. We will also explicitly decide what not to do, that is, we will figure out which features of the problem are not essential to a first iteration.

3.3.1   *Applying the results-driven process to data modeling*

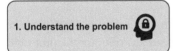

First, we need to understand the question. In this case, the question is vaguely "Who are our customers?" which would normally require some pushback for clarification. In this instance, whatever the actual analytical question about customers is, the data modeling step is fundamental to answering it. We must first consolidate the customer data from the three data sources.

> **TIP**   We could think about what additional data to augment it with to better fit the needs of the analytical questions. We know we want to end up with one row per customer, but we don't yet know if a summary of the customer's purchase history would be a useful addition. In this case, we don't want to spend time preemptively adding information to our data model because we think someone might ask for it down the line.

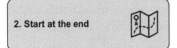

Our end product is quite well defined, but, specifically, starting from the end here means having an idea of the structure of the final data model, the existence of which will allow us to count customers to produce our minimum viable answer. We know that one of its most important properties should be that it contains one row per customer. That's the level of granularity we're aiming for. Any purchase data we augment it with would, therefore, need to be aggregated to the customer level; we couldn't include individual products purchased by a customer but could include their total spending, the date they first signed up, the number of unique purchases they made, and so forth.

Another aspect of looking ahead at our end result is to identify the schema of our final data model. What columns are common across our datasets? Are there columns we will have to drop before we combine the data sources, or are they important enough that we will accept some missing data in our final solution? In data modeling, these are all important aspects to think about up front, so we can keep them in mind while in the weeds of coding our solution, and we don't spend time manipulating data that we cannot use in the final data model.

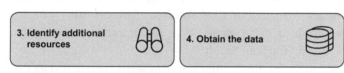

The datasets have been identified and provided for us in this case, so our "Identify" and "Obtain" steps have been done for us. However, in a real-world scenario, it would be prudent to think about any additional sources of customer data that might exist within our organization. This often includes spreadsheets kept by various sales managers on their computer desktops!

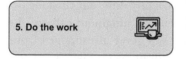

To actually do the data modeling task, here are some key steps to consider:

1 We would start by exploring all three datasets. We want to ascertain whether the columns contain what the data dictionaries have said. For example, are guest details always complete when we don't have a customer ID? We also want to see whether the values make sense. We're concentrating on customer data but might also want to see if the `price` column contains any unrealistic values. Are the date and time values all within the same period? Is there anything amiss with any of the postcode values? This is an iterative process, so we may not exhaust all our exploration at the beginning; some of these questions may only present themselves later on. We also don't want to spend too much time exploring columns we won't use.

2 Once we have verified some key assumptions about the data, one idea would be to deduplicate each dataset to just unique customers before merging them. This is especially true for purchases, where any time a customer buys multiple items, their details are repeated. We would also make some of the key decisions about differences in schema. If there is data that is only present in some of the sources, what do we do with it?

3 The next step is to combine these separate datasets; we want a dataset that contains all possible customer records. The combined dataset may contain duplicates. We can get rid of some obvious duplication by removing exact duplicates, which may arise if a customer record existed in both the customer database and the CRM data, and the records were otherwise identical. If the information in two customer records is identical, but the unique identifier differs, we would need to be careful. Casually removing a duplicate would result in the loss of what we might refer to as "data lineage," that is, the traceability of where our data originally came from. If we have a customer record for Jane Smith, it's good practice to keep all possible identifiers for that customer that we've encountered across datasets. Perhaps she is customer 8834 in one dataset and 931 in another, and we would want to know that somehow in our final data model. This not only makes it easier to trace her accounts back to their sources, but also increases trust in our final solution. Anyone using our data model knows the assumptions we've made about which customer accounts make up the customer "entity" for Jane Smith.

4 Next, we could look at deduplicating our combined customer data beyond simply identifying exact duplicates. Fuzzy string matching might be a good approach here; in this case, we compare two strings and judge them as identical if they almost are. When using fuzzy matching, typos are taken into account, and "London" and "Lodnon" are seen as the same string. Research in the field of record linkage and entity resolution may be helpful to read up on. These are entire topics dedicated to figuring out whether two slightly different versions of an entity are, in fact, the same. We would need to make a judgment call on whether this additional work has tangible benefits and is a good investment of our time. It might even be a task we leave for a second draft, as we may prefer to show our stakeholders our first findings before committing to this more complex step.

5 Finally, we would clean up the data model so that it has the schema we want, ensuring the column names are meaningful. Depending on how we choose to handle duplicate accounts, we may need to decide on a main account for each customer entity, for example.

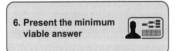

6. Present the minimum viable answer

The way to present a data model is by focusing on the implications of our work. Creating a small presentation outlining what we've done, how many customers we've found, and what assumptions our work is founded on would get more attention than giving access to the data model in the database. It is unlikely our stakeholders would ever use our data model to analyze data directly, anyway; the main benefit of the work is improved accuracy and more opportunities in customer analytics later on.

Presenting our findings also creates an opportunity to work with our stakeholders to make some of the analytical decisions together. Sometimes, we don't have the right intuition to choose between two seemingly similar options. A problem I have faced myself is when customers exist as companies in one database and individuals in another. I, as the analyst, shouldn't be the one that has the final say over whether "Jane Smith" is the same customer as her company "JS Motors"; that's a decision that needs wider business input, especially if the business is going to measure and track customer numbers over time. You can use the first iteration of your data model to present some of these key questions for your stakeholders to think about.

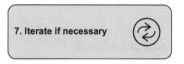

After getting feedback on your initial findings, it is usually apparent what the next iteration of your solution needs. In the context of the project, since we lack direct feedback from a stakeholder, iteration might mean you create a minimum viable data model quickly, perhaps stopping before doing any meaningful deduplication. Beyond allowing you to get feedback on your work quicker, getting to a minimum viable solution soon can give you the confidence that you're on the right track. You'll also have a solution in place that is easier to iteratively improve, rather than spending a long time on a more complex one, having nothing tangible to show for it until the end of a longer process. Alternatively, this might be the point at which it is apparent that there is no tangible business value in improving your solution further, so rather than iterating further, the project is considered complete.

3.3.2   Questions to consider

As you work through this project, here are some key questions to consider:

- What are the possible ways in which customers can be represented across these datasets? It may be helpful to list all scenarios (customers in CRM, customers who made a purchase, guest checkouts, etc.) to hone in on exactly what you will need to code.
- When you consider duplicates, how will linked accounts (i.e., a main account versus linked accounts) be represented?
- When deduplicating records, what fields do you want to use for deduplication? Are two people with the same name living at the same postcode necessarily the same person? How much do two customers' details need to differ before we consider them different people?

3.4   An example solution: Identifying customers from transactional data

Let's dive into the details of an actual example solution. I strongly recommend attempting the project yourself before reviewing the example solution. As with every project, the data files, as described in section 3.2, are in the supplementary materials. I also recommend reading this section even if you've got a solution you're happy with, not because the example solution is the only solution but because we can learn a lot from seeing how others approach the same problem.

3.4.1   *Developing an action plan*

We will first explore the data to see if our assumptions about it hold, whether any data is missing, and so on. Then, we will decide on a common schema for our datasets and trim them all down to this common schema, meaning we will have three smaller customer datasets—one from purchases, one from the customer database, and one from the CRM data—which are all structured the same way and can be easily combined. After combining the datasets, we will deduplicate our records to arrive at the best guess of our customer base.

3.4.2   *Exploring, extracting, and combining multiple sources of data*

We will explore each of the three datasets, extract common customer information from them, and combine them into one "master" view of customers. We will then look at deduplicating that combined dataset. Let's start with the raw purchases.

EXPLORING A NEW DATASET

We start by importing the necessary libraries and reading in the sales data:

```
import pandas as pd          ⎤  Imports necessary
import numpy as np        ◄──⎦  libraries

sales = pd.read_csv("./data/purchases.csv")   ◄──⎤  Reads in our purchases CSV
print(sales.shape)                          ◄──   ⎦  file as a pandas DataFrame

                                               Inspects the size of the DataFrame
```

The output of this code is (71519, 11), meaning just over 71,000 rows of data and 11 columns, so there are over 71,000 transactions in the purchases table. We know from the problem statement that guest checkouts will not make up all our transactions, so checking for missing data should at least reveal some missing guest information. The following code produces the output in figure 3.4, showing the count of missing values per column:

```
sales.isnull().sum()     ◄──⎤  A pandas trick to "add up"
                            ⎦  rows with missing values
```

```
event_time            0
product_id            0
category_id           0
category_code     16739
brand              5707
price                 0
session_id            0
customer_id       18448
guest_first_name  53071
guest_surname     53071
guest_postcode    53071
dtype: int64
```

Figure 3.4   Missing values in our purchases data

There are 18,448 missing customer IDs, which should relate to guest checkouts, and 53,071 missing guest values. Adding those up gives us 71,519, which is the total number of records, meaning that guest checkouts and registered user checkouts make up our entire dataset. There are seemingly no rows with either all this information missing or both being present, but we should verify this. First, let's create a new column to track guest checkouts, which happen when a customer ID is not provided:

```
sales["is_guest"] = sales["customer_id"].isnull()
```

Now, our is_guest column takes the Boolean value of True if the customer ID is missing. We can use this column to verify our assumption about the guest checkouts and the customer IDs being mutually exclusive. The first line of this code checks for cases where the transaction was a guest checkout, but we also had a customer ID, and the second returns cases where we had neither:

```
sales[sales["is_guest"] & sales["customer_id"].notnull()]
sales[(sales["is_guest"] == False) & sales["customer_id"].isnull()]
```

The output for both lines is presented in figure 3.5.

event_time	product_id	category_id	category_code	brand	price	session_id	(...)

Figure 3.5   The output of our code to check whether guest and registered user checkouts overlap

This is Python's way of telling us that there are no records for our criteria, meaning we can be sure that all rows are either a guest checkout or a purchase made by a registered customer. Next on our data quality agenda is checking what percentage of records are guest checkouts. This is not just for informational purposes, but also for us to get a sense of how many customer records we will have to infer. As guest checkouts are our weakest signal for a customer record, any guests we add to our customer database are assumed customers. They are inferred rather than concrete customer accounts.

For example, if someone entered John Smith as their guest checkout name, it could be because Mr. Smith was buying something on behalf of someone else, perhaps as a gift. Is John Smith the customer in this case? Or maybe it was someone using Mr. Smith's credit card, maybe one of his children. In this case, is the customer John Smith or the child? Either way, we have no more information to go on than the guest name, John Smith, and that is what we would need to put in the customer database. Counting the number of guest accounts is useful to determine what percentage of our customer data will be "assumed" cases like this. Using the is_guest column we created earlier, we can calculate its distribution:

```
sales["is_guest"].value_counts(normalize=True)
```

The output is shown in figure 3.6.

```
False     0.742055
True      0.257945
Name: is_guest, dtype: float64
```

Figure 3.6   The proportion of guest vs. registered user purchases

This tells us that 25% of the rows are guest checkouts, but we need to remember that one row represents a purchased *item*, not a customer record, so the proportion of customers who checked out as guests is not necessarily 25%. We can calculate this actual proportion:

```
guest_columns = ["guest_first_name", "guest_surname",
➥ "guest_postcode"]
unique_guests = sales[guest_columns].drop_duplicates()
print(len(unique_guests))
unique_customers = sales["customer_id"].unique()
cust_total = len(unique_customers) + len(unique_guests)
print(len(unique_guests) / (cust_total-1))
```

Gets a unique combination of guest columns

Gets all unique customer IDs

Subtracts 1 from the unique customer count because NULL is also counted

This prints a value of 8301 and another just under 0.25, meaning we have 8,301 unique combinations of guest columns, and once we extract unique customers, it turns out a quarter are indeed not registered and checked out as guests instead. This number won't be exact because there could be typos. We are assuming every combination of name and postcode is a unique customer, but a single customer making a typo during one of their checkouts would result in us double-counting them here. This, of course, assumes they are allowed to make a typo during the checkout process. We would need to know more about the actual e-commerce system to understand whether these guest columns relate to billing or credit card information, for example, where typos might cause the purchase to be rejected. Knowing the data-generating process is vital.

Let's summarize what we have so far. Figure 3.7 shows the progress we've made exploring the purchases dataset.

IDENTIFYING A COMMON STRUCTURE BETWEEN DATASETS

There are around 25,000 unique customer IDs, which represent registered customers, and another roughly 8,000 unique inferred guests, so from purchases alone, we estimate the upper bound of the number of customers to be around 33,000. I say upper bound because we will have to investigate duplicate accounts later, and this number may decrease if we find any. We also know that we have a first name, surname, and postcode available for guest checkouts. We will need to bear this in mind when we look at the other customer databases.

However, before we export our first intermediate dataset, we need to decide on a schema for our data model. We know our guest customers have names and postcodes,

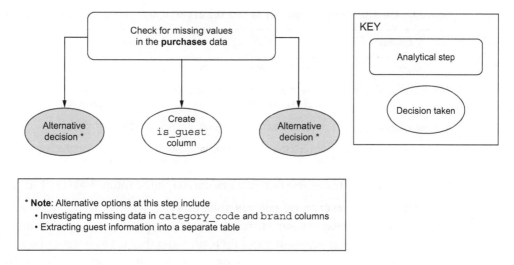

Figure 3.7   Progress in exploring the purchases dataset

and if we look at the data dictionary, we can see the customer and CRM datasets also have customer age. We don't really want to drop that column just because it is missing for guest accounts, so our final schema will include it.

It is generally a good idea to also keep track of where our records came from once they are combined into a single table. We could do this by adding a source column, which could have values of purchases, customer database, or CRM, but this structure would assume a record can only come from one place. We may encounter duplication, so a better choice is an indicator column for each data source, that is, a column to mark whether the record is present in the purchase data, another to indicate whether it's present in the customer database, and so on. These are mostly for data lineage purposes, so the source of the information is more transparent. We can also decide to explicitly track whether a record came from a guest checkout because this may be important later if a stakeholder wants to know what percentage of customers don't register when buying. Table 3.5 shows the final schema, which is what each of the three datasets needs to be transformed into.

Table 3.5   The data model schema that all data sources need to be transformed into

Column	Description
customer_id	The unique ID of the customer record, or NULL for guests.
first_name	Either from the customer or CRM tables or the guest information.
surname	Either from the customer or CRM tables or the guest information.
postcode	Either from the customer or CRM tables or the guest information.
age	From the customer or CRM tables, unavailable for guests.

Table 3.5   The data model schema that all data sources need to be transformed into *(continued)*

Column	Description
is_guest	True if the data comes from a guest checkout.
in_purchase_data	True if this customer record appears in the purchase table. It is not exclusive since the customer could also appear in the customer or CRM datasets.
in_crm_data	True if the customer record exists in the CRM database.
in_customer_data	True if the customer record exists in the customer database.

Let's go ahead and transform our first raw dataset, sales, into this desired structure.

RESTRUCTURING A DATASET TO THE COMMON STRUCTURE

The easiest way to export our customers from the purchase data is to extract the guests and non-guests separately and then combine them. These two subsets will not have the same structure because we have three columns for guests (first name, surname, and postcode) and for registered customers, we only have their IDs. We could join data from the customer and CRM tables to find the relevant names and postcodes for these IDs, or we could do that when we get around to exploring and manipulating the customer datasets. This choice is more personal preference than anything else. I've chosen to leave the joining until later, so for now, we will export incomplete data.

To export only the guests, we can filter using our is_guest column and export only the relevant columns:

```
guest_columns = ["guest_first_name", "guest_surname",
➥ "guest_postcode", "is_guest"]
guests = sales.loc[sales["is_guest"], guest_columns]
guests = guests.drop_duplicates()                          We drop duplicates
guests.head()                                              to ensure we only have
                                                           unique guest information.
```

The output is as presented in figure 3.8.

	guest_first_name	guest_surname	guest_postcode	is_guest
0	MICHAEL	MASON	RG497ZQ	True
2	COLE	WILKINSON	SW75TQ	True
3	MOHAMMED	RICHARDS	RG150RE	True
7	KIAN	MILLS	SW332TF	True
13	RUBY	OWEN	PO377YS	True

Figure 3.8   Guest data from the purchases table ready to be combined with customer data

For non-guest checkouts, we won't have these columns; we will have only a customer ID:

```
non_guests = (
  pd.DataFrame(
    sales.loc[sales["customer_id"].notnull(), "customer_id"]
      .unique()
      .astype(int),
    columns=["customer_id"]
  )
)
non_guests.head()
```

Customer ID is a single column, so we need to explicitly make it a DataFrame.

We extract unique customer IDs from non-guest rows.

The output is shown in figure 3.9.

	customer_id
0	7466
1	31266
2	534142828
3	1035
4	6985

Figure 3.9   Non-guest data from purchases, which is just a column of customer IDs

The data shown in figures 3.8 and 3.9 are of a different structure. However, when we combine them, we will have all the columns from both datasets and missing data where a column did not exist in one of the datasets:

```
sales_customers = pd.concat([non_guests,guests], axis=0, ignore_index=True)
```

First, we concatenate (or "union" if you are used to SQL terminology) our two datasets. Then, we rename our columns and remove the guest prefix:

```
new_col_names = ["customer_id", "first_name", "surname",
  "postcode", "is_guest"]
sales_customers = sales_customers.set_axis(new_col_names, axis=1)
```

We also want to make sure we don't have missing data, so we fill in the missing values for the is_guest column. Technically, we could leave it blank to indicate that someone isn't a guest, but explicitly using True/False values is clearer:

```
sales_customers["is_guest"] = sales_customers["is_guest"].fillna(False)
```

Now we add the in_purchase_data column we decided on for our schema:

```
sales_customers["in_purchase_data"] = True
```

Since we're working with text data, another important step is to ensure there is no trailing whitespace and that the names all use the same capitalization. This is so that customer names are treated as being the same even if one is lowercase and the other uppercase. We can use the `pandas` built-in `.str` accessor class, which lets us manipulate entire string columns:

```
for col in ["first_name", "surname"]:
    sales_customers[col] = sales_customers[col].str.lower().str.strip()

sales_customers["postcode"] = sales_customers["postcode"].str.strip()
```

Now, the customer data extracted from our purchases looks like figure 3.10.

	customer_id	first_name	surname	postcode	is_guest	in_purchase_data
0	7466.0	NaN	NaN	NaN	False	True
1	31266.0	NaN	NaN	NaN	False	True
2	534142828.0	NaN	NaN	NaN	False	True
3	1035.0	NaN	NaN	NaN	False	True
4	6985.0	NaN	NaN	NaN	False	True
...	...	...	...	...	...	...
33256	NaN	poppy	foster	M192EQ	True	True
33257	NaN	sophie	chapman	NW500AS	True	True
33258	NaN	scarlett	shaw	EX86QS	True	True
33259	NaN	michael	harrison	HR280TG	True	True
33260	NaN	skye	green	HR478ER	True	True

33261 rows × 6 columns

Figure 3.10 A preview of our customer data extracted from purchases

The first rows show the non-guest checkouts and the registered customers. For now, we have no names or postcodes for them because we decided to join those afterward. The last few rows in the preview show our guests, hence the missing customer ID.

Before we move on, let's summarize what we have done so far. Figure 3.11 shows the steps we took when exploring and reshaping the purchases dataset. Text that appears without shapes represents steps and decisions from previous sections.

We are now ready to move on and explore the customer datasets and merge them with the customer data we have just exported from our raw purchases.

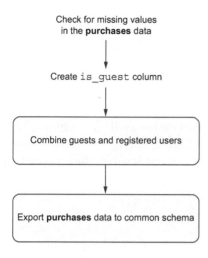

Figure 3.11 The steps we took on the purchases dataset

EXPLORING A SECOND DATASET

We know from the data dictionary that both customer datasets have the same schema. What we're looking for in both datasets is whether there is any missing data, whether the customer IDs are all filled in, and whether there are any duplicate records. Since customer ID is a unique identifier, we don't anticipate any duplicates, but you cannot assume anything. We start with the CRM data:

```
crm = pd.read_csv("./data/crm_export.csv")
print(crm.shape)
crm.head()
```

The shape of the dataset is `(7825, 5)`, meaning 7,825 rows and 5 columns. Figure 3.12 shows a preview of the CRM dataset.

	customer_id	first_name	surname	postcode	age
0	29223	Holly	Rogers	LS475RT	12
1	27826	Daniel	Owen	M902XX	5
2	7432	Eleanor	Russell	HR904ZA	34
3	2569	Paige	Roberts	DE732EP	61
4	9195	Matilda	Young	LS670FU	78

Figure 3.12 The first few rows of the raw CRM data

We check for missing data with the following code, the output of which is shown in figure 3.13:

```
crm.isnull().sum()
```

```
customer_id    0
first_name     0
surname        0
postcode       0
age            0
dtype: int64
```

**Figure 3.13   No missing data
in the CRM table**

The next bit of sanity checking is ensuring that customer IDs are unique. One way to do this is to group by the customer ID and find instances where there are multiple rows in a group. If customer IDs are unique, no records should be returned. Let's verify this:

```
crm.groupby("customer_id").size().loc[lambda x: x > 1]
```

Here we use `groupby` and `size` to count how many records we have per customer ID and use `loc` to filter instances where there is more than one. The Python output is `Series([], dtype: int64)`, which indicates no records were found, as the empty square brackets represent an empty collection in Python. This means customer IDs are indeed unique.

However, this does not mean that customer *details* are unique in the table. If we look at how many unique combinations of name, postcode, and age we have, we can see this:

```
print(len(crm))
print(len(crm.drop(columns="customer_id").drop_duplicates()))
```

The output is 7,825 and 7,419, respectively, meaning that while there are 7,825 rows in the CRM data, there are only 7,419 unique combinations of columns once we drop the customer ID, which indicates we have about 400 duplicate customer details where the same information is spread across multiple IDs. This might not mean 400 duplicate customers because we could also have multiple people with very common names living at the same postcode, but because we have also factored age into it, it is more likely these are all redundant duplicates. Incorrect duplicates, if there are any, are likely to be a very small percentage when we consider the size of the dataset, so it makes sense not to dwell on this, and for now, say that every unique combination of name, postcode, and age is a unique customer. The nature of data modeling work is that there will always be a margin of error.

Figure 3.14 summarizes what we have done so far with the CRM data.

JOINING DATASETS TO ENHANCE ONE WITH INFORMATION FROM ANOTHER
The next step is to transform the CRM data to the same schema as the customers from the purchase table, and we also need to enhance the registered customers in the purchase history with details from the CRM data. So far, we only have IDs for those customers, but we need their names, postcodes, and ages. Not all of them will be found in the CRM data, but we can join the two and populate as many rows as we can. We will

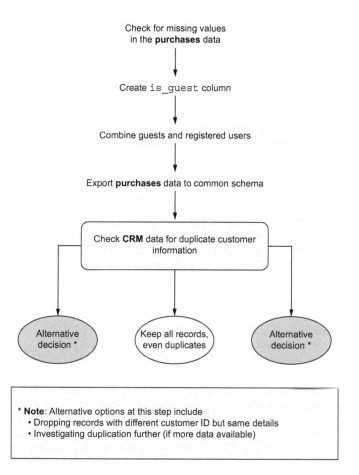

Figure 3.14   First steps in processing the CRM data

use a left join for this as that will ensure we keep all the rows in the original data regardless of whether we find a match in the other. The code for this is as follows, and the result is shown in figure 3.15:

```
sales_and_crm_customers = sales_customers.merge(crm,
➥ on="customer_id", how="left", suffixes=("_sales", "_crm"))
print(len(sales_and_crm_customers))
sales_and_crm_customers.isnull().sum()
```

One pandas-specific peculiarity is that columns that appear in both tables get an _x and _y suffix by default. We overrode this here to be more descriptive, so the ones with _sales are from the source data—the purchases—and the _crm suffix is given to the merged data, in this case, the CRM data.

Given that there were around 33,000 rows in the sales data and 26,000 rows missing from the newly added CRM customer columns, we can see we matched around

```
customer_id            8300
first_name_sales      24961
surname_sales         24961
postcode_sales        24961
is_guest                  0
in_purchase_data          0
first_name_crm        26147
surname_crm           26147
postcode_crm          26147
age                   26147
dtype: int64
```

Figure 3.15   Checking for missing values after merging the sales and CRM data

7,000 rows on customer ID. That is, customers in 7,000 purchases had their records stored in the CRM table. What we have now is a dataset where 7,000 customer records are in columns ending in _crm, which we should merge into the ones marked _sales, which contain customer data from guest checkouts. First, we define a filter to select only rows with a customer ID, thus excluding guests and rows with customer information in the crm-suffixed columns:

```
merged_customers_filter = (
  (sales_and_crm_customers["customer_id"].notnull())
    & ((sales_and_crm_customers["first_name_crm"].notnull())
      | (sales_and_crm_customers["surname_crm"].notnull()))
)
```

This filter can then be applied to identify these rows as having been found in the CRM data:

```
sales_and_crm_customers.loc[merged_customers_filter, "in_crm_data"] = True
sales_and_crm_customers.loc[~merged_customers_filter, "in_crm_data"] = False
sales_and_crm_customers["in_crm_data"].value_counts()
```

The output is shown in figure 3.16.

```
False    26147
True      7114
Name: in_crm_data, dtype: int64
```

Figure 3.16   Number of rows with customer information coming from the CRM data, after merging

This 7,114 number tallies with what we observed earlier, that around 7,000 rows have now had their customer information updated. Time to copy over data from crm-suffixed columns to our _sales suffixed ones and only keep the latter to get back to our original schema:

```
sales_and_crm_customers.loc[merged_customers_filter, ["first_name_sales",
  "surname_sales", "postcode_sales"]] = (
    sales_and_crm_customers.loc[merged_customers_filter, ["first_name_crm",
  "surname_crm", "postcode_crm"]]
```

```
    .values
)
```

Here, we simply copied over the first name, surname, and postcode to overwrite the missing values in `sales`-suffixed columns with CRM customer data in the `crm`-suffixed ones. Now we're ready to remove the latter:

```
sales_and_crm_customers = (
    sales_and_crm_customers
    .drop(columns=["first_name_crm", "surname_crm", "postcode_crm"])
    .rename(columns={
        "first_name_sales": "first_name",
        "surname_sales": "surname",
        "postcode_sales": "postcode"
    })
)
sales_and_crm_customers.head()
```

The output is shown in figure 3.17 and is what we'd expect. The schema is now the same as before, apart from a new `in_crm_data` flag, and the customer data from purchases has been enhanced with CRM data where possible.

	customer_id	first_name	surname	postcode	is_guest	in_purchase_data	age	in_crm_data
0	7466.0	NaN	NaN	NaN	False	True	NaN	False
1	31266.0	harley	palmer	HR250EJ	False	True	33.0	True
2	534142828.0	NaN	NaN	NaN	False	True	NaN	False
3	1035.0	NaN	NaN	NaN	False	True	NaN	False
4	6985.0	NaN	NaN	NaN	False	True	NaN	False

Figure 3.17 Combined purchase and CRM customer data

Immediately in the second row, we notice an example of a customer who purchased with a registered account, so they are not guests, but their details have been filled in via the CRM dataset. What remains is to check for and add customer details that exist in our CRM system but do not appear in our purchases. There may be reasons for this; perhaps those customers bought something on the phone, and those sales do not get recorded in the same place. Whatever the reason, it is a possibility that we need to account for to ensure full coverage.

USING SETS TO CROSS-REFERENCE TWO DATASETS

To find these records, we employ a Python trick to subtract one set of customer IDs from another, leaving us with the difference:

```
crm_ids_to_add = list(set(crm["customer_id"].unique())
    - set(sales_and_crm_customers["customer_id"].unique()))
print(len(crm_ids_to_add))
```

Here, "set" refers to the rigorous mathematical definition of a unique collection of items, and "difference" means the subtraction of one set from another, leaving us with only customer IDs that appear in the CRM data but not in purchases. The output tells us there are 711 such customers whose details need to be added to our growing customer dataset. We simply concatenate/union the data with the customers corresponding to the IDs we have just selected:

```
sales_and_crm_customers = (
    pd.concat([sales_and_crm_customers,
➥ crm[crm["customer_id"].isin(crm_ids_to_add)]],
            axis=0,
            ignore_index=True)
)
```

One final aspect of this data to clean up is that for these new customers, we don't have data for our source flags, so we fill them in with default values. Customers added from the CRM data will have their in_crm_data flag set to True, in_purchase_data as False, and since they weren't guests, is_guest as False. The output of the following code is shown in figure 3.18:

```
sales_and_crm_customers["is_guest"]
➥ = sales_and_crm_customers["is_guest"].fillna(False)
sales_and_crm_customers["in_purchase_data"]
➥ = sales_and_crm_customers["in_purchase_data"].fillna(False)
sales_and_crm_customers["in_crm_data"]
➥ = sales_and_crm_customers["in_crm_data"].fillna(True)

sales_and_crm_customers.isnull().sum()
```

```
customer_id         8300
first_name         17847
surname            17847
postcode           17847
is_guest               0
in_purchase_data       0
age                26147
in_crm_data            0
dtype: int64
```

Figure 3.18 After merging the CRM data and cleaning it, there are no missing values for our source flags.

Let's review what we have done with the CRM data before moving on. Figure 3.19 shows all the steps we have taken.

To summarize, we now have a customer dataset of all customers who made a purchase, including guest checkouts, as well as data from our CRM system, including customers who exist only in the CRM data and have no recorded purchases. We now need to repeat this process with data in the customer database, which is structurally similar to the CRM data.

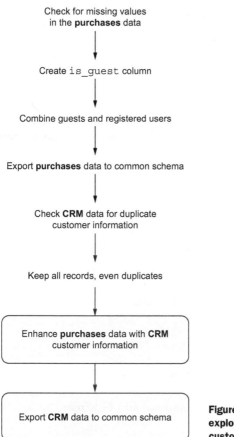

Figure 3.19 The steps we took to explore the CRM data and export customer information

EXPLORING A THIRD DATASET

Time to look at our customer database. The code will be similar to the one used to manipulate the CRM data but is included for completeness:

```
customers = pd.read_csv("./data/customer_database.csv")
print(customers.shape)
customers.head()
```

The output is (23476, 5), meaning we have over 23,000 customer records, which is significantly more than in our CRM data. A preview of what this data looks like is shown in figure 3.20.

The following code checks for missing data and produces the output shown in figure 3.21:

```
customers.isnull().sum()
```

	customer_id	first_name	surname	postcode	age
0	1641	Rhys	Richards	DE456EZ	45
1	24796	Maisie	Young	SW433XX	16
2	14358	Nathan	King	NW49TU	58
3	15306	Jack	Moore	NW908RR	26
4	24971	Alexander	Roberts	SW500HW	85

Figure 3.20 The first few rows of the customer data

```
customer_id    0
first_name     0
surname        0
postcode       0
age            0
dtype: int64
```

Figure 3.21 No missing data in the customer database

We sanitize our columns like we did for the CRM data:

```
for col in ["first_name", "surname"]:
    customers[col] = customers[col].str.lower().str.strip()

customers["postcode"] = customers["postcode"].str.strip()
```

Now, we can check whether customer ID is unique and how many unique combinations of customer information we have:

```
customers.groupby("customer_id").size().loc[lambda x: x>1]
```

This code yields the same output as in the CRM data, namely an empty Python collection, meaning there are no instances of the same customer ID appearing twice:

```
print("{} rows".format(len(customers)))
unique_customers = customers.drop(columns="customer_id").drop_duplicates()
print("{} unique combinations of customers".format(len(unique_customers)))
```

The output of the previous code tells us that 23,476 rows represent 19,889 unique combinations of customer details, so we potentially have around 3,500 duplicate records to handle. We will do this once all the customer data has been merged into a single table.

MERGING ALL OUR DATA SOURCES

The next step is to merge the customer information into the growing customer data by joining them. Again, we give the duplicate column names meaningful suffixes to show which table they came from:

```
all_customers = sales_and_crm_customers.merge(customers,
    on="customer_id", how="left", suffixes=("_sales", "_customers"))
all_customers.head()
```

The output of this merge is shown in figure 3.22.

	customer_id	first_name_sales	surname_sales	postcode_sales	is_guest	in_purchase_data
0	7466.0	NaN	NaN	NaN	False	True
1	31266.0	harley	palmer	HR250EJ	False	True
2	534142828.0	NaN	NaN	NaN	False	True
3	1035.0	NaN	NaN	NaN	False	True
4	6985.0	NaN	NaN	NaN	False	True

(continued)

	age_sales	in_crm_data	first_name_customers	surname_customers	postcode_customers	age_customers
0	NaN	False	eve	richards	HR90PT	45.0
1	33.0	True	NaN	NaN	NaN	NaN
2	NaN	False	NaN	NaN	NaN	NaN
3	NaN	False	luca	gibson	DE256NH	30.0
4	NaN	False	mia	rogers	HR662RP	43.0

Figure 3.22 The first few rows of the sales and CRM customers merged with the customer database

As with the CRM data, we have duplicates of the customer detail columns. We will now identify which rows were successfully merged with the customer database, mark them with a final flag `in_customer_data`, and copy those details over to the `_sales`-suffixed columns before finally removing the redundant columns and arriving at our final schema. The output for the following code is shown in figure 3.23:

```
merged_customers_filter = (
    (all_customers["customer_id"].notnull())
    & ((all_customers["first_name_customers"].notnull())
        | (all_customers["surname_customers"].notnull()))
)
all_customers.loc[merged_customers_filter, "in_customer_data"] = True
all_customers.loc[~merged_customers_filter, "in_customer_data"] = False
all_customers["in_customer_data"].value_counts()
```

```
True     22053
False    11919
Name: in_customer_data, dtype: int64
```

Figure 3.23 The distribution of the new flag, showing whether a customer's details appear in the customer database

Almost two-thirds of purchases relate to customers whose details are stored in the customer database. We can now update the original customer details, those with a _sales suffix, with details from the customer database:

```
update_filter = (                                    ←——| A filter to mark customers
    (all_customers["in_customer_data"])                  | whose details we copy over
    & (all_customers["first_name_sales"].isnull())
    & (all_customers["surname_sales"].isnull())
)

all_customers.loc[update_filter, ["first_name_sales",
➡ "surname_sales", "postcode_sales", "age_sales"]] = (
    all_customers.loc[update_filter, ["first_name_customers",
➡ "surname_customers", "postcode_customers", "age_customers"]].values
)                                                    ←——

all_customers = (                                    ←——|  We then
    all_customers                                            overwrite
    .drop(columns=["first_name_customers", "surname_customers",   those
    "age_customers", "postcode_customers"])                 customers'
    .rename(columns={                                       details.
        "first_name_sales": "first_name",
        "surname_sales": "surname",              Finally, we merge
        "age_sales": "age",                      the columns into
        "postcode_sales": "postcode"             the final schema.
    })
)
```

We also need to add any customers present in the customer database who do not appear in the purchases table:

```
customer_ids_to_add = list(set(customers["customer_id"].unique())
➡ - set(all_customers["customer_id"].unique()))
print(len(customer_ids_to_add))
```

This returns 1,423 additional customers to add:

```
all_customers = (
    pd.concat([all_customers,
➡ customers[customers["customer_id"].isin(customer_ids_to_add)]],
        axis=0,
        ignore_index=True)
)
```

Finally, we update the source flags to reflect their correct defaults if they are missing. Any newly added customers are not guests, didn't come from purchases or the CRM data, but are present in the customer database:

```
all_customers["is_guest"] = all_customers["is_guest"].fillna(False)
all_customers["in_purchase_data"]
➡ = all_customers["in_purchase_data"].fillna(False)
```

```
all_customers["in_crm_data"]
⇨ = all_customers["in_crm_data"].fillna(False)
all_customers["in_customer_data"]
⇨ = all_customers["in_customer_data"].fillna(True)
```

We can now inspect the final schema of our combined customer data model, shown in figure 3.24:

```
all_customers.head()
```

	customer_id	first_name	surname	postcode	is_guest	in_purchase_data	age	in_crm_data	in_customer_data
0	7466.0	eve	richards	HR90PT	False	True	45.0	False	True
1	31266.0	harley	palmer	HR250EJ	False	True	33.0	True	False
2	534142828.0	NaN	NaN	NaN	False	True	NaN	False	False
3	1035.0	luca	gibson	DE256NH	False	True	30.0	False	True
4	6985.0	mia	rogers	HR662RP	False	True	43.0	False	True

Figure 3.24 A preview of the customer data merged from all three sources

From figure 3.24, we can already understand the combinations of where customer data comes from. The third row shows us another edge case we had to be prepared for—a purchase from a registered customer whose details we do not have in either the CRM data or the customer database. We know very little about this customer, but they were given an ID, so their details may be in another system. As analysts, we would reach out internally to the business and find an explanation. Until then, we should keep these rows as they are potentially legitimate customer entities and should thus be counted in our data model.

Let's summarize all our steps so far. We explored three different sources of customer data, transformed them into the same schema, and finally merged them into a single table of customer information. Figure 3.25 shows all our steps so far.

Taking stock of what we have so far, we have merged our three sources of customer data, taking care to cover all eventualities, totaling 35,395 records. One step we will take before moving on to deduplication is to get a sense of the size of our various customer record types. There are four ways we could have added customers to our data model:

- *Identified customers*—Customers who made a purchase and their details are present in either the CRM data or the customer database
- *Guest checkouts*—Customers whose details come from what they entered as a guest
- *Unidentified customer IDs*—Customers with a valid ID but with no corresponding record in either customer dataset
- *Customers with no purchases*—Customers who are present in either customer dataset but do not appear in the purchases data

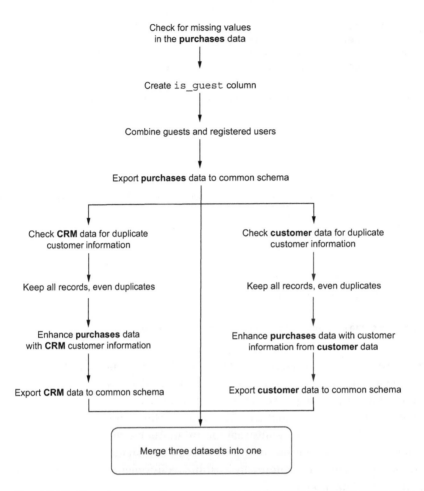

Figure 3.25   Steps to process three sources of customer data and finally merge them

These customer types are mutually exclusive, and their numbers should add up to the entire data model. We can verify this:

```
identified_customers = (
    all_customers[(all_customers["customer_id"].notnull())
                  & (all_customers["in_purchase_data"])
                  & ((all_customers["in_crm_data"])
                     | (all_customers["in_customer_data"]))]
)

guests = all_customers[all_customers["is_guest"]]

customer_ids_not_found = (
    all_customers[(all_customers["customer_id"].notnull())
                  & (all_customers["first_name"].isnull())
                  & (all_customers["surname"].isnull())]
)
```

```
customer_data_only = (
    all_customers[((all_customers["in_crm_data"])
                    | (all_customers["in_customer_data"])
                    )
                  & (all_customers["in_purchase_data"] == False)]
)

print(len(all_customers), len(identified_customers))
print(len(guests), len(customer_ids_not_found), len(customer_data_only))
```

The output is the following: 35,395 records in the entire data model, 23,713 of which are identified customers, 8,300 guests, 1,248 unidentified customer IDs, and 2,134 customers with no purchases. The first number is the sum of the others, so we can be confident we did not miss any of our eventualities, and they don't overlap. At this stage, we know there might be some duplication, so we move on to the final part of modeling our customer data—entity resolution.

3.4.3 Applying entity resolution to deduplicate records

One possible kind of duplication we might have is the same customer's details appearing in both the CRM data and the customer database. In this case, we might have rows in our data model that are exact duplicates, which are easy to drop:

```
print(len(all_customers))                              ⟵  Checks the count of rows
all_customers = all_customers.drop_duplicates()            before deduplicating
print(len(all_customers))                              ⟵  Checks the row count
                                                           again to see any impact
```

The output for both statements is the same—35,395 records—meaning there are no exact duplicates. In this case, this is because we updated our flags along the way. That is, customers present in multiple data sources simply have multiple source flags set to `True`, so there were no exact duplicates to drop.

One consideration at this point is that guest checkout customers are missing the age column. There is a choice to make here: Do we drop this column because our final data model would contain missing data, or do we include it but avoid using it for deduplication? If you're going to drop data, it's better to do it as late as possible, so it makes sense to keep that column. When we deduplicate the records, we can decide whether two customers with otherwise identical information, but one has their age filled in and the other doesn't, are the same customer.

FILLING IN MISSING DATA WITH UNIQUE IDENTIFIERS

Another decision we can make is whether to give guest accounts fake customer IDs rather than leaving them as missing data. When we get to the deduplication step, it is a good idea to link accounts together, that is, identify customer IDs that relate to the same underlying customer entity. With guest accounts, we cannot do this unless they also have unique identifiers, so it makes sense to give them their own IDs. One idea is to allocate a range of integers only for guest accounts. We can look at the existing IDs to see the current range:

```
all_customers["customer_id"].agg(["min", "max"])
```

The output tells us the current IDs range from the number 1 all the way to 9-digit integers, so a safe range would need to be well outside this. One option is to use negative numbers instead to identify each unique guest (i.e., each combination of guest customer data points). Negative IDs are unusual for unique identifiers, but the alternative approach of allocating an ID range for guests, say, in the 12-digit range, feels just as artificial. Another option could be to create alphanumeric identifiers, like a number preceded by a "G" for "guest," but since customer IDs are otherwise all integers, it's a personal choice not to branch out into the alphanumeric:

```
all_guests = all_customers[all_customers["is_guest"]].copy()
new_ids = np.arange(-1, -(len(all_guests) + 1), -1)          ⬅────┐
all_customers.loc[all_customers["is_guest"], "customer_id"] = new_ids    │
                                                                          │
                            We create an automatic range of values       │
                              starting from −1 and decreasing.   │
```

Now, our guest customers have IDs ranging from −1 to −8300. At this stage, we should have no duplicate records for customers that appeared in multiple datasets. However, we could still have duplicate records for the same customer if they somehow received two different customer IDs in different systems. Customer John Smith, with an ID of 123, might still be the same customer as John Smith, with an ID of 456.

Now, we are at the final deduplication phase; we might not be talking about a large percentage of duplicate records. As I mentioned when discussing iteration, in the first pass, we might even choose to ignore the duplication, in which case we already have our first customer data model. However, this is a task where we want to be as accurate as possible and would ideally reduce duplication to zero.

FINDING AND LINKING DUPLICATE RECORDS

The most straightforward initial deduplication approach is to say that if two customers have the same values for first name, surname, postcode, and age, they are the same customer. However, this might be a problem if we have a guest account who is the same customer as one already in the CRM system, which we wouldn't know if we included age in the comparison, as it would be missing for the guest record. Using only first name, surname, and postcode may be a combination good enough to start with. We can write some code now to find all customer IDs whose first name, last name, and postcode match exactly.

First, we create an object, `duplicates`, which is a list of all customer records that are identical to one another in the columns we specified. The `keep=False` parameter ensures we keep all relevant records, not just the duplicate ones. Having the `keep` parameter as anything else would drop the first instance and only keep the other rows, the duplicates:

```
columns_to_consider = ["first_name", "surname", "postcode"]

duplicates = all_customers[all_customers.duplicated(
➥ subset=columns_to_consider, keep=False)]
```

We can now create a lookup dictionary where each customer ID is linked to all the other records, which are its duplicates. A sample of this dictionary is shown in figure 3.26:

```
duplicate_dict = duplicates.groupby(columns_to_consider)['customer_id']
➥ .apply(list).to_dict()
```

```
{('aaliyah', 'harvey', 'SO760SX'): [22648, 27397],
 ('aaliyah', 'mills', 'PO872DJ'): [32561, 18324],
 ('aaliyah', 'morgan', 'M190JH'): [10157, 30899],
 ('aaliyah', 'robinson', 'DE533TL'): [1905, 31960],
```

Figure 3.26 A sample of the duplicate lookup dictionary

This dictionary tells us that, for example, there are two customer IDs for Aaliyah Harvey at postcode SO760SX: 22648 and 27397. We can use this dictionary to create a new column, `other_customer_ids`, where we store this list for accounts that have duplicates. A sample of the resulting data is shown in figure 3.27:

```
all_customers['other_customer_ids'] = all_customers.apply(
➥ lambda x: duplicate_dict.get((x['first_name'],
➥ x['surname'], x['postcode'])), axis=1)
```

	customer_id	first_name	surname	postcode	is_guest	in_purchase_data	age
0	7466	eve	richards	HR90PT	False	True	45.0
1	31266	harley	palmer	HR250EJ	False	True	33.0
2	534142828	NaN	NaN	NaN	False	True	NaN
3	1035	luca	gibson	DE256NH	False	True	30.0
4	6985	mia	rogers	HR662RP	False	True	43.0

(continued)

	in_crm_data	in_customer_data	other_customer_ids
0	False	True	None
1	True	False	[31266, 5411]
2	False	False	None
3	False	True	None
4	False	True	None

Figure 3.27 A sample of rows with the new `other_customer_ids` column

Figure 3.27 shows that, for example, Harley Palmer at postcode HR250EJ has two customer records: IDs 31266 and 5411. Strictly speaking, our other_customer_ids column should not be self-referential, so we should remove a customer's own ID from it. We can create a small function to do that and apply it to the rows with duplicates. Figure 3.28 shows the data after we run the following code. From this, we can notice an instance where a guest account for Max Moore, at postcode M902XX, is linked to a registered customer ID as a duplicate:

```
def remove_own_record(row):
    ids = list(row["other_customer_ids"])
    ids.remove(row["customer_id"])
    return ids

all_customers.loc[all_customers["other_customer_ids"].notnull(),
    "duplicate_customer_ids"] = (
      all_customers[all_customers["other_customer_ids"].notnull()]
    .apply(remove_own_record, axis=1)
)
```

	customer_id	first_name	surname	postcode	is_guest	in_purchase_data	age
1	31266	harley	palmer	HR250EJ	False	True	33.0
5	26434	bailey	richardson	SW988AF	False	True	31.0
6	28961	skye	johnson	M80NA	False	True	54.0
10	12586	max	moore	M902XX	False	True	20.0
12	22825	alicia	wood	SO879UN	False	True	24.0

(continued)

	in_crm_data	in_customer_data	other_customer_ids	duplicate_customer_ids
1	True	False	[31266, 5411]	[5411]
5	True	True	[26434, 27761]	[27761]
6	False	True	[28961, 12140]	[12140]
10	True	False	[12586, -6174, 32914]	[-6174, 32914]
12	False	True	[22825, 28495]	[28495]

Figure 3.28   The new duplicate_customer_ids **column**

As a reminder, what we want our database to contain is one row per customer, and each customer who has duplicate records has this fact marked somehow. The data, as it stands, has multiple rows for the same customer entity, one from the point of view of each, an example of which is shown in figure 3.29. Customers 31266 and 5411 are likely the same entity, and their duplication is recorded from both points of view.

	customer_id	first_name	surname	postcode	is_guest	in_purchase_data	age
1	31266	harley	palmer	HR250EJ	False	True	33.0
7208	5411	harley	palmer	HR250EJ	False	True	33.0

(continued)

	in_crm_data	in_customer_data	other_customer_ids	duplicate_customer_ids
1	True	False	[31266, 5411]	[5411]
7208	True	False	[31266, 5411]	[31266]

Figure 3.29   The same customer entity represented as two rows

There are two ways to tackle this problem. One is to delete one of the duplicate records entirely, thus reducing the data down to one row per entity. The duplicate_customer_ids column would still record the fact that this customer entity is referred to by multiple customer IDs, but the rest of the customer data for the duplicate ID would no longer be there. Ideally, each row would be a deduplicated customer record, but another option is to create an is_main flag against rows to identify them this way. The advantage is that all data lineage is preserved, and the downside is that you can't simply count the rows anymore; you would need to remember to filter on is_main each time. Choosing which representation is better for your data model will again depend on the context in which the data model will be used. Technically, if customers 1480 and 1481 are the same customer, they're the same customer *entity* but two distinct *records*, and my personal preference is to delete as little data as possible, so in the example solution, I've used the is_main flag approach.

Whichever representation you choose, you still need to decide which customer record is the main one. One method is to simply use the first one you encounter. It is unlikely to make a big difference, but a more principled way would be to use a better metric, like number of transactions, total spending, and so forth, to decide which customer record deserves "main" status.

The technical trick to create the flag is to generate a column that gives each duplicate a rank and a row number in the order they are encountered. Anything with a rank of 1 simply becomes a main account. This approach will work for duplicates and unique records, as the first instance of a combination of customer details will always have a rank of 1:

```
all_customers["rank"]
    = all_customers.groupby(columns_to_consider).cumcount()+1
```

Figure 3.30 shows the same duplicate pair as in figure 3.24, with the new `rank` column added.

	customer_id	first_name	surname	postcode	is_guest	in_purchase_data	age
1	31266	harley	palmer	HR250EJ	False	True	33.0
7208	5411	harley	palmer	HR250EJ	False	True	33.0

(continued)	in_crm_data	in_customer_data	other_customer_ids	duplicate_customer_ids	rank
1	True	False	[31266, 5411]	[5411]	1.0
7208	True	False	[31266, 5411]	[31266]	2.0

Figure 3.30 Our data with a new `rank` column

Now, we have one row per customer record, but to count distinct customer entities, we can create our `is_main` flag to make the data model more obvious. Once we've done this, we no longer need our `rank` column:

```
all_customers.loc[all_customers["rank"] == 1, "is_main"] = True
all_customers["is_main"] = all_customers["is_main"].fillna(False)
all_customers = all_customers.drop(columns="rank")
```

Finally, we can count the records:

```
print(f"Total customers in DB: {len(all_customers)}")
print(f"Of which {len(all_customers[all_customers['is_main']])}
➥ are unique/main records")
```

The output shows that out of 35,395 records, 27,394 are unique/main records. This assumes that two customers with the same name and postcode are the same customer and that there are only *exact* duplicates. To ensure our solution is as accurate as possible, given the data, we can try to match records that are *almost* identical.

USING ENTITY RESOLUTION TOOLS TO IMPROVE DEDUPLICATION

Once our dataset is deduplicated, around the 27,000 mark, we may wish to apply more advanced ideas in future iterations. One is fuzzy string matching to link accounts that differ by a simple typo. Another idea is to investigate whether you could use purchasing patterns to identify identical customers. In the case where two customers match on most columns but, say, differ in their age, you could use additional information like their purchases to decide whether they refer to the same customer. For this example, we'll identify accounts that are almost identical and see if that makes a difference. When it comes to more complex topics, such as record linkage, there is often a Python package we can use rather than implement any algorithms ourselves. In this case, we will use the Python Record Linkage Toolkit, which implements multiple algorithms for record deduplication and linking efficiently. An important aspect of being an analyst today is identifying when to use the work of others. We don't always need a deep understanding of the underlying algorithms and implementations before we use external libraries as long as we know what to expect from the output and can investigate problems when they occur.

Let's feed our data into this toolkit, a module called `recordlinkage`:

```
import recordlinkage
```

We can effectively follow the basic tutorial from the toolkit's data deduplication page (https://mng.bz/nRYa) and modify it to our needs. First, we index our dataset so that we don't try to compare every pair of records to each other but tell the code that two records at the same postcode should be tested for duplication. This assumes there are no typos in the postcode, which may not be the case, but it will make our code run much faster as there are fewer comparisons to make. Sometimes, we need to trade off accuracy and performance:

```
indexer = recordlinkage.Index()
indexer.block('postcode')
candidate_links
➥ = indexer.index(all_customers.set_index("customer_id"))
```

Creates an Index object

Marks postcode as a column to use for indexing

Applies the indexing to the data

We set the index to be the `customer_id` column because that way, our final dataset of matches will retain this name, as we will see. Next, we set up the comparison rules: How should our records be compared against each other? Should matches be exact or allowed to be fuzzy? We can also choose the algorithm with which to make a fuzzy comparison between strings. Here, we use the Damerau–Levenshtein method, which is a measure of *edit distance*, that is, the number of individual character edits required to get from one string to another. The higher the distance, the less similar the two strings are. Here, you could experiment with different comparison methods and observe the results:

```
compare = recordlinkage.Compare()
compare.string('first_name', 'first_name', method='damerau_levenshtein',
➥ threshold=0.85, label="first_name")
compare.string('surname', 'surname', method='damerau_levenshtein',
➥ threshold=0.85, label="surname")
compare.exact('postcode', 'postcode', label="postcode")
```

Creates a comparison object

Names should be fuzzy comparisons; anything over 85% similar is a match.

Postcodes should match exactly.

Now, we are ready to use our comparison rules to perform the pairwise comparisons. This creates a DataFrame containing all compared pairs and whether each of our comparison criteria was met. A sample of the output is shown in figure 3.31:

```
compare_vectors = compare.compute(candidate_links,
➥ all_customers.set_index("customer_id"))
```

customer_id_1	customer_id_2	first_name	surname	postcode
7523	7466	0.0	0.0	1
7492	7466	0.0	0.0	1
	7523	0.0	0.0	1
7518	7466	0.0	0.0	1
	7523	0.0	0.0	1

Figure 3.31   A sample of the output of our record linkage attempt

This sample shows that, for example, customer IDs 7523 and 7466 match on postcode but not on name. We can reduce this data down to only the cases where all comparisons returned a match:

```
matches = compare_vectors[compare_vectors.sum(axis=1) == 3]
```

The output is the same structure as figure 3.31 but with only perfect matches. Next, we should merge these customer IDs back to the original dataset and see if we've improved our record-linking attempts from before:

```
match_df = pd.DataFrame(          ⟵  Creates a new DataFrame containing
    data=matches.index.tolist(),      only the two columns of customer IDs
    columns=["customer_id_1", "customer_id_2"]
)
matched = all_customers.merge(match_df, left_on="customer_id",
➥ right_on="customer_id_1", how="left", suffixes=("_customers", "_matches"))  ⟵
matched = matched.merge(match_df, left_on="customer_id",
➥ right_on="customer_id_2", how="left", suffixes=("_customers", "_matches"))  ⟵
```

Joins customer data on the second customer ID

Joins customer data on the first customer ID

The matches dataset is already deduplicated in the sense that if customers 1 and 2 are duplicates, we do not have two records from each of their perspectives, so joining on both customer IDs means we ensure we have merged the main customer with all the duplicates found by recordlinkage. Figure 3.32 shows the relevant columns of our current merged data. There is an instance where both the duplicate_customer_ids column, created by looking for exact matches, and the new customer_id columns, created by the latest fuzzy matching attempt, agree with each other on records 5411 and 31226.

	customer_id	first_name	surname	postcode	other_customer_ids	duplicate_customer_ids
0	7466	eve	richards	HR90PT	None	NaN
1	31266	harley	palmer	HR250EJ	[31266, 5411]	[5411]
2	534142828	NaN	NaN	NaN	None	NaN
3	1035	luca	gibson	DE256NH	None	NaN
4	6985	mia	rogers	HR662RP	None	NaN

(continued)

	is_main	customer_id_1_customers	customer_id_2_customers	customer_id_1_matches	customer_id_2_matches
0	True	NaN	NaN	NaN	NaN
1	True	NaN	NaN	5411.0	31266.0
2	False	NaN	NaN	NaN	NaN
3	True	NaN	NaN	NaN	NaN
4	True	NaN	NaN	NaN	NaN

Figure 3.32 New columns added by merging the linked records back to our customer data model

One problem we need to resolve with this new merged data is that records with multiple duplicates are now repeated (e.g., customer ID 30730), as shown in figure 3.33.

	customer_id	first_name	surname	postcode	other_customer_ids	duplicate_customer_ids
4829	30730	harvey	robertson	NW436BL	[30730, 28816, 13817, 13814]	[28816, 13817, 13814]
4830	30730	harvey	robertson	NW436BL	[30730, 28816, 13817, 13814]	[28816, 13817, 13814]
4831	30730	harvey	robertson	NW436BL	[30730, 28816, 13817, 13814]	[28816, 13817, 13814]

(continued)

	is_main	customer_id_1_customers	customer_id_2_customers	customer_id_1_matches	customer_id_2_matches
4829	True	NaN	NaN	28816.0	30730.0
4830	True	NaN	NaN	13817.0	30730.0
4831	True	NaN	NaN	13814.0	30730.0

Figure 3.33 Three duplicates means three rows of data, which we need to merge into one

To merge these rows into a single row, as we have in the `duplicate_customer_ids` column, we can write a small function to collect all linked customer IDs for a given customer ID. We joined our linked pairs twice, so both the `customer_id_1_customers` and `customer_id_2_matches` columns could refer to our customer, and the `customer_id_2_customers` and `customer_id_1_matches` columns could refer to the duplicate ID:

```
def merge_duplicates(group):
    duplicate_list = []
    if np.isnan(group["customer_id_1_matches"].values[0]) == False:
        duplicate_list.extend(group["customer_id_1_matches"].tolist())
    if np.isnan(group["customer_id_2_customers"].values[0]) == False:
        duplicate_list.extend(group["customer_id_2_customers"].tolist())
    if len(duplicate_list) > 0:
        return sorted(list(set([int(x) for x in duplicate_list])))
    return np.nan

linkages = (
    matched
    .groupby("customer_id")
    .apply(merge_duplicates)
    .reset_index(name="linked_duplicates")
)
```

Our function collects the necessary values from multiple rows into a single list, and we apply this function to each customer ID, in turn, to reduce the dataset down to one row per customer ID again. The output is shown in figure 3.34.

	customer_id	linked_duplicates
0	-8300	NaN
1	-8299	[5652]
2	-8298	NaN
3	-8297	NaN
4	-8296	NaN

Figure 3.34 A preview of our customer IDs linked to their duplicates

We can use the `customer_id` column to merge this data back to our data model, so we have two sets of duplicates to compare side by side—the one that only uses exact matches and the latest one, which also uses fuzzy string matching:

```
all_customers = all_customers.merge(linkages, on="customer_id", how="left")
```

Our data now looks like that in figure 3.35.

Now, we can compare instances where the two columns `duplicate_customer_ids` and `linked_duplicates` do not agree. Figure 3.36 shows some of the rows as the output of the following code:

```
(
    all_customers[(all_customers["duplicate_customer_ids"].notnull())
            & (all_customers["linked_duplicates"].notnull())
            & (all_customers["duplicate_customer_ids"]
    != all_customers["linked_duplicates"])]
)
```

	customer_id	first_name	surname	postcode	is_guest	in_purchase_data	age
0	7466	eve	richards	HR90PT	False	True	45.0
1	31266	harley	palmer	HR250EJ	False	True	33.0
2	534142828	NaN	NaN	NaN	False	True	NaN
3	1035	luca	gibson	DE256NH	False	True	30.0
4	6985	mia	rogers	HR662RP	False	True	43.0

(continued)

	in_crm_data	in_customer_data	other_customer_ids	duplicate_customer_ids	is_main	linked_duplicates
0	False	True	None	NaN	True	NaN
1	True	False	[31266, 5411]	[5411]	True	[5411]
2	False	False	None	NaN	False	NaN
3	False	True	None	NaN	True	NaN
4	False	True	None	NaN	True	NaN

Figure 3.35 Customer data containing results of two different deduplication methods

	customer_id	first_name	surname	postcode	is_guest	in_purchase_data	age
2197	10383	scarlett	jackson	M284ZB	False	True	35.0
7203	19549	summer	anderson	RG546PY	False	True	47.0
9445	16969	georgia	scott	PO466DY	False	True	9.0
13277	5390	josh	simpson	HR235FS	False	True	81.0
14692	32354	josh	simpson	HR235FS	False	True	81.0

(continued)

	in_crm_data	in_customer_data	other_customer_ids	duplicate_customer_ids	is_main	linked_duplicates
2197	True	True	[10383, 10386]	[10386]	True	[10386, 27536, 28786]
7203	True	False	[19549, 19551]	[19551]	True	[19551, 28832]
9445	False	True	[16969, 16966]	[16966]	True	[16966, 32299]
13277	False	True	[5390, 32354]	[32354]	True	[32354, 33132]
14692	False	True	[5390, 32354]	[5390]	False	[5390, 33132]

Figure 3.36 Instances where the two deduplication methods disagree

Let's inspect one of these cases, shown in figure 3.37. We observe that, for Scarlett Jackson, two additional duplicate records were found by `recordlinkage`, one of them referring to a Sgarlett Jagkson and another to a Scariett Jackson. All of these are likely to be the same customer, so it makes sense to use the fuzzy method to find all possible duplicates.

	customer_id	first_name	surname	postcode	is_guest	in_purchase_data	age
2197	10383	scarlett	jackson	M284ZB	False	True	35.0
10596	27536	scariett	jackson	M284ZB	False	True	12.0
19538	28786	sgarlett	jagkson	M284ZB	False	True	35.0
24809	10386	scarlett	jackson	M284ZB	False	True	12.0

(continued)

	in_crm_data	in_customer_data	other_customer_ids	duplicate_customer_ids	is_main	linked_duplicates
2197	True	True	[10383, 10386]	[10386]	True	[10386, 27536, 28786]
10596	False	True	None	NaN	True	[10383, 10386]
19538	False	True	None	NaN	True	[10383, 10386]
24809	False	True	[10383, 10386]	[10383]	False	[10383, 27536, 28786]

Figure 3.37   An instance where the two deduplication methods found different results

Ultimately, there are just 13 cases where the two methods disagree, so it seems using `recordlinkage` only gave us a marginal improvement. However, we now have code for the future that can deduplicate our customer data more intelligently, and the accuracy of our results has improved.

Before we move on to the conclusions and recommendations, let's review the entire analysis process shown in figure 3.38. As with all analyses, your specific path may have diverged from the ones I chose.

Now that we have done the work and documented our analysis, let's move on to the conclusions and recommendations.

3.4.4   *Conclusions and recommendations*

Our initial problem statement asked for help counting customers. Our final data model has 35,395 rows corresponding to 27,394 unique customers, which fits our original estimate of "at most 33,000 customers." However, it is a more precise and therefore more useful number as it is a result of all the analysis we have done so far. This number may be different if you decide to use the results of the `recordlinkage` library to create a deduplicated data model.

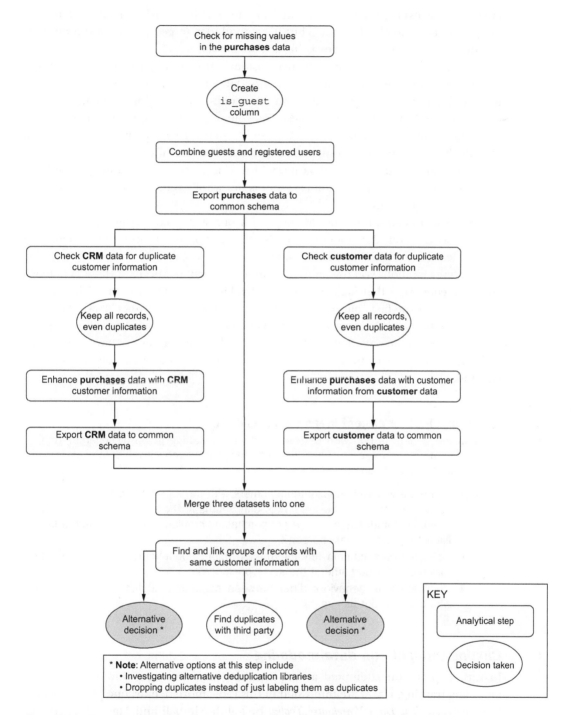

Figure 3.38 The entire analytical process diagram for this project

How do we assess the quality of the final solution? This is hard to quantify as there is no ground truth to check against, but it's a good idea to get a sense of the different amounts of completeness that exist in the data model.

For example, we have around 26,000 customer IDs in the purchase data that have no corresponding records in either customer dataset. This means we have 26,000 customers who have signed up to make a purchase online, but we don't have their details, and because they weren't using a guest checkout, we have nothing but a customer ID for them in our final data model. We could choose to drop them as incomplete records, but we would skew our measurement of the size of the customer base. It is better to understand that our data model varies in completeness and is suitable for some tasks—like counting customers—but is not wholly suitable for other tasks, such as customer segmentation.

This is a conclusion we should share with our stakeholders when presenting an analysis based on our data models. It is also the kind of uncertainty and ambiguity we need to learn to embrace and communicate.

Whatever methods you use, entity resolution is hard to automate 100%. There will always be edge cases that make the data model less than 100% accurate. The value in this task lies in the fact that once you have a "best guess" customer data model, you can be sure that all subsequent analyses, while not perfectly accurate, will be the best you can do given the data that you have. Also, each analysis does not have to start with defining what we mean by a customer since that work has already been done in the data model.

Activity: Further project ideas with this data

E-commerce data is rich with patterns and trends waiting to be discovered. Think about some other research questions that can be answered with this data. Here are some ideas to get you thinking:

- Is there a way to deduplicate customers with the same name based on their purchase history? If there are two John Smiths at the same postcode but different customer IDs and different purchasing profiles, does that make it less likely they're the same person?
- Does the data contain any information about households? Perhaps people with the same surname at the same postcode?
- Do purchasing behaviors differ between registered customers and people who checked out as guests?

3.5   *Closing thoughts on data modeling*

In this chapter, you attempted a data modeling task, perhaps without formal data modeling training. If you are interested in this topic more deeply, one place to start is the canonical *The Data Warehouse Toolkit* by Ralph Kimball and Margy Ross (Wiley, 2013). There are key data modeling concepts such as "star schemas" and "fact tables" to explore to get a deeper understanding of data modeling best practices. A less technical, more business-oriented approach would be to study the Business Event Analysis & Modeling (BEAM) technique. The idea behind it is that the core business entity to focus on is events that happen in the business lifecycle. Your data models would take the form of "customer buys product," where one record is one instance of a customer buying the product, complete with details about the customer, the product, and the purchasing event. Thinking in terms of events forces you to think about how the business actually works and, ultimately, the process that generated your raw data. A relevant text to explore would be *Agile Data Warehouse Design* (DecisionOne Press, 2011) by Lawrence Corr and Jim Stagnitto.

What is most important is that you consider the purpose, and therefore the necessary details, of your data and get into the habit of creating data models, which abstract away the complexities of the raw data into a more business-relevant form. This skill will come up in most of your analytical projects.

3.5.1 *Data modeling skills for any project*

In this chapter, we focused on the creation of new datasets, which we called data models. The specific skills learned for data modeling, which can be used for any problem, include

- Exploring multiple datasets to identify a common structure
- Reshaping a dataset to adhere to this common structure
- Identifying what form a data model should be stored in (e.g., wide or long)
- Joining multiple datasets to enhance one with information from another
- Cross-referencing two datasets (i.e., finding rows that appear in one but not the other)
- Combining smaller data models into a master data model
- Using simple methods to deduplicate records
- Using advanced methods, such as entity resolution tools, to deduplicate records

Summary

- Thinking about the purpose of a dataset helps identify the right structure for your data model.
- Data modeling is a crucial analyst skill that should be applied to create clean, defined, deduplicated, restructured, and usable data from raw datasets.
- Even basic analytical tasks such as counting are easier when the data is modeled correctly.
- Proper data modeling provides easy reuse of the same data to answer additional analytical questions by adjusting the level of granularity or providing wide or long looks at the data.

Metrics

At some point in your career, you will likely be asked to create and maintain a dashboard that tracks key performance indicators (KPIs) for the business. That's because there is so much going on in a business that simple, summary-level metrics are the most common way to measure and analyze what is happening. Rather than getting detailed verbal summaries from every business unit or employee, executives look at which direction figures such as turnover, profit, or margin are trending.

The metrics we choose define everything we do, from the executive board down to the individual analyst, so we need to be sure that they are well defined.

> **Real business case: Defining key business metrics**
>
> An important metric in the used car auction domain, where I worked for years, is conversion. The business had multiple analyses and dashboards dedicated to questions about conversion.
>
> Conversion was used to measure the percentage of cars in an auction we were able to sell for our customers, the vendors. This seems straightforward, but it turned out that people across the business did not agree on a definition of conversion, especially when aggregating multiple auction events. There was also a separate but related metric called "first-time conversion," which was even harder for stakeholders to agree on.
>
> What started as a simple metric turned into a large project where multiple areas of the business were corralled to define these fundamental terms. Metric definitions are crucial, and they form the basis of this chapter's project.

4.1   The importance of well-defined metrics

Sometimes, you will be asked to measure and track a metric that is insufficiently defined or ill suited to the problem. The first step in any analysis, and our results-driven approach, is to understand the problem—in this case, the metric we are being asked to measure. Words such as "best" (e.g., "what's the best month to run an advertising campaign?") are giveaways that something hasn't been properly defined.

Some of the common ways the use of metrics can go wrong are

- Overreliance on a metric has unintended consequences. An example would be social media platforms trying to maximize users' attention as their key metric. This incentivizes clickbait and content that elicits strong emotions.
- The metric doesn't incorporate every important element of the business. Schools being incentivized to maximize student attendance rather than the quality of education is one example.
- The metric doesn't measure the intended outcome. A common measure of customer satisfaction is the net promoter score or NPS. The way this score is calculated means only users who give a 9 or 10 out of 10 are deemed "promoters" and even scores of 8 out of 10 are discarded. This means it is possible to get a high average score but a low NPS, which can be misleading.

In each of these cases, the solution is to either choose a metric that better captures all aspects of the problem, choose additional metrics to complement the single chosen metric, or, ideally, choose both. We should always be skeptical of single metrics that claim to perfectly summarize a complex problem and look at solutions from different angles instead.

Single metrics can give us at-a-glance views of an entire business's operations, but the oversimplification often has consequences. A relevant aphorism, Goodhart's law, states, "When a measure becomes a target, it ceases to be a good measure." Once you start optimizing for a single metric, it becomes a bad metric to use as a measurement.

This does not mean using simplifying metrics is wrong, but only that we should understand the consequences.

The project in this chapter explores this idea; it is all about defining metrics based on a vague stakeholder request, so let's dive right in.

4.2   *Project 3: Defining precise metrics for better decision making*

Let's take a look at the project, in which we will be asked to define and calculate metrics to find the best-performing products. The data is available for you to attempt it yourself at https://davidasboth.com/book-code. You will find the datasets you can use to attempt the project, as well as the example solution in the form of a Jupyter notebook.

First, let's look at the problem statement and examine the business context.

4.2.1   *Problem statement*

In this scenario, you are a junior analyst working for an e-commerce startup, Online Odyssey Outlet. If you have already attempted the project in chapter 3, it is in fact the same sort of startup. The data will be of a similar, if not identical, structure.

> **NOTE** Thanks again to REES46 for providing the original transaction data (https://mng.bz/6eZo), which has only been altered for this project by filtering it to a manageable size by removing "view" events and only keeping registered users (those with a valid `user_id`).

The date is January 2020, and the startup has just been through its first winter sale. Senior stakeholders are interested in knowing which products performed best during the Christmas period so that they can streamline the products they advertise in future sale periods. You will do this by analyzing up to two months of events data, presented as two separate data sources with identical structures. Events refer not just to sales but to more general customer actions, such as viewing a product on the website or placing it into their virtual cart.

The challenge is that, when pressed, stakeholders aren't exactly sure what they mean by "best." In an initial brainstorming session, they highlight some aspects they care about when ranking their products:

- Volume of sales
- Total revenue from a single product
- Popularity, measured by the number of unique customers who bought a product
- Conversion, meaning the percentage of time a product is bought once it has been placed in the virtual shopping cart
- Products with increased performance from November to December

Your stakeholders do not assign weights to these factors, so their relative importance is unclear, but you should consider one or more of these metrics when presenting your findings. They are also open to suggestions for additional metrics that would help improve the performance of future sales.

4.2.2   Data dictionary

Table 4.1 shows the data dictionary for the events data, and figure 4.1 shows some sample data. The November and December events are in separate tables but have the same structure and are therefore easily combined.

Table 4.1   Data dictionary for events data

Column	Description
event_time	The date and time of the transaction
event_type	The type of the user event, either cart (the customer placed a product into their cart) or purchase (the customer bought the item)
product_id	The unique identifier of the product
category_id	The unique identifier of the product category
category_code	A code that describes the product's main and subcategories
brand	The brand of the product (if applicable)
price	The price of the product (listed price when adding to cart, or sold price when the event is purchase) in USD
user_id	The unique identifier of the registered customer
user_session	The unique identifier of the user's browsing session

	event_time	event_type	product_id	category_id
0	2019-11-01 00:00:14 UTC	cart	1005014	2053013555631882655
1	2019-11-01 00:00:41 UTC	purchase	13200605	2053013557192163841
2	2019-11-01 00:01:04 UTC	purchase	1005161	2053013555631882655
3	2019-11-01 00:03:24 UTC	cart	1801881	2053013554415534427
4	2019-11-01 00:03:39 UTC	cart	1005115	2053013555631882655

(continued)

	category_code	brand	price	user_id	user_session
0	electronics.smartphone	samsung	503.09	533326659	6b928be2-2bce-4640-8296-0efdf2fda22a
1	furniture.bedroom.bed	NaN	566.30	559368633	d6034fa2-41fb-4ac0-9051-55ea9fc9147a
2	electronics.smartphone	xiaomi	211.92	513351129	e6b7ce9b-1938-4e20-976c-8b4163aea11d
3	electronics.video.tv	samsung	488.80	557746614	4d76d6d3-fff5-4880-8327-e9e57b618e0e
4	electronics.smartphone	apple	949.47	565865924	fd4bd6d4-bd14-4fdc-9aff-bd41a594f82e

Figure 4.1   A snapshot of the events data

4.2.3 *Desired outcomes*

The output of the analysis should be recommendations of the best-performing products on whichever dimension(s) you choose. The recommendation could be for single product IDs or broader ones relating to brands or product categories, as long as your choice of best product is justified in your analysis. The recommendation could be presented to a stakeholder in any format. This could be a whole presentation deck, some choice visualizations, or even just data tables produced by your analysis tool.

> **Activity: Presentation**
>
> Think about how you would present your findings. What format would be most appropriate? What details would your stakeholders be most interested in hearing? Crucially, what unnecessary details would you want to leave out? Knowing how to summarize your work for the right audience is an important analyst skill to practice.

4.2.4 *Required tools*

For this chapter's example solution, I will use the Python library `pandas` to read and manipulate the datasets, the `numpy` library for additional numerical computations, and `matplotlib` to create visualizations. As with each of the projects, the specific technology you use does not matter as long as it satisfies the criteria for each project. For this project, you need a tool that can

- Load a dataset in the order of millions of rows from CSV files
- Create new columns and manipulate existing ones
- Combine (union) two datasets of the same structure
- Perform basic manipulation tasks such as sorting, grouping, and reshaping data
- Create data visualizations (optional)

4.3 *Applying the results-driven method to different metric definitions*

Let's use the results-driven approach again to break the problem down. In a problem that is as open ended as this one, it is particularly important to understand what our stakeholders want from the analysis. We need to understand the minimum viable answer that would be acceptable to present and could form the basis for future work iterations.

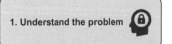

This step is always critical before starting the work itself, but even more so in open-ended questions like this one. What would it mean to focus on the different metrics the stakeholders have suggested?

- Focusing on volume alone could overinflate the importance of products that people simply buy in bulk more than others.

- Focusing on total revenue alone could overemphasize expensive products.
- Prioritizing popularity might simply reveal products that everyone buys, such as smartphones, clothes, or kitchen appliances. However, it might help distinguish the "better" products from similar ones in their category (i.e., we can assume almost everyone will buy a smartphone, but not the same one).
- Focusing on conversion would highlight products that people are less likely to change their minds on, but it is unclear if that has a direct relationship with "best performance" particularly.
- Comparing performance between November and December specifically would target the stakeholders' questions directly since they asked about best performers over the Christmas period.

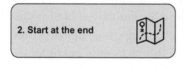 **2. Start at the end**

This step forces us to think about the output of our work before we even begin. In this case, the output has not been explicitly defined. However, we know that our minimum viable answer should contain

- Measurements of our chosen metrics at a product level (e.g., a table of total revenue in December by product, sorted in descending revenue order)
- A ranking so we can highlight top performers
- Justifications for which metrics were chosen
- A summary of our findings in tabular or visual form
- Recommendations for further iterations (if requested)

These end goals help us identify what to focus on during our analysis, so we are less likely to unnecessarily go down rabbit holes.

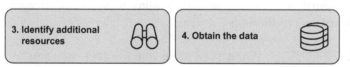 **3. Identify additional resources**   **4. Obtain the data**

As in chapter 3, our data has been provided for us, and there is nothing to explicitly identify or obtain. However, one task we might want to perform here is to check whether all the possible metrics can be measured with the available data. This can be done by looking at the data dictionary and verifying our assumptions during the analysis. One choice to make is whether to focus on December's events only or include the November data so that we can compare product performance before and during the Christmas period. In future iterations, we might also request data from the previous year to do a year-on-year comparison, which is not possible with the available data.

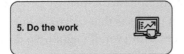

5. Do the work

During the analysis, some steps to consider are

- Merge the November and December data if we decide to investigate those comparison metrics.
- Explore the events data. We are specifically interested in questions like
  - What makes a product unique? Is its ID sufficient, and is the ID truly a unique identifier? Some product catalogs might have the same product ID listed multiple times for different color variants, in which case ID would not be sufficient as a unique identifier.
  - Are there any gaps in our data (e.g., dates for which we do not have events)? Identifying gaps would help us understand the limitations of the available data.
  - What are the generally best-performing categories/subcategories/brands? This will help determine if our later results make sense in context.
  - What is the distribution of product price? Are there outliers to investigate further? This is particularly important if we choose to explore product revenue.
  - What are some baselines for product popularity and conversion? Again, knowing the conversion rate for a typical product or how many people generally buy something will help put results into context.
- Aggregate the data to a product level since the raw data is at a transaction level
- Calculate the chosen metrics for each product
- Compare products across multiple metrics if we have chosen to measure more than one
- Summarize our findings in tabular or visual form
- Recommend further work in case stakeholders want to dive deeper into the problem based on our findings

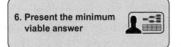

6. Present the minimum viable answer

When presenting our findings, we want to focus on summarizing our method, our chosen metrics, and the resulting best products. The important aspect to focus on is "so what?" Our findings should be presented in a way that suggests concrete action that can be taken. Telling a stakeholder that socks tend to sell well all year round with a spike of sales around Christmas is unlikely to be news to them. If we choose to create slides, we should aim for three to four slides with a natural flow, succinct messages, and appropriate visualizations. In our code, that means we should create visualizations that most effectively communicate our findings.

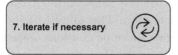

7. Iterate if necessary

We generally want to present our findings to a stakeholder as soon as we have a minimum viable answer. This might mean iterating before our analysis is complete. However, in this instance, the possible metrics to investigate are well defined, and we should have a value calculated for each metric across our products and perhaps summarized across categories and brands, too. That way, when discussing future iterations, we could focus on metrics beyond those already suggested.

4.3.1 Questions to consider

During this analysis, you should always be thinking about the following:

- What is the definition of each chosen metric? Words like "volume" or "revenue" sound self-explanatory, but they need to be strictly defined before they are calculated.
- What are the effects of choosing a particular metric as the definition for "best"? What should "best" measure, and how will our definition be useful to our stakeholders?

4.4 An example solution: Finding the best performing products

Let's go through an example solution to the problem. As with every project, I encourage you to attempt the project yourself before reviewing the solution and bear in mind this is one of many possible ways to tackle the problem. The order of the exploratory steps is not always important. You may choose to investigate different aspects of the data first compared to what I have chosen, and again, that is to be expected.

As for our action plan, we will first combine the November and December events and explore the combined data, resolving any data problems along the way. Next, we will aggregate the data to produce a product-level dataset. We can then define and calculate multiple metrics to see how product rankings differ among the different metrics. Finally, we will summarize our findings to see what initial recommendations we can make to our stakeholders.

4.4.1 Combining and exploring product data

Because our two datasets, November and December events, are identical in structure, we will explore the data only once they have been combined. Let's start there:

```
import pandas as pd
import numpy as np
import matplotlib.pyplot as plt

november = pd.read_csv("./data/november.csv.gz")
december = pd.read_csv("./data/december.csv.gz")

events = pd.concat([november, december], axis=0, ignore_index=True)
print(events.shape)
```

Here, we use the `pandas` library to concatenate the two datasets. If you are familiar with SQL, this is the equivalent of a union operation. The output of the code is `(7033125, 9)`, meaning we have over 7 million rows and nine columns of data.

Now it's time for some basic sanity checks of the data. Do we have any missing values? Figure 4.2 shows the output of looking for missing data:

```
events.isnull().sum()
```

```
event_time          0
event_type          0
product_id          0
category_id         0
category_code       0
brand          395108
price               0
user_id             0
user_session       27
dtype: int64
```

Figure 4.2   The number of rows with missing values for each column in our events data

We have some user sessions missing, which means we don't know which unique browsing session those 27 events belong to. That shouldn't affect our analysis as we're interested in products, so we can leave those rows in. The same goes for the `brand` column—missing values aren't necessarily a worry at this stage because we don't yet know to what extent we will use that information.

Let's start building our diagram to record our steps. So far, we completed the step shown in figure 4.3.

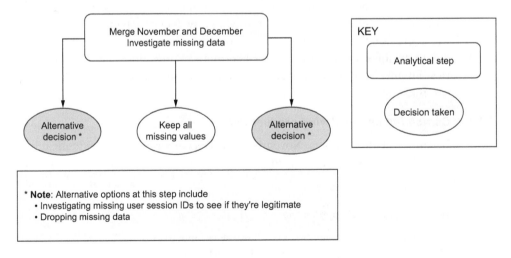

Figure 4.3   The first step in our analysis, visualized

It's time to move on and validate different assumptions in our data, including ones about the date range and product categorization.

VALIDATING ASSUMPTIONS IN THE DATA

Our next assumption is that we really do have November and December data, which we should verify independently. Figure 4.4 shows the output of checking for the date range in our data:

```
events["event_time"] = pd.to_datetime(events["event_time"],
    format="%Y-%m-%d %H:%M:%S %Z")
events["event_time"].agg(["min", "max"])
```

```
min    2019-11-01 00:00:14+00:00
max    2019-12-31 23:59:09+00:00
Name: event_time, dtype: datetime64[ns, UTC]
```

Figure 4.4   The date range in our data

Our data is in the expected range (November 1 through December 31), but we still don't know if we have event data for every single date in between. The following code calculates the number of unique days for each month, the output of which is shown in figure 4.5:

```
(
    events
    .assign(month=events["event_time"].dt.month,
            day=events["event_time"].dt.day)
    .groupby("month")
    ["day"]
    .nunique()
)
```

Using the assign function to create temporary columns for day and month

The nunique function calculates the number of unique days per month.

```
month
11    30
12    31
Name: day, dtype: int64
```

Figure 4.5   The unique number of days encountered per month

The output is what we'd expect, so we have at least one event for each day in our data. Finally, we also want to know if the number of events is consistent across these days. The following code calculates and visualizes this, and the output chart is shown in figure 4.6:

```
fig, axis = plt.subplots(figsize=(10, 6))

(
    events
    .assign(month=events["event_time"].dt.month,
            day=events["event_time"].dt.day)
```

```
        .groupby(["month", "day"])
        .size()
        .plot
        .bar(ax=axis)
)

labels = (
    pd.date_range(
        events["event_time"].dt.date.min(),
        events["event_time"].dt.date.max(),
        freq="D")
    .strftime("%b %d")
)

axis.set(title="Number of events per calendar day",
         xlabel="Number of rows",
         ylabel="Calendar day",
         xticklabels=labels)

plt.show()
```

Creates custom axis labels based on dates in the data

Formats labels as "month day" (e.g., "Nov 1")

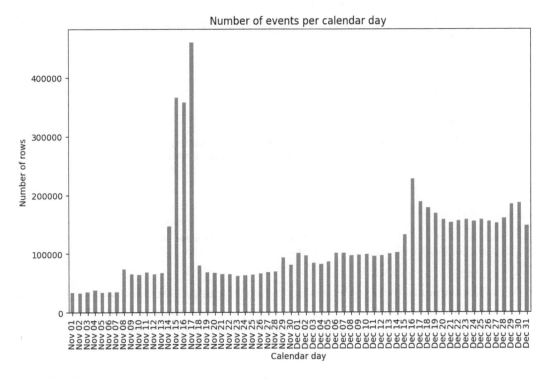

Figure 4.6 Number of events per calendar day, visualized

Our data clearly shows a wide range of volumes across the days. What we're interested in with this chart is whether there are any outliers in either direction. There are seven low-activity days, and they correspond to the first week of November. This could mean customers hadn't been using the platform as often yet, and knowing exactly when the startup launched the website would help put this into context. There are also three days of particularly high activity in mid-November. Again, this could be because of an organic increase in user engagement or a social media post that went viral. It could be artificial due to an advertising campaign that ran at that time, or there could have been a sale on. Without further information, we are only speculating, but it is the kind of speculating we would need to do upon seeing these results.

The next column to turn our attention to is the event type. What is the proportion of the different events in our data? Figure 4.7 shows the output of the following code:

```
events["event_type"].value_counts(dropna=False)
```

```
cart         5276372
purchase     1756753
Name: event_type, dtype: int64
```

Figure 4.7   The proportion of different event types

In a typical e-commerce environment, there is a funnel of events from users exploring, then placing items into a cart, and finally purchasing them. As expected, in this case, we observe that this funnel narrows, meaning we see much fewer purchase events than cart ones.

Time to turn our attention to the product catalog and investigate what kind of products the e-commerce platform offers. First, what is the typical price range for our products? Figure 4.8 shows the output of our investigation into prices:

```
fig, axis = plt.subplots()

(
    events["price"]
    .hist(bins=25, ax=axis)
)

axis.ticklabel_format(useOffset=False, style='plain')    ◁── Disables scientific notation

axis.set(title="Distribution of product price",
         xlabel="Product price ($)",
         ylabel="Frequency")

plt.show()
```

This output is common in price data, that is, a clustering of small values and a long skew to the right. This means most of our products are listed or sold under $500, with some outliers up to $2,500.

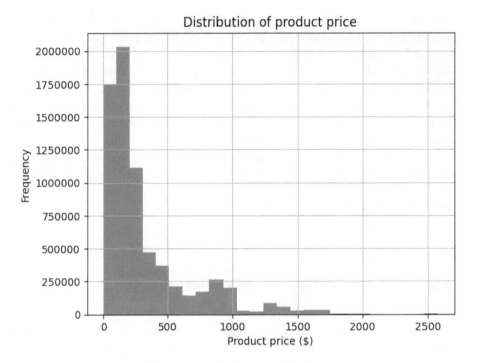

Figure 4.8　The distribution of product prices

What about brands? Figure 4.9 shows the top 10 brands obtained with the following code. Missing brands are intentionally not included:

```
events["brand"].value_counts().head(10)
```

```
samsung    1756284
apple      1368364
xiaomi      722125
huawei      263155
oppo        128661
lg          123581
sony         78615
artel        72124
lucente      69998
lenovo       59700
Name: brand, dtype: int64
```

Figure 4.9　Top 10 brands by number of events

At a glance, this suggests most of our user events are focused on the technology category. The actual makeup of our unique product catalog might differ, as might the top 10 brands if we only look at purchase events. Now that we've looked at brands, let's also take a look at product categories.

INVESTIGATING CONSISTENCY OF PRODUCT CATEGORIES

Are our products correctly categorized? This is a question that we should ask every time we have a dataset with IDs and associated assigned categories. One way to check this is to ask, do we have any product IDs that are assigned to multiple categories? The following code investigates this, and the output is shown in figure 4.10:

```
(
    events
    .groupby("product_id")
    ["category_code"]
    .nunique()
    .loc[lambda x: x > 1]
    .sort_values(ascending=False)
)
```

First, counts the number of unique category codes encountered per product ID

Finds instances where that count is more than 1

```
product_id
1000978        2
13900087       2
13900049       2
13900054       2
13900055       2
             ..
5701183        2
5701186        2
5701190        2
5701192        2
100028003      2
Name: category_code, Length: 12884, dtype: int64
```

Figure 4.10   The result of investigating products assigned to multiple categories

As we can see, almost 13,000 products are assigned to multiple categories. This suggests there is an error somewhere in our underlying product catalog. Let's look at the top category codes to investigate further. Figure 4.11 shows the output of looking at the top 10 most common category codes:

```
events["category_code"].value_counts().head(10)
```

```
construction.tools.light           1823398
electronics.smartphone             1577185
electronics.audio.headphone         240308
electronics.clocks                  233198
sport.bicycle                       231644
apparel.shoes                       212586
appliances.kitchen.refrigerators    190523
appliances.personal.massager        185601
appliances.environment.vacuum       170290
appliances.kitchen.washer           170121
Name: category_code, dtype: int64
```

Figure 4.11   Top 10 category codes by number of rows

This doesn't necessarily mean most of our products are in the "light construction tools" category because this is the number of events, not the number of unique products, but it does suggest a problem similar to the one we uncovered in figure 4.10. Let's look at how brand and category codes intersect by looking at the top 10 brands in this "light construction tools" category. The following code produces the output in figure 4.12:

```
(
    events
    .loc[events["category_code"] == "construction.tools.light", "brand"]
    .value_counts()
    .head(10)
)
```

```
samsung    727599
apple      521481
xiaomi     304546
huawei     149347
oppo        68446
vivo        10709
meizu        9093
honor        4389
nokia        3231
omron        3003
Name: brand, dtype: int64
```

Figure 4.12 Top 10 brands in the construction.tools.light category

Unless technology manufacturers have secretly branched out into construction tools, we have a problem with our product categories. Most of these brands are typically known for smartphones, and we can look at some examples to verify this. The following code finds all product IDs that have multiple codes against them so that we know which ones to focus on. Figure 4.13 shows a sample of this subset of product IDs:

```
dupe_product_ids = (
    events
    .groupby("product_id")
    ["category_code"]
    .nunique()
    .loc[lambda x: x > 1]
    .index
    .values
)

dupe_product_ids[:10]
```

```
array([1000978, 1001588, 1001618, 1001619, 1002098, 1002100, 1002101,
       1002225, 1002367, 1002482], dtype=int64)
```

Figure 4.13 A subset of product IDs with multiple assigned categories

From this subset of data, we can find instances where one category is "light construction tools" and see what other categories that product is assigned to. An example is shown in the following code and figure 4.14:

```
(
    events.loc[events["product_id"] == 1001588,
            "category_code"]
    .value_counts()
)
```

```
construction.tools.light    50
electronics.smartphone      22
Name: category_code, dtype: int64
```

Figure 4.14   Breakdown of categories for a particular erroneous product

In this instance, we have a smartphone that is also incorrectly categorized as a construction tool. We have a major decision to make now: How do we handle these products? We have several options:

- *Ignore this problem*—The downside is we won't be able to use the category code to investigate top-performing products since we know it is often incorrectly assigned.
- *Drop products that are incorrectly categorized*—The problem is this could be a significant portion of our data.
- *Fix the product categorization*—This seems like the best approach, but we might not have enough information to find the correct category for each product.

In reality, we would want more information about how these product categories came about and, ideally, fix the problem at the source. However, in this case, we only have this data to work with, so let's attempt a fix using the data we have.

CORRECTING INCONSISTENCIES IN DATA CATEGORIES

Our plan of action is to find products with duplicate categories, and for cases where one category is `construction.tools.light`, we use the other category. In instances where we have duplication that doesn't involve the `construction.tools.light` category, we would need to investigate accordingly or use the majority one. For example, if a product ID is mostly categorized as a refrigerator but is sometimes categorized as a smartphone, we overwrite the data so that the product ID is always in the refrigerator category. There is the danger that we incorrectly categorize some products, but we will also fix the problem with the construction tools category.

The following code defines a method to fix the category codes of a single product ID and applies it to all the duplicated product ID data. The output is a new category code for each of the affected product IDs, as shown in figure 4.15:

product_id_rows contains all rows for a product ID so we can find the two categories associated with this ID.

```python
def get_correct_category_code(product_id_rows):
    categories = product_id_rows["category_code"].value_counts()

    if "construction.tools.light" in categories.index:
        return categories.index.drop("construction.tools.light").values[0]
    else:
        return categories.index[0]

corrected_categories = (
    events[events["product_id"].isin(dupe_product_ids)]
    .groupby("product_id")
    .apply(get_correct_category_code)
    .reset_index(name="corrected_category")
)

corrected_categories.head()
```

Otherwise, return the majority category.

If one is construction.tools.light, return the other one.

	product_id	corrected_category
0	1000978	electronics.smartphone
1	1001588	electronics.smartphone
2	1001618	electronics.smartphone
3	1001619	electronics.smartphone
4	1002098	electronics.smartphone

Figure 4.15   A preview of the data we will use to correct product ID categories

As figure 4.15 shows, we have plenty of products that should be smartphones but aren't always categorized that way. Now, we will join this corrected category data to our original events dataset and overwrite the categories where the original and the corrected categories do not match. To verify our changes, we will look at the top category codes again and compare our results to figure 4.11. The following code produces a similar result, as shown in figure 4.16:

```python
events = events.merge(corrected_categories, on="product_id", how="left")
events.loc[events["corrected_category"].notnull(), "category_code"] = \
    events.loc[events["corrected_category"].notnull(), "corrected_category"]

events["category_code"].value_counts()
```

Now, our data mostly consists of smartphones, which is more in line with our findings around the most popular brands. It is important to note that we may have inflated the prevalence of smartphones because we made specific assumptions about how to fix

```
electronics.smartphone              3350680
sport.bicycle                        384120
appliances.personal.massager         254300
electronics.clocks                   228546
appliances.kitchen.refrigerators     214637
                                        . . .
apparel.skirt                           261
construction.tools.soldering            200
sport.diving                            144
computers.components.sound_card         118
auto.accessories.light                   41
Name: category_code, Length: 134, dtype: int64
```

Figure 4.16 A breakdown of category codes after applying our fixes

our data, which may not be correct. However, we do not have enough information in the available data to investigate this further.

Upon inspection, this category code column also contains a "main" category, corresponding to the first part of the string up to the first period character, that may be useful in our analysis, so let's isolate it. The output of the following code shows the breakdown of this main category, as shown in figure 4.17:

```
events["category"] = events["category_code"].str.split(".").str[0]

events = events.rename(columns={"category_code": "subcategory"})

events["category"].value_counts()
```

```
electronics    3908916
appliances     1250149
apparel         540955
sport           439029
computers       291790
furniture       216264
construction    144637
kids             98236
auto            89079
accessories     39350
country_yard     6106
medicine         5616
stationery       2998
Name: category, dtype: int64
```

Figure 4.17 A breakdown of the "main" category of products

This table further convinces us that most of our products are electronics of some kind. Before we continue to summarize our data at the product level, we will want to make sure that a particular product ID only ever refers to one product. We will come to this step soon. Before we move on, let's summarize our work so far. Figure 4.18 shows the steps we have taken and where our decisions could have diverged.

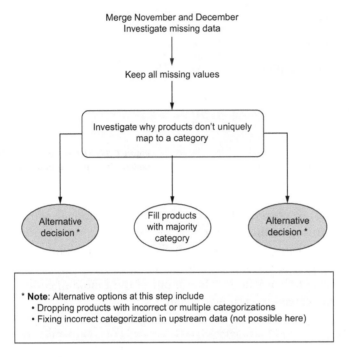

Figure 4.18   The steps in our analysis so far

Another way products are categorized is with their brand. We should also investigate whether there are any product IDs that have multiple brands against them. Considering that we have missing data for the brand column, this seems like a relevant step to take.

INVESTIGATE CONSISTENCY OF BRAND LABELS

Here, to investigate whether each product only has one brand attached to it, we follow a process very similar to when we did this for product categories. The output of the following code is shown in figure 4.19:

```
duplicated_brands = (
    events
    .assign(brand = events["brand"].fillna("No brand"))
    .groupby("product_id")
    ["brand"]
    .nunique()
    .loc[lambda x: x > 1]
    .index
)

print(len(duplicated_brands))

duplicated_brands[:10]
```

Temporarily fills missing brand data with a placeholder because the nunique function ignores missing values

```
1245
```

```
Int64Index([1001618, 1002310, 1002786, 1002877, 1003080, 1003224, 1003238,
            1003330, 1003604, 1003851],
           dtype='int64', name='product_id')
```

Figure 4.19   The result of investigating products labeled with multiple brands

There are 1,245 products in our catalog that have either two different brands against them or have the `brand` column missing some of the time. To clean this data up, we will apply logic similar to what we used for categories: for products with multiple brands against them, we pick the majority non-null brand. The following code block implements this logic, and the output is a mapping of product IDs to the brand they should be assigned to. A subset of this output is shown in figure 4.20:

> **product_id_rows contains all rows for a product ID, so we can find the brands associated with this ID. Using value_counts will give us only non-NA values.**

```
def get_correct_brand(product_id_rows):
    brand_counts = product_id_rows["brand"].value_counts(dropna=False)    ◄─┘

    if isinstance(brand_counts.index[0], str):
        return brand_counts.index[0]           ◄─┐  If there are no NA
                                                  │  values, just return the
                                                  │  majority brand.

    if len(brand_counts) == 1:
        return np.nan          ◄─┐  Now, if np.NaN is the
                                  │  only value, return it.

    return brand_counts.index[1]     ◄─┐  Otherwise, return
                                        │  the second value
corrected_brands = (                    │  (the majority non-
    events[events["product_id"].isin(duplicated_brands)]   │  null value).
    .groupby("product_id")
    .apply(get_correct_brand)
    .reset_index(name="corrected_brand")
)

corrected_brands.head()
```

	product_id	corrected_brand
0	1001618	apple
1	1002310	lg
2	1002786	apple
3	1002877	samsung
4	1003080	huawei

Figure 4.20   Product IDs against the brand to which they should be allocated

Similarly to how we handled categories, we can join these corrected brands to the original events data and overwrite the brand column where necessary.

CORRECTING INCONSISTENCIES IN BRAND LABELS

We do this with the following code, after which we verify whether there are any product IDs that still have multiple combinations of brand and category. The expected output is that there are no such product IDs, and the number of unique product ID, category, and brand combinations should match the number of unique product IDs. Running the following code block does not result in an assertion error, meaning the condition is met, and product IDs are finally categorized in a unique way:

```
events = events.merge(corrected_brands, on="product_id", how="left")
events.loc[events["corrected_brand"].notnull(), "brand"] = \
    events.loc[events["corrected_brand"].notnull(), "corrected_brand"]

assert (
    len(events[["product_id", "category", "subcategory", "brand"]]
        .drop_duplicates())
    ==
    events["product_id"].nunique()
)
```

In the remainder of the project, we will be working with product-level data, so a useful step is to give each product a more descriptive name, especially because we don't have a "product name" column. Each product ID should have a unique name, meaning the product ID should be a part of the name since that's what makes products unique in our dataset. We can combine the product's ID, brand, and category code to get a more readable string for each product. The following code does this, and an output of the data with this additional column is shown in figure 4.21:

```
def get_product_name(row):
    brand = ""                                    Only include
                                                  brand if it's
    if isinstance(row["brand"], str):      ◁───   available.
        brand = row["brand"]

    return f"{str(row['product_id'])} - {brand} {row['subcategory']}"

events["product_name"] = events.apply(get_product_name, axis=1)

events.head()
```

Finally, we may wish to export this modified data to an intermediate dataset, which we can use for analysis. Some of the operations so far may take a few minutes due to the size of the data, and we do not want that to be a bottleneck every time we come back to work on our analysis.

	event_time	event_type	product_id	category_id	subcategory
0	2019-11-01 00:00:14+00:00	cart	1005014	2053013555631882655	electronics.smartphone
1	2019-11-01 00:00:41+00:00	purchase	13200605	2053013557192163841	furniture.bedroom.bed
2	2019-11-01 00:01:04+00:00	purchase	1005161	2053013555631882655	electronics.smartphone
3	2019-11-01 00:03:24+00:00	cart	1801881	2053013554415534427	appliances.personal.massager
4	2019-11-01 00:03:39+00:00	cart	1005115	2053013555631882655	electronics.smartphone

(continued)

	brand	price	user_id	user_session	category	product_name
0	samsung	503.09	533326659	6b928be2-2bce-4640-8296-0efdf2fda22a	electronics	1005014 - samsung electronics.smartphone
1	NaN	566.30	559368633	d6034fa2-41fb-4ac0-9051-55ea9fc9147a	furniture	13200605 - furniture.bedroom.bed
2	xiaomi	211.92	513351129	e6b7ce9b-1938-4e20-976c-8b4163aea11d	electronics	1005161 - xiaomi electronics.smartphone
3	samsung	488.80	557746614	4d76d6d3-fff5-4880-8327-e9e57b618e0e	appliances	1801881 - samsung appliances.personal.massager
4	apple	949.47	565865924	fd4bd6d4-bd14-4fdc-9aff-bd41a594f82e	electronics	1005115 - apple electronics.smartphone

Figure 4.21 A snapshot of the new columns added to the events data

EXPORTING AN INTERMEDIATE DATA MODEL TO SEPARATE DATA CLEANING FROM ANALYSIS

It is good practice to separate the code that cleans the data from the code that analyzes it. One way to do this is to output the cleaned data to a separate file, which the analysis code can read directly.

The intermediate data can be any format, but *parquet* is useful because it is a compressed data format that stores type information, unlike other formats, such as CSVs. This means that when we read in a parquet file in the future, we do not have to convert date columns to date types as our code will already know about them:

```
events.to_parquet("./data/events.parquet.gz", compression="gzip")
```

Let's summarize this part of the analysis before moving on. Figure 4.22 shows the steps we have taken so far, up to the point where we exported our intermediate dataset. Notice that our investigations into categories and brands are represented side by side because they are independent of each other and could have been done in any order.

Now, we are ready to move on to part 2 of our solution, which is summarizing data to the product level and calculating all the relevant metrics.

4.4.2 Calculating product-level metrics

We have explored and cleaned our data and are now ready to start looking at our desired metrics. However, first we need to transform data to be at the right granularity.

CHANGING THE GRANULARITY OF THE DATA TO SUIT THE QUESTION

The raw data is at the event level, and we are interested in products, so we should aggregate the data to be one row per product. In doing so, we need to define various

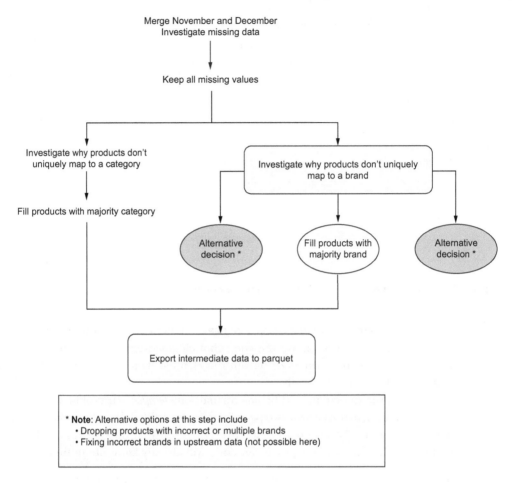

Figure 4.22   All the steps in part 1 of our analysis

aggregations to summarize data at the right level. To understand what aggregations we need, we must define our metrics precisely. Based on our project brief, the metrics we will calculate are

- *Volume*—The count of purchase events for a given product ID. We do not have a "quantity" column, meaning if a particular user bought the same product twice, there would be two separate rows in the data to indicate this. Therefore, counting rows that correspond to purchase events is how we can count the sales volume for a product.

- *Revenue*—The sum of the `price` column. We have no information about shipping costs, wholesale cost of products, or the amount of tax, so we can only calculate the gross total income from each product.

- *Popularity*—The number of unique users who bought a product. This will ignore cases where a single user bought multiples of a product but is a good proxy for popularity.
- *Change in performance*—For this, we will simply calculate each metric separately for November and December events.
- *Conversion*—Given the data, it will be defined as the number of purchase events as a percentage of cart events in a given period. That is, out of all the times someone put an item into a cart, what percentage became a purchase event? Ideally, we would also consider what percentage of viewed items turned into sales, but we do not have the data to answer that question.

Conversion is a tricky metric because the denominator can be interpreted in multiple ways. For example, if a user puts an item into the cart, removes it, then adds it again, and finally purchases it, we may have two events contributing to the denominator instead of one. Our choice of whether to deduplicate these events as a single instance or to use both rows will affect our conversion figures. Here, when calculating conversion, we will keep things simple and count all cart events as our denominator and all purchase events as our numerator.

Given the kinds of metrics we are interested in, our aggregations at a product level will include

- November and December data separately for month-on-month comparison
- Sum of the `price` column for revenue
- Count of rows for volume
- Number of unique users for popularity
- The difference between the monthly figures
- Number of cart and purchase events so we can calculate conversion

For all but the conversion metrics, we only need the purchase events. It is only when introducing conversion that we want to look at cart events as well. Therefore, to make our code more efficient, we will calculate most of the metrics on the purchases before calculating conversion metrics separately and joining them afterward.

To do this, we need to separate the cart events data from the purchase events:

```
purchases = events[events["event_type"] == "purchase"].copy()
carts = events[events["event_type"] == "cart"].copy()
```

Now, let's construct a league table (ranking system) of metrics at the individual product level step by step.

CALCULATING MULTIPLE METRICS AT ONCE

Creating this league table will be a dense piece of code because it is where we end up doing more of our calculations, so let's deconstruct it into its individual steps. First, we create new indicator columns to calculate monthly values. Indicators are columns that contain either a value or a fallback value like 0 if a row of data does not meet the desired criteria. In this case, november_revenue will contain the value from the price column if the event is in November. Otherwise, it will contain 0. Calculating the sum of this column for a given product ID will therefore give us the total revenue for November alone. The following code creates the indicator columns:

```
purchases
    .assign(
        november_count=np.where(purchases["event_time"].dt.month==11,
⇒ 1, 0),
        november_revenue=np.where(purchases["event_time"].dt.month==11,
⇒ purchases["price"], 0),
        november_user_id=np.where(purchases["event_time"].dt.month==11,
⇒ purchases["user_id"], np.nan),
        december_count=np.where(purchases["event_time"].dt.month==12,
⇒ 1, 0),
        december_revenue=np.where(purchases["event_time"].dt.month==12,
⇒ purchases["price"], 0),
        december_user_id=np.where(purchases["event_time"].dt.month==12,
⇒ purchases["user_id"], np.nan))
```

Next, we group our data by product ID and summarize these new indicator columns to get monthly revenue, row count, and unique user ID count:

```
.groupby(["product_id", "product_name"])
    .agg(november_volume=('november_count', 'sum'),
        november_revenue=('november_revenue', 'sum'),
        november_users=('november_user_id', 'nunique'),
        december_volume=('december_count', 'sum'),
        december_revenue=('december_revenue', 'sum'),
        december_users=('december_user_id', 'nunique')
    )
```

Finally, we create new columns that calculate the difference between November and December figures. This gives us all our desired metrics that only require the purchase events data. It is this dataset to which we will join our conversion metrics. Here is the final complete code block, and figure 4.23 shows a snapshot of the created league table:

```
purchases_league_table = (
    purchases
    .assign(
        november_count=np.where(purchases["event_time"].dt.month==11,
⇒ 1, 0),
        november_revenue=np.where(purchases["event_time"].dt.month==11,
⇒ purchases["price"], 0),
        november_user_id=np.where(purchases["event_time"].dt.month==11,
⇒ purchases["user_id"], np.nan),
        december_count=np.where(purchases["event_time"].dt.month==12,
⇒ 1, 0),
        december_revenue=np.where(purchases["event_time"].dt.month==12,
⇒ purchases["price"], 0),
```

```
        december_user_id=np.where(purchases["event_time"].dt.month==12,
    purchases["user_id"], np.nan))
    .groupby(["product_id", "product_name"])
    .agg(november_volume=('november_count', 'sum'),
        november_revenue=('november_revenue', 'sum'),
        november_users=('november_user_id', 'nunique'),
        december_volume=('december_count', 'sum'),
        december_revenue=('december_revenue', 'sum'),
        december_users=('december_user_id', 'nunique')
    )
    .assign(
        volume_diff=lambda x:
            x["december_volume"] - x["november_volume"],
        revenue_diff=lambda x:
            x["december_revenue"] - x["november_revenue"],
        users_diff=lambda x:
            x["december_users"] - x["november_users"])
    .reset_index()
)

purchases_league_table.head()
```

	product_id	product_name	november_volume	november_revenue	november_users
0	1000978	1000978 - samsung electronics.smartphone	20	6135.32	17
1	1001588	1001588 - meizu electronics.smartphone	6	766.29	5
2	1001605	1001605 - apple electronics.smartphone	0	0.00	0
3	1001606	1001606 - apple electronics.smartphone	0	0.00	0
4	1001618	1001618 - apple electronics.smartphone	36	18059.76	25

(continued)

	december_volume	december_revenue	december_users	volume_diff	revenue_diff	users_diff
0	16	4260.40	16	-4	-1874.92	-1
1	13	1652.55	12	7	886.26	7
2	18	9806.76	16	18	9806.76	16
3	11	5662.69	10	11	5662.69	10
4	7	4745.84	7	-29	-13313.92	-18

Figure 4.23   A snapshot of the purchases league table data

From this table, we get a lot of information at a glance, including

- Products that sold more in November than in December and vice versa
- Products that did not sell at all in November but did sell in December
- Products bought by more or fewer customers month-on-month

In some ways, we could even stop here and use this table to answer our questions by simply sorting it based on the column that we believe represents our metric for the best product. However, we also wanted to calculate conversion metrics first. The following code calculates the number of rows per event type for each product ID per month:

```
conversion_table = (
    pd.pivot_table(
        data=events.assign(month=events["event_time"].dt.month),
        index=["product_id", "product_name"],
        columns=["month", "event_type"],
        values="user_session",
        aggfunc="count"
    )
    .fillna(0)
    .set_axis(labels=["november_cart", "november_sold",
➥ "december_cart", "december_sold"],
            axis=1)
    .reset_index()
    .assign(november_conversion
➥ = lambda x: x["november_sold"] / x["november_cart"],
            december_conversion
➥ = lambda x: x["december_sold"] / x["december_cart"])
)

conversion_table.head()
```

Using the `pivot_table` function in `pandas` means this table would extend to counting any number of event types and could be used if we were to obtain data for view events as well. This isn't strictly necessary here, but it requires a bit of prophylactic coding to prepare for future eventualities. Figure 4.24 shows a snapshot of this conversion league table.

From this snapshot, we have already found a problem; this data will contain missing values. Having no cart or purchase events results in a missing value, rather than a zero, because strictly speaking, 0 conversion would mean we had cart events, and none of them resulted in a purchase. Whenever you calculate a division, you should also be prepared to encounter infinity values, which happen when you try to divide by zero.

For now, let's merge these two product league tables and ensure that product IDs are unique. Figure 4.25 shows the output when we look at the columns in this merged metrics dataset:

```
league_table = purchases_league_table.merge(conversion_table,
➥ on=["product_id", "product_name"], how="left")
assert len(league_table) == purchases["product_id"].nunique()
league_table.dtypes
```

	product_id	product_name	november_cart	november_sold
0	1000894	1000894 - texet electronics.smartphone	0.0	0.0
1	1000978	1000978 - samsung electronics.smartphone	60.0	20.0
2	1001588	1001588 - meizu electronics.smartphone	16.0	6.0
3	1001605	1001605 - apple electronics.smartphone	0.0	0.0
4	1001606	1001606 - apple electronics.smartphone	0.0	0.0

(continued)

	december_cart	december_sold	november_conversion	december_conversion
0	4.0	0.0	NaN	0.000000
1	58.0	16.0	0.333333	0.275862
2	37.0	13.0	0.375000	0.351351
3	42.0	18.0	NaN	0.428571
4	23.0	11.0	NaN	0.478261

Figure 4.24   A snapshot of the conversion league table data

```
product_id             int64
product_name           object
november_volume        int32
november_revenue       float64
november_users         int64
december_volume        int32
december_revenue       float64
december_users         int64
volume_diff            int32
revenue_diff           float64
users_diff             int64
november_cart          float64
november_sold          float64
december_cart          float64
december_sold          float64
november_conversion    float64
december_conversion    float64
dtype: object
```

Figure 4.25   Columns in our metrics table and their data types

Let's add these latest steps to our growing diagram to show our analytical steps. Figure 4.26 shows the latest version. I put the investigations of product brands and categories alongside one another to indicate that they happen independently and don't necessarily follow each other in a specific order.

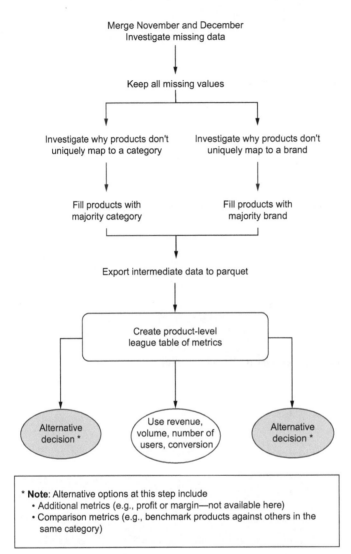

Figure 4.26   Steps taken so far up to the creation of the metrics league table

Now, we have all the metrics we could be interested in, and the next step is to look at products that perform well.

4.4.3   *Finding the best products using our defined metrics*

With all these metrics in place, how do we use them to find the "best" product? The answer is, as is often the case, it depends.

DEFINING METRICS BASED ON THE SPECIFIC QUESTION

We have multiple options, such as

- Picking a single metric to sort the league table by and thinking of the top N products as being the best.
- We could weight each metric by its relative importance, create a weighted combination of metric values to come up with a single value to define each product, and use that value to find the top N.
- If we care specifically about December performers, we could look at outliers in our difference metrics, such as the difference in volume between November and December.

There are many more options, but since the brief was specifically about the December sale period, we will focus our efforts on products that showed the biggest month-on-month increases. For which of the metrics should we focus on this difference? Our options are

- *Change in revenue*—Focusing on absolute revenue might mean expensive items skew our results.
- *Change in the number of unique users*—This might be a good measure for products that perform better month-on-month.
- *Change in volume*—This seems like a solid, logical place to start as simply selling more of an item month-on-month is an indicator of good performance.

We should first understand the typical month-on-month change in volume. Figure 4.27 shows the histogram produced by the following code:

```
fig, axis = plt.subplots()

league_table["volume_diff"].hist(bins=100, ax=axis)

axis.set(title="Distribution of month-on-month change in volume",
         xlabel="Change in volume from November to December",
         ylabel="Frequency")
```

Clearly, there are outliers that skew this histogram beyond usefulness. Let's zoom into the middle to see if the month-on-month change is centered around zero. The following code produces the histogram in figure 4.28:

```
fig, axis = plt.subplots()

league_table.loc[league_table["volume_diff"].between(-100,100),
➥ "volume_diff"].hist(bins=100, ax=axis)

axis.set(title="Distribution of month-on-month change in volume",
         xlabel="Change in volume from November to December",
         ylabel="Frequency")
```

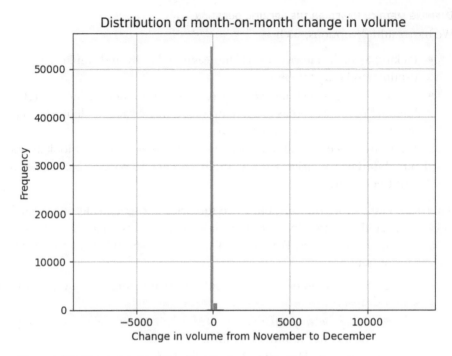

Figure 4.27   **Histogram of month-on-month change in product sales volume**

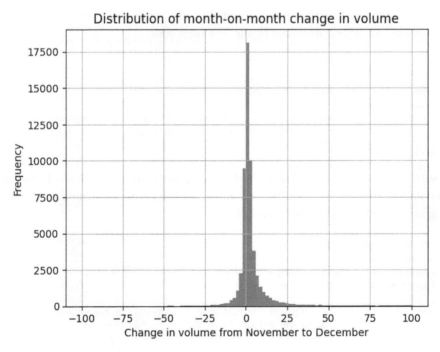

Figure 4.28   **A zoomed-in version of the histogram from figure 4.27**

Looking at this histogram more closely, we see that most products haven't changed much in sales volume month-on-month, and some products sold more, while others sold less. However, these are absolute values. Products that generally sell only a handful per month would be underrepresented in these graphs. Therefore, we should really calculate and look at the percentage change in sales volume. The following code calculates this value and produces a histogram of percentage change, as shown in figure 4.29. Note the code also removes missing percentage change values, as well as infinity values produced when dividing by zero:

```
league_table["volume_diff_pct"] = (
    100 * (league_table["volume_diff"] / league_table["november_volume"])
)

fig, axis = plt.subplots()

(
    league_table["volume_diff_pct"]
    .replace([np.inf, -np.inf], np.nan)
    .dropna()
    .loc[lambda x: x.between(-101,501)]
    .hist(bins=50, ax=axis)
)

axis.set(
    title="Distribution of month-on-month percentage change in volume",
    xlabel="% difference between sales in November and December",
    ylabel="Frequency"
)
```

This chart shows us that most products seem to have actually sold nothing in December versus November since a −100% change means zero items sold in December. There are also products that sold two, three, four, and five times more month-on-month. With percentage values, we need to be mindful of biases that can arise. For example, if we sold one of a product in November and five in December, that is a 500% change but is unlikely to be as significant as selling 1,000 of something when we sold only 500 in the previous month, although that is technically a smaller percentage change. One way to mitigate this problem is to exclude items that only typically sell a handful.

Before we continue our analysis, however, we should include additional product details in our league table so that when we identify high performers, we can look at what categories or brands they represent.

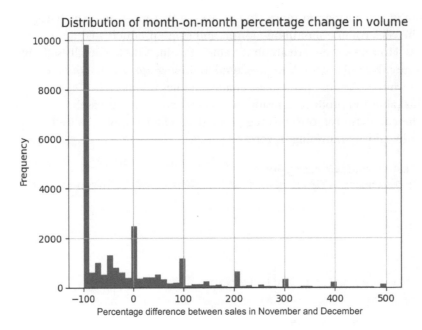

Figure 4.29   Distribution of percentage month-on-month change in sales volume

ITERATING ON OUR METRICS BASED ON OUR FINDINGS

We could have enhanced our products with this additional data when creating the league table, but we are doing it at this stage of the analysis in response to our desire to investigate further. The following code creates a product catalog, which we can join to our league table to add additional product details. Figure 4.30 shows a snapshot of this product catalog:

```
product_catalog = (
    events[["product_id", "product_name", "category_id", "subcategory",
 "brand", "category"]]
    .drop_duplicates(subset=["product_id", "product_name", "subcategory",
 "brand", "category"])
)

assert len(product_catalog) == events["product_id"].nunique()

print(product_catalog.shape)
product_catalog.head()
```

Now, we continue our analysis by defining cutoffs for how many of a particular product we must have sold to consider it when we look for top performers. Discounting

	product_id	product_name	category_id
0	1005014	1005014 - samsung electronics.smartphone	2053013555631882655
1	13200605	13200605 - furniture.bedroom.bed	2053013557192163841
2	1005161	1005161 - xiaomi electronics.smartphone	2053013555631882655
3	1801881	1801881 - samsung appliances.personal.massager	2053013554415534427
4	1005115	1005115 - apple electronics.smartphone	2053013555631882655

(continued)

	subcategory	brand	category
0	electronics.smartphone	samsung	electronics
1	furniture.bedroom.bed	None	furniture
2	electronics.smartphone	xiaomi	electronics
3	appliances.personal.massager	samsung	appliances
4	electronics.smartphone	apple	electronics

Figure 4.30   A snapshot of the product catalog

products that only sell a handful at a time means that high percentage change values are more likely to be meaningful:

```
DEC_VS_NOV_PCT_CUTOFF = 200
NOV_VOLUME_CUTOFF = 10
ONLY_DEC_VOLUME_CUTOFF = 100

december_high_performers = (
    pd.concat(
    [
        league_table[(np.isinf(league_table["volume_diff_pct"]) == False)
            & (league_table["november_volume"] > NOV_VOLUME_CUTOFF)
            & (league_table["volume_diff_pct"] > DEC_VS_NOV_PCT_CUTOFF)],
        league_table[(np.isinf(league_table["volume_diff_pct"]))
            & (league_table["december_volume"] > ONLY_DEC_VOLUME_CUTOFF)]
    ],
    axis=0,
    ignore_index=True)
    .merge(product_catalog.drop(columns="product_name"), on="product_id")
)

print(december_high_performers.shape)
```

Here, we defined some cutoffs that mean we only consider products that

- Sold at least twice as many in December as November
- Sold at least 10 in November
- Sold at least 100 in December

These cutoffs are somewhat arbitrary, and changing them will change our results, but they do ensure we only identify products that really did outperform themselves in December. Our particular choice of cutoffs resulted in 449 products. We could provide these directly to our stakeholders, or we could do further analysis to see what kinds of products show up more often as high performers. Let us look at the top categories, subcategories, and brands among these high-performing products. These are shown in figures 4.31 through 4.33, respectively:

```
from IPython.display import display

for col in ["category", "subcategory", "brand"]:
    print(col)
    display(december_high_performers[col].value_counts())
```

```
category

apparel         121
appliances      102
electronics      85
computers        36
furniture        32
kids             24
construction     20
sport            13
auto              8
country_yard      4
medicine          2
accessories       1
stationery        1
Name: category, dtype: int64
```

Figure 4.31 Top-performing product categories

```
subcategory

electronics.smartphone          43
apparel.shoes                   37
appliances.kitchen.coffee_grinder  33
apparel.shoes.sandals           28
appliances.personal.massager    26
                                ..
electronics.audio.microphone     1
apparel.shoes.ballet_shoes       1
kids.dolls                       1
appliances.personal.hair_cutter  1
stationery.cartrige              1
Name: subcategory, Length: 76, dtype: int64
```

Figure 4.32 Top-performing product subcategories

```
brand

lucente    56
xiaomi     31
sony       24
samsung    20
huawei     18
            ..
babyzen     1
palit       1
galaxy      1
gorenje     1
saeshin     1
Name: brand, Length: 128, dtype: int64
```

Figure 4.33 Top-performing product brands

It appears that smartphones, various kinds of clothing, and products made by Lucente top the rankings in terms of December's best performers. There are also some coffee grinders that appear to have performed well. In fact, digging into the results a bit more suggests that these coffee grinders account for most of Lucente's success in the league table. The following code shows the top unique combinations of category, subcategory, and brand, as shown in figure 4.34:

```
december_high_performers[["category", "subcategory", "brand"]]
    .value_counts().head(10)
```

```
category     subcategory                           brand
appliances   appliances.kitchen.coffee_grinder     lucente     33
electronics  electronics.smartphone                xiaomi      12
apparel      apparel.shoes                         sony        11
kids         kids.toys                             lucente     10
electronics  electronics.smartphone                huawei       9
                                                   samsung      8
apparel      apparel.shoes                         lg           7
computers    computers.peripherals.printer         lucente      7
furniture    furniture.kitchen.chair               xiaomi       6
electronics  electronics.smartphone                apple        6
dtype: int64
```

Figure 4.34 Top-performing products by category and brand

One aspect of this final table that might catch the eye is the presence of shoes made by Sony, which may warrant some investigation. They could be legitimate Sony-branded shoes or products categorized incorrectly.

We now have enough results to present to stakeholders. To recap, we have

- Combined the events datasets
- Cleaned up incorrectly categorized product data

- Calculated all possible metrics of interest
- Decided what to use as a measure of "best"
- Extracted the highest-performing products based on our chosen metric
- Investigated these high performers in more detail

Whichever metric(s) you chose, the process would have been similar to that shown in this example solution. We are unlikely to have reached the same conclusions because those depend entirely on your analytical choices throughout.

Let us briefly look at what happens when we use a different metric to define the best product and how that affects our results.

INVESTIGATING ALTERNATIVE METRIC DEFINITIONS

What happens if we decide the best products are the ones that converted the most cart events into purchase ones in the month of December? First, we use the following code to produce the histogram in figure 4.35, showing the distribution of December conversion:

```
fig, axis = plt.subplots()

(
    league_table[(np.isinf(league_table["december_conversion"]) == False)
    & (np.isnan(league_table["december_conversion"]) == False)]
    ["december_conversion"]
    .mul(100)
    .hist(bins=50, ax=axis)
)

axis.set(
    title="Distribution of December conversion",
    xlabel="Conversion (%)",
    ylabel="Frequency"
)
```

Most products convert at around the 30% mark, but a lot of products convert at 100% and even more. That latter option shouldn't be possible since we should logically not have more products purchased than were put into a cart. Let's investigate these records. The following code extracts only rows with over 99% conversion and excludes infinite values and other data errors. Using those results, we examine a single example of high conversion, shown in figure 4.36:

```
(
    league_table[(np.isinf(league_table["december_conversion"]) == False)
                & (np.isnan(league_table["december_conversion"]) == False)
                & (league_table["december_conversion"] > 0.99)]
    .sort_values("december_conversion", ascending=False)
    .head(20)
)
events[(events["product_id"] == 9200694)
    & (events["event_time"].dt.month == 12)]
```

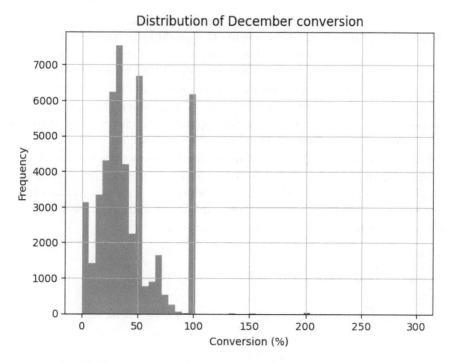

Figure 4.35   Distribution of conversion percentage in December

	event_time	event_type	product_id	category_id	subcategory
4698592	2019-12-17 13:01:28+00:00	cart	9200694	2232732104343421549	apparel.scarf
4698610	2019-12-17 13:01:38+00:00	purchase	9200694	2232732104343421549	apparel.scarf
5124731	2019-12-20 04:04:58+00:00	purchase	9200694	2232732104343421549	apparel.scarf
5192399	2019-12-20 10:56:30+00:00	purchase	9200694	2232732104343421549	apparel.scarf

(continued)

	brand	price	user_id	user_session	category	product_name
4698592	None	84.94	513304382	ecb28e2c-525d-4adb-998e-fd589d66ca86	apparel	9200694 - apparel.scarf
4698610	None	84.94	513304382	ecb28e2c-525d-4adb-998e-fd589d66ca86	apparel	9200694 - apparel.scarf
5124731	None	84.94	513304382	d607a412-9e1c-4ab4-89be-b4dd3fe8def1	apparel	9200694 - apparel.scarf
5192399	None	84.94	513304382	935b176b-19ee-47f1-8332-1144e970c495	apparel	9200694 - apparel.scarf

Figure 4.36   An example of raw data leading to over 100% conversion

There is a scarf that was bought three times by the same user on two different dates but with only one associated cart event. This could mean either a data error where we are missing two cart events or that we made incorrect assumptions about the data-generating process. When we said conversion should not be over 100%, we assumed a linear process where a user cannot make a purchase without putting an item into their cart. However, it is possible there is an "orders" page where a user could review their past orders and reorder products, while bypassing the cart screens. If this were the case, the data shown in figure 4.35 would not be unexpected.

As it stands, we have no way of knowing whether these instances are valid, so to get our top performers, we can simply restrict our data to under 100% conversion. Let us also stipulate some cutoffs and say that a product must have been bought by at least N users with a total of M sales to be included in our top conversion performers. The following code identifies the top performers, totaling 55 rows:

```
MIN_USERS = 5
MIN_PURCHASES = 10
CONVERSION_LOWER_LIMIT = 0.7

best_december_converters = (
    league_table[(np.isinf(league_table["december_conversion"]) == False)
            & (np.isnan(league_table["december_conversion"]) == False)
            & (league_table["december_conversion"]
    .between(CONVERSION_LOWER_LIMIT, 1))
            & (league_table["december_users"] > MIN_USERS)
            & (league_table["december_sold"] > MIN_PURCHASES)]
    .sort_values("december_conversion", ascending=False)
    .merge(product_catalog.drop(columns=["product_name"]),
    on=["product_id"])
)

print(best_december_converters.shape)
```

This means there are 55 products in total that were bought by at least five different users, totaling a minimum of 10 sales, and converted over 70% of their cart events to purchase ones. We could now look at what kinds of products these correspond to by looking at their categories. This output is shown in figure 4.37:

```
best_december_converters["category"].value_counts()
```

```
furniture        9
construction     8
computers        7
appliances       7
electronics      6
kids             6
apparel          6
auto             3
sport            2
accessories      1
Name: category, dtype: int64
```

Figure 4.37   Top-performing categories among highest-converting products

The results are quite different from the volume-based rankings. When conversion is considered the key metric, furniture and construction items come up as the highest performers. Looking into this deeper, using the following code gives us the output in figure 4.38:

```
best_december_converters.loc[best_december_converters["category"]
    .isin(["furniture", "construction"]), "subcategory"].value_counts()
```

```
construction.components.faucet    6
furniture.bedroom.bed             3
construction.tools.drill          2
furniture.bathroom.bath           2
furniture.bedroom.blanket         1
furniture.kitchen.table           1
furniture.universal.light         1
furniture.living_room.sofa        1
Name: subcategory, dtype: int64
```

Figure 4.38 Furniture and construction products that converted best in December

What this tells us is that once most people have identified a faucet, drill, or sofa, they will most likely go ahead and purchase it. Smartphones feature less in conversion-based rankings, perhaps indicating that people are unsure about their smartphone purchase even after placing the item in their cart.

Before summarizing our conclusions, let's recap the entire analysis process as a diagram to remind ourselves of the steps we took and where our choices might have diverged. Figure 4.39 shows the final diagram.

We are now ready to summarize our results in preparation for presenting them to our stakeholders.

PROJECT OUTCOMES

Based on these results, it looks like a safe bet to recommend to our stakeholders that classic Christmas present items like smartphones and kitchen appliances are likely to be high performers in December. The results based on conversion are less convincing since they only highlight products that people buy once they've added them to their cart, but they may not tell us anything about the success of those products.

As always, there are limitations to our analysis. We did not look at the correlation between product price and performance. It is possible that our data implicitly tells us when a sale was on, which we could identify by looking at products whose price suddenly dropped, and this could inform our decision about which products sell best during sale periods. We could also request additional pricing data, such as postage costs, tax, or item wholesale costs. This latter figure could tell us not just which products generate the most revenue but also which ones generate the highest profit.

Our restriction to two months of data also means our analysis is incomplete. Having more data would let us benchmark our products better and see which products

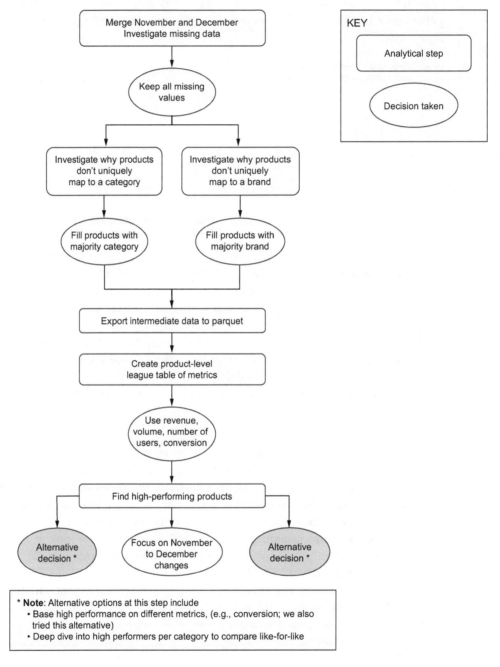

Figure 4.39   The final diagram showing all the steps and decision points in our analysis

deviate most from their average baseline performance. As it stands, we based this on a single month of data, which may be insufficient.

Our initial findings warrant a further discussion with our stakeholders, and hopefully, showing them the effects of choosing different metrics will help focus them on the ones that truly matter to them. When choosing what to present to them, it is important to consider whether our recommendations are actionable. Telling stakeholders that people generally buy the faucets they have identified is less likely to result in them taking action than telling them that smartphones increase their sales the most in the December period.

Activity: Further project ideas with this data

The e-commerce data in this chapter gives you plenty of opportunities to practice calculating and reflecting on different metrics. As with all projects, I recommend considering different research questions, such as

- What are some products whose prices fluctuate more than others? There is no reason to assume the same product ID sold for the same amount each time.
- Are there temporal patterns in the data (products that sell more or convert better on weekends than weekdays, for example)?
- You could go deeper into the product catalog and look for subcategories that perform better than others. What would "better" mean here?

4.5 Closing thoughts on metrics

As an analyst, you will encounter many projects like this one, where metrics will be insufficiently defined. Your job is not simply to perform the calculations given to you by a stakeholder, but to have a conversation with them to define metrics that are clear and measurable, given the available data, and that capture the right underlying concepts. We should generally be wary of summarizing complex problems into a single metric and should feel comfortable pushing back to help stakeholders create more usable problem definitions.

There are two avenues to explore these concepts further: one is to understand different business metrics generally so that business terminology is more familiar to you, and the other is to research metrics specific to the industry you work in.

How do you know what to read on the topic? As it turns out, generating reading lists for a new topic is a great use of generative AI tools, for example, large language models such as Open AI's ChatGPT. I gave it the following prompt:

Give me a reading list for someone who is interested in exploring different business metrics and their impact

ChatGPT was able to generate a reading list of books to explore metrics further. The list includes general works such as *The Balanced Scorecard: Translating Strategy into Action*

(Harvard Business School Press, 1996) by Robert S. Kaplan and David P. Norton, which "goes beyond financial metrics to measure various dimensions of organizational performance," or a title focusing on a more specific domain, social media, in *Measure What Matters: Online Tools For Understanding Customers, Social Media, Engagement, and Key Relationships* (Wiley, 2011) by Katie Delahaye Paine.

While not all recommendations by the AI might be usable, employing it to kick-start the research process is one way in which it becomes a valuable tool in the analyst's toolkit.

4.5.1 *Skills for defining better metrics for any project*

In this chapter, our biggest challenge was turning a vague request into measurable metrics that we could analyze. The key skills learned for defining metrics that are applicable to any similar project include

- Ensuring that definitions within the data are consistent (e.g., the same product is always assigned to the same category)
- Exporting intermediate versions of the data to separate exploration and cleaning from analysis
- Changing the granularity of the data to suit the question (e.g., summarizing transaction-level data to the product level)
- Calculating multiple metrics to investigate the problem from different angles
- Iterating on our chosen metrics once we have some initial findings
- Investigating alternative metrics to present to our stakeholders for a more complete picture

Summary

- Choosing the right metric is a vital professional skill for analysts to develop.
- Any metric you choose to measure performance will affect the entire analysis path.
- Be wary of summarizing complex problems into a single metric.
- Definitions of key metrics should be unambiguous to avoid analytical errors.

Unusual data sources

This chapter covers

- Thinking of data beyond what is available in structured formats
- Using all the data sources available to you creatively, regardless of their format
- Navigating the tradeoff between time spent and value added when working with additional data sources

Most datasets you will encounter in your career are not as clean and structured as those provided in a learning environment. The reality is that it's often the analyst who must search for the right data, which may be hidden in complicated spreadsheets or hidden even further in unstructured, nontraditional data sources. This chapter is about practicing the creativity of identifying and using novel and unstructured data sources to answer interesting analytical questions.

Structured vs. unstructured data

For the sake of clarity, when I use the words "structured" and "unstructured" to describe a dataset, I mean tabular, two-dimensional data versus everything else. Analysts typically work with structured data—something with rows and columns that can be opened in Excel or something that sits in a database and could conceivably be opened in Excel. Unstructured data is anything that isn't in a rows and columns format, ranging from documents or raw audio to free text or a binary data format.

In this project, you will be working with unstructured PDF files containing structured data tables. The semantics of whether we call this data unstructured, structured, semi-structured, or something else does not change the fact that working with PDFs is not the same as working with tabular data. That is the structured versus unstructured difference with which we are dealing in this chapter.

5.1   *Identifying novel data sources*

I always advocate starting with a problem to solve. This is no different when thinking about additional data sources to use for your analysis. Once you have a clear problem statement, it is easier to understand what data sources you still need. This is why identifying and obtaining data are steps 3 and 4, and not steps 1 and 2, of the results-driven approach.

What data is available to you will vary between workplaces, but generally, the kinds of data that may be helpful to consider are

- Data generated by typical business processes, such as emails.
- Data in operational systems, if this is not already available.
- Self-hosted data, meaning data people create for themselves, such as spreadsheets on people's computer desktops. These are important only if people rely on them for decision making. Otherwise, they may just be less accurate versions of existing operational data. One example is salespeople tracking their own client pipeline outside of the company CRM.
- Industry data, such as market statistics published by a central body.
- Government statistics, published as open data.
- White papers, public documents that summarize research on a given topic in an accessible way, created either internally or by a competitor.

Real business case: Extracting published industry data from PDFs

In many sectors, leading industry bodies publish market statistics, which are often the best indicators of the state of the market over time. Many of these statistics are published as tabular data, usually Excel files. However, in the past, I have had to resort to finding less structured forms of important statistics and writing my own PDF data extraction code. This is an experience every aspiring analyst should go through, hence the inclusion of this project.

5.1.1 Considerations for using new datasets

There are some general considerations when deciding to use an additional data source to augment your analysis:

- Does this data source integrate with existing data? Can we join or merge this dataset with the one we are already using or is that not required? There will be instances where salespeople record their sales in their own spreadsheets, either outside the "official" CRM or alongside it. Would it be possible to join the data in their own custom spreadsheet to the data in the CRM system? Is there a common client identifier, like an ID, present in both datasets? If not, can we still link clients across those datasets somehow, such as by name? Refer to chapter 3 for a specific example of just such a problem.

- How much effort is it to extract structured data from this data source? This might involve manipulating an unstructured format and creating a tabular representation or taking a structured dataset that has a different format from our existing data and therefore requires work to change and rename columns to match the format we need. Either way, it is important to estimate the effort involved in this work before deciding to use a new data source:
  - A subset of this question is, do you currently have the expertise to manipulate this data? Not having worked with a particular data format is not a deal-breaker, but learning the necessary skills factors into estimating the effort involved.
  - A related consideration is, does your tool support this data format? If you are used to working solely in Excel, for example, it may be harder to manipulate unusual data formats, but a programming language such as Python or R may have a relevant library that is easy to install and use.

- What is the value of this additional data? What questions can you answer with it that you couldn't answer before? Knowing this will help determine whether the effort will be worth it.

- Does this data create additional dependencies? Will this additional data be used as a one-off, or is it something that will require engineering resources to continuously ingest and store?

5.2 Project 4: Analyzing film industry trends using PDF data

Let's take a look at the project in which we will extract structured data from PDF files to understand the effects of the COVID-19 pandemic on the film industry. We will look at the problems our stakeholders want to solve and the data sources they have provided. Section 5.3 will dive into how to approach this problem using the results-driven approach as well as some technical considerations when handling PDF files. As with every project, there is a section dedicated to a step-by-step example solution, which can be found in section 5.4. As usual, our solutions will likely diverge, especially if you are not using Python, since I explore some Python-specific ways to read data tables from PDFs.

The data is available at https://davidasboth.com/book-code. You will find the files with which you can attempt the project, as well as the example solution in the form of a Jupyter notebook.

5.2.1   *Problem statement*

In this scenario, you are working for EchoTale Analytics, a research firm in the entertainment industry. Their primary mission is to publish analytical pieces about the evolution of the entertainment industry, and you have been placed in charge of a project in their film division. Specifically, the firm wants to publish a white paper about how the COVID-19 pandemic has affected the film industry. They don't currently have a more focused topic, so your task is to complete and present the preliminary research. Since the target is a white paper, the priority is to be able to tell a story that would be interesting to a film-loving audience.

The firm works exclusively with external data sources, and for this project, they have given you PDF reports from the British Film Industry's (BFI) Research and Statistics Unit (RSU), called Statistical Yearbooks. These Yearbooks contain annual summaries of statistics about the film industry, including embedded data tables. Most of the data relates to the film industry in the United Kingdom, but some global statistics are included as well. The data goes back almost 20 years, and naturally, the format of the PDF report is not consistent.

> **NOTE**   Thanks to the BFI RSU and specifically John Sandow, senior research and data analyst, for permission to use the PDF reports.

To complete this project, you will need to

- Identify the dimensions along which the film industry is analyzed in the Yearbooks
- Decide how far back to extract data, as well as what constitutes pre-COVID and post-lockdown periods
- Extract the necessary underlying data
- Analyze the film statistics to arrive at a narrative that could be useful to your stakeholders in preparing their white paper

Your stakeholders' priority is that the findings are interesting and unexpected. They already assume cinema admissions dropped during the pandemic period and went down to zero during lockdowns, and they do not want to publish a white paper with such obvious statistics. They would prefer you explore things such as

- Have admissions recovered post-lockdown differently in different countries?
- What genres of films were popular before and after the pandemic period? Has this changed since lockdown restrictions were lifted?
- Which distributors have experienced the biggest change post-pandemic?
- Has there been a change in people's attitudes toward independent films?

You will spend most of the time in the analysis portion of this project exploring trends pre- and post-lockdowns and comparing them to identify the most marked changes, which are the ones most likely to be interesting to your stakeholders.

5.2.2   Data dictionary

This project does not have an explicit data dictionary, which is a common problem in the real world. Even if you do not create a data dictionary, you will need to note down the types of data present in each Yearbook before deciding on what data to focus on. Some aspects of the data may only be present in older or newer Yearbooks, but you will need your data to be consistently available in all the documents you end up using.

One aspect of the documents that will make your work a bit easier is that the data is in tables that can be extracted with the right tools. An example of such a table is shown in figure 5.1.

Table 1 Box office results for the top 20 films released in the UK and Republic of Ireland, 2021

Rank	Title	Country of origin	Box office gross (£ million)	Widest point of release	Opening weekend gross (£ million)	Distributor
1	No Time to Die*	UK/USA	96.7	791	25.8	Universal
2	Spider-Man: No Way Home*	USA	92.8ª	694	31.9	Sony
3	Dune*	USA/Can	22.0	691	5.9	Warner Bros
4	Shang-Chi and the Legend of the Ten Rings	USA/Aus	21.3	671	5.8	Walt Disney
5	Peter Rabbit 2: The Runaway*	Aus/USA	20.5	648	4.6	Sony
6	Black Widow	UK/USA	18.8	653	7.0	Walt Disney
7	Venom: Let There Be Carnage	UK/USA	18.1	610	6.2	Sony
8	Free Guy	USA	16.9	655	2.6	Walt Disney
9	Fast & Furious 9	UK/USA	16.5	614	6.1	Universal
10	Eternals	UK/USA	14.9	651	5.5	Walt Disney
11	The Suicide Squad	USA	14.3	649	3.3	Warner Bros
12	Space Jam: A New Legacy	USA	12.9	640	1.4	Warner Bros
13	Jungle Cruise	USA	12.5	612	2.3	Walt Disney
14	A Quiet Place Part II	USA	11.8	625	3.6	Paramount
15	Ghostbusters: Afterlife*	USA/Can	11.5	662	4.3	Sony
16	The Addams Family 2*	USA/Can	10.3	676	2.0	Universal
17	The Croods: A New Age	USA	10.0	659	0.7	Universal
18	House of Gucci*	UK/USA	9.9	712	2.4	Universal
19	The Conjuring: The Devil Made Me Do It	USA	9.6	516	2.7	Warner Bros
20	Cruella	UK/USA	9.5	585	1.5	Walt Disney

Figure 5.1   An example data table from a Statistical Yearbook PDF file

> **Activity: Creating a data dictionary**
>
> Try writing a data dictionary for the data you end up using. Often, analysts write dictionaries for data they end up using because they're the first to use it for analysis. It's good practice to create this document for future users of the data, which includes a future version of you!

5.2.3 *Desired outcomes*

The output of your analysis should be recommendations about potential topics for the white paper. The recommendations should be specific, so if you think there is a story about how people prefer different film genres since lockdown restrictions were lifted, your analysis should contain specific conclusions about which genres were popular before and after. Your recommendations should also be supported by visualizations, which may be included in the final white paper. As an additional consideration, you could also think about how your data extraction method, whether that is code or a specific tool, could be reused for future versions of this project.

5.2.4 *Required tools*

For the example solution in this chapter, I used the Python libraries `pandas` and `matplotlib` to explore and visualize the data. To extract the data from the PDFs in the first place, I ended up using the Python library `pdfplumber`, but I will discuss other options. Your chosen tools may be different, and as with every project, the tool is less important than the process, but the tool you select must be able to

- Read a PDF file and extract tabular data from it into a more typical format, such as a CSV file
- Load multiple datasets from CSV or Excel files
- Combine two or more datasets
- Perform basic data manipulation tasks, such as sorting, grouping, and reshaping data
- Create data visualizations

I have opted to stay within my Python toolkit for this chapter as well, but I will discuss some other options at your disposal. You may choose to extract the data from the PDFs with a tool outside of your regular toolkit, in which case your usual tools only need to satisfy the latter bullet points and not necessarily the first one.

5.3 *Applying the results-driven method to extracting data from PDFs*

There is a lot of uncertainty in this project, partly due to the unknown and inconsistent structure of the PDF files and partly due to the vagueness of our stakeholders' requests. Using the results-driven approach, we can formulate an action plan.

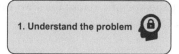

Our stakeholders haven't given us much direction, so our understanding of the problem is incomplete at this stage. Our first iteration needs to focus on identifying common data tables across multiple years of the Yearbooks and analyzing what we have at our disposal. Once we start looking at pre-COVID and post-lockdown trends, we will have more information about what the main topic of our analysis will be.

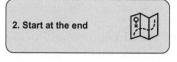

Even though we don't know precisely what the white paper topic will be, we do know that we need to focus on comparing the same data in different time periods. Our minimum viable answer will focus on this comparison. Even this information gives us an idea of the final output of our work, which we can work toward.

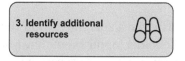

In this project, the identification stage will be crucial. This is where we explore the PDFs and note down common data themes we could explore. Once we have done that, we can move on to extracting only the specific data we need. This will save us time in the long run because extracting all the data tables and only then exploring them would take longer.

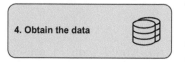

You could argue the data was obtained when our stakeholder provided the PDF files, but as we have seen, there is plenty of work to do before we have a structured dataset to explore. Not all projects following the results-driven approach will result in the same time spent on each section. In this project, I envisage this step taking up a large portion of our time.

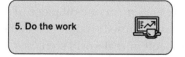

Let's sketch out the steps we will take, building on the steps discussed in section 5.2.1:

- First, we will open the PDF Yearbooks in descending year order and note the data tables available to us. There is no substitute for actually looking at our data before opening our analysis tools to get a sense of what we're working with.
- Next, we will decide how far back we are aiming to go in time. We do not have a lot of data to establish post-lockdown trends, and we don't want to spend too long looking at data that's too far in the past.
- We can then decide on which aspects of the data we will be able to extract for analysis. This will depend on what is available consistently over the period we've settled on.

- The next step will be to find and extract the specific data tables we need and save them in a structured format, such as CSVs.

> ### Activity: Reusable methods
> When you get to this point, think about how reusable your chosen extraction method is. Whether you manually extract the data or write a script to do it, it is possible that you will need to do it again in a future iteration. Thinking about reusability up front is a good practice to save yourself time in the long run.

- At this point, we can analyze the data by examining pre- and post-lockdown trends along the dimensions we have identified, whether that is changes in genre, admissions for independent films, or something else.
- Finally, we will settle on a story to present to our stakeholders for inclusion in the white paper.

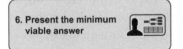

We cannot simulate the actual interaction you would have with a stakeholder upon presenting your findings. We can, however, practice preparing for such an interaction by considering the follow-up questions you might hear, given the work you present, and prepare your answers to them. Being ready with suggestions for future iterations leads to more productive stakeholder conversations.

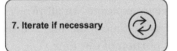

In this instance, we would want to present to our stakeholders as soon as we have solid evidence for one or more of our findings. What constitutes "solid" is not necessarily a question of statistical significance but more an intuition about what kind of story our stakeholders would be interested in hearing and publishing. This analysis, like others, is not a one-off piece of work you deliver; it is a conversation. The idea behind what to present is part of an analyst skill set that can only be developed by immersing yourself in real-world scenarios.

5.4   An example solution: Effects of the COVID-19 lockdown periods on the film industry

Let's tackle an example solution for this problem. Reading my solution is more valuable once you have attempted the project yourself. Remember, our solutions may differ. You may end up doing things in a different order as well.

We will begin by inspecting our PDFs to see what kind of data is consistently available across multiple years. Once we have made a decision on which datasets to focus on, we will find a PDF extraction method and make sure it can reliably extract tables of data from our PDFs. In the second part, we will analyze our newly created structured data to answer some of our stakeholders' questions.

5.4.1 Inspecting the available data

The very first step is to decide which years of data to look at. If we look at the available files, a snapshot of which is shown in figure 5.2, we notice that the Yearbook used to be a single file per year until 2018, after which the files are broken down by category. However, files from 2018 onward also seem to have a "master" document, for example, the one titled "2018—BFI Statistical Yearbook."

Name

2014 - BFI Statistical Yearbook 2014 - 919.pdf

2016 - BFI Statistical Yearbook 2016 - 917.pdf

2017 - BFI Statistical Yearbook 2017 - 916.pdf

2018 - Audiences - 913.pdf

2018 - BFI Statistical Yearbook 2018 - 903.pdf

2018 - Distribution and exhibition - 908.pdf

2018 Film at the cinema - 905.pdf

2018 - Film education and industry employment - 911.pdf

2018 - Home entertainment - 914.pdf

2018 - Public investment in film in the UK - 910.pdf

2018 - Screen sector certification and production - 907.pdf

2018 - UK film economy - 909.pdf

2018 - UK film market as a whole - 912.pdf

2018 - UK films and British talent worldwide - 906.pdf

2019 - Audiences - 900.pdf

2019 - BFI yearbook 2019 - 888.pdf

2019 - Distribution and exhibition - 894.pdf

2019 - Film at the cinema - 891.pdf

Figure 5.2 A snapshot of the available PDF files

We also appear to be missing the file for 2015 entirely, which would contain data for 2014. That's a problem we need a solution for if we want to go back further in time.

NOTE The years indicated in the files are actually for the previous year, meaning the file called "2018 Statistical Yearbook" contains data for 2017.

We can choose to extend our time period later, but for now, we will aim for the minimum amount of data that will get us pre- and post-lockdown trends. The first COVID lockdowns were in early 2020, so we definitely want 2019 at a minimum. Since we're interested in patterns, more data would be better, so we'll include two years pre-COVID: 2018 and 2019. This also means we only include years where the format of the documents is consistent.

A longer-term review would give us more information, but we want to balance time and complexity, so two years will suffice for our first iteration. If we were to go further back in time, which would be pre-2017, we would want to make sure that the categories in the single documents match those that are broken out into separate files from 2018 onward. That is, is there data for audiences, distribution, public investment, and so forth available?

Most of the lockdown restrictions were eased in 2021, so everything beyond that will be the "post-lockdowns" period, and we will need to decide how to categorize data in 2021.

Since we want our data to start in 2018, we will start with the 2019 Yearbook. Let's see what tables of data are available. Looking at the table of contents, partially shown in figure 5.3, we see that the subheadings match the individual files for 2019, which suggests all the necessary data might be contained in this single file.

The file contains a mixture of text, charts, infographics, and data tables.

IDENTIFYING WHAT DATA TO EXTRACT

Looking at the data tables, just for admissions alone, we have statistics for the following:

- Total admissions by country
- Monthly admissions in the United Kingdom
- Admissions by UK region
- Annual admission figures all the way back to 1935

Beyond this, we also have data for broad categories such as

- Gross box office revenue
- Top films of the year
- Countries of origin
- Genre
- Directors
- Independent films
- Distributors

Contents

Figure 5.3   A partial view of the table of contents from the 2019 Yearbook

Even just looking at these data tables inspires many directions for our analysis. Since the data is for a white paper, we should choose categories that are likely to contain interesting stories. Of course, we don't know up front, but intuition and domain expertise can help us choose a path that is more likely to yield results. Intuition like that is built only with lots of practice. We will focus on

- Admission patterns
- Distribution of genres
- Market share across distributors

Choosing these categories means we can ask whether seasonal patterns have changed over time, whether people now prefer different genres, and which if any, distributor has come out of the pandemic as the winner in terms of market share.

Let's summarize our work so far since we have just reached the first key decision point. Figure 5.4 shows the current step and the alternative options.

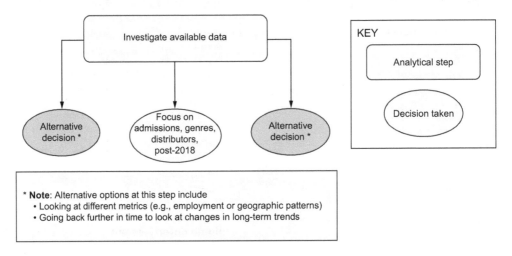

Figure 5.4   The first step and decision point in the analysis

Now, we can identify exactly which tables to look for in all our files to make sure we have the right data each year. For simplicity, let's limit ourselves to one data table per category. Figures 5.5–5.7 show the data tables in the 2019 document that we will search for in post-2019 files.

Based on our decision to focus on admissions, genres, and distributors, we can see the necessary data exists in just three tables. We can verify that these data tables exist for years beyond 2018 in their respective Yearbooks. If we had encountered a difference in structure, we would have had to investigate whether the same information was present in each table and ensure their structures matched so that we could combine them across multiple years into single files.

5.4.2   *Extracting data from PDFs*

Now that we know what data tables we need, we have multiple options to extract them. We could

- Manually copy a limited amount of our data from the PDFs
- Use a dedicated PDF extraction tool
- Find PDF extraction capabilities for our preferred tool (e.g., Python)

Table 2 Monthly UK cinema admissions, 2017 and 2018

Month	2017 (million)	2018 (million)	% +/- on 2017
January	15.0	16.2	8.0
February	16.5	16.1	-2.3
March	16.2	13.5	-16.2
April	15.6	15.5	-0.9
May	11.3	13.7	21.0
June	9.6	10.4	8.6
July	17.8	15.6	-12.3
August	14.5	19.2	32.8
September	10.8	10.1	-6.0
October	12.1	16.0	32.6
November	14.1	14.8	5.4
December	17.2	15.7	-8.7
Total	**170.6**	**177.0**	**3.7**

Source: CAA, comScore

Note: Figures may not sum to totals due to rounding.

Figure 5.5   Monthly UK admissions from the 2019 Yearbook

Table 17 Films released in the UK and Republic of Ireland by genre, 2018 (ranked by gross box office)

Genre	Number of releases	% of releases	Gross box office (£ million)	% of total box office	Top performing title
Action	77	9.8	361.3	27.7	Avengers: Infinity War
Animation	46	5.8	242.2	18.6	Incredibles 2
Drama	246	31.3	154.1	11.8	A Star Is Born
Comedy	144	18.3	88.3	6.8	Johnny English Strikes Again
Biopic	5	0.6	78.5	6.0	Bohemian Rhapsody
Musical	5	0.6	67.0	5.1	Mamma Mia! Here We Go Again
Family	10	1.3	60.3	4.6	Mary Poppins Returns
Fantasy	4	0.5	57.6	4.4	Fantastic Beasts: The Crimes of Grindelwald
Horror	38	4.8	57.1	4.4	A Quiet Place
Adventure	10	1.3	36.4	2.8	Ready Player One
Sci-fi	14	1.8	30.8	2.4	Solo: A Star Wars Story
Thriller	42	5.3	30.6	2.3	The Equalizer 2
Crime	10	1.3	17.9	1.4	Widows
Romance	17	2.2	11.8	0.9	The Guernsey Literary and Potato Peel Pie Society
Documentary	112	14.2	9.3	0.7	Free Solo
War	3	0.4	1.3	0.1	Journey's End
Western	2	0.3	0.1	<0.1	Sweet Country
Mystery	2	0.3	0.1	<0.1	Dark River
Total	**787**	**100.0**	**1,304.8**	**100.0**	

Source: comScore, BFI RSU analysis

Note: Figures/percentages may not sum to totals due to rounding.

Figure 5.6   Releases and revenue by genre from the 2019 Yearbook

Table 1 Distributor share of box office, UK and Republic of Ireland, 2018

Distributor	Market share (%)	Films on release in 2018	Box office gross (£ million)
Walt Disney	23.6	24	325.6
Universal	19.5	40	268.5
20th Century Fox	14.5	28	199.3
Warner Bros	13.9	31	191.4
Sony	10.7	33	146.8
Paramount	4.8	12	66.0
eOne Films	3.2	22	43.9
StudioCanal	2.8	31	38.4
Lionsgate	1.5	21	21.2
Entertainment	1.1	9	15.6
Top 10 total	95.5	251	1,316.8
Others (128 distributors)	4.5	715	61.4
Total	**100.0**	**966**	**2,695.0**

Source: comScore

Notes:

The total number of films on release differs from Table 5 as it includes all films shown in cinemas in 2018, including titles first released in 2017.

Box office gross = cumulative box office total for all films handled by the distributor in the period 1 January 2018 to 31 December 2018.

Figures may not sum to sub-totals/totals due to rounding.

Figure 5.7   Market share by distributor from the 2019 Yearbook

Table 5.1 shows the tradeoffs of these different approaches.

Table 5.1   Comparing PDF extraction techniques

Option	Pros	Cons
Manually copying data from PDFs into Excel	▪ Quick for a small amount of data	▪ Cannot be automated ▪ Does not scale to more data
Dedicated PDF extraction tool, either web or desktop based	▪ Likely to be accurate ▪ Web-based tool requires no installation	▪ May not be free ▪ Privacy concerns if uploading files to the web ▪ Hard to automate ▪ May not scale to multiple files
Finding PDF capabilities in our current tool	▪ Allows automation and scales to many files ▪ No need to leave/change our preferred tools	▪ Current toolkit may not have such capabilities ▪ If there are few files and a one-off task, it might be quicker to extract data manually.

Whatever option we settle on, we still need to go through the process of choosing a tool, implementing it/setting it up, and using it to extract the data from the PDFs. Let's look at each step in detail, starting with choosing the right tool with the help of AI.

CHOOSING A **PDF** EXTRACTION METHOD

There is a lot of uncertainty in these options. Working with a specific task that we only have to perform rarely is a perfect use case for AI tools. Figure 5.8 shows the OpenAI GPT-3.5 model's partial answer to the following prompt:

> *What are my options for easily extracting data tables from PDFs into a machine-readable format? The suggested options must be free, open source, and can include Python libraries.*

First, it is important to remember that because these tools are evolving rapidly, the same prompt will give us different results depending on which AI tool we use and when we use it. We can see that ChatGPT recommends a mix of Python libraries and non-Python options as requested, which gives us plenty to explore. However, when investigating one of the non-Python options, it turns out the GitHub link for Tabby-PDF is incorrect. In this case, we can find it ourselves, but it is a reminder that AI tools sometimes hallucinate in their suggestions, and they could even recommend tools that don't exist.

Let's also use the AI tool to help us to start with one of the libraries. When asked, "Of the Python options, which one is the easiest to set up with the fewest dependencies?" its suggestion is to start with `tabula-py`, as it has the fewest dependencies. However, its dependency is to install a Java Runtime Environment, which is something we may prefer not to do. Its next suggestion, the `pdfplumber` library, has no such external dependencies, but its documentation suggests that table extraction features are a "plus." Another suggestion, `camelot`, specializes in data table extraction, but according to ChatGPT, it is harder to set up due to its own external dependencies. So, we shouldn't take the AI's answer as perfect; it should be the start and not the end of the process.

Weighing up our options, let's settle on trying `pdfplumber` first because other Python libraries that are easier to install are its only dependencies. If its table-reading capabilities do not give us the results we require, we can always try another library, but we will favor simplicity in our first attempt.

Installing `pdfplumber` can be done using any package manager you use, whether that is `pip`, `conda`, or `poetry`. As these tools install dependent libraries automatically, there is little for us to do in this step. However, if you choose to use a different tool for PDF extraction, this step may be more involved.

1. **Tabula-py:**
   - Tabula-py is a Python library that allows you to extract tables from PDFs into CSV or DataFrame formats. It's built on top of the Java-based Tabula project.
   - GitHub: https://github.com/chezou/tabula-py

2. **PDFPlumber:**
   - PDFPlumber is a Python library specifically designed for extracting text and tables from PDFs. It's built on top of PDFMiner and provides a simple way to extract tables into data structures.
   - GitHub: https://github.com/jsvine/pdfplumber

3. **Camelot-py:**
   - Camelot-py is another Python library that can extract tables from PDFs. It's designed to handle both text-based and scanned PDFs.
   - GitHub: https://github.com/camelot-dev/camelot

4. **PyMuPDF (MuPDF):**
   - PyMuPDF is a Python binding for the MuPDF library, which can be used to extract text and table data from PDFs.
   - GitHub: https://github.com/pymupdf/PyMuPDF

5. **PDFMiner:**
   - PDFMiner is a low-level Python library for extracting text and data from PDF files. While it's more complex than some other options, it provides a lot of flexibility.
   - GitHub: https://github.com/pdfminer/pdfminer.six

6. **TabbyPDF:**
   - TabbyPDF is an open-source tool for extracting tables from PDFs. It provides a graphical user interface (GUI) that makes it easier to work with.
   - GitHub: https://github.com/TabbyPDF/tabby

7. **pdftotext (Poppler):**
   - If you're comfortable with command-line tools, you can use `pdftotext`, which is part of the Poppler library. It can convert PDFs to plain text, and then you can parse the text to extract tables.
   - Poppler GitHub: https://gitlab.freedesktop.org/poppler/poppler

Figure 5.8   A list of options for PDF data extraction suggested by ChatGPT

Now that we've decided on a method, let's summarize our process until this point before moving on to the actual extraction step. Figure 5.9 shows the process so far.

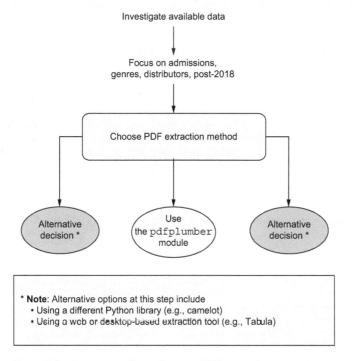

Figure 5.9   Steps up until settling on a PDF extraction method

Let's now use our chosen tool to extract the structured data from our PDFs.

Using our chosen tool to extract data from PDFs

After installing `pdfplumber`, let's start by importing our libraries:

```
import numpy as np
import pandas as pd

import pdfplumber

from IPython.display import display
```

This might be the first time we use the `pdfplumber` library, so to get started, we would read its documentation to understand how to open a PDF and extract tables from it. Because we will extract multiple tables from multiple pages across multiple documents, we should write a reusable function that performs the extraction of one or more tables from one or more pages of a single PDF. This function needs to open a

PDF file, extract all the tables in the pages we specify, and return them as pandas Data-Frames ready for analysis.

Let's start with the extraction code. Given a specified path and a page number, the following code will open the PDF, enumerate through the pages, and extract all the tables it identifies:

```
pdf_path = "./files/2019 - BFI yearbook 2019 - 888.pdf"
page_num = 11


page_tables = []


with pdfplumber.open(pdf_path) as pdf:
    page = pdf.pages[page_num-1]
    page_tables = [t.extract() for t in page.find_tables()]


page_tables
```

page_tables is a list of lists of lists(!) extracted from special Table objects.

At this point, the `page_tables` variable is a list that contains lists of lists. The output is shown in figure 5.10.

```
[[['Month', '2017 (million)', '2018 (million)', '% +/- on 2017'],
  ['January', '15.0', '16.2', '8.0'],
  ['February', '16.5', '16.1', '-2.3'],
  ['March', '16.2', '13.5', '-16.2'],
  ['April', '15.6', '15.5', '-0.9'],
  ['May', '11.3', '13.7', '21.0'],
  ['June', '9.6', '10.4', '8.6'],
  ['July', '17.8', '15.6', '-12.3'],
  ['August', '14.5', '19.2', '32.8'],
  ['September', '10.8', '10.1', '-6.0'],
  ['October', '12.1', '16.0', '32.6'],
  ['November', '14.1', '14.8', '5.4'],
  ['December', '17.2', '15.7', '-8.7'],
  ['Total', '170.6', '177.0', '3.7']]]
```

Figure 5.10 A table extracted by `pdfplumber` from a single PDF page

Each row of the table is a list of strings, starting with the column headers. These rows are themselves in a list, representing a single table. Using the `page.find_tables()` function means we end up with a list of these tables. Hence, our data structure is a list of lists of lists. Luckily, pandas makes it easy for us to convert this to a list of Data-Frames, as shown in the following code snippet:

```
table = page_tables[0]
pd.DataFrame(table[1:-1], columns=table[0])
```

These code snippets can then be extended to work across multiple pages, and with a few additional print statements and logical checks, the entire function is shown in the following code snippet, a portion of the output of which is shown in figure 5.11:

```
def extract_tables(pdf_path, pages=None, print_tables=True):
    """
    Extract all tables found in a PDF.

    `pdf_path`: file path pointing to the PDF
    `pages`: the page number(s) to read
    `print_tables`: whether to also print out
    all the tables that are found (default: True)

    returns: a list of pandas DataFrames
    """

    if not pages:
        pages = []

    print(f"Reading {pdf_path}")

    tables = []

    with pdfplumber.open(pdf_path) as pdf:
        for page_num in pages:
            page = pdf.pages[page_num-1]

            page_tables = [t.extract() for t in page.find_tables()]

            df = [pd.DataFrame(table[1:-1], columns=table[0])     ◁─┐
    for table in page_tables]

            tables.extend(df)

    print(f"{len(tables)} tables found.")

    if len(tables) > 0:
        if print_tables:
            for index, df in enumerate(tables):
                print(f"\n#######################\n\tTable
    {index}\n#######################\n")
                display(df)

    return tables

tables = extract_tables("./files/2019 - BFI yearbook 2019 - 888.pdf",
    pages=[11,34,70])
```

> In each case, the variable table is now a list of lists and the first list contains the column headers.

The variable `tables` that stores the output of our function is now a list of DataFrames, each representing one table extracted from a PDF. It's time to apply this function to our

```
Reading ./files/2019 - BFI yearbook 2019 - 888.pdf
3 tables found.

###########################
        Table 0
###########################
```

	Month	2017 (million)	2018 (million)	% +/- on 2017
0	January	15.0	16.2	8.0
1	February	16.5	16.1	-2.3
2	March	16.2	13.5	-16.2
3	April	15.6	15.5	-0.9
4	May	11.3	13.7	21.0

Figure 5.11   **A part of the output of our** `extract_tables` **function**

PDFs and extract the data we need. We will walk through this for 2018 data, but for completeness, all the data extraction code is included in the supplementary code listings.

First, we identify the page numbers of interest and use our function to extract the admissions, genre, and distributor data:

```
tables_2018 = extract_tables("./files/2019 - BFI yearbook 2019 - 888.pdf",
    pages=[11,34,70])
```

The full admissions data is shown in figure 5.12.

	Month	2017 (million)	2018 (million)	% +/- on 2017
0	January	15.0	16.2	8.0
1	February	16.5	16.1	-2.3
2	March	16.2	13.5	-16.2
3	April	15.6	15.5	-0.9
4	May	11.3	13.7	21.0
5	June	9.6	10.4	8.6
6	July	17.8	15.6	-12.3
7	August	14.5	19.2	32.8
8	September	10.8	10.1	-6.0
9	October	12.1	16.0	32.6
10	November	14.1	14.8	5.4
11	December	17.2	15.7	-8.7

Figure 5.12   **2018 admissions data as extracted from our PDF**

One important aspect of this data that we notice is that the columns themselves do not tell us the year this data belongs to. This will be important when we combine admissions data over multiple years, so we will add a Year column. We also do not need 2017 data or the percentage change, so we can drop those columns. A sample of the modified admissions data is shown in figure 5.13:

```
admissions_2018 = (
    tables_2018[0]
    .iloc[:,[0, 2]]
)

admissions_2018.columns = ["Month", "Admissions (million)"]

admissions_2018.insert(0, "Year", 2018)

admissions_2018.head()
```

	Year	Month	Admissions (million)
0	2018	January	16.2
1	2018	February	16.1
2	2018	March	13.5
3	2018	April	15.5
4	2018	May	13.7

Figure 5.13 A snapshot of the modified admissions data

Moving onto genres, the second table in our extracted list of DataFrames contains the data we need, as shown in figure 5.14.

	Genre	Number of\nreleases	% of\nreleases
0	Action	77	9.8
1	Animation	46	5.8
2	Drama	246	31.3
3	Comedy	144	18.3
4	Biopic	5	0.6

(continued)

	Gross box\noffice\n(£ million)	% of total\nbox office	Top performing title
0	361.3	27.7	Avengers: Infinity War
1	242.2	18.6	Incredibles 2
2	154.1	11.8	A Star Is Born
3	88.3	6.8	Johnny English Strikes Again
4	78.5	6.0	Bohemian Rhapsody

Figure 5.14 Genre breakdown for 2018 as extracted from the PDF

As opposed to the admissions data, this breakdown is by genre and relates to the entire year of 2018. We still need to add a Year column to differentiate genres across years, but we need to remember that this dataset has a different level of granularity. Again, we do not need all the columns, and we will need to clean up the column names to remove the \n newline characters. The following code snippet produces the modified genre data, a snapshot of which is shown in figure 5.15:

```
genres_2018 = (
    tables_2018[1]
    .drop(columns=[tables_2018[1].columns[2], tables_2018[1].columns[4]])
)

genres_2018.insert(0, "Year", 2018)

genres_2018.columns = ["Year", "Genre", "Number of releases",
⇒ "Gross box office (£ million)", "Top performing title"]

genres_2018.head()
```

	Year	Genre	Number of releases	Gross box office (£ million)	Top performing title
0	2018	Action	77	361.3	Avengers: Infinity War
1	2018	Animation	46	242.2	Incredibles 2
2	2018	Drama	246	154.1	A Star Is Born
3	2018	Comedy	144	88.3	Johnny English Strikes Again
4	2018	Biopic	5	78.5	Bohemian Rhapsody

Figure 5.15   The modified genre data from 2018

Finally, moving on to distributors, the data directly extracted from the PDF is shown in figure 5.16.

In this case, all our columns will be useful, and we need to add the Year column again. We should also remove row 10, as it is a total of the rows above it, which would skew our calculations if we left it in. The following code modifies the data to suit our needs, and a snapshot of the modified data is shown in figure 5.17:

```
distributors_2018 = (
    tables_2018[2]
    .drop(index=[10])          ⟵── Drops the "top
)                                   10 total" row

distributors_2018.insert(0, "Year", 2018)

distributors_2018.columns = ["Year", "Distributor", "Market share",
⇒ "Films on release", "Box office gross (£ million)"]

distributors_2018.head()
```

	Distributor	Market share\n(%)	Films on release\nin 2018	Box office gross\n(£ million)
0	Walt Disney	23.6	24	325.6
1	Universal	19.5	40	268.5
2	20th Century Fox	14.5	28	199.3
3	Warner Bros	13.9	31	191.4
4	Sony	10.7	33	146.8
5	Paramount	4.8	12	66.0
6	eOne Films	3.2	22	43.9
7	StudioCanal	2.8	31	38.4
8	Lionsgate	1.5	21	21.2
9	Entertainment	1.1	9	15.6
10	Top 10 total	95.5	251	1,316.8
11	Others (128 distributors)	4.5	715	61.4

Figure 5.16 The raw distributors data, as extracted from the PDF

	Year	Distributor	Market share	Films on release	Box office gross (£ million)
0	2018	Walt Disney	23.6	24	325.6
1	2018	Universal	19.5	40	268.5
2	2018	20th Century Fox	14.5	28	199.3
3	2018	Warner Bros	13.9	31	191.4
4	2018	Sony	10.7	33	146.8

Figure 5.17 The modified distributor data for 2018

NOTE Repeating this process for subsequent years shows some differences. In 2019, there are two admissions tables on the same page, so we need to explicitly choose the right one. Also, in the 2022 Yearbooks, the tables are spread across multiple PDFs. Extracting these tables is the same process for all the years, but these minor differences are what make PDF data extraction complicated.

Every dataset of the same type across the years is structured identically, so we do not need to do any additional cleaning before being able to combine them. The following code shows how we combine the annual admissions datasets into a single one:

```
admissions = pd.concat([admissions_2018, admissions_2019,
    admissions_2020, admissions_2021],
    ignore_index=True,
    axis=0)
```

To ensure we have the right amount of data, we perform a quick sanity check to see how many rows of monthly data we have per year. We are expecting exactly 12 rows per year, which is verified in the output shown in figure 5.18:

```
admissions["Year"].value_counts()
```

```
2018    12
2019    12
2020    12
2021    12
Name: Year, dtype: int64
```

Figure 5.18   Verifying that we have 12 rows of admissions data for each year

Finally, we write the combined admissions data into its own file:

```
admissions.to_csv("admissions.csv", index=False)
```

The process for combining and exporting genre and distributor data is identical, and we end up with three files that we are ready to analyze.

5.4.3   *Analyzing the data extracted from PDFs*

Now that we have our data extracted from our PDFs and combined, we can start exploring it to find stories to use in our white paper. We will take each dataset at a time, starting with admissions. We could continue the code, meaning we would already have our admissions data as a variable, but I have chosen to explicitly separate the extraction and analysis processes. In the accompanying resources, you will find the process split into two Jupyter notebooks. For the analysis portion, we will start a new Jupyter notebook using the data created in the first one.

There are multiple benefits to separating extraction from analysis:

- Extraction and analysis can be worked on separately as long as the extraction step produces the output the analysis step expects.
- You save time by not having to rerun the extraction steps every time the analysis changes.
- Steps can be more easily maintained because they are logically decoupled from each other.

In general, when you see an opportunity to create a cleaner solution by separating logical steps from each other, you should take it. Anyone looking at your work in the future, including yourself, will be grateful for the extra effort you put in early on.

ENHANCING EXTRACTED DATA WITH CUSTOM LOGIC

We start by reading in the admissions data and taking a look at it. The following code produces the output in figure 5.19:

```
import pandas as pd
import matplotlib.pyplot as plt
import datetime
```

```
admissions = pd.read_csv("admissions.csv")
print(admissions.shape)
admissions.head()
```

	Year	Month	Admissions (million)
0	2018	January	16.2
1	2018	February	16.1
2	2018	March	13.5
3	2018	April	15.5
4	2018	May	13.7

Figure 5.19 A snapshot of the admissions data

The dataset is small because it is a single monthly value across only a few years. However, it is sufficient to divide into three periods: pre-COVID lockdowns, during COVID lockdowns, and post-COVID lockdowns. We do this by creating a date column with the right data type. The output of the following code is shown in figure 5.20:

```
COVID_START_DATE = datetime.datetime(2020, 3, 1)
LOCKDOWN_END_DATE = datetime.datetime(2021, 7, 1)

admissions["date"] = (
    "1 " +
    admissions["Month"] +
    " " +
    admissions["Year"].astype(str)
)
```

We define variables to mark cutoff points for COVID periods.

Our data has no days, so we arbitrarily set dates to the first of the month.

```
admissions["date"] = pd.to_datetime(admissions["date"], format="%d %B %Y")
admissions.head()
```

	Year	Month	Admissions (million)	Date
0	2018	January	16.2	2018-01-01
1	2018	February	16.1	2018-02-01
2	2018	March	13.5	2018-03-01
3	2018	April	15.5	2018-04-01
4	2018	May	13.7	2018-05-01

Figure 5.20 Verifying that our newly added Date column is as expected

Next, we define cutoff points for the three periods and apply them to the data. We also use the Categorical data type in pandas to ensure the correct order is observed when sorting; otherwise, these periods would be sorted alphabetically. Then, we verify that this new column is distributed as we'd expect and that we haven't left any missing data. The output of the following code is shown in figure 5.21:

```
admissions.loc[admissions["date"] < COVID_START_DATE, "covid_period"]
⟼ = "pre-COVID"
admissions.loc[admissions["date"].between(COVID_START_DATE,
⟼ LOCKDOWN_END_DATE, "left"), "covid_period"] = "during COVID"
admissions.loc[admissions["date"] >= LOCKDOWN_END_DATE, "covid_period"]
⟼ = "post-lockdowns"

admissions["covid_period"] = (
    pd.Categorical(
        admissions["covid_period"],
        categories=["pre-COVID", "during COVID", "post-lockdowns"],
        ordered=True
    )
)

admissions["covid_period"].value_counts(dropna=False)
```

```
pre-COVID          26
during COVID       16
post-lockdowns      6
Name: covid_period, dtype: int64
```

Figure 5.21   Number of rows per different COVID period

We can now plot monthly admissions and mark each COVID period with a different color and line style using the following code, which produces the plot in figure 5.22:

```
fig, axis = plt.subplots(figsize=(10, 6))

linestyles = ["solid", "dotted", "dashed"]

for idx, covid_period in
⟼ enumerate(admissions["covid_period"].value_counts().index):
    (
        admissions
        .query(f"covid_period=='{covid_period}'")
        .set_index("date")
        ["Admissions (million)"]
        .plot(ax=axis, label=covid_period, linestyle=linestyles[idx])
    )

axis.set(
    title="Monthly cinema admissions over time",
    ylabel="Admissions (millions)"
)

axis.legend()

plt.show()
```

At first glance, there are missing months due to the lockdown periods, and after the last lockdown was lifted, it appears that admissions have started to return to pre-pandemic levels. If we had more post-lockdown data, we could also examine whether seasonal patterns are similar to what they were before the pandemic.

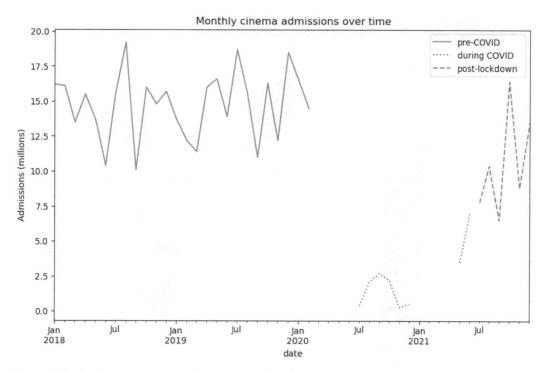

Figure 5.22   Admissions across multiple COVID periods

If we were to look at the average monthly admissions in the three periods, we could examine this further. The following code does this and produces the output shown in figure 5.23:

```
fig, axis = plt.subplots()

admissions_by_period = (
    admissions
    .groupby("covid_period")
    ["Admissions (million)"]
    .agg(["mean", "median"])
)

for i, metric in enumerate(admissions_by_period.columns):
    hatch = "/" if i == 0 else "\\\\"
    color = "C0" if i == 0 else "C1"
    admissions_by_period[metric].plot(kind="bar", ax=axis, position=i,
                                      hatch=hatch, label=metric,
                                      width=0.2, color=color)

axis.set(
    title="Average monthly cinema admissions during COVID periods",
    ylabel="Admissions (millions)",
```

Different colors for different metrics

Different hatch patterns for different metrics

```
        xlabel="Period",
        xticklabels = admissions_by_period.index
)

axis.legend()

plt.show()
```

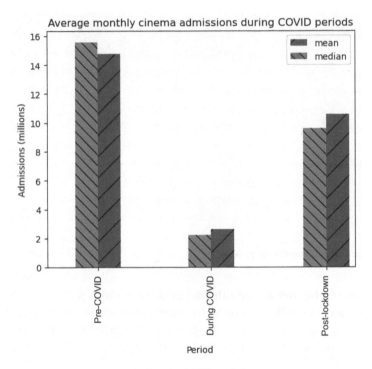

Figure 5.23 Average admissions by COVID period

The reason for looking at both the mean and the median is to investigate whether the data is skewed in either direction. That is, do pre-COVID or post-lockdown months tend to have outliers in either direction? Looking at histograms of monthly admissions by period investigates this further. The following code produces the histograms shown in figure 5.24:

```
fig, axes = plt.subplots(1, 2, figsize=(10, 6), sharey=True)

(
    admissions
    .loc[admissions["covid_period"] == "pre-COVID", "Admissions (million)"]
    .hist(bins=10, ax=axes[0])
)

axes[0].set(
    title="Distribution of monthly admissions pre-COVID",
```

```
    xlabel="Admissions (million)",
    ylabel="Frequency"
)


(
    admissions
    .loc[admissions["covid_period"] == "post-lockdowns",
➡   "Admissions (million)"]
    .hist(ax=axes[1])
)

axes[1].set(
    title="Distribution of monthly admissions post-lockdowns",
    xlabel="Admissions (million)"
)

plt.show()
```

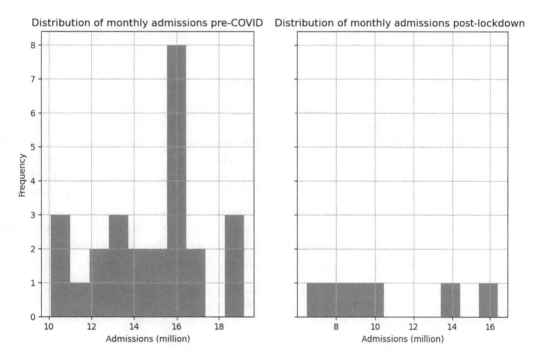

Figure 5.24   Histograms of admissions pre-COVID and post-lockdowns

There is not a lot of post-lockdown data, but we can observe that there are more months with fewer admissions, which is what we'd expect given the slow recovery. Pre-COVID, we expected approximately 15–17 million admissions per month, with a few outliers in both positive and negative directions. As it stands, there is not much of a story to tell about post-lockdown admissions habits, except for noting that admissions look to be trending toward pre-COVID levels again by the end of 2021.

INVESTIGATING CHANGES IN TRENDS OVER TIME USING DATA FROM MULTIPLE SOURCES
Now, let's see what genres were popular on either side of the pandemic period. First, let's read in and examine our data. Figure 5.25 shows a snapshot of rows produced by the following code:

```
genres = pd.read_csv("genres.csv")
print(genres.shape)
genres.head()
```

	Year	Genre	Number of releases	Gross box office (£ million)	Top performing title
0	2018	Action	77	361.3	Avengers: Infinity War
1	2018	Animation	46	242.2	Incredibles 2
2	2018	Drama	246	154.1	A Star Is Born
3	2018	Comedy	144	88.3	Johnny English Strikes Again
4	2018	Biopic	5	78.5	Bohemian Rhapsody

Figure 5.25   A snapshot of rows from the genre dataset

There are two things to note. First, this dataset is small since it is a handful of genres recorded over just a few years. Second, this dataset is at an annual level, not a monthly one, which changes our definitions of COVID periods. Specifically, we must accept that the first couple of months of 2020 data will be allocated as "during COVID" even though they occurred before the first lockdown, and we need to decide what to do with 2021 data. 2021 still had lockdowns, but the second half of the year is useful data about post-lockdown trends, which we wouldn't want to throw away. We will err on the side of keeping 2021 as "post-lockdowns" and categorizing 2020 as the only "during COVID" year. The following code does this and produces the output in figure 5.26:

```
genres.loc[genres["Year"] < 2020, "covid_period"] = "pre-COVID"
genres.loc[genres["Year"] == 2020, "covid_period"] = "during COVID"
genres.loc[genres["Year"] > 2020, "covid_period"] = "post-lockdowns"

genres["covid_period"].value_counts(dropna=False)
```

```
covid_period
pre-COVID       35
during COVID    16
post-lockdowns  16
Name: count, dtype: int64
```

Figure 5.26   Distribution of rows per COVID period in the genres dataset

Glancing at the data, we might notice that the gross box office column has non-numeric values, namely <0.1, to indicate genres that totaled less than £100,000. To calculate revenue by genre, for example, we need this column to be numeric. We could convert that value to zero, but that would be misleading, and it is not the same value as 0.1, which is a value also present in our data. To indicate low revenue, we can add a placeholder value of, say, 0.05:

```
genres.loc[genres["Gross box office (£ million)"] == "<0.1",
    "Gross box office (£ million)"] = 0.05
genres["Gross box office (£ million)"] =
    genres["Gross box office (£ million)"].astype(float)
```

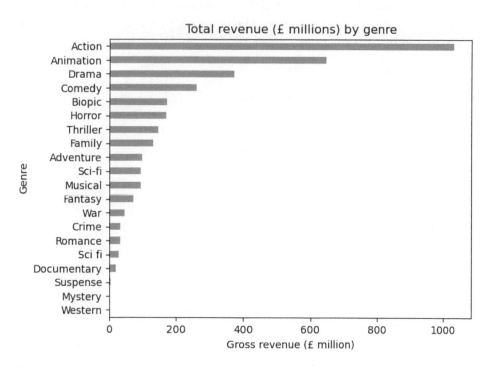

Figure 5.27   Total revenue by genre

Now, we can look at total revenue by genre in our dataset. The output of the following code is shown in figure 5.27:

```
fig, axis = plt.subplots()

(
    genres
    .groupby("Genre")
    ["Gross box office (£ million)"]
    .sum()
    .sort_values()
```

```
    .plot
    .barh(ax=axis)
)


axis.set(
    title="Total revenue (£ millions) by genre",
    xlabel="Gross revenue (£ million)"
)

plt.show()
```

It seems that people like action and animation films the most. What we really want to see is this same distribution by year. We could also look at it by COVID period, but let's look at the more granular picture. The following code achieves this and produces the output in figure 5.28:

```
years = genres["Year"].unique()

fig, axes = plt.subplots(1, len(years),
    figsize=(3*len(years),8), sharex=True)

for idx, year in enumerate(years):
    (
        genres[genres["Year"] == year]
        .groupby("Genre")
        ["Gross box office (£ million)"]
        .sum()
        .sort_values()
        .plot
        .barh(ax=axes[idx])
    )

    axes[idx].set(
        title=f"Revenue by genre ({year})"
    )

plt.tight_layout()
plt.show()
```

That gives quite a clear picture. Action films are the most popular, regardless of year. Comedy films historically haven't done as well pre-COVID, but there has been a rise in their popularity in 2021. Here are some theories about this result:

- Animated films take years of effort, and if animators weren't working at any point during COVID, that would have delayed the release of animated films in 2021.
- Comparatively, comedies are probably cheaper to make, though that's a question for the domain experts.
- People possibly prefer light-hearted relief in post-lockdown times.

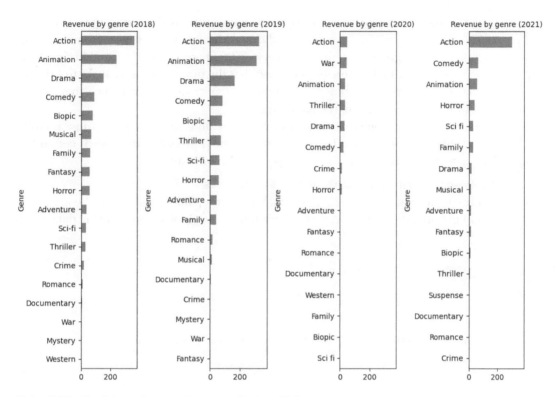

Figure 5.28   Breakdown of revenue by genre across multiple years

Let's test that first assumption. If our theory holds, we should see fewer releases in the animation genre in 2021. Figure 5.29 shows the output of this investigation:

```
(
    genres[genres["Genre"] == "Animation"]
    .groupby("Year")
    ["Number of releases"]
    .sum()
)
```

```
Year
2018    46
2019    40
2020    19
2021    38
Name: Number of releases, dtype: int64
```

Figure 5.29   Number of animation releases over time

There were almost as many films released in the animation genre in 2021 as in 2019, so our theory doesn't explain why the revenue of that genre dropped. Another interesting point from figure 5.28 is the popularity of war films in 2020:

```
genres[(genres["Genre"] == "War") & (genres["Year"] == 2020)]
```

Looking into it, we find that the top-performing title in this category was the film *1917*, which was released in January 2020. Although the revenue from this film accounts for its high place in the rankings in 2020, it was released before the first lockdowns, so it doesn't tell us anything beyond that the filmmakers were lucky to bring in the revenue before the lockdown happened. It certainly isn't evidence that people liked films about war during the pandemic.

In summary, it appears that although action films are by far the most popular genre, comedies experienced a growth in revenue post-lockdowns. This is certainly a finding worth bringing to a domain expert to find out more.

RESOLVING DIFFERENT ENTITY NAMES ACROSS DATA SOURCES

Our final question relates to distributors. Which companies came out of the lockdown period grossing the most revenue for their films? Let's look at our available data in figure 5.30:

```
distributors = pd.read_csv("distributors.csv")
print(distributors.shape)
distributors.head()
```

	Year	Distributor	Market share	Films on release	Box office gross (£ million)
0	2018	Walt Disney	23.6	24	325.6
1	2018	Universal	19.5	40	268.5
2	2018	20th Century Fox	14.5	28	199.3
3	2018	Warner Bros	13.9	31	191.4
4	2018	Sony	10.7	33	146.8

Figure 5.30   A snapshot of the distributors dataset

For each distributor, we have their revenue market share, number of films released, and total gross box office revenue per year. Let's assign our COVID periods again. Figure 5.31 shows the number of rows of data we have per COVID period:

```
distributors.loc[distributors["Year"] < 2020, "covid_period"] = "pre-COVID"
distributors.loc[distributors["Year"] == 2020, "covid_period"]
➥ = "during COVID"
distributors.loc[distributors["Year"] > 2020, "covid_period"]
➥ = "post-lockdowns"

distributors["covid_period"].value_counts(dropna=False)
```

```
covid_period
pre-COVID           22
during COVID        11
post-lockdowns      11
Name: count, dtype: int64
```

Figure 5.31   Number of rows per COVID period in the distributors data

We should also verify that the market share column adds up to 100% each year. Figure 5.32 shows whether this is the case:

```
distributors.groupby("Year")["Market share"].sum()
```

```
Year
2018    100.1
2019     99.9
2020    100.1
2021    100.2
Name: Market share, dtype: float64
```
Figure 5.32   Total market share per year

The Statistical Yearbooks explicitly mention rounding errors, which are probably responsible for the numbers in figure 5.32. Let us now look at market share by distributor for each year of our data. The easiest way to do this with `pandas` is to create a pivot table where each column is a different distributor, and each row is a different year. This way, when we call the `plot` function, we see one line per distributor over time. Let's see what this reshaping of our data does. The following code produces the pivot table shown in figure 5.33:

```
(
    distributors
    .groupby(["Year", "Distributor"])
    ["Market share"]
    .sum()
    .unstack()
)
```

Distributor	20th Century Fox	20th Century Fox°	Entertainment	Entertainment Film Distributors	Entertainment One	Lionsgate	Other distributors (137)	Other distributors (143)	Others (128 distributors)	Others (Total 130 distributors)
Year										
2018	14.5	NaN	1.1	NaN	NaN	1.5	NaN	NaN	4.5	NaN
2019	NaN	5.7	NaN	NaN	3.8	4.2	NaN	NaN	NaN	4.6
2020	NaN	NaN	NaN	4.3	15.9	4.5	NaN	7.5	NaN	NaN
2021	NaN	NaN	NaN	NaN	1.4	1.8	3.2	NaN	NaN	NaN

Figure 5.33   A snapshot of the pivot table aggregating across distributors and years

There are a number of data problems that become obvious. We need to merge the two separate values for 20th Century Fox, merge the "Other" categories into a single name so they get a single line over time, and investigate the various distributors with "Entertainment" in the name. Upon investigation, it appears Entertainment One and eOne Films, which both appear in our data, are the same entity (https://www .entertainmentone.com/about-eone/). Entertainment Film Distributors is a legitimately separate entity from Entertainment One, but we don't have evidence of whether the distributor marked simply "Entertainment" should be merged into any other category. We will leave it on its own. After these corrections, we can look at how many years each distributor is represented in our data. The result of this is shown in figure 5.34:

```
distributors["Distributor"] = (
    distributors["Distributor"].replace({
        "20th Century Fox*": "20th Century Fox",
        "eOne Films": "Entertainment One"
    })
)

distributors.loc[distributors["Distributor"].str.startswith("Other"),
➥ "Distributor"] = "Other"

distributors["Distributor"].value_counts()
```

Walt Disney	4
Universal	4
Warner Bros	4
Sony	4
Paramount	4
Entertainment One	4
StudioCanal	4
Lionsgate	4
Other	4
20th Century Fox	2
STX Entertainment	2
Entertainment	1
Entertainment Film Distributors	1
Shear Entertainment*	1
Park Circus	1
Name: Distributor, dtype: int64	

Figure 5.34   **Number of years each distributor is present in our data**

We can also use this result to decide whether to plot all distributors. We are particularly interested in change over time, so we should keep only distributors that appear in all years of our data. This will potentially omit distributors who went out of business during or because of the pandemic. These could be analyzed further separately:

```
distributors_to_keep = (
    distributors["Distributor"]
    .value_counts()
    .loc[lambda x: x == distributors["Year"].nunique()]
    .index
)
```

We can use these distributors to recreate our pivot table and see how market share compares across years:

```
distributors_pivot = (
  distributors
```

```
.query("Distributor in @distributors_to_keep")
.assign(Year=distributors["Year"]
       .apply(lambda x: datetime.datetime(x, 1, 1))     ◁─────── Converts each
      )                                                          year to the first of
.groupby(["Year", "Distributor"])                                January to make it
["Market share"]                                                 a date type
.sum()
.unstack()              ◁────┤ One row per year, one
)                            column per distributor
```

Visually, it's easier to read the pivot table if years go across columns, so let's transpose the data and examine the output shown in figure 5.35:

```
distributors_pivot.transpose()
```

Year	2018-01-01	2019-01-01	2020-01-01	2021-01-01
Distributor				
Entertainment One	3.2	3.8	15.9	1.4
Lionsgate	1.5	4.2	4.5	1.8
Other	4.5	4.6	7.5	3.2
Paramount	4.8	5.9	8.0	3.7
Sony	10.7	9.3	15.6	22.2
StudioCanal	2.8	1.0	4.5	0.5
Universal	19.5	13.9	12.5	30.6
Walt Disney	23.6	37.9	14.3	21.2
Warner Bros	13.9	12.4	11.7	14.4

Figure 5.35   Distributor market share (%) over time

From this pivot table, we can conclude the following:

- Walt Disney completed their purchase of 20th Century Fox in 2019, yet this did not translate to a large increase in market share even in 2021.
- Sony achieved the biggest increase in market share post-lockdown, doubling their market share from 2018, but Universal also increased their market share from pre-COVID levels.
- Apart from Sony and Universal, the distributors with bigger market share roughly returned to pre-COVID levels of market share in 2021. Some smaller ones, like StudioCanal, failed to reach pre-COVID levels.

Initial speculation about these results might be that the bigger distributors are the ones that have the resources to bounce back from even a global pandemic, whereas smaller distributors will likely struggle more with this.

Before summarizing our findings, let's review the whole process, including places where our latest step could have diverged. Figure 5.36 shows the whole process.

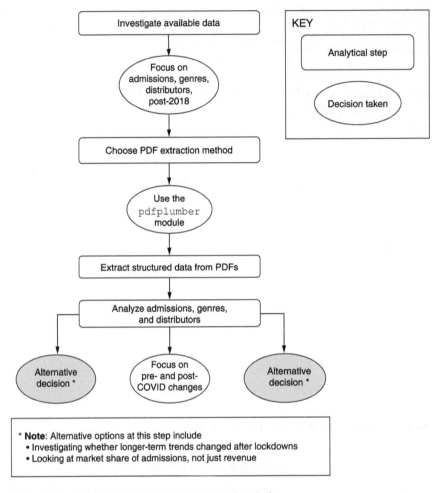

Figure 5.36   The final steps taken in the example solution

Let's now review our findings and summarize our recommendations to our stakeholders.

5.4.4   *Project conclusions and recommendations*

What do our results mean for the white paper?

- UK-level admissions data does not tell a very interesting story beyond admissions looking like they are reaching pre-COVID levels. An additional year of data would help clarify post-lockdown trends, as would looking at admissions at a more granular level, such as by region or film type.

- There is a difference in the breakdown of genres post-lockdowns, certainly enough of a difference to investigate this angle further.
- Distributors follow general market trends where larger entities bounce back from COVID more easily than smaller ones.

The limitations of our analysis extend mostly to a lack of data. We do not have a lot of post-lockdown data to compare with past trends, so our conclusions can only be tentative. Our data is focused on the United Kingdom, so it does not give a global picture. However, we can assume the research firm we work for would have more granular data for us to investigate our findings further. There is enough in our conclusions to have a conversation with our domain experts, but the first round of analysis does not suggest we have enough to support a white paper.

One benefit of this analysis, whether or not it leads to a published paper, is that we have written a data pipeline to extract data from the BFI's published statistics. Having this data in a format that is ready to be analyzed will yield value for future projects. Sometimes, cleaning data in this way can be a valuable contribution in itself.

Activity: Further project ideas with this data

The PDF files included in this chapter are a treasure trove of information about the film industry. This project focused on the effects of the pandemic, but there are many other angles to explore and many research questions that could be answered. Here are some ideas to get you started:

- How have people's preferences of genre evolved over time?
- Is there a pattern in what kind of independent films is successful?
- How have attendance figures changed over time in different countries? Are movie-goers changing the same way everywhere?

5.5 Closing thoughts on exploring novel data sources

There are two takeaways from this chapter. One is that you will encounter situations where you need to learn a specific, narrow skill to extract data from an unusual format. This is a good opportunity to learn about more esoteric parts of your existing toolkit, such as its PDF-extracting capabilities. AI tools can accelerate this learning process, and this chapter's project is an example of where depth is not required. To successfully complete the project in this chapter, you did not need to become an expert in PDF extraction or optical character recognition, the process of converting an image to a machine-readable text form. You only needed to find the relevant library and code snippets to extract tabular data from a PDF. It is an example of learning enough to stay focused on the end result and no more.

Second, the broader takeaway is that data is available in many forms. Knowing that our tools make it possible to extract data from unusual, unstructured sources will expand the potential data available to us for our analyses. It allows us to generate more creative solutions to problems, which will help us add more value with our work.

5.5.1   *Skills for exploring unusual data sources for any project*

In this chapter, we explored a new source of data, namely, PDF files. The specific skills required for unusual data sources, and more broadly for exploring new data sources, which can be used for any problem, include

- Finding the relevant data in unstructured files, such as PDFs
- Identifying existing tools to extract data from a novel source
- Using AI tools such as ChatGPT to learn about specific tools for specific data formats
- Using new tools to extract data from unstructured sources into structured formats (e.g., data from PDFs into CSV files)
- Enhancing extracted data with custom logic (e.g., pre- and post-COVID lockdown periods)
- Investigating trends by extracting similar data from multiple sources over time (e.g., the same annual report across multiple years)
- Resolving differences across multiple similar data sources (e.g., names of production companies changing over time but relating to the same entity)

Summary

- Identifying novel and unstructured data sources is a core skill of a good analyst.
- Considering new data sources in your analysis may introduce nontabular or unstructured data requiring effort to clean up: time you should consider when including them.
- Telling the story that's in the data, rather than the one our stakeholders asked for in their problem statement, is critical to avoid misleading ourselves.
- Focusing on the problem to solve rather than the data increases the chances that any additional data you consider will be relevant.

Categorical data

This chapter covers

- Determining the best approach to handle categorical data
- How to avoid common mistakes when working with categorical data
- Analyzing categorical data with the right methods to investigate patterns and associations

Sometimes, you may encounter data that is not numeric, and your typical analysis methods won't apply. Instead, this data represents groups or categories with values limited to a set number of options. Customer locations, departments, and demographics are typical sources of such discrete values. We call this *categorical* data, and it is common in most datasets.

Methods suitable for numeric or continuous data are not appropriate for categorical data. Knowing the correct way to handle categorical data will broaden your toolbox and ensure you use the right tool for the job when your data is mostly categorical. In this chapter, we will review common tools for handling categorical data before diving into the project.

6.1   *Working with categorical data*

One of the first tasks in any analysis is understanding your data. In a tabular dataset, every column of data will be one of two types: continuous or categorical. This distinction doesn't apply to unstructured data, such as audio or video files, but most analysts work mostly with tabular data. Regardless of what the values in these columns represent, they will either be on a continuous scale or part of a discrete set. Sometimes, it is not even obvious whether a column is categorical if the entries are numeric. Let's look at an example dataset.

Figure 6.1 shows a snapshot of a dataset used widely in the machine learning community for teaching purposes. The original data was created by Jánosi et al. (1988) and is available at https://mng.bz/vKo7. It is a medical dataset of different patient measurements, also showing whether the patients had coronary heart disease. The associated data problem is to use the measurements to predict whether a patient has coronary heart disease.

	age	sex	cp	trestbps	chol	fbs	restecg	thalach	exang	oldpeak	slope	ca	thal	condition
0	69	1	0	160	234	1	2	131	0	0.1	1	1	0	0
1	69	0	0	140	239	0	0	151	0	1.8	0	2	0	0
2	66	0	0	150	226	0	0	114	0	2.6	2	0	0	0
3	65	1	0	138	282	1	2	174	0	1.4	1	1	0	1
4	64	1	0	110	211	0	2	144	1	1.8	1	0	0	0

Figure 6.1   A preview of the UCI heart disease dataset

The first two columns, `age` and `sex`, are easier to identify as continuous and categorical, respectively. Even though `sex` is numeric, we treat it the same as if the values were text (e.g., "male" or "female"). For example, taking a numeric average of this column is not the same as calculating the average age of our patients would be. We call this type of categorical column *nominal* because there is no natural ordering among the categories. Other examples include color or political parties.

Categorical data can also be *ordinal*, where categories do have a natural order but are not on a numerical scale. Examples include sizes (e.g., small, medium, and large) or survey responses (e.g., values between "strongly disagree" and "strongly agree"). For completeness, table 6.1 shows the breakdown of the different types of data we can encounter.

Table 6.1   An overview of the different types of data

Name	Categorical or continuous?	Properties	Example
Nominal	Categorical	Data has discrete values, and categories are not ordered.	Colors, political parties

Table 6.1 An overview of the different types of data *(continued)*

Name	Categorical or continuous?	Properties	Example
Ordinal	Categorical	Data has discrete values, and categories have a natural order, but spacing is uneven between categories.	T-shirt sizes (S/M/L), survey responses (good versus bad)
Interval	Continuous	Values are spaced evenly, but zero is not an absence of the measurement.	Temperature
Ratio	Continuous	Values are spaced evenly, and zero means an absence of the measurement.	Height, weight

NOTE The word "ratio" in these definitions is not to be confused with the meaning where two measurements are compared to each other, like the ratio of new versus returning customers. In this case, "ratio" is the technical term for a continuous variable that starts at zero, where zero indicates an absence of that quantity. You can have a negative temperature but not a negative height, which is the distinction between "interval" and "ratio" quantities.

Back to the heart disease example. What about the other columns beyond `age` and `sex`? If we just inspect the data types when importing it, we observe that all columns are numeric. Figure 6.2 shows sample Python output to verify this.

```
age           int64
sex           int64
cp            int64
trestbps      int64
chol          int64
fbs           int64
restecg       int64
thalach       int64
exang         int64
oldpeak     float64
slope         int64
ca            int64
thal          int64
condition     int64        Figure 6.2   The data types in the
dtype: object              heart disease data
```

From this information so far, we might conclude that because our columns are numeric, all of our data must be continuous. However, upon closer inspection, we find that a few of our columns only take a small number of discrete values. For example, figure 6.3 shows the breakdown of values in the `slope` column.

Although this is an integer column, there are only three discrete values. These values correspond to whether a patient's exercise-related tests were done on an upward or downward slope or none at all. This column is, therefore, categorical, specifically, nominal.

```
0      139
1      137
2       21
Name: slope, dtype: int64
```

Figure 6.3   Breakdown of values of the `slope` column in the heart disease dataset

This might seem like a trivial finding, but if we were to treat this column as continuous, we might perform erroneous calculations with it, such as taking an average. We might get an average slope value of 0.6, but it would be meaningless. It does not represent a value halfway between 0, upsloping, and 1, flat, because the numbering is arbitrary. Changing the numbers we assign to each category would change this result and its interpretation.

> **Real business case: Enhancing analyses with categorical data**
>
> Used cars that go through auctions have all sorts of data entered about them, and a lot of them are categorical. Transmission type, fuel type, make, and model are all categorical values and are fundamental to understanding the used car market. The models I built for predicting the price of a used car or the likelihood that it will sell all heavily relied on these categorical values.
>
> Our team was also periodically asked to look at whether the color of a car had any effect on its value. This not only involved manipulating a categorical `color` column but also extracting those categories from a free text field where people could enter anything for the color of the car!

How do we then treat categorical data? Let's review some differences between methods for continuous versus categorical data.

6.1.1   *Methods for handling categorical data*

Let's look at some key methods for analyzing continuous and categorical data. When we are working with continuous data, we are specifically interested in

- The range of our values
- The distribution of our values
- The presence of outliers
- Associations between continuous values

To explore these properties, the tools we have at our disposal are

- Summary statistics (minimum, maximum, mean, median, etc.)
- Histograms and box plots to investigate range and distribution
- Scatter plots and correlation measures to investigate relationships between continuous variables

When it comes to categorical data, not all of these methods apply. Let's revisit the heart disease dataset for an example where treating categorical values as continuous leads us astray.

One mistake we might make is to use the categorical `slope` variable in a regression model as if it were continuous, that is, in a scenario where we try to predict someone's risk of heart disease based on the slope of the apparatus while testing them. We might end up with a result that would be interpreted as "for every unit increase in slope, the likelihood of our patient having heart disease goes up by 7%." This is a valid interpretation for continuous measures like age, where every additional year of someone's age increases the risk of heart disease. However, what does a "unit increase" in the slope value mean? Since the numbering is arbitrary, it doesn't actually mean anything, and the whole problem is formulated incorrectly.

The correct treatment of the `slope` column for regression would be to convert it to binary indicator variables, each column representing one of the possible discrete values in a categorical column. In our slope example, we would create columns that represent whether each patient had a 0, 1, or 2 for their slope value, so we would create three columns, one for each possible slope value. The value of these columns would be 0 or 1, depending on whether the slope value was 0, 1, or 2. These binary columns would, therefore, be mutually exclusive since the `slope` column could only ever be one value. This is also referred to as *one-hot encoding*, and the results of this in our scenario are shown in figure 6.4 alongside the original `slope` column.

NOTE   You might have also seen the term "dummy variables" to describe this format. Technically, dummy variables are one-hot encodings with one of the columns dropped, but the idea is the same.

	slope	slope_0	slope_1	slope_2
0	1	0	1	0
1	0	1	0	0
2	2	0	0	1
3	1	0	1	0
4	1	0	1	0
...	...	...	...	...
292	0	1	0	0
293	1	0	1	0
294	1	0	1	0
295	0	1	0	0
296	0	1	0	0

297 rows × 4 columns

Figure 6.4   The original slope column and three new columns created by applying one-hot encoding

From this format, we can still infer the value of the `slope` column for each patient, but now, these columns are also valid as inputs to a regression model. This is just one example where there is a method specifically suited for categorical data. In general, for categorical data, we are interested in

- The frequency distribution of our values
- Associations between our categorical values and other values, both continuous and categorical

Some methods that specifically tackle these attributes for categorical data are

- Grouping and aggregation
- Bar charts to visualize the frequency distribution
- Pivot tables and crosstabs to compare cooccurrences of two categorical columns
- Histograms and box plots colored by a categorical column to show the distribution of a continuous variable across different categories

There are many other methods to investigate continuous and categorical data, some of which we will explore in more detail in the chapter. One common source of categorical values, which we will work with, is survey response data.

6.1.2 *Working with survey data*

Survey data has its own specific considerations beyond the fact that it is a common source of categorical columns. As we're doing our analysis, we will need to consider the following:

- Survey data is self-reported, meaning it will have special kinds of biases. People might choose to omit answers for personal reasons or answer untruthfully. Participants who answer the survey are likely the kinds of people who willingly answer surveys, which again means a biased sample.
- Data might be missing for different reasons than in other datasets. Missing data could indicate an unwillingness to answer specific questions, users exiting the survey halfway through, or questions that are unavailable to the user based on answers to other questions (e.g. follow-ups to elaborate if they answered yes to something).
- Many answers will be on a Likert scale, where participants choose one of typically five answers ranging from "strongly disagree" to "strongly agree." This means we will be working with ordinal values—categories that have a natural order but not a consistent numeric scale.

The takeaway is that we should not underestimate the importance of knowing our data, and a key aspect of that is knowing the correct type of each of our columns and the source of the data itself. Let's now put this to the test in this chapter's project.

6.2 Project 5: Analyzing a survey to understand developer attitudes toward AI tools

Let's now look at our project, in which we will analyze survey responses to understand how software developers are using AI tools. Most of the data is categorical because the source is a survey that contained lots of multiple-choice questions resulting in categorical values. We will look at the problem statement, the data dictionary, the outputs we should aim for, and what capabilities our tools need to tackle this problem. We will then go through a detailed plan using our results-oriented framework before diving into an example solution.

The data is available for you to attempt it yourself at https://davidasboth.com/book-code. You will find the files with which you can attempt the project, as well as the example solution in the form of a Jupyter notebook.

6.2.1 Problem statement

In this scenario, you are working as an analyst for AI Dev Elite, an AI startup focused on creating generative AI tools for people who write code, such as software developers. They are struggling to focus their product idea, so they have asked you to research how coders are currently using generative AI tools. They want to identify people's pain points and find a market gap to exploit.

They have two hypotheses they would like you to test:

- New versus experienced coders are using these tools differently.
- People's opinions on the usefulness and trustworthiness of current AI tools depend on their experience, job role, and what specifically they use the tools for.

As much as they would love to access the queries people are typing into these tools directly, they have identified the Stack Overflow Developer Survey as a good source of information for the first iteration of this project. In this survey, developers disclosed details about their jobs, current tools, and usage of and attitudes toward generative AI tools. It is from these survey results that they want us to test their hypotheses.

NOTE   Thank you to Stack Overflow for making their Developer Survey results available here: https://insights.stackoverflow.com/survey, under the Open Database License (ODbL).

6.2.2 Data dictionary

The data dictionary for this dataset comes in two parts, both included in the supplementary materials:

- There is a question-by-question breakdown, `survey_results_schema.csv`, documenting which question a column contains answers for. Some questions' answers are spread across multiple columns.
- There is also a PDF copy of the survey itself. With this, you can directly observe the data-generating process, which is rare.

I recommend looking at the survey to start with because that will put the columns in both the data dictionary and the data itself into context. Seeing the survey questions directly will help identify the questions of interest for the analysis. Then, you can use the `survey_results_schema.csv` file to find the associated column name(s) in the answer data. Figure 6.5 shows an excerpt of this lookup file.

	A	B	C	D	E	F
1	qid	qname	question	force_resp	type	selector
14	QID276	LearnCode	How do you learn to code? Select all that apply.	FALSE	MC	MAVR
15	QID281	LearnCodeOnline	What online resources do you use to learn to code? Select all that ap	FALSE	MC	MAVR
16	QID306	LearnCodeCoursesCert	What online courses or certifications do you use to learn to code? Se	FALSE	MC	MAVR
17	QID32	YearsCode	Including any education, how many years have you been coding in t(	FALSE	MC	DL
18	QID34	YearsCodePro	NOT including education, how many years have you coded professi(	FALSE	MC	DL
19	QID31	DevType	Which of the following describes your current job, the one you do m(	FALSE	MC	SAVR
20	QID29	OrgSize	Approximately how many people are employed by the company or o(	FALSE	MC	SAVR
21	QID278	PurchaseInfluence	What level of influence do you, personally, have over new technolog}	FALSE	MC	SAVR
22	QID322	TechList	When thinking about new technology purchases at your organizatio(	FALSE	MC	SAVR

Figure 6.5 An excerpt of the mapping document used as a data dictionary

As figure 6.5 shows, the question about how many years someone has coded professionally is referenced in the answer data as `YearsCodePro`. This is how we identify all the relevant columns for analysis in the example solution.

6.2.3 *Desired outcomes*

Since our stakeholders have specific hypotheses, our analysis should focus on these. We need to do some general exploration of the data to identify missing values and so on, but our focus is on the specifics of the request. Our minimum viable answer should be evidence to support or refute these hypotheses. Therefore,

- Our conclusions should include whether there is a difference in the use of AI across different levels of experience.
- We should communicate the factors that affect a person's opinion of, and trust in, AI tools, as supported by the survey data.

6.2.4 *Required tools*

As with most chapters, as long as your toolkit can read, explore, and visualize data, it will be suitable to complete this project. In the example solution, I use Python, the `pandas` library for data exploration, and `matplotlib` and `seaborn` for visualization. I also introduce some statistical functions from the `scipy` library when investigating associations within the data. The checklist for this project is, therefore, that your tool can

- Load multiple datasets from CSV or Excel files
- Combine two or more datasets
- Perform basic data manipulation tasks, such as sorting, grouping, and reshaping data

- Create data visualizations
- Produce statistical analysis, specifically of categorical data, but this is optional

6.3 *Applying the results-driven method to analyzing the developer survey*

Let's now see how we keep our result in focus and formulate a results-oriented action plan. We can follow the steps of the results-driven process to explore the data with our stakeholders' requests and hypotheses in mind.

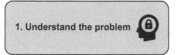

First, we need to understand what our stakeholders want from this analysis. Their initial aim is to find evidence to support or contradict their initial theories, but their ultimate goal is to find a market gap to exploit with an AI product. We can keep these two aims in mind when analyzing the data to ensure our results are valuable.

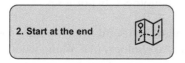

From our stakeholders' request, we know there are two kinds of output to create:

- Evidence for whether there is a difference in the use of AI tools between developers of different experience levels
- Analysis of the factors that determine someone's score when assessing the usefulness and trust of AI tools

As always, having a results-oriented focus means we can ignore certain paths our analysis could take if those paths do not serve us in finding an answer to our specific questions. In practice, this means ignoring questions in the survey that are not related to experience, usefulness, or trust in AI tools or a factor that could likely be linked to these.

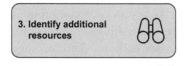

In this project, the identification of the data source has been done for us. This is not an uncommon scenario, and as ever, we are working within the limitations of the available data.

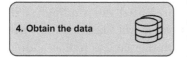

There is one question to resolve at this stage, which is whether we want to look at surveys that happened before 2023 (currently the latest version). We have more than a single survey available to us, so we could choose to include past years as well. However, there are two arguments against doing this. First, we want a minimum viable answer, which means erring on the side of using less data to start with. Second, the use of AI tools has only really taken off in 2023, so earlier data may not give us more information to help our specific analysis.

Having thought about the problem before diving in, this is the part where we formulate the action plan for the analysis. We broadly want to take the following steps:

- Read the survey to ascertain the exact questions that were asked.
- Examine the data dictionary and our data to see how questions relate to columns in the data.
- Explore the data by looking at the usual properties, such as missing data, outliers, and similar.
- Identify the questions and columns that relate to our research questions.
- Analyze the relationship between our variables and the AI-related outcomes we are interested in.
- Summarize our findings in light of our stakeholders' hypotheses.

TIP   This is a project where statistical tests might be useful since we have specific hypotheses to investigate. Rightly or not, stakeholders like asking whether something is statistically significant, and this is a chance to provide them with an actual answer.

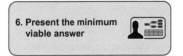

In this step, we want to present the evidence to support or refute our stakeholders' hypotheses, which were the following:

- There is a difference in the use of AI across different levels of experience.
- The factors that affect a person's opinion of and trust in AI tools are their level of experience, job role, and what specifically they use the tools for.

We specifically want to provide the most complete answer that can still be supported by our data. We do not want our stakeholders to take action on recommendations that are not based on robust findings, so unless we are confident in an association that we found, we should use appropriate language. Phrases such as "the data suggests" are generally preferred over words like "prove" or "shows."

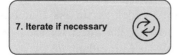

Once we have presented our findings, a discussion with our stakeholders will likely lead to further questions to explore in the data, as well as additional data sources that would help our analysis. Our goal is to get to this point sooner rather than later, so we should only include the minimum amount of complexity in our first iteration.

6.4 An example solution: How do developers use AI?

Let's now step through an example solution for this problem. As always, if you attempt the project yourself before reading this section, you will find it more valuable since you can compare the two solutions, with the usual caveat that our solutions may differ simply due to the choices we made.

The first order of business is to decide which columns represent the questions we're interested in and, therefore, which we will focus on. Next, we will look at a high-level, general exploration of the data before looking at what affects developers' attitudes toward AI.

6.4.1 Exploring categorical data

Usually, in an analytical project, the first step is to look at the available data. However, we have a rare opportunity to see the data-generating process itself by looking at the survey that generated our dataset. Upon scrolling through it, here are some initial observations:

- Most questions are not mandatory, which means we can expect lots of missing data.
- There are questions about age, number of years of experience coding, and job title, which look immediately relevant.
- Every question relating to a specific tool or technology includes options to mark them as "currently using" and "hoping to use next year," and AI-related questions also include "interested in using" and "not interested in using," as well as just "currently using." Having all these options means we can cross-reference answers to find deeper relationships.
- The way that participants can mark how favorable and trustworthy they deem AI tools to be is to use a Likert scale, which is the technical name for survey questions that allow positive, neutral, and negative answers and that represent ordinal data.
- The README file states that "Free response submissions have been removed," which is unfortunate as we will be missing answers to the survey question "Please describe how you would expect your workflow to be different, if at all, in one year as a result of AI advancements." Also, we will not see answers to questions that have an "other" option where participants can elaborate.

We will no doubt revisit the survey itself when we have questions about the data, but for now, we have enough of a sense of it to start our exploration. Let's see a snapshot of how the survey questions relate to rows in our dataset:

```
import pandas as pd
import seaborn as sns
import matplotlib.pyplot as plt

survey = pd.read_csv("./data/survey_results_public.csv.gz")
print(survey.shape)
survey.head()
```

The output of this code tells us that we are working with 89,000 survey responses, a sample of which is shown in figure 6.6.

	ResponseId	Q120	MainBranch	Age	Employment	RemoteWork	CodingActivities	EdLevel
0	1	I agree	None of these	18-24 years old	NaN	NaN	NaN	NaN
1	2	I agree	I am a developer by profession	25-34 years old	Employed, full-time	Remote	Hobby;Contribute to open-source projects;Boots...	Bachelor's degree (B.A., B.S., B.Eng., etc.)
2	3	I agree	I am a developer by profession	45-54 years old	Employed, full-time	Hybrid (some remote, some in-person)	Hobby;Professional development or self-paced l...	Bachelor's degree (B.A., B.S., B.Eng., etc.)
3	4	I agree	I am a developer by profession	25-34 years old	Employed, full-time	Hybrid (some remote, some in-person)	Hobby	Bachelor's degree (B.A., B.S., B.Eng., etc.)

Figure 6.6   A snapshot of the raw survey data

From this snapshot, we can already see that

- There will be missing values, as predicted.
- Most answers, even age, are categorical data represented as text.
- Answers to multiple-choice questions are stored as semicolon-separated strings. There are multiple ways this kind of data could have been stored, so it's good to establish which representation we're facing.

Let's dig into the missing data a bit more.

INVESTIGATING MISSING DATA

Ideally, we should find that only nonmandatory questions will have missing answers. Is this the case? Figure 6.7 shows a snapshot of the table showing the number of missing values for each column:

```
survey.isnull().sum()
```

This shows us that, for example, the participant unique identifier and the age columns both have no missing data. The `MainBranch` column represents the answer to the survey question, "Which of the following options best describes you today? For the purpose of this survey, a developer is 'someone who writes code.'" Age was one of the

```
ResponseId                    0
Q120                          0
MainBranch                    0
Age                           0
Employment                 1286
                            ...
ProfessionalTech          47401
Industry                  52410
SurveyLength               2699
SurveyEase                 2630
ConvertedCompYearly       41165
Length: 84, dtype: int64
```

Figure 6.7 Missing values for each column

questions we were interested in and was mandatory in the survey. So far, so good. As it happens, we have the data dictionary in a machine-readable format, so we can cross-reference it with the data to see which mandatory questions actually have missing data. Figure 6.8 is a snapshot of the data dictionary dataset:

```
data_dict = pd.read_csv("./data/survey_results_schema.csv")
data_dict.head(10)
```

	qid	qname	question	force_resp	type	selector
0	QID16	S0	\<div>\<span style="font-size:19px;">\<strong>Hel...	False	DB	TB
1	QID12	MetaInfo	Browser Meta Info	False	Meta	Browser
2	QID310	Q310	\<div>\<span style="font-size:19px;">\<strong>You...	False	DB	TB
3	QID312	Q120		True	MC	SAVR
4	QID1	S1	\<span style="font-size:22px; font-family: aria...	False	DB	TB
5	QID2	MainBranch	Which of the following options best describes ...	True	MC	SAVR
6	QID127	Age	What is your age? *	True	MC	MAVR
7	QID296	Employment	Which of the following best describes your cur...	False	MC	MAVR
8	QID308	RemoteWork	Which best describes your current work situation?	False	MC	SAVR
9	QID297	CodingActivities	Which of the following best describes the code...	False	MC	MAVR

Figure 6.8 A snapshot of the data dictionary dataset

We have a `qname` column, which should match the column names in our answer data. We also have the question itself, seemingly in either text or HTML form, and whether the question was mandatory, represented in the `force_resp` column. Looks like we have enough to cross-reference these files, but it's worth checking our assumption about the `qname` column. A neat trick in Python is to compare the column names using sets.

Set theory does not often appear in a data science curriculum, but knowing a couple of tricks with sets, which are collections that only contain unique values, can help in specific cases like this one. We will create a set of both the column names in our answer data and the values in the `qname` column of the data dictionary dataset and see where they overlap.

```
len(set(survey.columns).intersection(set(data_dict["qname"])))
```

The output is 50, meaning there are 50 columns that appear in both sets. That's promising, but we also want to know which columns don't overlap. Subtracting one set from another in Python actually gives us this difference. The output of this code is a collection of 34 columns in our answer data that are unaccounted for in the data dictionary, a sample of which is shown in figure 6.9:

```
set(survey.columns) - set(data_dict["qname"])
```

```
{'AIDevHaveWorkedWith',
 'AIDevWantToWorkWith',
 'AINextNeither different nor similar',
 'AINextSomewhat different',
 'AINextSomewhat similar',
 'AINextVery different',
 'AINextVery similar',
 'AISearchHaveWorkedWith',
 'AISearchWantToWorkWith',
 'AIToolCurrently Using',
 'AIToolInterested in Using',
 'AIToolNot interested in Using',
```

Figure 6.9   A sample of columns unaccounted for in the data dictionary

On inspection, a lot of these look like multiple-choice options for the same questions. For example, the survey question, "Which parts of your development workflow are you currently using AI tools for, and which are you interested in using AI tools for over the next year? Please select all that apply," has checkbox options for "Currently using," "Interested in using," and "Not interested in using," the answers to which are recorded across the three columns. Figures 6.10 and 6.11 show the format of the question as it appears in the survey and how the answers are represented in the data, respectively.

For each column of checkboxes in the survey, there is a corresponding column in the data, the value of which is all the AI use cases that were ticked for that column. That is, the participant represented in the second row in figure 6.11 said they are currently using AI tools for writing code and committing and reviewing code.

It looks like we cannot easily match all our columns to the data dictionary, so another option is to look at what is mandatory according to the data dictionary and check whether all the related columns have any missing answer data. Figure 6.12 shows the mandatory columns according to the data dictionary:

```
data_dict[data_dict["force_resp"] == True]
```

Which parts of your development workflow are you currently using AI tools for, and which are you interested in using AI tools for over the next year? Please select all that apply.

	Currently using	Interested in using	Not interested in using
Learning about a codebase	☐	☐	☐
Project planning	☐	☐	☐
Writing code	☐	☐	☐
Documenting code	☐	☐	☐
Debugging and getting help	☐	☐	☐
Testing code	☐	☐	☐

Figure 6.10   The question about AI tools as it appears in the survey

	AIToolCurrently Using	AIToolInterested in Using	AIToolNot interested in Using
0	NaN	NaN	NaN
1	Writing code;Committing and reviewing code	Learning about a codebase;Writing code;Debuggi...	NaN
2	NaN	NaN	NaN
3	NaN	NaN	NaN
4	Learning about a codebase;Writing code;Documen...	Project planning;Testing code;Committing and r...	NaN

Figure 6.11   The same question represented in the survey answer data

	qid	qname	question	force_resp	type	selector
3	QID312	Q120		True	MC	SAVR
5	QID2	MainBranch	Which of the following options best describes ...	True	MC	SAVR
6	QID127	Age	What is your age? *	True	MC	MAVR
11	QID25	EdLevel	Which of the following best describes the high...	True	MC	SAVR
22	QID6	Country	Where do you live? <span style="font-weight: b...	True	MC	DL
23	QID50	Currency	Which currency do you use day-to-day? If your ...	True	MC	DL
39	QID266	NEWSOSites	Which of the following Stack Overflow sites ha...	True	MC	MAVR
46	QID314	AISelect	Do you currently use AI tools in your developm...	True	MC	SAVR
54	QID299	TBranch	<span style="font-size:16px;">Would you like t...	True	MC	SAVR

Figure 6.12   The mandatory columns according to the data dictionary

At a minimum, each row in our answer data should have a value for age, highest education level, country, currency, and whether the participant currently uses AI tools in their workflow. Therefore, we should have no missing data in the EdLevel column. Is this the case? Figure 6.13 shows the output of the following code:

```
survey[survey["EdLevel"].isnull()]
```

	ResponseId	Q120	MainBranch	Age	Employment	RemoteWork	CodingActivities	EdLevel
0	1	I agree	None of these	18-24 years old	NaN	NaN	NaN	NaN
70	71	I agree	None of these	45-54 years old	NaN	NaN	NaN	NaN
304	305	I agree	None of these	18-24 years old	NaN	NaN	NaN	NaN
733	734	I agree	None of these	45-54 years old	NaN	NaN	NaN	NaN
875	876	I agree	None of these	45-54 years old	NaN	NaN	NaN	NaN

Figure 6.13   Rows where the education level is missing, which should never be the case

Clearly, there are missing answers to mandatory questions. One suspicious element here is that where EdLevel is missing, every answer seems to be missing. Perhaps these are completely erroneous examples. Let's identify how many missing columns there are for each participant that has a missing value for the EdLevel column. Figure 6.14 shows the output:

```
survey[survey["EdLevel"].isnull()].isnull().sum(axis=1).sort_values()
```

```
0          80
65302      80
65252      80
65037      80
64859      80
            ..
43794      80
43573      80
43567      80
43519      80
89159      80
Length: 1211, dtype: int64
```

Figure 6.14   The number of missing values per row where EdLevel is missing

This tells us that wherever `EdLevel` is missing, there are precisely 80 missing values, which implies that these are survey responses with all answers missing and can be safely removed. Specifically, anywhere with all survey answer columns missing can be dropped:

```
survey = survey.dropna(subset=survey.columns[4:], how="all")
```

Let's revisit our cross-referencing and look at all columns in our answer data that have no missing values. We can manually cross-check this against the mandatory questions, using figure 6.12, and see whether there are any questions whose corresponding columns have missing data. The following code produces the output shown in figure 6.15:

```
survey.isnull().sum().loc[lambda x: x==0]
```

```
ResponseId      0
Q120            0
MainBranch      0
Age             0
EdLevel         0
Country         0
NEWSOSites      0
AISelect        0
dtype: int64
```

Figure 6.15 The list of columns with no missing data

If we cross-reference this with the table in figure 6.12, it appears that the `Currency` column is the only mandatory question left that has missing data. Let's again see if there is a pattern in the missingness. Are there the same number of missing values when `Currency` is missing? Figure 6.16 shows the output of the following code:

```
survey[survey["Currency"].isnull()].isnull().sum(axis=1)
```

```
9        33
35       51
46       42
47       52
49       36
         ..
89173    16
89176    37
89180    33
89181    54
89182    30
Length: 22639, dtype: int64
```

Figure 6.16 The number of missing values for each row where `Currency` is missing

There does not appear to be a pattern here. It suggests that although there are over 20,000 missing answers for the mandatory `Currency` question, this might be a technical error of some sort. Perhaps there could be other factors influencing this, such as certain countries where the currency data is missing more often. Either way, our initial research questions do not rely on this column, so this is a good place to decide not to pursue this line of inquiry further for now. Let's summarize our process so far. Our first decision point was to investigate and drop missing values, as illustrated by figure 6.17.

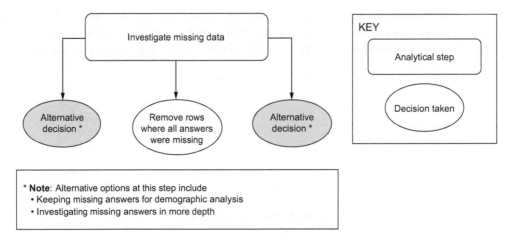

Figure 6.17   The first step of our analysis, visualized

Let's now explore our AI-related columns in a bit more detail.

6.4.2   Analyzing categorical survey data

First, we should understand what proportion of people are even using AI tools. A quick chart reveals the answer to this, shown in figure 6.18:

```
fig, axis = plt.subplots()

(
    survey["AISelect"]
    .value_counts(dropna=False)
    .plot
    .barh(ax=axis)
)

axis.set(title="Answers to the question:\n'Do you currently
➥ use AI tools in your development process?'",
        xlabel="Number of responses")

plt.show()
```

There are many directions we could continue from here. We could, for example, find out what demographics or job roles AI tool users have versus those who don't use

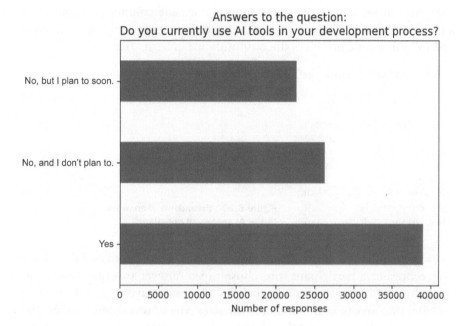

Figure 6.18 The distribution of answers to whether participants use AI tools

them. However, since we are focused on our end result, we can realize that this is not the question we are trying to answer. We are only interested in the subpopulations that already use AI tools, and we are more focused on how they use them. Having said that, an angle we are interested in is how people view the trustworthiness of AI tools, so it might be interesting to see if there is a difference in attitudes between participants who use AI and those who don't.

INVESTIGATING LIKERT DATA IN SURVEY ANSWERS

For the question of how AI users feel about the tools, we first want to use the AISent column, which reveals the answer to the question shown in figure 6.19.

How favorable is your stance on using AI tools as part of your development workflow?

- ○ Very favorable
- ○ Favorable
- ○ Indifferent
- ○ Unfavorable
- ○ Very unfavorable
- ○ Unsure

Figure 6.19 The question about AI sentiment

Now, we can look at the distribution of the `AISent` column to identify how people answered. Since this question is not mandatory, we expect to find some missing data. The following code produces the output shown in figure 6.20:

```
survey["AISent"].value_counts(dropna=False)
```

```
Favorable              29863
NaN                    26472
Very favorable         17050
Indifferent            10147
Unsure                  2471
Unfavorable             1698
Very unfavorable         272
Name: AISent, dtype: int64
```

Figure 6.20   Breakdown of answers to the AI sentiment question

As expected, there are lots of missing answers. These are not bad data; by and large, they represent a participant who chose not to answer this question, so we can fill this value in with a placeholder, such as "no answer given." Another, more Python-specific, step we can take is to make the data type of this column explicitly categorical. This will allow us to set the ordering of the values so that whenever they appear in a data table or a chart, they are not ordered alphabetically. We do all this using the pandas `Categorical` data type. The output of the following code is shown in figure 6.21:

```
survey["AISent"] = (
    pd.Categorical(
        survey["AISent"].fillna("No answer given"),
        categories=['No answer given', 'Unsure',
                    'Very unfavorable', 'Unfavorable',
                    'Indifferent', 'Favorable', 'Very favorable'],
        ordered=True)
)

survey["AISent"].value_counts(dropna=False).sort_index()
```

```
No answer given      26472
Unsure                2471
Very unfavorable       272
Unfavorable           1698
Indifferent          10147
Favorable            29863
Very favorable       17050
Name: AISent, dtype: int64
```

Figure 6.21   Breakdown of AI sentiment answers after converting to a `Categorical` data type

One choice I had to make was what order the values appear in. It is mostly my personal preference that I chose to put the "no answer given" option first and start the remaining answers from negative to positive sentiment. However, it is still a choice we have to make at this point. Now, we can compare the distribution of these answers across the groups of AI tool users, nonusers, and aspiring users.

USING PIVOT TABLES TO CROSS-REFERENCE CATEGORICAL VALUES

Comparing answers about favorability across different groups of AI tool users involves cross-referencing two categorical variables. In pandas, one appropriate method is crosstab, and the following code produces the output in figure 6.22:

```
pd.crosstab(
    index=survey["AISelect"],        ← Rows represent whether the
    columns=survey["AISent"]              participant is an AI tool user.
)                                    ← Columns represent answers
                                          to the AI sentiment question.
```

AISent AISelect	No answer given	Unsure	Very unfavorable	Unfavorable	Indifferent	Favorable	Very favorable
No, and I don't plan to.	26221	0	0	0	0	0	0
No, but I plan to soon.	155	1762	129	927	5858	10790	3089
Yes	96	709	143	771	4289	19073	13961

Figure 6.22 Comparing whether AI users or non-users view AI tools favorably

We can immediately notice that whoever said they don't use AI did not give a follow-up answer either because the follow-up didn't make sense, or the survey actively hid the option. We could stop here and try to make further sense of this table, as it's not too large. However, I would err on the side of not staring at tables of numbers for very long and creating visualizations instead.

VISUALIZING PIVOT TABLES WITH HEATMAPS

Visualizing a table of numbers is usually a good opportunity for a heatmap, which the seaborn library can provide. I have chosen a grayscale option that translates to print, but any sequential colormap would do.

A note on color scale terminology

When deciding on colors for a visualization and multiple colors are involved, we need to make a choice of colormap, that is, the range of colors present in the visualization. Our choices are sequential, diverging, or categorical (also called nominal or qualitative).

Sequential colormaps gradually change in lightness to represent a continuous scale. The lightness is proportional to the size of the measurement; an example is the greyscale colormap, such as the one used in figure 6.23. The darker colors indicate more people falling into a category.

(continued)

Diverging colormaps include multiple colors, which gradually change in lightness depending on the direction. Lightness is still used to indicate strength, but the hue also indicates direction. An example is negative values being red and positives being blue, with larger values being darker red or blue, respectively.

Categorical colormaps are used when different parts of a visualization need to be distinct colors. They are usually used in pie or bar charts where each slice or bar is a completely different color. The colors are purely for visual separation and are not to be interpreted numerically.

I have also anchored the minimum and maximum points at 0 and 1, respectively, because that is the scale we are working with. Figure 6.23 shows the generated heatmap:

```
fig, axis = plt.subplots()

sns.heatmap(
    data=pd.crosstab(
        index=survey.loc[survey["AISelect"]
 != "No, and I don't plan to", "AISelect"],
        columns=survey.loc[survey["AISelect"]
 != "No, and I don't plan to", "AISent"],
        normalize="index"
    ),
    cmap="Greys",
    vmin=0,
    vmax=1,
    square=True,
    annot=True,
    ax=axis
)

fig.suptitle("How favorably do different people view AI tools?")

axis.set(
    xlabel="How favorable is your stance on using AI tools?",
    ylabel="Do you currently use AI tools?"
)

plt.show()
```

NOTE This is a good opportunity to incorporate some programming best practices into our analysis. We will undoubtedly create more heatmaps like this, and the difference between them will be the data and the axis labels. The other options will remain the same, so we should create a reusable function that can generate a heatmap without duplicating our code. Problems of code quality are generally beyond the scope of these projects.

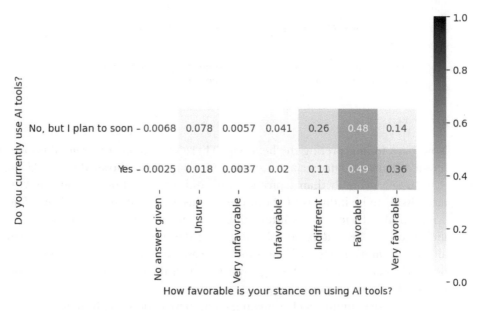

Figure 6.23   Heatmap showing the favorability of AI tools among users and aspiring users

The modified code to produce the heatmap from figure 6.23 looks like the following. We will reuse this `create_heatmap` method throughout the solution:

```
def create_heatmap(data, square=True):
    fig, axis = plt.subplots()                        ⟵⎤ The function only needs
                                                        ⎥ the data table and an
    sns.heatmap(                                        ⎥ optional way to make the
        data=data,                                      ⎦ heatmap square or not.
        cmap="Greys",
        vmin=0,
        vmax=1,
        square=square,
        annot=True,
        ax=axis
    )                                           ⎤ We return the Figure and Axis
                                                ⎥ objects to allow custom axis
    return fig, axis              ⟵⎦ labels and titles.

fig, axis = create_heatmap(
    pd.crosstab(
        index=survey.loc[survey["AISelect"]
⇨  != "No, and I don't plan to", "AISelect"],
        columns=survey.loc[survey["AISelect"]
⇨  != "No, and I don't plan to", "AISent"],
        normalize="index"
```

```
            )
        )

fig.suptitle("How favorably do different people view AI tools?")

axis.set(
    xlabel="How favorable is your stance on using AI tools?",
    ylabel="Do you currently use AI tools?"
)

plt.show()
```

Now, back to interpreting the heatmap. There seem to be a couple of noticeable differences between current and aspiring AI users. First, those who use AI tools view them more favorably than aspiring users, and those who do not yet use AI tools are more likely to be indifferent about them. This is perhaps not surprising. The lack of cynicism about the tools is interesting; it seems very few developers view the tools unfavorably. This might be selection bias; developers filling in this survey might already be more likely to have good use cases for AI tools and, therefore, higher opinions. Let us see how these groups fare with the question about the trustworthiness of the tools' outputs.

The AIBen column also has missing data, so we choose to fill these in and create an ordered Categorical column again. The following code then produces the output in figure 6.24:

```
survey["AIBen"] = (
    pd.Categorical(
        survey["AIBen"].fillna("No answer given"),
        categories=['No answer given', 'Highly distrust',
                    'Somewhat distrust', 'Neither trust nor distrust',
                    'Somewhat trust', 'Highly trust'],
        ordered=True
    )
)

survey["AIBen"].value_counts(dropna=False).sort_index()
```

```
No answer given                26577
Highly distrust                 3350
Somewhat distrust              13330
Neither trust nor distrust     18837
Somewhat trust                 24128
Highly trust                    1751
Name: AIBen, dtype: int64
```

Figure 6.24   The distribution of trust in AI tools

Although most participants viewed AI tools favorably, there is more of a spread when it comes to trusting their outputs. The crosstab comparing these answers across AI users and aspiring users is achieved with the following code and shown in figure 6.25:

```
pd.crosstab(
    index=survey["AISelect"],
    columns=survey["AIBen"]
)
```

	No answer given	Highly distrust	Somewhat distrust
No, and I don't plan to	26221	0	0
No, but I plan to soon	202	1303	5975
Yes	154	2047	7355

(continued)

	Neither trust nor distrust	Somewhat trust	Highly trust
No, and I don't plan to	0	0	0
No, but I plan to soon	8085	6764	381
Yes	10752	17364	1370

Figure 6.25   Comparing AI trustworthiness across different users

Again, we can exclude nonusers and generate a heatmap of the crosstab, as shown in figure 6.26:

```
fig, axis = create_heatmap(
    pd.crosstab(
        index=survey.loc[survey["AISelect"]
    != "No, and I don't plan to", "AISelect"],
        columns=survey.loc[survey["AISelect"]
    != "No, and I don't plan to", "AIBen"],
        normalize="index"
    )
)

fig.suptitle("How much do different people trust the output of AI tools?")

axis.set(
    xlabel="How much do you trust the accuracy of the output from AI tools?",
    ylabel="Do you currently use AI tools?"
)

plt.show()
```

Active users of AI tools trust their outputs more and distrust them less, although very few people are comfortable saying they *highly* trust them. Aspiring users are more on the fence and have answered "neither trust nor distrust" more often. Again, it is not surprising, but it validates some basic assumptions.

Before moving on to investigate different aspects of the data, let's review our process so far. Figure 6.27 shows the steps taken so far.

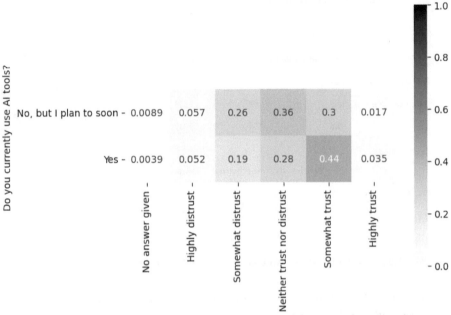

Figure 6.26   Heatmap comparing AI trustworthiness across AI tool users and aspiring users

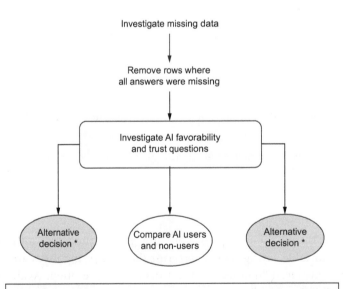

Figure 6.27   Visualizing our analysis so far

Now, it's time to dive deeper into what people are using AI tools for.

TRANSFORMING CATEGORICAL DATA INTO INDICATOR VARIABLES

For this portion, we will focus only on those who answered yes to the question about whether they use the tools. Let's remind ourselves about the format of the answers to the question about which parts of the development workflow they are using AI tools for. Figure 6.28 shows part of the related survey question.

Which parts of your development workflow are you currently using AI tools for, and which are you interested in using AI tools for over the next year? Please select all that apply.

	Currently using	Interested in using	Not interested in using
Learning about a codebase	☐	☐	☐
Project planning	☐	☐	☐
Writing code	☐	☐	☐
Documenting code	☐	☐	☐
Debugging and getting help	☐	☐	☐
Testing code	☐	☐	☐

Figure 6.28   A snapshot of the survey question about what participants are using AI tools for

Figure 6.29 shows a snapshot of the column that represents the answers in semicolon-delimited string form. The data was selected with the following code:

```
(
    survey.loc[survey["AISelect"] == "Yes", "AIToolCurrently Using"]
    .dropna()
    .head(10)
)
```

```
1                   Writing code;Committing and reviewing code
4         Learning about a codebase;Writing code;Documen...
5                      Writing code;Debugging and getting help
6                      Writing code;Debugging and getting help
7         Project planning;Writing code;Debugging and ge...
9                      Writing code;Debugging and getting help
11                             Writing code;Testing code
13                     Writing code;Debugging and getting help
15                                            Writing code
16                                            Writing code
Name: AIToolCurrently Using, dtype: object
```

Figure 6.29   A snapshot of the data used to store answers to how people use AI tools

This is not a format we can work with directly. Typically, we would spread the available answers out as indicator variables, binary columns to represent whether each possible answer was checked. This next step, one-hot encoding, where we convert this string column into indicator variables, is a purely technical one, which makes it a perfect place to turn to AI tools if you don't already know how to do the transformation with your existing tools. Let's see this in action.

I asked ChatGPT the following:

> *I have a pandas DataFrame that contains a column of values corresponding to multiple choice options from a survey question. The values are not exclusive, so they can contain multiple answers delimited by a semicolon. A sample value would be "option 1; option 2; option 3." I want to turn this into multiple indicator columns, one for each value, so I should have columns called "option 1," "option 2," etc., each being a binary indicator of whether that value was present in the original column. What is the pandas code for this?*

Its answer started with, "You can achieve this by using the `str.get_dummies` method in pandas to create indicator columns for each option in the multiple-choice column," which turned out to be exactly the method I was after. It also suggested some code snippets, as shown in figure 6.30.

```
import pandas as pd

# Sample DataFrame with a column containing multiple choice options
data = {'Options': ["option 1; option 2; option 3",
                    "option 2; option 4",
                    "option 1; option 3",
                    "option 4"]}

df = pd.DataFrame(data)

# Use str.get_dummies to create indicator columns
indicator_columns = df['Options'].str.get_dummies(sep='; ')

# Rename the indicator columns to match the option names
indicator_columns.columns = [f"option {col}" for col in indicator_columns.co

# Concatenate the indicator columns with the original DataFrame
df = pd.concat([df, indicator_columns], axis=1)

# Drop the original 'Options' column if needed
# df.drop('Options', axis=1, inplace=True)

print(df)
```

Figure 6.30   Code snippets suggested by ChatGPT

One tweak I had to make was changing the separator from "; " to ";" because our data doesn't have the trailing space between the semicolon-delimited values. Other than that, the `str.get_dummies` function is exactly what we are after. The following code generates the indicator columns shown in figure 6.31:

```
ai_tool_indicators = (
    survey.loc[survey["AISelect"] == "Yes", "AIToolCurrently Using"]
    .str.get_dummies(sep=";")
)
ai_tool_indicators
```

	Collaborating with teammates	Committing and reviewing code	Debugging and getting help	Deployment and monitoring	Documenting code
1	0	1	0	0	0
4	0	0	1	0	1
5	0	0	1	0	0
6	0	0	1	0	0
7	0	0	1	0	0

(continued)

	Learning about a codebase	Other (please describe)	Project planning	Testing code	Writing code
1	0	0	0	0	1
4	1	0	0	0	1
5	0	0	0	0	1
6	0	0	0	0	1
7	0	0	1	0	1

Figure 6.31 A snapshot of the newly created indicator columns

To reiterate, each column represents one of the checkbox rows from figure 6.28, and a value of 1 means that the checkbox was ticked under the "Currently using" column. If we were to repeat this for "Interested in using" and "Not interested in using," we would end up with three times as many indicator variables, essentially one column per checkbox under that question.

Experience might tell us that when separating delimited strings, we could end up with trailing spaces in column names, so let's check and fix that:

```
ai_tool_indicators.columns = [c.strip() for c in ai_tool_indicators.columns]
```

One benefit of indicator variables is that the sum of each column represents the number of people who ticked a particular checkbox, and the mean of each column represents the percentage. Let's look at the percentage of participants who checked each option. Remember, this is now only AI users telling us what they currently use AI tools for. The following code produces the chart in figure 6.32:

```
fig, axis = plt.subplots()

(
    ai_tool_indicators
    .mean()
    .sort_values()
    .plot
    .barh(ax=axis)
)

axis.set(
    title="What are AI users using their AI tools for?",
    xlabel="% of users who ticked that option"
)

plt.show()
```

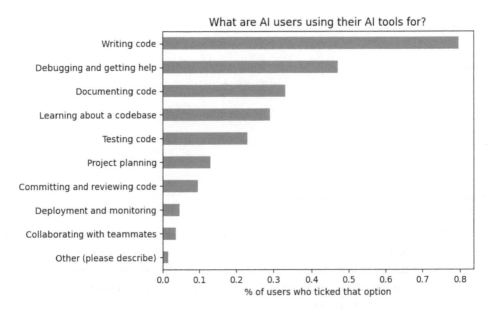

Figure 6.32 Bar chart showing what percentage of AI users ticked each "Currently using" option

Most developers are using AI tools to write and debug code, but there are other tangential use cases that are popular, such as testing code, project planning, and even documenting code. We can add the indicator columns to our original data and keep a filtered dataset of only AI users for use in the remaining investigations. Figure 6.33 shows a snapshot of the data after the following manipulations:

```
survey_ai_users = (
    pd.concat([survey, ai_tool_indicators], axis=1)
    .dropna(subset=ai_tool_indicators.columns, how="any")
)
```

concat will, by default, match on indices.

```
assert len(survey[survey["AISelect"] == "Yes"]) == len(survey_ai_users)

survey_ai_users.head()
```

	ResponseId	Q120	MainBranch	Age	Employment
1	2	I agree	I am a developer by profession	25-34 years old	Employed, full-time
4	5	I agree	I am a developer by profession	25-34 years old	Employed, full-time;Independent contractor, fr...
5	6	I agree	I am a developer by profession	35-44 years old	Employed, full-time
6	7	I agree	I am a developer by profession	35-44 years old	Employed, full-time
7	8	I agree	I am a developer by profession	25-34 years old	Employed, full-time

```
(continued, some columns hidden for clarity)
```

	Committing and reviewing code	Debugging and getting help	Deployment and monitoring	Documenting code
1	1.0	0.0	0.0	0.0
4	0.0	1.0	0.0	1.0
5	0.0	1.0	0.0	0.0
6	0.0	1.0	0.0	0.0
7	0.0	1.0	0.0	0.0

Figure 6.33 A snapshot of the combined data of AI users

Let's see how favorable and trustworthy participants judge AI to be depending on what they use the tools for. Our "start at the end" philosophy is helpful here. We want a table where each row is one of the AI tool use cases (e.g., "Writing code"), and each column is one of the favorability options. Each cell then represents the count, or better, the percentage, of those who said they use AI tools for a particular purpose and answered a particular way for favorability. This should show us whether there is a difference in opinion across different users' profiles.

CONVERTING DATA TO A LONG FORMAT FOR EASIER ANALYSIS

Cross-referencing the different use cases with favorability opinions requires some reshaping of our data. This is another use case for an AI tool to tell us how to do this, but this time, let's attempt it ourselves and compare notes with our AI tool afterward. What we want is data in a long format, which will make it easier to generate the right crosstab. See chapter 3 for more details on wide versus long data in the context of data modeling. The following code creates a long-form version of one of the multiple-choice options cross-referenced against favorability, and the output is shown in figure 6.34:

```
(
    survey_ai_users[survey_ai_users["Collaborating with teammates"] == 1]
```

```
    .groupby("AISent")
    .size()
    .reset_index(name="count")
    .assign(option="Collaborating with teammates")
)
```

	AISent	count	option
0	No answer given	0	Collaborating with teammates
1	Unsure	19	Collaborating with teammates
2	Very unfavorable	10	Collaborating with teammates
3	Unfavorable	12	Collaborating with teammates
4	Indifferent	99	Collaborating with teammates
5	Favorable	534	Collaborating with teammates
6	Very favorable	703	Collaborating with teammates

Figure 6.34 AI tools favorability across people who use them for collaboration

If we had this dataset for every option combined into one long table, we could reshape it into the crosstab we need. Let's loop through the options and build up this long table:

```
tool_favorability_dfs = []                              ⟵  Loops through
for col in ai_tool_indicators.columns:                      all indicators
    option_df = (
        survey_ai_users[survey_ai_users[col] == 1]
        .groupby("AISent")
        .size()
        .reset_index(name="count")                      ⟵  Generates the aggregation
        .assign(option=col)                                 similar to figure 6.32 and
    )                                                       tracks in a list
    tool_favorability_dfs.append(option_df)

options_vs_favorability = pd.concat(                    ⟵  Combines the list into
    tool_favorability_dfs,                                  one DataFrame
    axis=0,
    ignore_index=True
)

print(options_vs_favorability.shape)
```

The output is (70, 3), meaning we have 70 rows now, corresponding to the 10 indicator columns with seven possible favorability answers each. We can now use this data to create a crosstab of percentages, as planned. The following code does this and produces the crosstab in figure 6.35:

```
favorability_crosstab = (
    pd.crosstab(index=options_vs_favorability["option"],
                columns=options_vs_favorability["AISent"],
```

```
        values=options_vs_favorability["count"],
        aggfunc="sum",
        normalize="index")
)
favorability_crosstab
```

AISent option	No answer given	Unsure	Very unfavorable	Unfavorable	Indifferent	Favorable	Very favorable
Collaborating with teammates	0.000000	0.013798	0.007262	0.008715	0.071895	0.387800	0.510530
Committing and reviewing code	0.000788	0.011298	0.003678	0.008408	0.068050	0.392801	0.514976
Debugging and getting help	0.000651	0.014156	0.002658	0.013614	0.077019	0.464555	0.427347
Deployment and monitoring	0.001119	0.013423	0.006711	0.009508	0.064318	0.381991	0.522931
Documenting code	0.000386	0.011417	0.002314	0.010723	0.076294	0.446810	0.452056
Learning about a codebase	0.000441	0.014009	0.003348	0.012335	0.078767	0.441322	0.449780
Other (please describe)	0.000000	0.034542	0.010363	0.044905	0.143351	0.436960	0.329879
Project planning	0.000785	0.012753	0.003335	0.010202	0.066706	0.404159	0.502060
Testing code	0.000556	0.011889	0.003444	0.010556	0.067778	0.433222	0.472556
Writing code	0.000385	0.014166	0.002634	0.014102	0.085927	0.485400	0.397385

Figure 6.35   Crosstab of favorability vs. different AI tool use cases

This is now a table that is hard to interpret in its current form, so let's generate a heat-map of this, too. The final heatmap is shown in figure 6.36:

```
fig, axis = create_heatmap(
    favorability_crosstab.round(2)
)

fig.suptitle("How favorably do people who use AI for different purposes
⇒ view AI tools?")

axis.set(xlabel=None, ylabel=None)

plt.show()
```

This is much easier to interpret than the raw data table. There does not seem to be a big difference across use cases, but there are some observations we can make:

- Even when we break the data out into use cases, AI users generally view their tools favorably.
- Those who use the tools for project planning, collaborating, committing and reviewing code, and deployment and monitoring grade the AI tools as "very favorable" the most.
- The biggest "indifferent" category is "Other," but we do not have the underlying data, so we cannot investigate this further.

How favorably do people who use AI for different purposes view AI tools?

	No answer given	Unsure	Very unfavorable	Unfavorable	Indifferent	Favorable	Very favorable
Collaborating with teammates	0	0.01	0.01	0.01	0.07	0.39	0.51
Committing and reviewing code	0	0.01	0	0.01	0.07	0.39	0.51
Debugging and getting help	0	0.01	0	0.01	0.08	0.46	0.43
Deployment and monitoring	0	0.01	0.01	0.01	0.06	0.38	0.52
Documenting code	0	0.01	0	0.01	0.08	0.45	0.45
Learning about a codebase	0	0.01	0	0.01	0.08	0.44	0.45
Other (please describe)	0	0.03	0.01	0.04	0.14	0.44	0.33
Project planning	0	0.01	0	0.01	0.07	0.4	0.5
Testing code	0	0.01	0	0.01	0.07	0.43	0.47
Writing code	0	0.01	0	0.01	0.09	0.49	0.4

Figure 6.36   Heatmap comparing favorability across different AI tool use cases

Before moving on, let's briefly look at how ChatGPT suggested we solve this particular technical challenge.

USING AI TOOLS TO IMPROVE OUR ANALYSIS

Whenever something takes two or three discrete steps, I get the feeling that there is an easier way to do it, which is where AI tools can help improve our technical knowledge.

> **NOTE**   It is important to remember that AI tools like ChatGPT are just that—tools. This makes them interchangeable over time. You might not use this specific AI tool, and there will undoubtedly be more advanced ones created in the future. Feel free to substitute all references to ChatGPT with whichever AI tool you prefer.

In this case, ChatGPT's answer was very similar; it suggested building up a DataFrame by looping through the options. Figure 6.37 shows ChatGPT's answer. I did not integrate its suggestion or dig into the specific differences between it and my code; all I was looking for was whether there was a single `pandas` method I overlooked for doing this transformation. As it turns out, AI tools can do no better than looping through the different options.

2. To calculate the percentage of each satisfaction score for each option, you can use the following code:

```python
# Create a DataFrame with satisfaction values as columns and initialize them to 0
satisfaction_columns = df['satisfaction'].unique()
satisfaction_df = pd.DataFrame(0, index=df.columns[:-1], columns=satisfaction_columns)

# Iterate through each option column and calculate percentages
for option in df.columns[:-1]:
    # Group by the option column and calculate the percentage of each satisfaction scor
    grouped = df.groupby([option, 'satisfaction']).size().unstack(fill_value=0)

    # Calculate the total count of each option
    total_count = df[option].sum()

    # Calculate the percentage and update the satisfaction_df
    percentage_df = (grouped / total_count) * 100
    satisfaction_df.loc[option] = percentage_df.loc[1]  # Use loc[1] to select rows whe

# Fill NaN values with 0 (for options where no one ticked that option)
satisfaction_df.fillna(0, inplace=True)
```

Figure 6.37   ChatGPT's approach to creating the options vs. favorability crosstab

Previously, the question about the trustworthiness of the output generated more interesting findings, so let us repeat this latest crosstab and heatmap process for the AIBen column as well. The following code generates the long-format data, a snapshot of which is shown in figure 6.38:

```
tool_trust_dfs = []
for col in ai_tool_indicators.columns:
    option_df = (
        survey_ai_users[survey_ai_users[col] == 1]
        .groupby("AIBen")
```

```
        .size()
        .reset_index(name="count")
        .assign(option=col)
    )
    tool_trust_dfs.append(option_df)

options_vs_trust = pd.concat(tool_trust_dfs, axis=0, ignore_index=True)

print(options_vs_trust.shape)
options_vs_trust.head()
```

	AIBen	count	option
0	No answer given	2	Collaborating with teammates
1	Highly distrust	43	Collaborating with teammates
2	Somewhat distrust	143	Collaborating with teammates
3	Neither trust nor distrust	317	Collaborating with teammates
4	Somewhat trust	705	Collaborating with teammates

Figure 6.38   A snapshot of long-format data comparing AI tool use case options with trustworthiness

This generates 60 rows of data, 10 use cases with six trustworthiness options each. Now, we can create the crosstab and heatmap generated by the following code. The final heatmap is shown in figure 6.39:

```
trust_crosstab = (
    pd.crosstab(index=options_vs_trust["option"],
                columns=options_vs_trust["AIBen"],
                values=options_vs_trust["count"],
                aggfunc="sum",
                normalize="index")
)

fig, axis = create_heatmap(
    trust_crosstab.round(2)
)

fig.suptitle("How much do people who use AI for different purposes
➡ trust the output of AI tools?")

axis.set(xlabel=None, ylabel=None)

plt.show()
```

From this heatmap, it appears that most users "somewhat trust" the AI tools' outputs, with not much difference across use cases. Having the data about the "Other" category would be interesting, as that is where the trustworthiness varies the most.

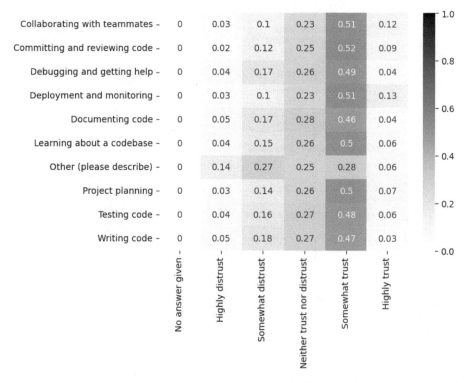

Figure 6.39   Heatmap of different AI tool use cases vs. view on trustworthiness

> **NOTE**   One limitation of using this multiple-choice data is we are double-counting anyone who said they use AI for more than one purpose. It's not a deal breaker for our analysis, but it's good to be aware that our categories are not mutually exclusive.

Before continuing our analysis, let's recap the steps so far, including the latest one, where we investigated opinions of AI across different use cases. Our latest steps are shown in figure 6.40.

Next, we are interested in the profiles of AI tool users (e.g., what job titles they have).

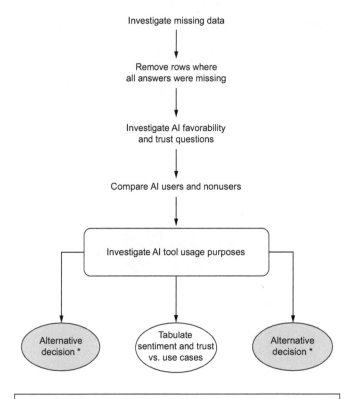

Figure 6.40 Steps taken in the analysis up to investigating AI tool usage

RECATEGORIZING DATA FOR CLARITY

There are further nuances we can explore in this data. People who said they use AI to write code may use it for very different purposes. Despite the name, the survey was not just completed by developers. Other job roles are also included, so it's worth exploring whether attitudes toward AI vary along those roles. First, let's look at the distribution of values in the DevType column, but only for people who are using AI tools. The results produced by the following code are shown in figure 6.41:

```
survey_ai_users['DevType'].value_counts(dropna=False)
```

As we'd expect, most participants are developers with a long tail of other jobs ranging from data roles to research, marketing, and even management. For our purposes, we can probably combine a few of these categories, at least for our first iteration. To identify if different job roles use AI differently, we can get away with grouping all

```
Developer, full-stack                              12316
NaN                                                 5509
Developer, back-end                                 5499
Developer, front-end                                2622
Other (please specify):                             1221
Developer, mobile                                   1126
Student                                             1106
Developer, desktop or enterprise applications       1087
Data scientist or machine learning specialist        953
Engineering manager                                  823
Senior Executive (C-Suite, VP, etc.)                 681
DevOps specialist                                    600
Academic researcher                                  571
Engineer, data                                       534
Research & Development role                           500
Developer, embedded applications or devices          486
Cloud infrastructure engineer                        467
Data or business analyst                             349
Developer, game or graphics                          326
System administrator                                 257
Project manager                                      232
Developer, QA or test                                231
Blockchain                                           200
Product manager                                      183
Educator                                             174
Security professional                                171
Engineer, site reliability                           160
Developer Experience                                 139
Designer                                             122
Scientist                                            100
Developer Advocate                                    98
Hardware Engineer                                      80
Database administrator                                65
Marketing or sales professional                       54
```

Figure 6.41   Distribution of job roles among participants who use AI tools

developers into a single group to start with. Let's see which of these groups could go into our larger "developer" group. The result of the following code is shown in figure 6.42:

```
devtypes = (
    survey_ai_users
    .dropna(subset=["DevType"])
    .query("DevType.str.startswith('Developer')")
    .loc[:,"DevType"]
)

devtypes.value_counts()
```

Most of these roles can go in a single "Developer" category, except the last two: "Developer experience" and "Developer advocate." These are developer-adjacent roles with more of a people focus with responsibilities such as creating and engaging with communities and not necessarily writing a lot of code. Let's group the rest of the developer

```
Developer, full-stack                              12316
Developer, back-end                                 5499
Developer, front-end                                2622
Developer, mobile                                   1126
Developer, desktop or enterprise applications       1087
Developer, embedded applications or devices          486
Developer, game or graphics                          326
Developer, QA or test                                231
Developer Experience                                 139
Developer Advocate                                    98
```

Figure 6.42 Distribution of different developer roles among AI tool users

roles into a single category. Specifically, in Python, we can create a dictionary that matches each of these roles with the "new" category they should belong to:

```
devtype_map = {}

dev_exclusions = ["Developer Experience", "Developer Advocate"]

dev_devtypes = [col for col in devtypes.value_counts().index
➥ if col not in dev_exclusions]

for col in dev_devtypes:
    devtype_map[col] = "Developer"
```

Looking at our list in figure 6.42 again, we see a few engineering roles that could be grouped together, so let's also do that. The following code produces the output in figure 6.43:

```
eng_devtypes = (
    survey_ai_users
    .dropna(subset=["DevType"])
    .query("DevType.str.contains('engineer', case=False)")
    .loc[:,"DevType"]
)

eng_devtypes.value_counts()
```

```
Engineering manager              823
Engineer, data                   534
Cloud infrastructure engineer    467
Engineer, site reliability       160
Hardware Engineer                 80
Name: DevType, dtype: int64
```

Figure 6.43 Distribution of engineering roles among AI tool users

All of these roles can go under one "Engineer" category for now, except the management one. Let's make that change and then look at the distribution of our new, more compact job category column. The following code produces the result in figure 6.44:

```
for col in ['Engineer, data', 'Cloud infrastructure engineer',
            'Engineer, site reliability', 'Hardware Engineer']:
    devtype_map[col] = "Engineer"

survey_ai_users["job_category"]
⇒ = survey_ai_users["DevType"].replace(devtype_map)

survey_ai_users["job_category"].value_counts(dropna=False)
```

```
Developer                                        23693
NaN                                               5509
Engineer                                          1241
Other (please specify):                           1221
Student                                           1106
Data scientist or machine learning specialist      953
Engineering manager                                823
Senior Executive (C-Suite, VP, etc.)               681
DevOps specialist                                  600
Academic researcher                                571
Research & Development role                         500
Data or business analyst                           349
System administrator                               257
Project manager                                    232
Blockchain                                         200
Product manager                                    183
Educator                                           174
Security professional                              171
Developer Experience                               139
Designer                                           122
Scientist                                          100
Developer Advocate                                  98
Database administrator                              65
Marketing or sales professional                     54
```

Figure 6.44 Distribution of a new `job_category` column

Now, we can create a crosstab similar to those we created previously, this time, to cross-reference job roles with AI use cases. First, we transform the data to a long format and then create our crosstab. Finally, we create a heatmap to make the results easier to investigate. The following code goes through these steps and produces the heatmap in figure 6.45:

```
tool_job_dfs = []                          Cross-reference job
                                           categories with AI
for col in ai_tool_indicators.columns:     ⟵  use cases.
    option_df = (
        survey_ai_users[survey_ai_users[col] == 1]
        .dropna(subset="job_category")
        .groupby("job_category")
        .size()
        .reset_index(name="count")
        .assign(option=col)
    )
    tool_job_dfs.append(option_df)

options_vs_jobs = pd.concat(tool_job_dfs, axis=0, ignore_index=True)
```

```
job_crosstab = (
    pd.crosstab(index=options_vs_jobs["option"],
                columns=options_vs_jobs["job_category"],
                values=options_vs_jobs["count"],
                aggfunc="sum",
                normalize="columns")
    .transpose()
)
```
◁——— **Reshapes into a crosstab**

```
fig, axis = create_heatmap(
    job_crosstab.round(2),
    square=False
)
```
◁——— **Finally, plots the heatmap**

```
fig.suptitle("What do different job roles use AI for?")

axis.set(xlabel=None, ylabel=None)

plt.show()
```

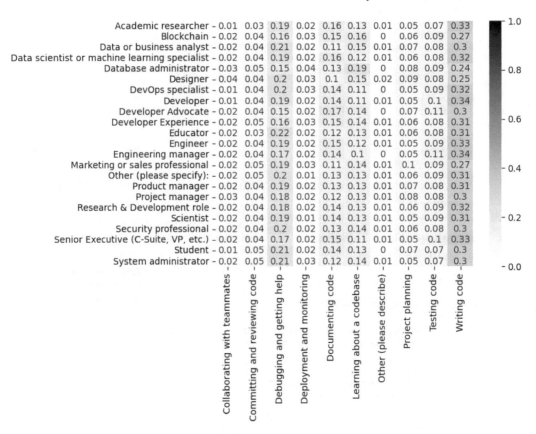

Figure 6.45   Heatmap showing AI use cases across different job roles

The heatmap gives us some insights into usage patterns:

- About 30% of people use AI tools for writing code, with database administrators, marketing and sales professionals, and designers being exceptions.
- Database administrators use AI for learning about a codebase more than others. Apart from them, other job roles that use AI for this the most are the ones that generally write less code, such as marketing or product functions.
- While developer advocates also use AI for writing code, they also score the highest in using it for documentation, which can be an important aspect of the role.

These few observations aside, participants seem to use AI tools more or less in the same way. Let's recap our steps again, including this latest step for investigating job roles. Figure 6.46 shows the latest step diagram.

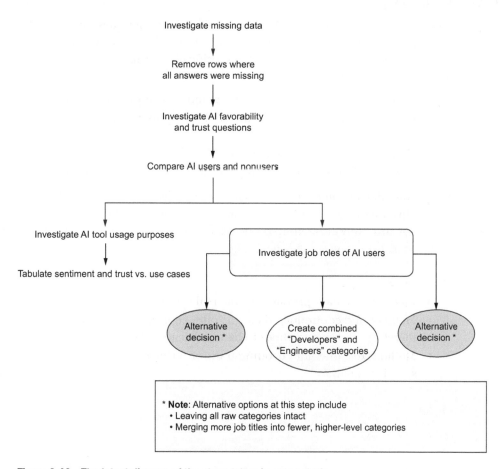

Figure 6.46   The latest diagram of the steps taken in our analysis

Note that once we clean up the AI sentiment and trust-related columns, certain parts of our analysis can be done in parallel. Figure 6.46 illustrates this since it is not necessary to compare AI tool usage and trust and favorability before investigating AI users' job roles. This highlights the fact that sometimes an analysis is not completely linear.

Let's export the data we will need to explore the questions further in the next chapter:

```
survey.to_parquet("../chapter-7/data/survey.parquet.gz",
➥compression="gzip", index=False)
survey_ai_users.to_parquet("../chapter-7/data/survey_ai_users.parquet.gz",
➥compression="gzip", index=False)
```

Let's now review everything that we have accomplished so far and identify what else we need to do to finish getting to a minimum viable answer in the next chapter.

6.4.3   *Project progress so far*

So far, we have answered one of the two main stakeholder questions, namely, whether developers' opinions on the usefulness and trustworthiness of current AI tools depend on their experience, job role, and what specifically they use the tools for. We have analyzed the survey to conclude that

- Users of AI tools generally view them more favorably than nonusers.
- Users of AI tools also trust the tools' outputs more than nonusers say they would.
- Help with writing and debugging code is the most popular use case for AI tools.
- People in different job roles report using AI tools for different purposes.

In the following chapter, we will continue the project by addressing the second stakeholder hypothesis, which is that new and experienced coders use these tools differently. For this, we will need methods that combine continuous and categorical data and perform appropriate statistical tests.

Summary

- Categorical data is prevalent in the real world.
- Methods for continuous data are often not appropriate for categorical data; therefore, knowing methods to handle categorical data is important for analysts.
- Methods like one-hot encoding transform categorical data into a format better suited for analysis.

Categorical data: Advanced methods 7

This chapter covers

- Combining continuous and categorical data in an analysis
- Converting continuous data to categorical when appropriate to do so
- Analyzing categorical data with advanced methods, such as statistical tests

In this chapter, we will continue exploring the value of categorical data. In chapter 6, we explored survey data, which was mostly categorical, and answered some of our stakeholders' questions with methods appropriate for categorical data. As a reminder, the data and example solution files for this project are available at https://davidasboth.com/book-code.

This chapter dives into more advanced methods: performing statistical tests with categorical data and combining continuous and categorical data. We will first recap the project brief from the previous chapter and summarize the work done so far before continuing with the analysis.

7.1   *Project 5 revisited: Analyzing survey data to determine developer attitudes to AI tools*

To recap, we are analyzing the Stack Overflow Developer Survey to determine how coders are using AI tools. Our stakeholders are interested in testing two of their hypotheses:

- New and experienced coders are using these tools differently.
- People's opinions on the usefulness and trustworthiness of current AI tools depend on their experience, job role, and what specifically they use the tools for.

We have answered the second part by exploring, reshaping, and summarizing categorical columns in our survey data. The next section describes the available data.

7.1.1   *Data dictionary*

The data dictionary for this dataset comes in two parts, both included in the supplementary materials:

- There is a question-by-question breakdown, `survey_results_schema.csv`, documenting which question a column contains answers for. Some questions' answers are spread across multiple columns.
- There is also a PDF copy of the survey itself. With this, you can directly observe the data-generating process, which is rare.

Let's revisit our desired outcomes, so we know what result to aim toward.

7.1.2   *Desired outcomes*

Our stakeholders have specific hypotheses, and our analysis should focus on them. We have already done some general exploration of the data to identify elements like missing values. Our minimum viable answer should be evidence to support or refute the main hypotheses. Therefore,

- Our conclusions should include whether there is a difference in the use of AI across different levels of experience.
- We should communicate the factors that affect a person's opinion of, and trust in, AI tools, as supported by the survey data.

Before continuing our analysis, let's revisit the work we have done in the previous chapter.

7.1.3   *Summary of the project so far*

In chapter 6, we

- Explored the survey questions to find the ones relevant to our analysis
- Investigated missing data
- Analyzed both AI users' and nonusers' trust and views on favorability of AI tools
- Explored the different purposes for which AI users use these tools and how different usage purposes affect users' trust

- Investigated the different job roles among respondents and how trust and favorability vary across these roles

Figure 7.1 shows the work done so far.

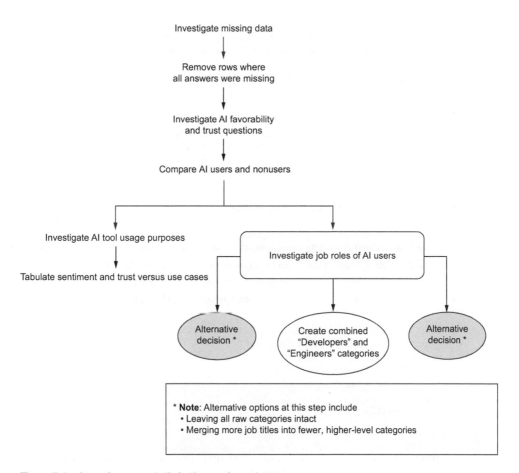

Figure 7.1   Steps in our analysis in the previous chapter

In this chapter, we will answer questions about the respondents' levels of experience. We are interested in whether having more coding experience changes opinions on AI tools and whether experienced users have different use cases than beginner coders.

7.2   *Using advanced methods to answer further questions about categorical data*

It is reasonable to believe that more experienced coders need different kinds of help from AI tools than more junior developers. Let's see the values in the `YearsCodePro` column, which asks how many years the respondent has been coding. The output of the following code, which starts with reading in data exported at the end of the previous chapter, is shown in figure 7.2:

```
import pandas as pd
import matplotlib.pyplot as plt
import seaborn as sns
survey = pd.read_parquet("./data/survey.parquet.gz")
survey_ai_users = pd.read_parquet("./data/survey_ai_users.parquet.gz")

survey_ai_users["YearsCodePro"].unique()
```

```
array(['9', '4', '21', '3', '15', nan, 'Less than 1 year', '10', '2', '6',
       '14', '7', '5', '16', '20', '11', '12', '19', '8', '50', '27',
       '13', '1', '18', '44', '22', '25', '24', '17', '26', '37', '30',
       'More than 50 years', '23', '32', '39', '28', '35', '36', '33',
       '34', '41', '31', '40', '38', '29', '43', '42', '45', '48', '47',
       '49', '46'], dtype=object)
```

Figure 7.2   Different values for `YearsCodePro`

This column should be numeric but is actually stored as text because of those two values: "less than 1 year" and "more than 50 years." Since the rest of the values are not binned, we should make this column numeric. We can replace those two text values with 0 and 50, respectively, without compromising the data too much:

```
survey_ai_users["YearsCodePro"] = (
    survey_ai_users["YearsCodePro"]
    .replace({
        'Less than 1 year': 0,
        'More than 50 years': 50
    })
    .astype(float)
)
```

NOTE In later versions of `pandas`, 2.0 and beyond, there are actually nullable integer types—that is, numbers that represent integers but can also be missing. For the example solutions, for compatibility reasons, I am using a version before 2.0, which only allows the `float` type, that is, decimal numbers, to contain missing values.

Now that we have a numeric `YearsCodePro` column, let's observe its distribution. The resulting histogram is shown in figure 7.3:

```
survey_ai_users["YearsCodePro"].hist(bins=20)
```

Most participants have less than 10 years of experience, with a long tail out toward 50. Now, if we were to test the relationship between this continuous value and another, we could simply calculate the correlation. However, we are trying to compare this against

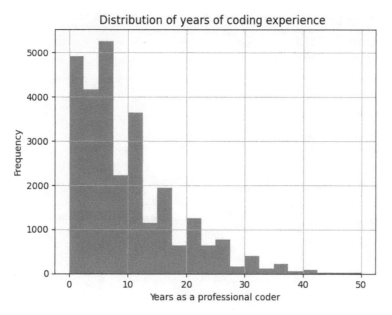

Figure 7.3 **Distribution of AI users' coding experience**

categorical data, such as how favorably someone views AI, so correlation in the traditional sense does not apply. One idea is to separate out this histogram of experience or similar visualizations of distribution, such as box plots, by the different answers to the favorability question. Let us look at an example using something the Python library `seaborn` calls "boxenplots," which are similar to box-and-whisker plots but with more information. The following code results in the plot in figure 7.4:

```
fig, axis = plt.subplots()

sns.boxenplot(
    data=survey_ai_users,
    x="YearsCodePro", y="AISent",
    color="gray",
    ax=axis
)

axis.set(
    title="Distribution of years of experience across
⇨ answers to the favorability question",
    xlabel="Years of coding experience",
    ylabel="How favorably do you view AI tools?"
)

plt.show()
```

This plot tells us that the highest median years of experience is in the unfavorable group. That is, the ones who view AI tools unfavorably are, on average, the more

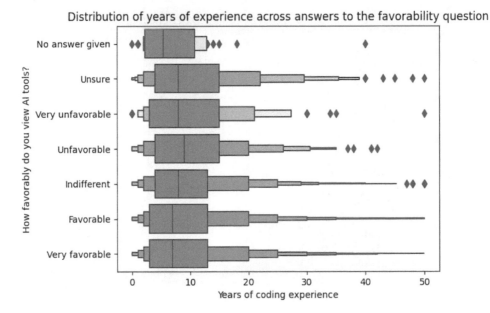

Figure 7.4 **Distribution of experience across different answers to the AI favorability question**

experienced coders. However, this median value is not a lot higher than for other groups, and each group has a lot of variance. Let's now look at how much different experience levels trust the output of AI tools. The following code produces the box-enplot in figure 7.5:

```
fig, axis = plt.subplots()

sns.boxenplot(
    data=survey_ai_users,
    x="YearsCodePro", y="AIBen",
    color="gray",
    ax=axis
)

axis.set(
    title="Distribution of years of experience across
    answers to the trust question",
    xlabel="Years of coding experience",
    ylabel="How much do you trust the output of AI tools?"
)

plt.show()
```

Again, those who gave the more negative answers tend to have more experience on average. The difference is possibly higher than with favorability and also suggests that more experienced coders are less likely to trust the output of such tools. What we

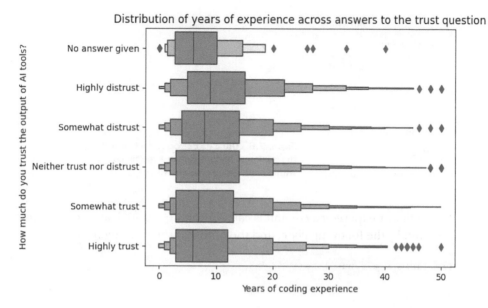

Figure 7.5   Distribution of years of experience across answers to the trust question

really want to know is the opposite question: rather than what is the distribution of experience across different answers, we want to know, what is the distribution of different answers across experience levels?

For this, we need another crosstab-to-heatmap process, this time comparing years of experience and answers to the favorability and trust questions. However, we can only do this if "years of experience" is represented as a categorical value.

7.2.1   *Binning continuous values to discrete categories*

We start by putting the continuous measure into categorical bins. Let's create six logical bins in total, but remember that your choice of bins will affect the result. Bins can be created manually, like in the following example, but can also be based on the data. One such method would be using quantiles, which would ensure each bin has the same amount of data. The following code bins our data and verifies the minimum and maximum years of experience within each bin, using the output shown in figure 7.6:

```
exp_bins = pd.cut(survey_ai_users["YearsCodePro"],
            bins=[-1, 0, 2, 5, 10, 20, 50],
            labels=["0", "1-2 years", "3-5 years",
                    "6-10 years", "11-20 years",
                    "over 20 years"]
        )

survey_ai_users.groupby(exp_bins)["YearsCodePro"].agg(["min", "max"])
```

	min	max
YearsCodePro		
0	0.0	0.0
1–2 years	1.0	2.0
3–5 years	3.0	5.0
6–10 years	6.0	10.0
11–20 years	11.0	20.0
Over 20 years	21.0	50.0

Figure 7.6 Our `YearsCodePro` bins with the minimum and maximum experience within each group also shown

Now that our experience column is categorical, we can look at its distribution. This is achieved by the following code, and the output is shown in figure 7.7:

```
fig, axis = plt.subplots()

(
    exp_bins
    .value_counts()
    .sort_index()
    .plot
    .bar(ax=axis)
)

axis.set(
    title="Distribution of years of experience (binned)",
    xlabel="Years of experience",
    ylabel="Frequency"
)

plt.show()
```

As shown by figure 7.7, most participants have less than 10 years of coding experience, with 6–10 years being the most common. Unlike the different AI tool use cases, this experience value is in a single column and is not spread across multiple indicators. That makes our crosstab creation much simpler because we are simply cross-tabulating two categorical columns. The following code achieves this and produces the output in figure 7.8:

```
exp_vs_sent = pd.crosstab(
    index=exp_bins,
    columns=survey_ai_users["AISent"],
    normalize="index"
)

exp_vs_sent
```

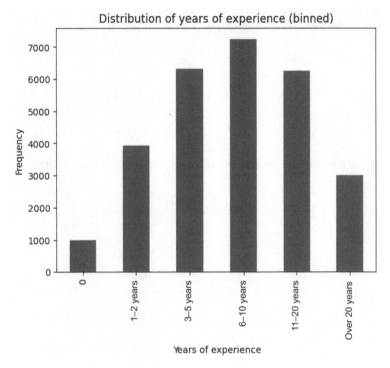

Figure 7.7   Distribution of the newly binned years of experience data

AISent YearsCodePro	No answer given	Unsure	Very unfavorable	Unfavorable	Indifferent	Favorable	Very favorable
0	0.001	0.015	0.004	0.018	0.104	0.506	0.352
1–2 years	0.003	0.017	0.004	0.015	0.101	0.510	0.350
3–5 years	0.002	0.015	0.002	0.016	0.105	0.489	0.372
6–10 years	0.001	0.017	0.004	0.019	0.113	0.476	0.370
11–20 years	0.002	0.017	0.003	0.023	0.112	0.484	0.358
Over 20 years	0.000	0.022	0.004	0.021	0.108	0.475	0.370

Figure 7.8   Crosstab of experience vs. answers to the favorability question

As with previous examples, this is better explored as a heatmap, which is produced by the following code and shown in figure 7.9:

```
fig, axis = create_heatmap(
    exp_vs_sent.round(2)
)
```

This function was defined in chapter 6.

```
fig.suptitle("How favorably do people with different
➥ amounts of coding experience view AI?")

axis.set(
    xlabel=None,
    ylabel="Coding experience"
)

plt.show()
```

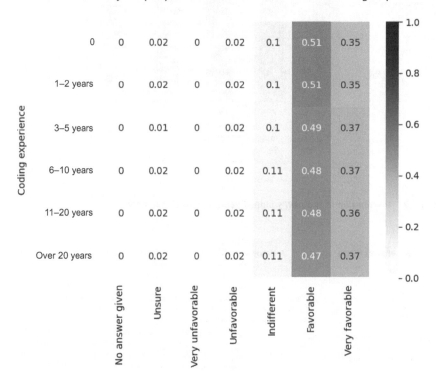

Figure 7.9   Heatmap of favorability vs. experience

While figure 7.4 showed that those who rated AI tools unfavorably were slightly more experienced cohorts, when flipping the question, it appears that the answers of most cohorts are distributed equally. What about trust in AI tools? The following code creates both the crosstab and heatmap, and the latter is shown in figure 7.10:

```
exp_vs_trust = pd.crosstab(
    index=exp_bins,
    columns=survey_ai_users["AIBen"],
    normalize="index"
)
```

```
fig, axis = create_heatmap(
    exp_vs_trust.round(2)
)

fig.suptitle("How much do people with different
➥ amounts of coding experience trust the output of an AI?")

axis.set(
    xlabel=None,
    ylabel="Coding experience"
)

plt.show()
```

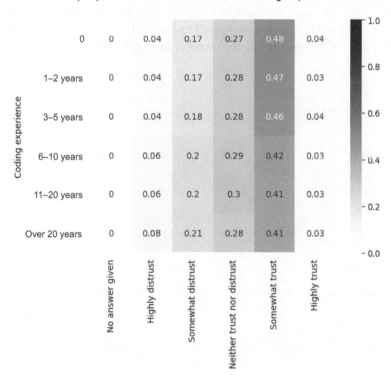

Figure 7.10 Coding experience vs. trust shown as a heatmap

This heatmap paints a picture similar to that of figure 7.5. It seems that the more experience someone has, on average, the less trust they have in the outputs of AI tools. This is a great place to consider the use of a statistical test. We want to know whether this finding is statistically significant. Specifically, our hypothesis is that the continuous measure of "years of experience" affects someone's answer to the question about trust in AI tools' output.

7.2.2   *Using statistical tests for categorical data*

Most statistical tests covered in data education are designed for continuous measures. However, there are statistical tests specifically for categorical data or a mix of data types. This is a perfect example of something you might be aware of but not have the required specific knowledge until you need it for a project. It is, therefore, something with which you can turn to an AI tool. Let's see what ChatGPT says when asked the question, "What methods can I use to measure the association between a continuous and an ordinal variable?"

It gives multiple approaches, including visualizations that we have already performed. It summarizes its recommendations with "If you're interested in the overall strength and direction of the relationship, Spearman's rank correlation or Kendall's Tau can be useful." These sound like good places to start.

Both of these methods are rank based, meaning they do not use the ordinal values directly but use their rank among all answers. This might again be something you haven't done with your specific tool before, and an AI tool could give you a relevant

```python
import pandas as pd
from scipy.stats import spearmanr

# Create a sample DataFrame with 'age' and 'satisfaction_score' columns
data = {
    'age': [25, 30, 35, 40, 45, 50, 55, 60, 65, 70],
    'satisfaction_score': [4, 3, 2, 5, 3, 4, 2, 5, 1, 3]
}

df = pd.DataFrame(data)

# Calculate the rank of 'satisfaction_score'
df['satisfaction_score_rank'] = df['satisfaction_score'].rank()

# Calculate Spearman's correlation
correlation, p_value = spearmanr(df['age'], df['satisfaction_score_rank'])

print(f"Spearman's Correlation: {correlation}")
print(f"P-value: {p_value}")

if p_value < 0.05:
    print("There is a statistically significant correlation.")
else:
    print("There is no statistically significant correlation.")
```

Figure 7.11   ChatGPT's code snippet to calculate Spearman's rank correlation

code snippet. Figure 7.11 shows ChatGPT's answer when prompted to give sample code to calculate Spearman's rank correlation with Python.

Obviously, this code snippet isn't directly useable, but it requires just a few modifications. Let's apply ChatGPT's code to our own and calculate Spearman's rank correlation, as well as Kendall's Tau value, which can be done in a similar manner. Two minor points to make here are that we have to drop any missing data for this analysis and ignore cases where no answer was given to the trust question since that value doesn't fit into the ordinal nature of the answers. First, we will create the ranking, and then calculate the two statistical metrics. The output, the final printout, is shown in figure 7.12:

```
trust_exp_data = (
    survey_ai_users
    .dropna(subset=["YearsCodePro", "AIBen"], how="any")
    .loc[survey_ai_users["AIBen"] != "No answer given", :]
)

trust_rank = (
    pd.Series(
        trust_exp_data["AIBen"]
        .factorize(sort=True)[0]
    )
    .rank()
)

from scipy.stats import spearmanr, kendalltau

correlation, p_value = spearmanr(
    trust_exp_data["YearsCodePro"],
    trust_rank
)

print("Spearman's\n", correlation, p_value)

correlation, p_value = kendalltau(
    trust_exp_data["YearsCodePro"],
    trust_rank
)

print("Kendall's tau\n", correlation, p_value)
```

```
Spearman's
 -0.0650445414009189 2.6886332522054823e-27
Kendall's tau
 -0.05052236119624125 2.5557806077186822e-27
```

Figure 7.12 Output of our statistical tests

In both tests, a correlation value close to zero means the association between variables is weak. The second value in both printouts is the p-value, a proxy for the significance of the result. A value close to zero means it is extremely unlikely we would see these results in a world where our base, or "null," hypothesis is true. That is to say, in a world where we assume there is no association between experience and trust score, how likely are we to calculate the association value at which we arrived? The lower this likelihood, the more confident we can be that our correlation value is robust. A low p-value means we are inclined to reject the null hypothesis, meaning we accept that the association we find, or lack of it, is statistically significant.

In this case, the statistical tests tell us there is significant evidence to suggest there is no link between experience and trust scores. The correlation values are negative, which would suggest experienced users distrust AI more, but the values are close to zero, meaning the association is weak. We are still free to explore this association further, but if a stakeholder insists on asking about statistical significance, we have an answer ready.

Let's review the process so far, including the parallel strands that comprised our analysis, as shown in figure 7.13.

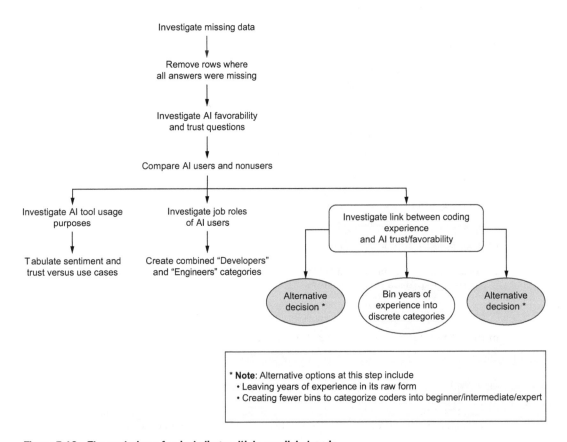

Figure 7.13   The analysis so far, including multiple parallel strands

The final point of inquiry before summarizing our results is to look at what developers are not interested in using AI tools for.

7.2.3   *Answering a new question from start to finish*

Looking at what developers are not interested in requires all the skills we have gained so far throughout this project. The survey specifically allows participants to tick a box for whether each use case is something they're not interested in, so we can look at this data directly. This will be useful in determining if a market opportunity actually exists. Since the answers to this question are recorded the same way as those for which participants are currently using AI tools for, we can go through the process shown in chapter 6:

1 Create indicator variables for each AI use case (this time from the `AIToolNot interested in Using` column).
2 Add the indicators to the survey data for AI users only.
3 Create a long-form dataset cross-referencing job role with the use cases people aren't interested in.
4 Use this long-form dataset to create a crosstab.
5 Visualize this crosstab as a heatmap.

Let's start with the indicator variables, after which we can look at which use cases people are least interested in, as shown in the bar chart in figure 7.14:

```
ai_not_interested_indicators = (
    survey.loc[survey["AISelect"] == "Yes", "AIToolNot interested in Using"]
    .str.get_dummies(sep=";")
)


fig, axis = plt.subplots()

(
    ai_not_interested_indicators
    .mean()
    .sort_values()
    .plot
    .barh(ax=axis)
)

axis.set(
    title="What do AI users NOT want to use AI for?",
    xlabel="% of participants who ticked that option"
)

plt.show()
```

Previous findings, such as the heatmap in figure 6.45 in the previous chapter, showed that very few people are using AI for collaboration, and figure 7.14 reinforces this. Participants explicitly said they don't imagine using AI tools for collaboration with humans, and around a quarter also aren't interested in using them for project planning or deployment and monitoring. It seems there are specific tasks that people do not want to delegate to AI tools. Finally, let's do our long-form data transformation to

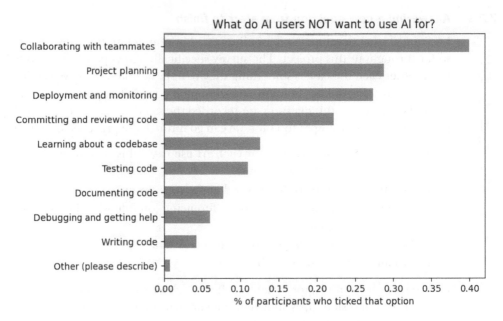

Figure 7.14   Which use cases people are most disinterested in using AI for

arrive at a heatmap to break this last analysis down by job role. This final heatmap is shown in figure 7.15:

```
ai_users_not_int = (
    pd.concat([survey, ai_not_interested_indicators], axis=1)
    .dropna(subset=ai_not_interested_indicators.columns, how="any")
)

ai_users_not_int["job_category"]
➥ = ai_users_not_int["DevType"].replace(devtype_map)      ⬅— This mapping of job
                                                              roles was defined
                                                              in chapter 6.

not_interested_job_dfs = []

for col in ai_not_interested_indicators.columns:          ⬅— Cross-references AI
    option_df = (                                            "anti-" use cases
        ai_users_not_int[ai_users_not_int[col] == 1]        with job categories
        .dropna(subset="job_category")
        .groupby("job_category")
        .size()
        .reset_index(name="count")
        .assign(option=col)
    )
    not_interested_job_dfs.append(option_df)

not_interested_options_vs_jobs = pd.concat(not_interested_job_dfs,
➥axis=0, ignore_index=True)
```

```
job_not_int_crosstab = (
    pd.crosstab(index=not_interested_options_vs_jobs["option"],
                columns=not_interested_options_vs_jobs["job_category"],
                values=not_interested_options_vs_jobs["count"],
                aggfunc="sum",
                normalize="columns")
    .transpose()
)
```

◄── **Reshapes into a crosstab**

```
fig, axis = create_heatmap(
    job_not_int_crosstab.round(2),
    square=False
)
```

◄── **Finally, visualizes as a heatmap**

```
fig.suptitle("What do different job roles NOT want to use AI for?")

axis.set(xlabel=None, ylabel=None)

plt.show()
```

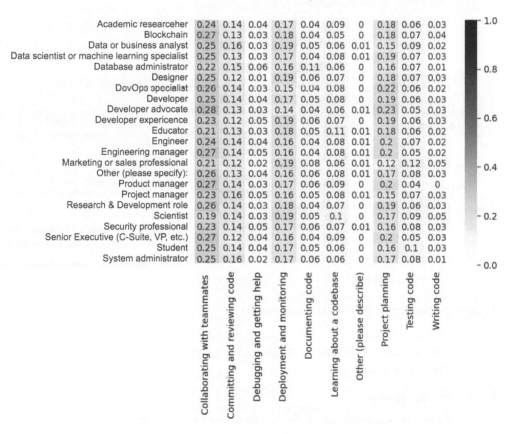

Figure 7.15 Heatmap comparing AI uses cases that different job roles are not interested in

This final heatmap reveals that the reluctance to use AI for human collaboration, project planning, and deployment and monitoring is constant across job roles. There are some differences, such as marketing professionals scoring testing code the highest out of all job roles as something they don't want to use AI for.

Before summarizing our results, let's summarize our analytical process, visualizing the four parallel strands we pursued to get a minimum viable answer to all our stakeholders' questions. Figure 7.16 shows this diagram.

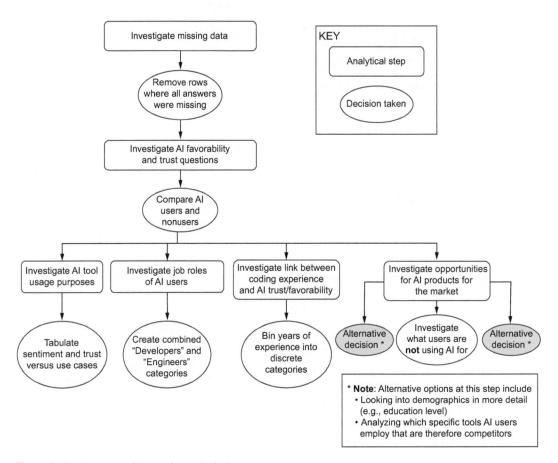

Figure 7.16 Summary of the entire analytical process

Now, it's time to summarize what we found and decide what to communicate back to our stakeholders.

7.2.4 Project results

Rather than summarize all our findings, let's focus on the ones directly related to our initial questions. Our stakeholders' initial hypotheses were that

- New and experienced coders are using these tools differently.
- People's opinions on the usefulness and trustworthiness of current AI tools depend on their experience, job role, and what specifically they use the tools for.

To answer these points, in our analysis, we found that

- Writing and debugging code are the most popular AI use cases, but there is undeniable variation in what different job roles currently use AI tools for.
- There are clearly use cases for AI that people are less interested in.
- Existing users of AI tools seem to favor and trust these tools more than aspiring users.
- There is little evidence that a developer's years of experience affects trust in AI tools.

What can we recommend in terms of market gaps to exploit? We have seen that those who actively use AI tools are more likely to view them more positively than potential users, so marketing the benefits of these tools is crucial. The market will already be saturated with AI-driven coding tools, so we should focus on the popular but less well-served use cases. Examples of this would include learning about a codebase, documenting existing code, and testing. We have also seen which gaps don't exist; it does not seem sensible to pursue AI-driven collaboration or project management tools.

These findings are more than enough for an initial stakeholder review, but there are plenty of avenues in the data to explore the viability of an AI-driven discovery/documentation tool further, such as

- There is a question about how often someone can find information within their business. We could cross-reference people who answered "often" with the current and future use cases to gauge interest in such a tool.
- There is also a question about how long people spend searching for information. Again, this could be cross-referenced with answers about AI tools and use cases.
- Finally, there is a question about how often people need help from their team, which again could be explored as a way to get people interested in AI assistance.

During our analysis, we also encountered some limitations in our data worth communicating to our stakeholders. The data is heavily biased toward developers, specifically those active on Stack Overflow. Even the README file for the dataset notes that "highly engaged users on Stack Overflow were more likely to notice the links for the survey and click to begin it." This is not necessarily a bad case of selection bias since the target audience of our startup overlaps with engaged Stack Overflow users. We are missing the presence of developers who aren't active online, and it would be worth quantifying this population and investigating other means of capturing their pain points and opinions.

We also do not have access to some of the free text answers, which would have given us deeper insight into how people are using and want to use AI tools. Creating our own qualitative survey or interviews could help us get a better understanding of our target market but would incur significant costs compared to using an existing survey.

> ### Activity: Further project ideas with this data
>
> The survey data used in this chapter has more dimensions that can be explored. As with all projects, I recommend taking the time to consider different research questions that could be answered. Here are some ideas to get you started:
>
> - Is there a relationship between the tools that developers use and their opinions and usage of AI? There are survey questions about programming languages and other related tools that we did not explicitly explore in the project.
> - There is a question about the industry the developer currently works in, which opens up opportunities to compare results across industries. Are some industries more forward-thinking with regard to AI than others?
> - At the start of the survey, there are questions about how developers prefer to learn. Do answers to these questions relate to different stances toward AI?

It is worth highlighting that we have just scratched the surface of what information is available in the survey data, but our results-driven approach meant we only explored avenues that were immediately relevant to the question at hand. That is the value of starting with the end result in mind and having something concrete to work toward.

7.3   *Closing thoughts on categorical data*

The prevalence of categorical data in real business scenarios should not be underestimated. Any operational system where data entry consists of multiple-choice options or dropdowns, customer surveys with discrete options, or data that contains hierarchies such as countries, regions, or departments will generate categorical data. Knowing the relevant options to treat this data correctly is crucial, especially because, in basic training, there is typically little time devoted to the subject. In trying to bridge the gap between training and the real world, understanding how to specifically handle categorical data, such as knowing methods like one-hot encoding, will go a long way.

Finally, let's look at the skills covered by this chapter that are necessary for working with categorical data.

7.3.1   *Skills for working with categorical data for any project*

In this chapter, we had to change our approach because we were dealing with survey data that contains many categorical variables. The specific skills that are required for working with categorical data, which can be used for any problem involving survey data and categorical values, include

- Understanding why data would be missing in a survey context (e.g., people deciding to omit certain answers)

- Deciding on a natural order for ordinal variables, such as survey answers on a Likert scale
- Using pivot tables to cross-reference two categorical variables and, optionally, visualizing them with heatmaps
- Splitting multiple answers into separate columns (e.g., for multiple-choice questions that allow more than one selection)
- Turning categorical data into binary indicator variables for use in analyses via one-hot encoding
- Reshaping data from a wide to a long representation for easier cross-tabulation
- Using AI tools, such as ChatGPT, to continuously improve how we work
- Manipulating existing categories (e.g., combining similar ones) to add clarity to our analysis
- Choosing when to prefer categorical over continuous data, such as binning a continuous "Age" column into fewer, broader categories
- Identifying the right statistical test to use based on our data types

Summary

- Advanced methods such as appropriate statistical tests can help answer more detailed questions about categorical data.
- Binning continuous data to be categorical can enhance our analysis.
- Choosing the right visualizations for categorical data is crucial to investigating our data and communicating our findings.
- When working with survey data, it is important to understand how survey questions map to columns in our dataset.

Time series data: Data preparation

This chapter covers

- Preparing time series data for analysis
- Determining what subset of time series data to use
- Cleaning time series data by handling gaps and missing values
- Analyzing patterns in time series data

Most datasets you will come across have a time component. If the process to generate the data involves taking the same measurement at recurring intervals, the data is called *time series data*. An example is measuring the yearly GDP of a country or the output of machinery in a production line. However, even something seemingly static, such as a customer database, has a time component if we look at the date customer records were created. We might not explicitly think of the data as a time series, but using this time component allows us to unlock additional insights in our data. For example, you could analyze the rate at which new customer records are being created or what times of the day your operations team are inputting data into the database.

> **Real business case: Forecasting**
>
> The project covered by chapters 8 and 9 was inspired by multiple forecasting projects I have worked on and the fact that most data analysis curricula spend proportionally little time on the topic of working with temporal data.
>
> In late 2020, I had to provide forecasts for where the used car market was heading after the initial COVID lockdown restrictions were lifted in the United Kingdom. Accurately forecasting an entire market is hard enough, but the added complexity of having patchy data for the lockdown period and having to forecast in a scenario no one had encountered before made this project particularly difficult.
>
> In the end, we arrived at a prediction using a combination of fundamental forecasting principles, some concrete assumptions about the pandemic, and domain knowledge from our experts. It was a good example of a project where technical skills weren't enough to solve the business problem.

Working with time series data is more than knowing how to work with date formats. It involves extracting time-related components from data, handling time data at different resolutions, handling gaps, forecasting into the future, and working out whether the data can be forecasted at all.

Knowing how to extract temporal patterns from your data is a vital skill in the real world and one that we will practice in this chapter through the project.

8.1 Working with time series data

A time series is a repeated measurement taken at different, ideally uniform, time intervals. A typical tabular dataset, such as a customer dataset, will contain one row per customer, and each column will represent a different property of a customer, such as age, employment status, address, and so forth. A time series, however, typically contains fewer columns: one to represent the date of a measurement and one or more columns to represent the individual measurement value at that time. Each row, therefore, represents the same measurement, and it is the measurement time that makes each row unique.

8.1.1 The hidden depth of time series data

Let's take a simple example—customer satisfaction over time. Imagine one of those smiley-face-based satisfaction surveys you can find at airports, supermarket checkouts, or any other public place. As a customer walks by, they can press a smiley face to indicate their level of satisfaction. They see smiley faces, and the database records a simple value from 1 to 5 on a Likert scale to measure the value from most dissatisfied to most satisfied. Table 8.1 shows an example of what this dataset might look like.

To capture satisfaction over time, you just need a timestamp and the satisfaction value. If you had such a system set up across multiple locations, you might also find a location ID column, but the data wouldn't be more complex than that.

Table 8.1   An example of a time series dataset

Date	Satisfaction score
2023-11-01 11:03:55	4
2023-11-01 11:17:02	5
2023-11-01 13:41:11	3
2023-11-01 14:06:43	4

What kind of analysis could we do with what is, at first glance, a very simple dataset? We could

- Use clusters of rows as a proxy to identify busier periods
- Calculate average satisfaction over time at various levels of granularity (daily, weekly, monthly, etc.)
- Investigate trends and seasonal patterns in the data (if customers are more satisfied at different points of the day or different days of the week)
- Find anomalies where satisfaction rose or dropped to unexpected levels
- Cross-reference this with other data to identify how satisfaction relates to external factors, such as special events
- Compare satisfaction scores across different locations where that data is available

The fact that most of these questions can be answered with just two to three columns of data shows the hidden depth that time series data can have.

8.1.2   *How to work with time series data*

What does it mean to work with time series? When exploring time data, we care about a lot of the same things as when exploring tabular data. We want to understand each column, ensure data types are consistent, and check for missing values. However, there are also specific considerations for time data:

- What is the granularity of the time series? Is it consistent?
- Are there any gaps in the time series? Are these gaps there by design?
- Is there a trend in the data?
- Are there seasonal patterns?
- Are there any outliers worth investigating?

Once you have explored your time series dataset and want to proceed to forecasting, there are additional considerations:

- What is the right granularity for forecasting? This will depend partly on how much noise there is in the data. Hourly data might be too noisy, and although daily averages might be smoother and easier to forecast, there might not be enough data at a daily level.

- Does the time series contain autocorrelation: do past values inform future values? There are statistical tests for this, and time series models will take advantage of this property.

- Is the time series stationary? Some time series models require the data to be stationary, which means having a roughly constant mean and variance over time. In reality, a lot of time series have some trend and seasonality, so we either need to handle those directly or use forecasting models that take care of them for us.

- Can any outliers be explained by external factors? For example, are certain spikes in your sales data due to one-off special sale days, like Black Friday? These external factors, technically "exogenous variables," can be used in many forecasting models to improve predictions.

A final note on forecasting: the most important question you should ask is, "How will the forecast be used?" This requires answering these questions:

- How often are forecasts required?
- What is the required granularity of the forecasts?
- How far into the future should the forecasts go?
- What does an acceptable level of accuracy look like?
- What is the value of an accurate forecast in business terms? What is, therefore, the return on investment of additional work to improve existing forecasts?
- Will the data required by the forecasting model be available in time?

Answers to these questions will inform your analytical decisions at least as much as the technical considerations. When completing this project, and as with any project, you should always focus on the business outcomes you are trying to improve.

8.2 Project 6: Analyzing time series to improve cycling infrastructure

Let's look at the project in which we will analyze road traffic data to understand where cycling infrastructure should be improved. In this chapter, we will explore the available data and prepare it for analysis, which will happen in chapter 9.

The data is available for you to attempt the project yourself at https://davidasboth .com/book-code. You will find the data you can use for the project, as well as the example solution in the form of a Jupyter notebook.

This project is all about using time series data to find answers to our business questions. As usual, we will start by looking at the problem statement, the data dictionary, the outputs we are aiming for, and what tools we need to tackle the problem. We will then formulate our action plan using the results-oriented framework before diving into the example solution.

8.2.1   *Problem statement*

You have been hired to work on a new government initiative, Bikes4Britain, which aims to improve cycling infrastructure in the United Kingdom. The aim of the first phase of the project is to identify the most suitable places around the country to improve infrastructure for cyclists. Specifically, your stakeholders are looking for recommendations of places with either substantial existing or increasing cycling traffic.

They want to start with open data sources and have identified the Department for Transport's road traffic statistics (https://roadtraffic.dft.gov.uk) as a way to measure cycling traffic across the country. This is the dataset we will use in this project to look for patterns and make recommendations.

> **NOTE**   Data originally taken from https://roadtraffic.dft.gov.uk/downloads. Thank you to the Department for Transport for making this data available under the Open Government Licence.

The data we will use from the Department's statistics is the raw count data. This is a record of raw counts of vehicles that passed a particular counting location at various times. Some of the datasets are too high-level, such as area-level annual summaries, and some of them are estimates, such as the estimated annual average daily flows data (AADFs). The raw count dataset contains data at the most granular level, and we can always aggregate it to higher levels (e.g., annual values) if needed.

8.2.2   *Data dictionary*

Before we think further about the project, we should take a look at what data we have available. The data dictionary document (https://mng.bz/4ajw) is included in the project files, and table 8.2 shows the columns in detail. The data dictionary is shown as is, without modification from the original.

Table 8.2   The data dictionary, showing all column definitions

Column name	Definition
Count_point_id	A unique reference for the road link that links the AADFs to the road network
Direction_of_travel	Direction of travel
Year	Counts are shown for each year from 2000 onwards
Count_date	The date when the actual count took place
Hour	The time when the counts in question took place, where 7 represents between 7 a.m. and 8 a.m., and 17 represents between 5 p.m. and 6 p.m.
Region_id	Website region identifier
Region_name	The name of the region that the count point (CP) sits within
Region_ons_code	The Office for National Statistics code identifier for the region

Table 8.2   The data dictionary, showing all column definitions *(continued)*

Column name	Definition
Local_authority_id	Website local authority identifier
Local_authority_name	The local authority that the CP sits within
Local_authority_code	The Office for National Statistics code identifier for the local authority
Road_name	The road name (for instance, M25 or A3)
Road_category	The classification of the road type (see data definitions for the full list)
Road_type	Whether the road is a major or minor road
Start_junction_road_name	The road name of the start junction of the link
End_junction_road_name	The road name of the end junction of the link
Easting	Easting coordinates of the CP location
Northing	Northing coordinates of the CP location
Latitude	Latitude of the CP location
Longitude	Longitude of the CP location
Link_length_km	Total length of the network road link for that CP (in kilometers)
Link_length_miles	Total length of the network road link for that CP (in miles)
Pedal_cycles	Counts for pedal cycles
Two_wheeled_motor_vehicles	Counts for two-wheeled motor vehicles
Cars_and_taxis	Counts for cars and taxis
Buses_and_coaches	Counts for buses and coaches
LGVs	Counts for LGVs
HGVs_2_rigid_axle	Counts for two-rigid axle HGVs
HGVs_3_rigid_axle	Counts for three-rigid axle HGVs
HGVs_4_or_more_rigid_axle	Counts for four or more rigid axle HGVs
HGVs_3_or_4_articulated_axle	Counts for three- or four-articulated axle HGVs
HGVs_5_articulated_axle	Counts for five-articulated axle HGVs
HGVs_6_articulated_axle	Counts for six-articulated axle HGVs
All_HGVs	Counts for all HGVs
All_motor_vehicles	Counts for all motor vehicles

The data dictionary shows that we have data about the day and time that vehicle counts were recorded. There is a column specifically recording the count of bicycles, as well as plenty of information about the stretch of road where the counting took place. We can already see that we will be able to look at vehicle counts at different locations as separate time series since we satisfy the definition of a time series by having both date and time information, as well as the same measurement taken at different time intervals.

8.2.3   Desired outcomes

The output of the project is a recommendation of which area, or areas, to concentrate on for further analysis. These might be areas that already have a lot of high bicycle traffic, or they might be areas where cycling is on the rise or forecasted to have high cycling demand in the future. Our recommendation will likely contain suggested additional datasets we could incorporate to continue the analysis. There is likely more that we would like to know about these areas before any infrastructure work is undertaken, and we should outline this additional work to our stakeholders.

As this project spans multiple chapters, the desired outcome of this chapter, which is the data preparation part, is a filtered and cleaned version of the raw data, ready to be analyzed. The outcome of chapter 9 will then be the results of the analysis and final recommendations.

8.2.4   Required tools

As with most projects, your data analysis toolkit needs to read, explore, and visualize data to be suitable for the project. In the example solution, I use Python and the pandas and matplotlib libraries for data exploration and visualization, respectively. In the following chapter, I also introduce some time series functions from the statsmodels library when investigating time-specific aspects of the data and the pmdarima module for automatically choosing the best forecasting model. For this project, your tool should be able to

- Load a large dataset from a CSV or Excel file containing millions of rows
- Perform basic data manipulation tasks, such as filtering, sorting, grouping, and reshaping data
- Create data visualizations
- Produce statistical analysis, specifically of time series data
- Optionally create forecasts based on time series data

8.3   Applying the results-driven method to analyzing road traffic data

Let's now see how we will address this problem in a results-driven way and formulate our action plan. We will follow the steps of the results-driven process to explore the data with our stakeholders' requests and areas of interest in mind.

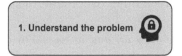

Do we fully understand the problem statement? Our stakeholders are interested in seeing how the number of cyclists has changed over time and across different areas. We know that's the part of the data we will focus on. However, their request is not as specific as we might like.

We need to define key terms, such as what it means for a place to be suitable for upgrading the cycling infrastructure. Is it somewhere where there are already a lot of cyclists? Or do we want to find places with potentially lower cycling traffic but where cycling is increasing the most over time? In that case, what are our criteria for "increasing"? If we can forecast our time series, we might even be able to make recommendations based on predicted future traffic.

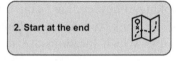

Let's now think about the end result. We must focus on patterns in cycling traffic, so there will be parts of the data we can largely ignore for our analysis. Knowing that we are interested in a particular aspect of the data will help us at the start when we are figuring out where to go next after the standard exploratory steps.

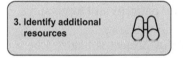

This is the step in which we decided to use the raw count data over the other available datasets. Again, this was driven directly by the problem statement. Area-level annual summaries are too high level to tease out cycling traffic, and using estimated measurements reduces the usefulness of our findings, leaving us with the raw count data to analyze. In this case, we do not have to make further decisions about which dataset to download, as the entire raw dataset comes as one file.

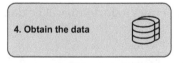

As with most of the projects, the data has already been downloaded, but no other changes have been made to it to best simulate the experience of exploring it for the first time. In the real world, obtaining the data might be a surprising obstacle, especially if you need permission, and there are privacy and governance concerns. This is not the case here, as we are working with open government data.

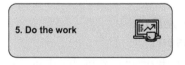

Let's now think about the steps we will take in our analysis. Before we turn our attention to the recommendation portion, we need to explore the dataset thoroughly. Specifically, we want to

- *Investigate the granularity of our data*—What does one row represent? Is it one row per location per day or something else? The granularity of data is one of the first things to investigate because it informs all other data transformations, like aggregations.

- *Understand the coverage of the data both geographically and in time*—For example, because the dataset is not a single time series but many, we need to know if every available location has the same amount of data.
- *Identify gaps in the time series*—Does every location have measurements at constant intervals? This is important to ensure we have enough of a sample at each location and is also a critical requirement for forecasting. Most forecasting algorithms do not work with gaps in the data or inconsistent intervals.
- *Investigate the distribution of bicycle counts*—What is a typical cycling volume for one row of data? Knowing this will immediately help identify the places with the highest cycling traffic.
- *Look at temporal patterns*—This includes looking at how cycling traffic fluctuates at different times of day, different days of the week, and across multiple years. Are there seasonal patterns we can identify? Which locations are showing a growing trend in cycling traffic?
- *Reduce the search space*—By this I mean we may not be able to analyze every location in equal detail because of gaps. We may have to filter the data down to locations that have more complete records across a longer time horizon, especially if we are interested in looking for temporal patterns and forecasting.

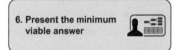

The output of this project is likely to be a combination of line charts and conversations. Line charts are the de facto time series visualization tool because they best represent the temporal component of an analytical result. We will likely end up creating other visualizations, too, but this is a project where the first iteration will spark a lot of conversation with our stakeholders. As we identify the limitations of the available data, we will be able to make recommendations about other datasets, and deciding on which ones to focus on will be done in collaboration with our domain experts.

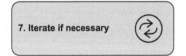

Since the dataset focuses narrowly on traffic volume, there will be multiple angles to explore after our initial recommendations. In the example solution, we'll explore some of these possible directions in which we could take a future iteration.

8.4   An example solution: Where should cycling infrastructure improvements be focused?

Now, it's time to look at an example walkthrough of analyzing this data. As always, I strongly recommend attempting the project yourself first. The example solution will be more relevant if you have your own analysis to compare it to. It bears repeating that the solution is not *the* solution, just one series of decisions you could make and conclusions you could reach along the way. Use it to generate more ideas and gain a different perspective on how you could have approached the same project brief.

Knowing what our end goal is and having thought about the various steps we want to take, our action plan will start with investigating the data. Only then will we understand what specific questions we can answer with what's available. Then, we can focus on looking for patterns and trends in cycling behavior and perhaps even attempt to forecast cycling trends into the future.

8.4.1   Investigating available data and extracting time series

As with any data problem, our first step is to look at the data itself. We know what columns to expect, but seeing a few sample rows will help us understand. We'll import the necessary libraries and examine a few rows of data. The output is shown in figure 8.1:

```
import pandas as pd
import numpy as np
import matplotlib.pyplot as plt

traffic = pd.read_csv("./data/dft_traffic_counts_raw_counts.csv.gz")
print(traffic.shape)
traffic.head()
```

	Count_point_id	Direction_of_travel	Year	Count_date	hour
0	749	E	2014	2014-06-25 00:00:00	7
1	749	E	2014	2014-06-25 00:00:00	8
2	749	E	2014	2014-06-25 00:00:00	9
3	749	E	2014	2014-06-25 00:00:00	10
4	749	E	2014	2014-06-25 00:00:00	11

(for clarity, not all columns are shown)

	HGVs_3_or_4_articulated_axle	HGVs_5_articulated_axle	HGVs_6_articulated_axle	All_HGVs	All_motor_vehicles
0	4.0	13	12.0	52.0	935.0
1	7.0	18	20.0	79.0	1102.0
2	9.0	17	19.0	74.0	773.0
3	7.0	18	17.0	89.0	778.0
4	3.0	16	24.0	85.0	875.0

Figure 8.1   A glimpse of the first few rows of traffic count data

The shape of the data is `(4815504, 35)`, meaning we have 35 columns and close to 5 million observations. From the columns, we can tell that this isn't a single time series. It is, in fact, lots of time series at various "count points," that is, measurement locations. Measurements at each count point can be treated as a separate time series, but we also have the option to aggregate by region, local authority, or even different time periods. From our data dictionary, we can also tell that we will be interested in the Pedal_cycles column, which measures the number of bicycles observed in a measurement period.

INVESTIGATING TIME SERIES COMPLETENESS

Let's examine the data to see how complete it is. First, we will look at missing data. The following code produces the output in figure 8.2:

```
traffic.isnull().sum()
```

```
Count_point_id                      0
Direction_of_travel                 0
Year                                0
Count_date                          0
hour                                0
Region_id                           0
Region_name                         0
Region_ons_code                     0
Local_authority_id                  0
Local_authority_name                0
Local_authority_code                0
Road_name                           0
Road_category                       0
Road_type                           0
Start_junction_road_name      2634972
End_junction_road_name        2634912
Easting                             0
Northing                            0
Latitude                            0
Longitude                           0
Link_length_km                2632824
Link_length_miles             2632824
Pedal_cycles                        0
Two_wheeled_motor_vehicles          0
Cars_and_taxis                      1
Buses_and_coaches                   5
LGVs                                0
HGVs_2_rigid_axle                   4
HGVs_3_rigid_axle                   1
HGVs_4_or_more_rigid_axle           2
HGVs_3_or_4_articulated_axle        1
HGVs_5_articulated_axle             0
HGVs_6_articulated_axle             1
All_HGVs                            9
All_motor_vehicles                 15
dtype: int64
```

Figure 8.2 Missing values per column in the traffic data

It looks like the records are mostly complete, with only road names and lengths missing a significant amount. This might have something to do with the different road types since not all roads in the country, and therefore, in the dataset, necessarily have a name. We will leave them missing since we have no reason to believe those rows are erroneous. There is a small number of measurements missing, which we will assume can be filled with zeros with the following code:

```
measurement_cols = [
    'Pedal_cycles', 'Two_wheeled_motor_vehicles',
    'Cars_and_taxis', 'Buses_and_coaches',
    'LGVs', 'HGVs_2_rigid_axle', 'HGVs_3_rigid_axle',
    'HGVs_4_or_more_rigid_axle', 'HGVs_3_or_4_articulated_axle',
    'HGVs_5_articulated_axle', 'HGVs_6_articulated_axle',
    'All_HGVs', 'All_motor_vehicles'
]

for col in measurement_cols:
    traffic[col] = traffic[col].fillna(0)
```

For completeness, we can also investigate what regions are covered by the data by inspecting the `Region_name` column. The following code produces the output in figure 8.3:

```
traffic["Region_name"].value_counts()
```

```
South East                   770532
North West                   562092
East of England              534120
South West                   478668
West Midlands                467604
Yorkshire and the Humber     413616
London                       393588
East Midlands                384516
Scotland                     298368
Wales                        286476
North East                   225924
Name: Region_name, dtype: int64
```

Figure 8.3 Distribution of regions in the traffic data

It looks like the data covers England, Scotland, and Wales, as well as various regions in England. Before moving on with our investigation, let's start building the diagram to document the analysis. Figure 8.4 shows the first step, in which we had to make a decision about missing values.

Our next question is concerning granularity: What precisely does one row of data represent?

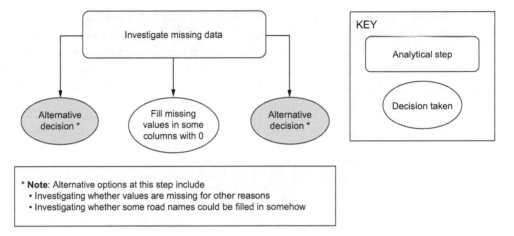

Figure 8.4   The first step in the analysis

INVESTIGATING TIME SERIES GRANULARITY

It is important to establish what one row of our data represents. It is a measurement at a particular time and location, but what specific combination of columns makes a row unique? We can test this by counting the number of rows for the combination of columns we believe to be unique and verifying if that matches the number of rows in the entire dataset.

> **A note on composite primary keys**
>
> When multiple columns make a record unique, this is called a *composite primary key*. It is when uniqueness does not come from a single ID column but a combination of more than one column. For example, customer IDs might not be unique if multiple customer databases are combined. In that case, the customer ID and the source database name might be what makes a record unique.
>
> This is another way in which foundational training can differ from the real world. In reality, databases often have complex structures, including composite primary keys.

The unique key, in this case, must at least contain Count_point_id, the Count_date, and therefore also the Year. There is also an hour column, suggesting the data is at an hourly granularity. If we assume these columns are the composite key, we can count the unique combinations and verify that they match the row count:

```
len(traffic[["Count_point_id", "Year", "Count_date",
➡ "hour"]].drop_duplicates())
```

This gives us 2435120, which is too few rows and suggests there is another column we haven't taken into account. The fact that this number is roughly half of the data suggests the column we are looking for typically has two values, so for every hour at every location, there is also another kind of measurement. Looking at the columns, this could be the `Direction_of_travel`, meaning traffic is counted separately in both directions at each location. Let's add that column to the key to see if it matches the number of rows:

```
len(traffic[["Count_point_id", "Year", "Count_date",
➥ "hour", "Direction_of_travel"]].drop_duplicates())
```

This returns `4815480`, which is much closer to the number of rows, suggesting we have found the right combination of columns, but the data contains duplicates. Let's investigate these. The following code finds duplicate keys and produces the output in figure 8.5:

```
duplicate_groups = (
    traffic
    .groupby(["Count_point_id", "Year", "Count_date",
➥ "hour", "Direction_of_travel"])
    .size()
    .loc[lambda x: x > 1]
)

duplicate_groups
```

It looks like there are two locations with duplicate measurements on two dates. We want to ascertain whether the measurements are also duplicated or whether the rows are perfect duplicates. We do this by taking one of the keys as an example and looking at which values the duplicate rows differ in. The following code does this and produces the output in figure 8.6:

```
example_dupes = (
  traffic[
    (traffic["Count_point_id"] == 7845)        ⟵ Finds a specific example of a duplicate
      & (traffic["Count_date"] == "2014-09-03 00:00:00")
      & (traffic["hour"] == 7)
      & (traffic["Direction_of_travel"] == "W")
  ]
)

(
  example_dupes
  .eq(example_dupes.shift(-1))                  ⟵ Uses the shift method to check whether values are equal in both rows
  .iloc[0]
  .loc[lambda x: x == False]
)
```

This tells us that for that location and date, the columns that differ are the ones measuring how many vehicles passed by. Let's look at the specific measurements to

```
Count_point_id  Year  Count_date                 hour  Direction_of_travel
7845            2014  2014-09-03 00:00:00        7     W                      2
                                                 8     W                      2
                                                 9     W                      2
                                                 10    W                      2
                                                 11    W                      2
                                                 12    W                      2
                                                 13    W                      2
                                                 14    W                      2
                                                 15    W                      2
                                                 16    W                      2
                                                 17    W                      2
                                                 18    W                      2
77043           2003  2003-06-18 00:00:00        7     S                      2
                                                 8     S                      2
                                                 9     S                      2
                                                 10    S                      2
                                                 11    S                      2
                                                 12    S                      2
                                                 13    S                      2
                                                 14    S                      2
                                                 15    S                      2
                                                 16    S                      2
                                                 17    S                      2
                                                 18    S                      2
dtype: int64
```

Figure 8.5 Duplicate records with the same composite primary key

```
Two_wheeled_motor_vehicles        False
Cars_and_taxis                    False
Buses_and_coaches                 False
LGVs                              False
HGVs_2_rigid_axle                 False
HGVs_3_rigid_axle                 False
HGVs_4_or_more_rigid_axle         False
HGVs_3_or_4_articulated_axle      False
HGVs_5_articulated_axle           False
HGVs_6_articulated_axle           False
All_HGVs                          False
All_motor_vehicles                False
Name: 24372, dtype: bool
```

Figure 8.6 Columns where values don't match in the example duplicate rows

determine how different they are. The following code extracts these columns. The returned data contains many columns, and by default, they are not all shown. Even if we could show them all, which is possible to do, they wouldn't fit horizontally on the screen without the need to scroll. One trick is to take a row or two of data and *transpose* it to show it as only one or two columns instead. We'll do this here, and the output is shown in figure 8.7:

```
(
  example_dupes[[
    'Two_wheeled_motor_vehicles', 'Cars_and_taxis', 'Buses_and_coaches',
    'LGVs', 'HGVs_2_rigid_axle', 'HGVs_3_rigid_axle',
    'HGVs_4_or_more_rigid_axle', 'HGVs_3_or_4_articulated_axle',
    'HGVs_5_articulated_axle', 'HGVs_6_articulated_axle', 'All_HGVs',
    'All_motor_vehicles']]
  .transpose()
)
```

	24372	24384
Two_wheeled_motor_vehicles	9.0	8.0
Cars_and_taxis	1567.0	1115.0
Buses_and_coaches	7.0	9.0
LGVs	185.0	168.0
HGVs_2_rigid_axle	30.0	29.0
HGVs_3_rigid_axle	5.0	6.0
HGVs_4_or_more_rigid_axle	5.0	1.0
HGVs_3_or_4_articulated_axle	6.0	1.0
HGVs_5_articulated_axle	2.0	4.0
HGVs_6_articulated_axle	10.0	13.0
All_HGVs	58.0	54.0
All_motor_vehicles	1826.0	1354.0

Figure 8.7   Side-by-side comparison of duplicate records

The values are quite different for the same combination of location and measurement date and time, so we are now confronted with a decision to make. What are our options when handling these duplicates?

- Should we combine the values somehow? This would make sense if these were partial measurements, but we have no evidence of this, and the numbers are too similar.
- Is one of them newer data, making the other row obsolete, in which case we should drop the first row? This is possible, but if it's the case, we have no way of knowing which would be the newer measurement apart from assuming the one

that appears later is more recent. This feels like a strong assumption to make with no evidence.

- We could drop these rows entirely, but this would introduce a gap into some of our time series, which is problematic for time series analysis.
- We could average the counts across the two records. This preserves the time series and keeps our numbers in the right ballpark, but we are essentially making up data this way.

There is no correct answer here. Each choice has its own assumptions and consequences. We will err on the side of preserving the time series and go with the averaging approach. While this does make up measurements that were not actually recorded, these duplicates are a small enough percentage of the overall data not to make this a big problem.

To combine these duplicates, we can group our data by the composite key, creating one group per unique identifier and averaging the measurement rows. In most cases, since the keys are unique, we will be averaging a single row, leaving it unaffected. The only additional trick is to handle missing columns. Our road name and link length columns, which form part of the composite key, contain missing values. The `pandas` library in particular will not group the records correctly when some grouping columns are missing.

To avoid this, we will temporarily fill missing values with a placeholder, do the deduplication, and remove the placeholder values afterward. For the `Road_name` column, we can use the text "PLACEHOLDER," but for the numeric columns, we need to find a value that doesn't already appear in the data. Negative numbers work well here, but we should double-check that there aren't already negative values for link length for whatever reason:

```
print(traffic["Link_length_km"].min(),
      traffic["Link_length_miles"].min())
```

The output is 0.1 and 0.06, respectively, telling us that there are no negative values, and we can use one as a placeholder. The process for deduplication is therefore the following:

- Replace missing values with placeholders.
- Group by all columns except the measurements.
- Within each group, which is mostly one row each, average the measurement values.
- In the grouped and aggregated dataset, replace placeholders with missing data again.

The following code does this and verifies that we have reduced the number of rows to the number of unique groups:

```
TEXT_PLACEHOLDER = "PLACEHOLDER"
NUMBER_PLACEHOLDER = -9999

group_cols = [
  'Count_point_id', 'Direction_of_travel', 'Year', 'Count_date', 'hour',
  'Region_id', 'Region_name', 'Region_ons_code', 'Local_authority_id',
  'Local_authority_name', 'Local_authority_code', 'Road_name',
  'Road_category', 'Road_type', 'Start_junction_road_name',
  'End_junction_road_name', 'Easting', 'Northing', 'Latitude',
  'Longitude', 'Link_length_km', 'Link_length_miles'
]

traffic_deduped = (
  traffic
  .assign(
    Start_junction_road_name = lambda df_:
    df_["Start_junction_road_name"].fillna(TEXT_PLACEHOLDER),
    End_junction_road_name = lambda df_:
    df_["End_junction_road_name"].fillna(TEXT_PLACEHOLDER),
    Link_length_km = lambda df_:
    df_["Link_length_km"].fillna(NUMBER_PLACEHOLDER),
    Link_length_miles = lambda df_:
    df_["Link_length_miles"].fillna(NUMBER_PLACEHOLDER)
  )
  .groupby(group_cols)
  .mean(numeric_only=True)
  .reset_index()
  .assign(
    Start_junction_road_name = lambda df_:
    df_["Start_junction_road_name"].replace(TEXT_PLACEHOLDER, np.nan),
    End_junction_road_name = lambda df_:
    df_["End_junction_road_name"].replace(TEXT_PLACEHOLDER, np.nan),
    Link_length_km = lambda df_:
    df_["Link_length_km"].replace(NUMBER_PLACEHOLDER, np.nan),
    Link_length_miles = lambda df_:
    df_["Link_length_miles"].replace(NUMBER_PLACEHOLDER, np.nan)
  )
)

print(traffic.shape, traffic_deduped.shape)
```

The output is `(4815504, 35) (4815480, 35)`, where the second pair of values shows us that we have reduced the data down to one row per unique combination of columns in the composite primary key. This feels like a lot of work to remove a few duplicates, but the presence of duplicates can cause multiple problems with analysis, so it is best to address them.

Figure 8.8 shows the latest version of our process, including the steps we have just taken to merge duplicate records.

So far, we've investigated and handled missing data and ensured we understand its granularity. Now, it's time to look at the coverage.

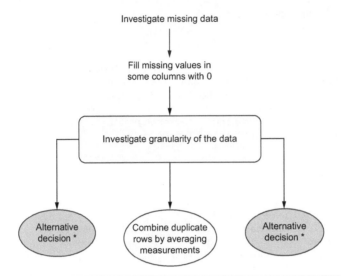

Figure 8.8 The diagram of our analysis two steps in

INVESTIGATING TIME SERIES COVERAGE

When I say we will look at the coverage, in this instance, I mean the date range of values in the data. We've looked briefly at geographic coverage, and now we want to investigate the following:

- What is the date range of the data in general?
- Does the date range vary across smaller time series (e.g., per location)?
- Are there consistent measurement intervals in the data?
- Are there gaps in any of the time series?

Answers to these questions will determine not only the quality of our final analysis but also whether we need to focus on certain parts of the country purely because of a lack of consistent data coverage everywhere. First, let's understand the date range of the data after we convert the Count_date column to be the right type. The output is shown in figure 8.9:

```
traffic["Count_date"] =
➥ pd.to_datetime(traffic["Count_date"], format="%Y-%m-%d %H:%M:%S")
traffic["Count_date"].agg(["min", "max"])
```

```
min   2000-03-17
max   2022-11-02
Name: Count_date, dtype: datetime64[ns]
```

Figure 8.9 The date range of the entire dataset

The output of this code is that the first date encountered in the dataset is March 2000, and the latest is November 2022. We have 20-year coverage, though it remains to be seen whether this is consistent across measuring locations. We want to know

- Does every location have 20 years of data?
- Are there gaps in any of the time series of the different locations?

One way to investigate this is to calculate the first and last date per location, calculate the difference, and investigate the distribution of this difference number. This will tell us how long each location-specific time series is at a glance. The following code achieves this, and the output is shown in figure 8.10:

```
coverage_by_point = (
    traffic
    .groupby("Count_point_id")
    ["Count_date"]
    .agg(["min", "max"])
    .assign(coverage_years = lambda x: (x["max"] - x["min"]).dt.days / 365)
    .sort_values("coverage_years", ascending=False)
)

coverage_by_point
```

Count_point_id	min	max	coverage_years
36583	2000-03-24	2022-10-21	22.591781
57775	2000-03-22	2022-10-13	22.575342
60024	2000-03-21	2022-10-11	22.572603
70222	2000-03-17	2022-10-05	22.567123
38544	2000-03-17	2022-10-03	22.561644
...	...	...	...
940862	2008-10-02	2008-10-02	0.000000
940867	2009-03-20	2009-03-20	0.000000
940868	2008-04-14	2008-04-14	0.000000
940869	2009-09-07	2009-09-07	0.000000
804572	2018-07-12	2018-07-12	0.000000

42517 rows × 3 columns

Figure 8.10 Coverage (in years) by location

This table tells us a few important things:

- *Coverage varies a lot across locations.* There are locations with a single day's worth of measurements and some that have data for the entire 22-year period.
- *Measurement dates vary.* This wasn't obvious looking at the data initially, but it turns out there is no consistent start or end point for any of the measurement time series.

To get a better sense of the distribution of these values, let's create a histogram. The following code produces the histogram in figure 8.11:

```
fig, axis = plt.subplots()

coverage_by_point["coverage_years"].hist(bins=50, ax=axis)

axis.set(
    title="Distribution of coverage (years) by location",
    xlabel="Date range (number of years)",
    ylabel="Frequency"
)

plt.show()
```

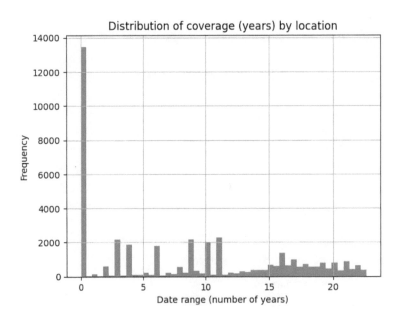

Figure 8.11 Histogram showing coverage in years across different locations

It looks like locations overwhelmingly have a coverage of near zero. That is, most locations only have one day of measurement to their name. This presents a problem because the data in those locations does not constitute much of a time series, except for hourly measurements on a single day. That's not enough data to draw much insight from. Again, we are facing the following choice:

- Do we include locations with only one day of measurements? Doing so means we don't lose a lot of coverage, but we also can't answer questions about increasing trends in those areas.
- Do we focus only on locations with enough data? This will mean we have more robust results but for far fewer locations and areas.

This is a good decision point to remind ourselves of our framework. We want to be results driven and have the research question at the forefront of our minds. We will likely need to follow up our recommendations with further work and certainly wouldn't want to base any infrastructure decisions on sparse data. On that basis, we will seek to trim down the data to keep only the time series that have the most data, the highest coverage, and no gaps.

> **NOTE**   This is one of those decisions that will drastically affect how different our solutions will be. If your results don't match mine, do not assume it is because you have made a mistake. We might have just made different decisions, leading to different results. As long as those decisions and their key assumptions are documented, different results may be equally valuable and useful.

Whenever we investigate missing data, we want to know whether there are any patterns in the gaps. Is any specific factor causing a part of our data to be missing? In this instance, we are working with low coverage instead of missing data, but the idea holds. Let's investigate whether there are certain areas of the country that have less coverage. Why could this be?

- Some locations may have been added to the "traffic measurement program" later than others.
- There might be logistic difficulties with measuring in certain locations.
- New roads have been built around newly built housing estates, and measurements could not have started at an earlier date.

Whatever the reason, we want to know whether low coverage is randomly distributed across the country or whether there is a pattern we should be aware of. Let's use the table from figure 8.10 to focus on location points with only one day of data. We will drop duplicate rows for the same location ID because we want to look at how they are distributed and not at their granular measurements. Figure 8.12 shows the number of locations with only one day of coverage, split by region, as obtained by the following code:

Locations with only one day of measurements are referred to as "zero" because the difference between the first and last measurement dates is zero.

```
zero_location_ids = coverage_by_point
    [coverage_by_point["coverage_years"] == 0].index

zero_locations = (
    traffic[traffic["Count_point_id"].isin(zero_location_ids)]
    .drop_duplicates("Count_point_id")
)
```

```
print(len(zero_locations))
zero_locations["Region_name"].value_counts()
```

```
South East                    1906
East of England               1724
South West                    1656
North West                    1571
Yorkshire and the Humber      1262
West Midlands                 1256
East Midlands                 1089
Scotland                       942
London                         829
North East                     713
Wales                          512
Name: Region_name, dtype: int64
```

Figure 8.12   **Number of locations with one day of data across regions**

There is variation here, but we must not fall into the trap of using absolute numbers to make a judgment. It might simply be that the South East has more single-day locations than Wales because there are more location points. Let's calculate these as a percentage of the total number of locations in each region to get a fair comparison.

First, we calculate the number of location points by region and then use that number to calculate the numbers in figure 8.12 as a percentage. The following code calculates the locations by region, as shown in figure 8.13:

```
location_sizes = (
    traffic
    .groupby("Region_name")
    ["Count_point_id"]
    .nunique()
)
```

```
Region_name
East Midlands                 3405
East of England               4666
London                        3329
North East                    2022
North West                    5063
Scotland                      3376
South East                    6097
South West                    4451
Wales                         2338
West Midlands                 4132
Yorkshire and the Humber      3642
Name: Count_point_id, dtype: int64
```

Figure 8.13   **Number of count points by region**

The following code joins the two tables together and produces the output table shown in figure 8.14:

```
(
    location_sizes
    .reset_index()
    .merge(
        zero_locations["Region_name"]
            .value_counts()
            .reset_index(name="count")
            .rename(columns={"index": "Region_name"}),
        on="Region_name"
    )
    .rename(columns={
        "Count_point_id": "total_points",
        "count": "number_of_zeros"
    })
    .assign(pct_zeros = lambda x: x["number_of_zeros"] / x["total_points"])
)
```

	Region_name	total_points	number_of_zeros	pct_zeros
0	East Midlands	3405	1089	0.319824
1	East of England	4666	1724	0.369481
2	London	3329	829	0.249024
3	North East	2022	713	0.352621
4	North West	5063	1571	0.310290
5	Scotland	3376	942	0.279028
6	South East	6097	1906	0.312613
7	South West	4451	1656	0.372051
8	Wales	2338	512	0.218991
9	West Midlands	4132	1256	0.303969
10	Yorkshire and the Humber	3642	1262	0.346513

Figure 8.14   Number of total locations and single-day locations per region

If there was a real problem with single-day locations being limited to only certain regions, we would find considerable variation in this table. As it stands, the percentage of locations that only have data on a single date is consistent across the regions, with only Wales and London being noticeably lower. We could investigate this much deeper, but in the spirit of getting to our result, we will assume we are satisfied that the existence of single-day locations is just something that happens everywhere and is not something to address directly.

Now that we have looked at missing data, granularity, and coverage, let's turn our attention to gaps. Gaps are a problem when it comes to time series, so we want to reduce our data to locations where we can get a longer and complete time series.

INVESTIGATING GAPS IN TIME SERIES

We've established that different locations have tracked data since a different starting point and for varying lengths of time. To identify gaps, we can't just count the number of unique dates seen at a location; we need to calculate the difference between each encountered date and the previously encountered date and flag any cases with more than a one-day gap.

Let's first look at the number of data points per location per date to get an idea whether there might be continuity problems. The following code calculates this and produces the table in figure 8.15:

```
points_and_dates = (
    traffic
    .groupby(["Count_point_id", "Count_date"])
    .size()
    .reset_index()
    .sort_values(["Count_point_id", "Count_date"])
)

points_and_dates.head()
```

	Count_point_id	Count_date	0
0	51	2004-05-21	24
1	51	2012-10-17	24
2	51	2020-10-02	24
3	52	2002-09-24	24
4	52	2011-10-04	24

Figure 8.15 Number of data points per location ID and per date

This table shows us something important. We made an incorrect assumption that measurements are taken daily across a year. The data is daily in its granularity, but there is only one day of measurement data for each year. We hadn't sliced the data in the right way before to find this earlier, but this gives us a clearer picture of what we have.

To understand whether there might be gaps, first, we can check how many unique values there are for the Year column in each location. Those that have 23 are the ones that have measurements in every year between 2000 and 2022, inclusive. We will focus only on locations that have at least 10 years of data, but that's somewhat arbitrary. We could also restrict time series that are complete for the most recent 5 to 10 years. Here, we'll choose completeness over recency, and the following code calculates this and outputs the result in figure 8.16:

```
num_years_by_point = (
    traffic
    .groupby("Count_point_id")
    ["Year"]
```

```
     .nunique()
     .loc[lambda x: x > 10]
     .sort_values(ascending=False)
)

num_years_by_point
```

```
Count_point_id
26010      23
46010      23
46008      23
16008      23
56047      23
           ..
943254     11
943258     11
943260     11
943262     11
942247     11
Name: Year, Length: 4959, dtype: int64
```

Figure 8.16   Distribution of the number of unique calendar years per location

Let's also look at the time series for the first of those locations to get a sense of what a complete time series looks like in our data. The following code produces the plot in figure 8.17:

```
fig, axis = plt.subplots()

LOCATION_ID = "26010"

(
    traffic
    .query(f"Count_point_id == {LOCATION_ID}")
    .groupby("Count_date")
    ["All_motor_vehicles"]
    .sum()
    .plot(ax=axis)
)

axis.set(
    title=f"Number of vehicles over time (location {LOCATION_ID})",
    xlabel="Date",
    ylabel="Number of vehicles (total)"
)

plt.show()
```

This is the total number of vehicles seen at a particular location on the day counting took place each year. There are already some interesting aspects, such as the dip in 2020 due to the COVID-19 lockdowns.

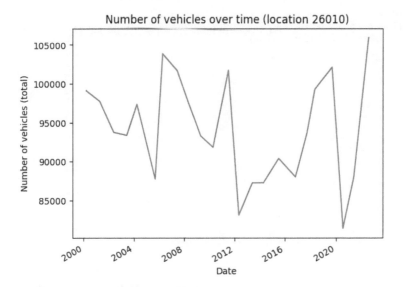

Figure 8.17   An example time series for location 26010

The next step is to filter our location list to only the time series that have no gaps. To do this, we will ensure our data is sorted and create a temporary column to capture the year of the previous row so that we can find instances where the gap between a row and the previous one is more than a year. The following code adds these additional columns, and a snapshot of the new `gaps` DataFrame is shown in figure 8.18:

```
long_count_points = num_years_by_point.index

gaps = (
    traffic
    .query("Count_point_id in @long_count_points")
    [["Count_point_id", "Year"]]
    .drop_duplicates()
    .sort_values(["Count_point_id", "Year"])
    .assign(
        prev_year= lambda x: x["Year"].shift(),
        diff= lambda x: x["Year"] - x["prev_year"]
    )
)

gaps.head()
```

These new columns help us identify places where the previously encountered measurements were from more than one year ago. In the highlighted section of figure 8.18, we can notice that there was no measurement at location ID 501 in the year 2018, so the gap between rows is two years. When the next location ID is encountered,

	Count_point_id	Year	prev_year	diff
2702896	501	2000	NaN	NaN
2526432	501	2001	2000.0	1.0
2320148	501	2002	2001.0	1.0
2642988	501	2004	2002.0	2.0
1444969	501	2006	2004.0	2.0
528811	501	2009	2006.0	3.0
3353634	501	2010	2009.0	1.0
3028085	501	2011	2010.0	1.0
2669418	501	2012	2011.0	1.0
2977261	501	2013	2012.0	1.0
693	501	2014	2013.0	1.0
35044	501	2015	2014.0	1.0
623	501	2016	2015.0	1.0
336999	501	2017	2016.0	1.0
4054701	501	2019	2017.0	2.0
4677828	501	2020	2019.0	1.0
4791625	501	2022	2020.0	2.0
2706196	502	2000	2022.0	-22.0
2556240	502	2001	2000.0	1.0
2296884	502	2002	2001.0	1.0

Figure 8.18 A snapshot of the new gaps DataFrame, with important rows highlighted

the gap can become negative when the last year of the previous location ID is later than the first year of the next location ID.

To identify gaps, we could simply filter this dataset down to where the diff column is greater than 1. However, we might encounter edge cases where the next location ID happens to start two years after the previous one, and we would erroneously mark it as having a gap.

To make sure we filter gaps properly, we also need to track the location ID of the previous column so that when we encounter a gap greater than one year, we also check whether the location ID is still the same. The following code does this, and some of the rows with problematic gaps are shown in figure 8.19:

```
gaps = (
    gaps
    .assign(
```

```
         prev_id= lambda x: x["Count_point_id"].shift()
     )
     .query("diff > 1 and Count_point_id == prev_id")
)

gaps.head()
```

	Count_point_id	Year	prev_year	diff	prev_id
2642988	501	2004	2002.0	2.0	501.0
1444969	501	2006	2004.0	2.0	501.0
528811	501	2009	2006.0	3.0	501.0
4054701	501	2019	2017.0	2.0	501.0
4791625	501	2022	2020.0	2.0	501.0

Figure 8.19 Some of the rows representing problematic gaps in the time series

We can now use this gaps DataFrame to find all the unique location IDs that we want to exclude from our final time series data. This is done with the following code. A part of the resulting DataFrame is shown in figure 8.20:

```
gap_ids = gaps["Count_point_id"].unique()

all_time_series_raw = (
    traffic
    .query("Count_point_id in @long_count_points \
    and Count_point_id not in @gap_ids")
)

all_time_series_raw.head()
```

Figure 8.20 now shows filtered rows from the original, raw traffic DataFrame. It contains only location IDs that have at least 10 years of continuous, gap-free data. Let's now aggregate this to actually be a time series summarized at a location level so that we better understand how much data we are left with. The following code performs this aggregation, and figure 8.21 shows the first few rows of our newly aggregated data:

```
all_time_series = (
    all_time_series_raw
    .groupby(["Count_point_id", "Count_date"])
    ["All_motor_vehicles"]
    .sum()
    .reset_index()
)

print(all_time_series["Count_point_id"].nunique())
all_time_series.head()
```

	Count_point_id	Direction_of_travel	Year	Count_date	hour
2488	931855	E	2016	2016-06-06	7
2489	931855	E	2016	2016-06-06	8
2490	931855	E	2016	2016-06-06	9
2491	931855	E	2016	2016-06-06	10
2492	931855	E	2016	2016-06-06	11

(for clarity, not all columns are shown)

	HGVs_3_or_4_articulated_axle	HGVs_5_articulated_axle	HGVs_6_articulated_axle	All_HGVs	All_motor_vehicles
2488	0.0	0	0.0	1.0	233.0
2489	0.0	1	0.0	7.0	437.0
2490	0.0	0	1.0	5.0	250.0
2491	0.0	0	0.0	2.0	261.0
2492	0.0	0	0.0	4.0	282.0

Figure 8.20   A snapshot of rows from the filtered traffic data

1419

	Count_point_id	Count_date	All_motor_vehicles
0	6003	2000-03-31	87479.0
1	6003	2001-06-25	74103.0
2	6003	2002-05-21	72377.0
3	6003	2003-06-05	91505.0
4	6003	2004-06-16	90564.0

Figure 8.21   A snapshot of filtered traffic data now aggregated as an annual time series

This is now one row per location ID and measurement date. As the top of figure 8.21 shows, we still have data for just over 1,400 unique location IDs. These are now all-time series where there are measurements every year, so it is a time series with no gaps.

To be precise, we have a time series showing the total number of vehicles that passed a count point in a single day in a particular year. There is only one day where measurements take place each year. This is an important detail because it leads to some caveats:

- Figure 8.21 shows that measurements are not taken on the same day each year. If we want to investigate traffic patterns over time, the measurements should at least be taken around the same time of year because, otherwise, we might be comparing summer traffic to winter traffic, for example. One option is to keep only time series where the measurements are consistently taken around the same time of year.

- Following this, whichever part of the year our measurements are taken from will introduce bias. Cycling patterns for locations where only winter measurements exist might not be helpful when cycling is likely reduced everywhere around that time of year.

- If the date *is* the same each year, that might actually be a problem because we might be comparing different days of the week, even weekdays to weekends.

Let's check that last point. What days of the week is the data spread across? The following code investigates this, and the output is shown in figure 8.22:

```
(
    all_time_series_raw[["Count_date"]]
    .drop_duplicates()
    ["Count_date"]
    .dt.weekday
    .value_counts(normalize=True)
    .sort_index()
)
```

```
0     0.186194
1     0.203293
2     0.205193
3     0.200127
4     0.205193
Name: Count_date, dtype: float64
```

Figure 8.22   The percentage of rows across different days of the week

This tells us that roughly 20% of rows are spread across Tuesday to Friday, with slightly less on Mondays. Because we are counting days of the week starting with Monday as zero, we now also know there are no weekends in our remaining data, so that's one concern we've alleviated.

We can still use this data as a proxy for traffic over time to help us hone in on locations that have interesting cycling traffic patterns, but we must be fully aware of the limitations, especially when presenting results to our stakeholders.

Before moving on to the analysis of these time series, our final step is to see what would happen if we were to keep only time series where every measurement was made in the same month each year.

FINDING TIME SERIES RECORDED AT THE SAME TIME EACH YEAR

The following code identifies the location points where measurements were only ever made in the same month every year. Figure 8.23 shows the output:

```
same_month_time_series = (
    all_time_series
    .assign(month=lambda x: x["Count_date"].dt.month)
    .groupby("Count_point_id")
```

```
    ["month"]
    .nunique()
    .loc[lambda x: x == 1]
)

print(len(same_month_time_series))

same_month_time_series.head()
```

```
691
Count_point_id
900056    1
919150    1
930188    1
931832    1
931837    1
Name: month, dtype: int64
```

Figure 8.23   Location IDs where only the same month was encountered

Keeping this filter would halve our data but still leave us just under 700 time series. We should verify that the time series associated with these location IDs do indeed only contain the same month. We'll take the first location ID as an example, but in reality, we'd want to spot-check a few cases. The following code examines the time series for the count point with ID 900056, and the output is shown in figure 8.24.

```
all_time_series[all_time_series["Count_point_id"] == 900056]
```

	Count_point_id	Count_date	All_motor_vehicles
324	900056	2007-05-14	10097.0
325	900056	2008-05-12	10278.0
326	900056	2009-05-11	10367.0
327	900056	2010-05-10	8705.0
328	900056	2011-05-16	7769.0
329	900056	2012-05-14	8435.0
330	900056	2013-05-13	8107.0
331	900056	2014-05-12	8798.0
332	900056	2015-05-11	8896.0
333	900056	2016-05-09	7508.0
334	900056	2017-05-15	7671.0
335	900056	2018-05-14	8818.0
336	900056	2019-05-20	9491.0

Figure 8.24   Time series data for location ID 900056

Figure 8.24 shows that for all 13 years that traffic was counted at location 900056, it was always done in May. This makes the measurements more comparable year on year. Let's now export this data to an intermediate file to separate the cleaning process from the analysis.

EXPORTING ONLY COMPLETE TIME SERIES DATA

Exporting an intermediate version of your data is a good habit to get into, especially if you have a lot of raw data, and cleaning and transforming it takes a bit of time.

We want to keep the raw version of the data filtered down to just the location IDs we have identified. We'll use the Parquet format as it is compact and preserves data types. This file will be the starting point for the analysis in chapter 9. The following code creates this exported file:

```
ids_to_export = same_month_time_series.index

(
    traffic
    .query("Count_point_id in @ids_to_export")
    .to_parquet("time_series.parquet.gz", compression="gzip")
)
```

8.4.2   Project progress so far

Before we move on to the analysis portion of the project in chapter 9, let's recap what we have achieved in this chapter, which was the data preparation part of the project. Here's what we know about our data:

- One row represents measurements taken at a single location, in a single hour on a particular date in a particular direction. A combination of these columns makes a record unique.
- For every location, we have a maximum of one unique day of measurements for a given calendar year.
- The number of years where measurements were taken varies significantly across location IDs. This means there is both inconsistent coverage and gaps in many of our time series.
- Apart from missing roughly half of the road name and length data, there are no significant missing values.

To mitigate some of the problems, we have extracted only locations with the longest and most complete time series to focus on in part 2 of our analysis. Figure 8.25 shows the analysis steps we have taken and the decisions we have made so far.

This diagram documents our process so far, and we will use the output of this chapter, a filtered version of the raw traffic data, as the starting point for the analysis in chapter 9.

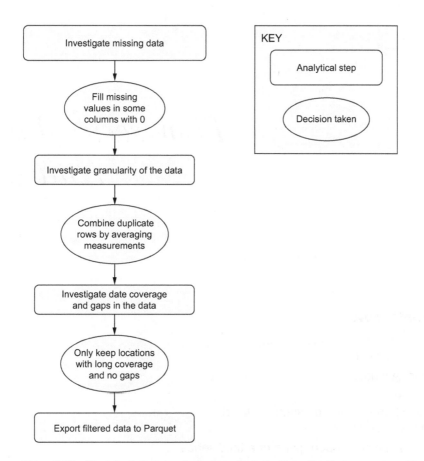

Figure 8.25 The latest diagram of our steps, including investigating coverage and handling gaps

Summary

- Time series data can seem simple yet contain complexity and hidden value.
- Understanding how to manipulate time data broadens your data analysis toolkit.
- The granularity of the available time series determines the analysis we can perform. For example, daily patterns cannot be determined from monthly data.
- Time series analysis works best if there are no gaps in the data.
- If there are gaps, they need to be handled either by smoothing over them or estimating what the values in the gaps should be.

Time series data: *Analysis*

9

In this chapter, we continue exploring the value of time series data. In chapter 8, we explored raw time series data and decided which records to keep before analyzing the time series further. This chapter is about the second part of the process: analyzing time series data to look for patterns, as well as decomposition and forecasting. We will first recap the project brief from the previous chapter and summarize the work done so far before continuing with the analysis.

9.1   Project 6 revisited: Analyzing time series to improve cycling infrastructure

We prepared our data, and it is ready for analysis. But before we start the analysis, let's recap the problem statement and the data dictionary from the previous chapter. The data is available for you to attempt the project yourself at https://davidasboth.com/book-code. You will find the files that you can use for the project, as well as the example solution in the form of a Jupyter notebook. The notebook for this chapter picks up where chapter 8 left off.

9.1.1   Problem statement

You have been hired to work on a new government initiative, Bikes4Britain, which aims to improve cycling infrastructure in the United Kingdom. The aim of the first phase of the project is to identify the most suitable places around the country to improve infrastructure for cyclists. Specifically, your stakeholders are looking for recommendations of places with either already existing or increasing cycling traffic. They want to start with open data sources and have identified the road traffic statistics of the Department for Transport (the homepage is https://roadtraffic.dft.gov.uk) as a way to measure cycling traffic across the country.

> **NOTE:**   The dataset we will use in this project to look for patterns and make recommendations was originally taken from https://roadtraffic.dft.gov.uk/downloads. Thank you to the Department for Transport for making this data available under the Open Government Licence.

The data we are using from the Department for Transport's statistics is the raw count data. This is a record of raw counts of vehicles that passed a particular counting location at various times. Some of the datasets are too high-level, such as area-level annual summaries, and some of them are estimates, such as the estimated annual average daily flows data (AADFs). The raw count dataset contains data at the most granular level, and we can always aggregate it to higher levels (e.g., annual values) if needed.

9.1.2   Data dictionary

The data dictionary document, originally obtained from https://mng.bz/4ajw, is included in the project files, and table 9.1 shows the columns in detail.

Table 9.1   The data dictionary, showing all column definitions

Column name	Definition
Count_point_id	A unique reference for the road link that links the AADFs to the road network
Direction_of_travel	Direction of travel
Year	Counts are shown for each year from 2000 onwards

Table 9.1   The data dictionary, showing all column definitions *(continued)*

Column name	Definition
Count_date	The date when the actual count took place
Hour	The time when the counts in question took place where 7 represents between 7 a.m. and 8 a.m. and 17 represents between 5 p.m. and 6 p.m.
Region_id	Website region identifier
Region_name	The name of the region that the CP sits within
Region_ons_code	The Office for National Statistics code identifier for the region
Local_authority_id	Website local authority identifier
Local_authority_name	The local authority that the CP sits within
Local_authority_code	The Office for National Statistics code identifier for the local authority
Road_name	The road name (for instance, M25 or A3)
Road_category	The classification of the road type (see data definitions for the full list)
Road_type	Whether the road is a 'major' or 'minor' road
Start_junction_road_name	The road name of the start junction of the link
End_junction_road_name	The road name of the end junction of the link
Easting	Easting coordinates of the CP location
Northing	Northing coordinates of the CP location
Latitude	Latitude of the CP location
Longitude	Longitude of the CP location
Link_length_km	Total length of the network road link for that CP (in kilometers)
Link_length_miles	Total length of the network road link for that CP (in miles)
Pedal_cycles	Counts for pedal cycles
Two_wheeled_motor_vehicles	Counts for two-wheeled motor vehicles
Cars_and_taxis	Counts for cars and taxis
Buses_and_coaches	Counts for buses and coaches
LGVs	Counts for LGVs
HGVs_2_rigid_axle	Counts for two-rigid axle HGVs
HGVs_3_rigid_axle	Counts for three-rigid axle HGVs
HGVs_4_or_more_rigid_axle	Counts for four or more rigid axle HGVs
HGVs_3_or_4_articulated_axle	Counts for three- or four-articulated axle HGVs

Table 9.1 **The data dictionary, showing all column definitions** *(continued)*

Column name	Definition
`HGVs_5_articulated_axle`	Counts for five-articulated axle HGVs
`HGVs_6_articulated_axle`	Counts for six-articulated axle HGVs
`All_HGVs`	Counts for all HGVs
`All_motor_vehicles`	Counts for all motor vehicles

In the example solution, we will use a smaller, cleaned, and filtered version of the raw data as a starting point, which we created in chapter 8. This has the same structure as the raw data, so the data dictionary in table 9.1 is still applicable.

9.1.3 *Desired outcomes*

The output of the project is a recommendation of which area, or areas, to concentrate initial efforts on. These might be areas that already have a lot of high cycle traffic, or they might be areas where cycling is on the rise or forecasted to have high cycling demand in the future. Our recommendation will likely contain suggestions to incorporate additional datasets to continue the analysis. There is probably more that we would like to know about these areas before any infrastructure work is undertaken, and we should outline this additional work to our stakeholders.

The output of the example solution from the chapter 8 was an intermediate dataset, which was cleaned and filtered for analysis. The output of the part of the analysis covered by this chapter will be the conclusions and recommendations we set out.

9.2 *Where should cycling infrastructure improvements be focused?*

Before we start analyzing our time series data, let's recap the work we did in the previous chapter to prepare the data for analysis. Figure 9.1 shows the diagram of the work done so far, highlighting where alternative decisions could have been made.

Now, it's time to look at an example walk-through of the analysis portion of the project. As always, I strongly recommend attempting the project yourself first. The example solution will be more relevant if you have your own analysis to compare it to. It bears repeating that the solution is not the solution, just one series of decisions you could make and conclusions you could reach along the way. Use it to generate more ideas and gain a different perspective on how you could have approached the same project brief.

9.2.1 *Analysis of time series data*

So far, we have cleaned up our raw traffic data and filtered it down so that we have a long, complete time series of traffic counts. Now it's time to focus our efforts on the problem at hand by looking specifically at cycling.

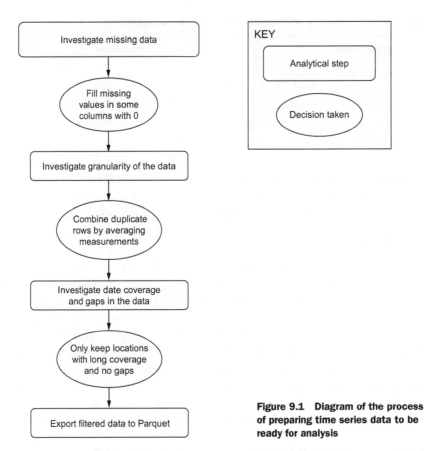

Figure 9.1   **Diagram of the process of preparing time series data to be ready for analysis**

CALCULATING DISTRIBUTIONS IN TIME SERIES DATA

At the end of chapter 8, we exported the data to a Parquet file to separate the data cleaning from the analysis. This section, therefore, begins with reading the same exported data again.

We know that in the data, there was a single day in each calendar year when measurements took place. We want to look at long-term trends, so the hourly granularity introduces noise that we want to remove by summarizing data annually. Let's start there. The following code does this, and a sample of the output is shown in figure 9.2:

```
import pandas as pd
import numpy as np
import matplotlib.pyplot as plt
traffic = pd.read_parquet("./data/time_series.parquet.gz")

cycling = (
    traffic
    .groupby(["Count_point_id", "Year"])
    ["Pedal_cycles"]
    .sum()
```

```
    .reset_index()
)

cycling.head()
```

	Count_point_id	Year	Pedal_cycles
0	900056	2007	24
1	900056	2008	19
2	900056	2009	38
3	900056	2010	17
4	900056	2011	8

Figure 9.2 A snapshot of annual counts of cycles at each location

This data is now one row per location ID per calendar year. Figure 9.2 shows a location with cycling traffic, but there is a possible problem; many of the location IDs might barely have any cycling traffic. To check this, we will look at the distribution of the total number of bicycles seen per location ID across all years. First, we will aggregate the data again to remove the annual values and be left with one row per location ID. This data is created using the following code and shown in figure 9.3:

```
cycling_totals = (
    cycling
    .groupby("Count_point_id")
    ["Pedal_cycles"]
    .sum()
)

cycling_totals.head()
```

```
Count_point_id
900056    259
919150    274
930188    133
931832    351
931837    102
Name: Pedal_cycles, dtype: int64
```

Figure 9.3 Total number of bicycles seen per location ID

Now, we can investigate the distribution of these values to get a feel for just how many locations have little or no cycling traffic. We anticipate the data to be heavily skewed to the right, meaning most values are likely to be around zero with a long tail of higher values. To account for this, we will add more bins to the histogram to hopefully better understand the spread of the data. The following code creates the histogram presented in figure 9.4:

```
fig, axis = plt.subplots()

cycling_totals.hist(bins=50, ax=axis)

axis.set(
    xlabel="Frequency",
    ylabel="Total cycling traffic",
    title="Distribution of total cycling traffic by location ID"
)

plt.show()
```

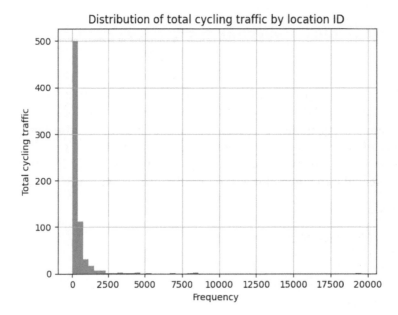

**Figure 9.4
Distribution of total
cycling traffic**

As expected, a lot of locations have recorded almost no cycling traffic. Let's focus on locations with over a certain amount of total cycling traffic. How do we know what value to use as a cutoff (i.e., consider only locations with over X bikes seen over time)? We should understand the quartiles of these values to get a sense of what cutoff values would constitute the top 25% or 50% of the data. The following code does this, and the output is shown in figure 9.5:

```
cycling_totals.describe()
```

This tells us that half of the locations have recorded 216 or more bicycles in total. Since we have focused on locations with at least 10 years of coverage, this translates to between 10 and 20 bicycles on average per measurement date. Whether that is enough traffic to warrant investigation and recommendations will depend on the business, so for this problem, we will make an assumption about what level of traffic is high enough for us to focus on.

```
count         691.000000
mean          455.458755
std          1090.329617
min             5.000000
25%           101.000000
50%           216.000000
75%           421.000000
max         19561.000000
Name: Pedal_cycles, dtype: float64
```

Figure 9.5 Descriptive statistics for the total cycling traffic values

Before we start cutting this data down, let's understand it a bit more. Where, for example, is the most cycling traffic? The following code produces the output in figure 9.6 and shows the top 10 location IDs by cycling traffic:

```
cycling_totals.sort_values(ascending=False).head(10)
```

```
Count_point_id
942489        19561
942321         8542
944649         8344
942319         7932
941061         6668
946751         5319
942951         4468
942735         4439
942853         4427
945985         4034
Name: Pedal_cycles, dtype: int64
```

Figure 9.6 Top 10 location IDs by total cycling traffic

We have a location with over 19,000 bicycles recorded and many more with thousands. Personally, I like to put more context around tables like this, so let's examine the specific location ID at the top of this table.

INVESTIGATING INDIVIDUAL DATA POINTS FOR MORE CONTEXT

Because our data contains many columns, we can use the trick of transposing it to show it as a single column instead. The following code does this, and we can review a single row of data as a vertical table, as shown in figure 9.7. For space reasons, some of the final columns are omitted from the figure but are present in the solution notebook:

```
(
    traffic[traffic["Count_point_id"] == 942489]
    .head(1)
    .transpose()
)
```

This is a minor road of some sort in Islington, which is a borough in North London. Specifically, which road this relates to is not mentioned. There are Road_name and

	91722
Count_point_id	942489
Direction_of_travel	N
Year	2014
Count_date	2014-09-19 00:00:00
hour	7
Region_id	6
Region_name	London
Region_ons_code	E12000007
Local_authority_id	96
Local_authority_name	Islington
Local_authority_code	E09000019
Road_name	U
Road_category	MCU
Road_type	Minor
Start_junction_road_name	None
End_junction_road_name	None
Easting	531449
Northing	182918
Latitude	51.52988
Longitude	-0.106402

Figure 9.7   The location ID with the highest cycling traffic (part of a single row of data transposed as a column)

Road_category columns that should tell us more, but they are not informative here. Let's look at the data dictionary to understand what these specific values mean. As a reminder, the data dictionary is included in the chapter's materials as a PDF. Table 9.2 shows the values we can expect in the Road_category column.

Table 9.2   Data dictionary for the Road_category column

Category	Category description
PM	M or class A principal motorway
PA	Class A principal road

Table 9.2   Data dictionary for the `Road_category` column *(continued)*

Category	Category description
TM	M or class A trunk motorway
TA	Class A trunk road
M	Minor road
MB	Class B road
MCU	Class C or unclassified road

From this, we can gather that the top cycling location is a very minor or unclassified road. A note in the data dictionary says, "Unclassified roads (referred to as 'U' in datasets) include residential roads both in urban and rural situations," so this is likely a residential road since Islington is not a rural location. These are the pieces of additional context you have as an analyst if you have relevant domain knowledge. If in doubt, ask a domain expert.

If we really want to understand a particular location in the data, we have latitude and longitude coordinates we can use. The values for this location are (51.52988, -0.106402), which, when put into a map, show the map point displayed in figure 9.8.

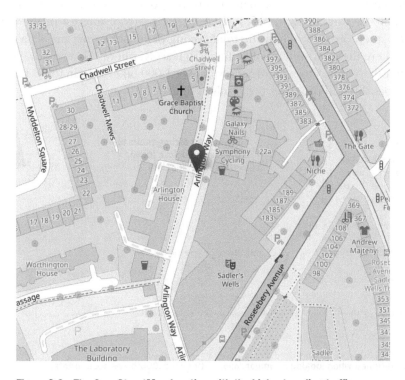

Figure 9.8   The OpenStreetMap location with the highest cycling traffic

Activity: Bring your data to life
In this project, whenever you want to find out more about a location ID, you can find it on a map with its coordinates. I encourage you to find opportunities to do so and even look at them with Google Street View, for example. As analysts, we don't often get the chance to add this much context to our data points, so we should make the most of it!

Without knowing more about this particular location, we can only guess why it has by far the highest cycling traffic in the data. Some ideas include

- It could simply be that the bicycle shop visible on the map, "Symphony Cycling," is on this street.
- This area might be particularly high in cyclists, but perhaps there is nothing special about this residential street, and any surrounding street would have yielded similar results.
- This might be a popular shortcut for cyclists looking to avoid the traffic on the surrounding larger roads on their cycling commute.
- There might be some bias around how counting points are chosen in the first place. Perhaps this location was chosen *because* of its high cycling traffic.

Whatever the reason, this poses many interesting questions, one of which is, is all cycling traffic on minor roads, or are there major roads of interest in the data? To answer this question, we will join the total cycling data back to the raw data and find locations where the total amount of cycling is at least X, where X is a value we set. Let's see whether there were any major roads with over 1,000 bikes seen in total. The following code does this and produces the result in figure 9.9:

```
(
  traffic
  .merge(                          Converts the cycling totals to
    cycling_totals               a DataFrame before joining
      .reset_index()          ◄─┘  to the raw traffic data
      .rename(columns={
        "Pedal_cycles": "Total_cycles"
      }),
    on="Count_point_id"
  )
  .query("Total_cycles > 1000 and Road_type=='Major'")
)
```

Count_point_id	Direction_of_travel	Year	Count_date	hour	Region_id	Region_name	Region_ons_code	Local_authority_id

0 rows × 36 columns

Figure 9.9   No rows returned when looking for major roads with over 1,000 bikes seen in total

This tells us that there are no instances of major roads where over 1000 bikes are seen in total. What if we lower that threshold to 100? This means major roads with only 5–10 bikes seen in a given day on average. The following code does this and produces the result in figure 9.10:

```
bikes_100_plus = (
    traffic
    .merge(
        cycling_totals
            .reset_index()
            .rename(columns={"Pedal_cycles": "Total_cycles"}),
        on="Count_point_id"
    )
    .query("Total_cycles > 100 and Road_type=='Major'")
)

bikes_100_plus
```

Count_point_id	Direction_of_travel	Year	Count_date	hour	Region_id	Region_name	Region_ons_code	Local_authority_id

0 rows × 36 columns

Figure 9.10   Traffic data for locations on major roads with over 100 total bikes seen

Even when we only consider 100 bikes in total, there does not seem to be bike traffic on major roads, at least not in the cut-down version of the data we are using. It is therefore likely that, in this analysis, we will not focus on recommending improvements to the cycling infrastructure along major roads. However, perhaps the lack of cycling traffic is an interesting finding itself—something to discuss with our stakeholders as a deeper investigation into how cyclists are having to circumvent major roads may be interesting to them.

Let's add our investigation into the distribution of cycling traffic to our analysis diagram, the latest version of which is shown in figure 9.11.

Focusing on the data at hand, let's now start looking at locations of interest based on their cycling traffic patterns, starting with locations where cycling has increased since data was first captured.

FINDING TIME SERIES THAT CONTAIN UPWARD TRENDS

Our first step is to define what we mean by "on the rise." Do we want to see cycling increase year-on-year consistently for a location to qualify? Since we only have a day's worth of data each year, there will be noise, so this criterion might be too strict. Let's look for locations where the latest measurement figure was higher than the first. It's a crude proxy for "increase in cycling," but we can filter the data down to the locations with the largest increase.

To achieve this, we need to take the rows for each location ID separately, ensure they are in chronological order, and then take the difference between the first and

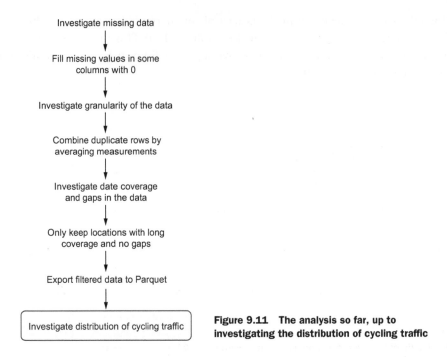

Figure 9.11   The analysis so far, up to investigating the distribution of cycling traffic

last rows. We should calculate both absolute and percentage changes to sanity-check our results. We also need to account for division by zero errors when calculating percentage change. The following code calculates both absolute and percentage change between the first and last values for each location, ending up with the dataset shown in figure 9.12:

```
def cycling_diff(group):
    return group.values[-1] - group.values[0]
```
Defines a function to calculate the difference between the first and last values encountered in a group

```
def cycling_diff_pct(group):
    if group.values[0] == 0:
        return np.inf
    diff = group.values[-1] - group.values[0]
    return diff / group.values[0]
```
Defines a function to calculate the change as a percentage

Accounts for division-by-zero errors

```
cycling_diffs = (
    cycling
    .sort_values(["Count_point_id", "Year"])
    .groupby("Count_point_id")
    .agg(
        diff=("Pedal_cycles",cycling_diff),
        diff_pct=("Pedal_cycles",cycling_diff_pct)
    )
)

cycling_diffs
```
Applies these two functions to every location ID group

	diff	diff_pct
Count_point_id		
900056	-10	-0.416667
919150	-1	-0.083333
930188	-2	-0.400000
931832	-10	-0.526316
931837	2	0.666667
...	...	...
990173	23	0.425926
990546	-17	-0.944444
990551	4	0.173913
990552	38	19.000000
996188	12	4.000000

691 rows × 2 columns

Figure 9.12 Absolute and percentage difference of cycling totals for each location

We have a variety of results here. There will be infinite values where the first measurement date yielded no bicycles, as well as instances of both positive and negative change over time. Before investigating this table further, it's a good idea to verify our calculations. Let's look at one of the locations and see if the raw data supports the change values we calculated. The following code does this to produce the result in figure 9.13:

```
cycling[cycling["Count_point_id"] == 900056]
```

We found that in 2007, there were 24 bicycles encountered and only 14 in 2019, which is a reduction of 42%, which figure 9.12 also shows. We can spot-check a few more examples to convince ourselves that our calculations are correct. Then, we can look at some of the highest increases in cycling traffic in percentage terms. The following code does this and produces the table in figure 9.14:

```
biggest_diffs = (
    cycling_diffs
    [np.isinf(cycling_diffs["diff_pct"]) == False]      ◁─┐ Removes infinity
    .sort_values("diff_pct", ascending=False)             │ values from
    .head(10)                                             │ consideration
)

biggest_diffs
```

	Count_point_id	Year	Pedal_cycles
0	900056	2007	24
1	900056	2008	19
2	900056	2009	38
3	900056	2010	17
4	900056	2011	8
5	900056	2012	23
6	900056	2013	5
7	900056	2014	19
8	900056	2015	13
9	900056	2016	32
10	900056	2017	14
11	900056	2018	33
12	900056	2019	14

Figure 9.13   Raw annual cycling data for location 900056

Count_point_id	diff	diff_pct
931883	29	29.000
990552	38	19.000
943399	139	17.375
944961	16	16.000
943595	14	14.000
947607	14	14.000
946565	24	12.000
946375	12	12.000
943535	21	10.500
949735	10	10.000

Figure 9.14   The locations with the highest percentage change in cycling

> **WARNING** When encountering division-by-zero scenarios, make sure you understand how your chosen tool represents infinity. In `pandas`, we use `np.inf`, a specific value from the `numpy` library. It is considered greater than all other integers when sorting, so in this instance, we make sure to remove those rows from consideration before sorting.

We have some interesting cases to investigate. It's time to plot these time series rather than relying on numeric calculations to determine interesting patterns. The following code produces the plot in figure 9.15. I have included only a few of the time series for clarity:

```
fig, axis = plt.subplots(figsize=(10, 6))

biggest_diff_ids = biggest_diffs.index

ids_to_plot = [943399, 931883, 946565, 990552]

diffs_to_plot = (
    cycling
    .query("Count_point_id in @ids_to_plot")
)

markers = ["o", "s", "P", "^"]

for i, point_id in enumerate(diffs_to_plot["Count_point_id"].unique()):
    point_series = cycling[cycling["Count_point_id"] == point_id]
    (
        point_series
        .set_index("Year")
        ["Pedal_cycles"]
        .plot(ax=axis,
              label=point_id,
              marker=markers[i],
              alpha=0.8)
    )

axis.set(
    xlabel="Year",
    ylabel="Pedal cycles encountered",
    title="Cycling traffic for locations with the highest increase"
)

axis.legend()

plt.show()
```

This shows that there are genuine increases in cycling traffic at various locations. We should, however, look at this problem from different angles because the nature of our data—the fact that we count vehicles on a single day each year—is such that all values

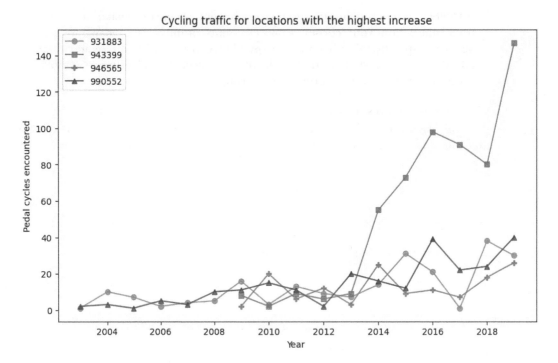

Figure 9.15   Some locations with the highest increase in cycling traffic

are subject to bias. There could be special events such as road closures, public holidays, or just varying patterns across weekdays that could explain these increases. Let's add this latest step to our growing analysis diagram, shown in figure 9.16.

Another angle we could consider is finding locations where cycling makes up a significant percentage of overall traffic.

IDENTIFYING TIME SERIES WITH CERTAIN CHARACTERISTICS

Let's look at how we can calculate cycling as a percentage of overall traffic. We've been using the `Pedal_cycles` column to count cyclists and `All_motor_vehicles` to count all traffic. However, the phrase "motor vehicles" suggests that perhaps bikes aren't included. This is something we need to verify before calculating anything. The data dictionary in table 8.1 doesn't answer this question as it just says that the column measures "counts for all motor vehicles." Fortunately, the PDF version includes more information. Page 10 contains a section called "Types of vehicle," under which there is the following: "All motor vehicles: All vehicles except pedal cycles." Figure 9.17 shows the relevant section of the document.

As suspected, to get the total number of vehicles seen, including bikes, we need to add those columns together. We also want to weight recent observations, so we will only take the last date for each location point. In some cases, this may be a few years in

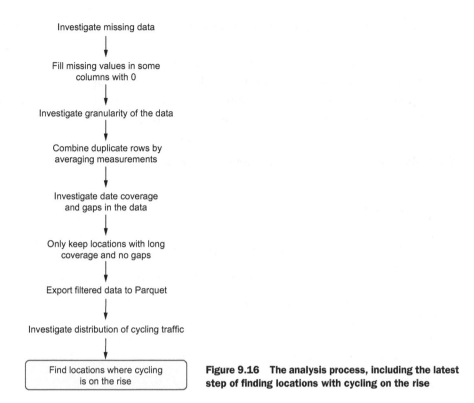

Figure 9.16 The analysis process, including the latest step of finding locations with cycling on the rise

Types of vehicle

Category	Category Description
All_MV	All Motor Vehicles
2WMV	Two-wheeled motor vehicles (e.g. motorcycles etc)
Car	Cars and Taxis
LGV	Light Goods Vans
HGV	Heavy Goods Vehicle total
HGVR2	2-rigid axle Heavy Goods Vehicle
HGVR3	3-rigid axle Heavy Goods Vehicle
HGVR4	4 or more rigid axle Heavy Goods Vehicle
HGVA3	3 and 4-articulated axle Heavy Goods Vehicle
HGVA5	5-articulated axle Heavy Goods Vehicle
HGVA6	6 or more articulated axle Heavy Goods Vehicle
PC	Pedal Cycles

The definitions for the vehicle types included in the traffic census are as follows:

All motor vehicles: All vehicles except pedal cycles.

Figure 9.17 A screenshot of the part of the data dictionary referring to what "all motor vehicles" means

the past, but it will at least give us only the most recent data. The steps in the following code are as follows:

1 Filter the traffic data to the *last observed date for each location ID.*
2 *Calculate the total traffic* by adding the relevant columns together.
3 *Group the data by location ID* to reduce the granularity to one row per location.
4 *Sum* the total traffic column and the bikes column.
5 *Calculate cycling as a percentage* for each location.

What follows is Python code for this, and a snapshot of the resulting dataset is shown in figure 9.18:

```
annual_bike_traffic = (
    traffic
    [traffic['Count_date']
 == traffic.groupby('Count_point_id')['Count_date'].transform('max')]
    .assign(
        all_traffic=lambda x: x["Pedal_cycles"] + x["All_motor_vehicles"]
    )
    .groupby(["Count_point_id", "Year"])
    [["Pedal_cycles", "all_traffic"]]
    .sum()
    .assign(
        pct_cycles = lambda x: x["Pedal_cycles"] / x["all_traffic"]
    )
    .sort_values("pct_cycles", ascending=False)
)

annual_bike_traffic.head()
```

Count_point_id	Year	Pedal_cycles	all_traffic	pct_cycles
942489	2019	1748	2004.0	0.872255
945923	2019	352	522.0	0.674330
941061	2019	769	1466.0	0.524557
945955	2019	245	684.0	0.358187
944077	2019	64	183.0	0.349727

Figure 9.18   Total traffic and cycling as an absolute and percentage value for each location

Figure 9.18 shows each location ID, the most recent year for which we have data, and the traffic calculations, including the percentage of traffic attributed to cycling. We can already notice some locations with a high percentage of cycling traffic. Let's investigate one of those examples in more detail. We will zoom in on just the first row from figure 9.18 and identify its location. The output is shown in figure 9.19.

```
(
  traffic[(traffic["Count_point_id"] == 942489)
    & (traffic["Year"] == 2019)]
  .head(1)
  .transpose()
)
```

	4337551
Count_point_id	942489
Direction_of_travel	S
Year	2019
Count_date	2019-09-20 00:00:00
hour	9
Region_id	6
Region_name	London
Region_ons_code	E12000007
Local_authority_id	96
Local_authority_name	Islington
Local_authority_code	E09000019
Road_name	U
Road_category	MCU
Road_type	Minor
Start_junction_road_name	None
End_junction_road_name	None
Easting	531449
Northing	182918
Latitude	51.529879
Longitude	-0.106402

Figure 9.19 A specific location with a high cycling traffic percentage

If we looked at this point on a map, we would find the same location we saw in figure 9.7. This is in fact the same suburban street in Islington, North London, that had the highest volume of cycling traffic in absolute terms. It's useful to see the same result verified from a different angle.

> **NOTE** Take a minute to look into some of the other locations that came up with high cycling traffic in the table produced in figure 9.6. Do you notice any patterns?

Looking at some of these locations, we see they all seem to be small suburban streets, perhaps being used as commuting shortcuts. Figure 9.20 shows the process so far, highlighting the fact that we are doing some investigations in parallel, with the results coming together at the end.

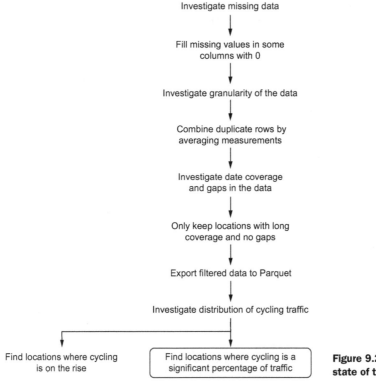

Figure 9.20   The current state of the analysis

Following our train of thought about some of these top locations, commuter pathways seem like a useful avenue to explore further, so let's move our focus to that.

IDENTIFYING TEMPORAL PATTERNS WITHIN TIME SERIES

To investigate commuting patterns, we will do two things:

- Look at the most popular times of day for cycling at each location. In other words, what hour(s) of the day do people cycle the most?
- Once we understand this, we will identify locations where cycling traffic is highest during commuting hours.

The first item requires us to calculate the average cycling traffic per hour. We can decide whether to average the results across all years of data or keep focusing on only the latest figures. Both approaches have pros and cons. Averaging across the entire data will negate possible changes in behavior over time if people don't commute by bicycle the same way they did 10–20 years ago. Using only the most recent data means we amplify any particular biases that may have occurred that year (e.g., road closures that were otherwise not present). We still want to bias toward recency, so we will go with the latter option. A more sophisticated idea might be to perform a weighted average over time, weighting recent measurements higher than older ones.

What does this particular calculation process look like? We will perform the following steps:

1 *Filter the cycling data to the most recent year for each location*—This will give us an up-to-date view on cycling patterns.
2 *Calculate the percentage of bike traffic that occurred in each hour of the day*—Using a percentage means comparable results regardless of the popularity of the location.
3 *Visualize the distribution of these percentage values by hour*—Using our "start at the end" approach, we imagine the final visualization. In this case, it will be a series of box plots, each representing an hour of the day and individual points representing the percentage of bike traffic in that hour of the day for a location.

From a technical perspective, the tricky point here is the first step. We need to count the total amount of cycling traffic per location while simultaneously comparing hourly values to that daily total. This requires us to have both hourly and daily values side by side. If you are a SQL user, this would be achieved with a *window function* using the `PARTITION BY` keyword. In `pandas`, we need to do something slightly different, in fact, so different that we can enlist the help of our favorite LLM.

I asked ChatGPT how to achieve this, and its first result suggested calculating hourly and daily totals separately and then joining the two tables by location ID. This is a perfectly good approach, but I specifically asked about using a window function-like approach. Figure 9.21 shows the part of the conversation where I steered ChatGPT to the result I wanted.

You

OK so I see you calculated the daily total first, then joined it back to the raw data.

Is there a way to do this in one go, like you would with window functions and the PARTITION BY operator in SQL? Or does pandas not support that?

ChatGPT

Yes, you can achieve this in one go using pandas by applying a window function-like operation with the "**transform**" method. You can partition the data by 'LocationID' and then calculate the total count for each date within each partition. Here's the code to do that:

Figure 9.21   A snippet of a conversation with ChatGPT about window functions in `pandas`

Therefore, we can use the `transform` method to achieve the desired result, which is to create a column alongside the raw data that captures the total daily cycling traffic for each location ID. Let's first filter our traffic to include only the most recent date for each location:

```
traffic_max_dates = (
    traffic[
        traffic['Count_date']
        == traffic.groupby('Count_point_id')['Count_date'].transform('max')
    ]
    .copy()
)
```

We will now aggregate this `traffic_max_dates` DataFrame to one row per location per hour. The following code does this and produces the output in figure 9.22:

```
cycling_daily_hourly = (
    traffic_max_dates.groupby(
        ["Count_point_id", "Count_date", "hour"]
    )
    ["Pedal_cycles"]
    .sum()
    .reset_index()
)

cycling_daily_hourly.head()
```

	Count_point_id	Count_date	hour	Pedal_cycles
0	900056	2019-05-20	7	2
1	900056	2019-05-20	8	0
2	900056	2019-05-20	9	0
3	900056	2019-05-20	10	0
4	900056	2019-05-20	11	2

Figure 9.22   Hourly cycling traffic per location for only the latest date for each location

Now, we need to create a column to measure total cycling traffic alongside this data to be able to calculate the percentage of cycling traffic attributable to each hour of the day for each location. This is where we use the trick that ChatGPT has shown us. The following code adds this column and calculates the percentage of traffic per hour, resulting in the data in figure 9.23:

```
cycling_daily_hourly['TotalDailyCount'] = (
    cycling_daily_hourly
    .groupby(['Count_point_id', 'Count_date'])
    ['Pedal_cycles']
```

```
    .transform('sum')
)
```

Transform calculates the total amount of traffic per location ID, so we can add it as an extra column without requiring an additional join.

```
cycling_daily_hourly['hourly_pct'] = (
    cycling_daily_hourly['Pedal_cycles']
    / cycling_daily_hourly['TotalDailyCount']
)

cycling_daily_hourly
```

	Count_point_id	Count_date	hour	Pedal_cycles	TotalDailyCount	hourly_pct
0	900056	2019-05-20	7	2	14	0.142857
1	900056	2019-05-20	8	0	14	0.000000
2	900056	2019-05-20	9	0	14	0.000000
3	900056	2019-05-20	10	0	14	0.000000
4	900056	2019-05-20	11	2	14	0.142857
...	...	...	...	...	...	...
8287	996188	2019-05-23	14	0	15	0.000000
8288	996188	2019-05-23	15	2	15	0.133333
8289	996188	2019-05-23	16	1	15	0.066667
8290	996188	2019-05-23	17	2	15	0.133333
8291	996188	2019-05-23	18	0	15	0.000000

8292 rows × 6 columns

Figure 9.23 Hourly data with additional percentage calculations appended

This is an instance where we want to verify those daily counts and percentage values before continuing. Let's look at that first example, location 900056. First, we calculate the latest date for that location from the raw data to ensure we have the right data:

```
traffic_max_dates.loc[
    traffic_max_dates["Count_point_id"] == 900056, "Count_date"].max()
```

The output is 2019-05-20, which tallies with the table in figure 9.23. Now, we want to look at all the raw data for that location ID and date to see whether the total cycling count really was 14 and, therefore, whether the percentages are also correct. The following code finds the raw data, which is shown in figure 9.24:

```
(
    cycling_daily_hourly
    [
```

```
        (cycling_daily_hourly["Count_point_id"] == 900056)
        & (cycling_daily_hourly["Count_date"] == "2019-05-20")
    ]
)
```

	Count_point_id	Count_date	hour	Pedal_cycles	TotalDailyCount	hourly_pct
0	900056	2019-05-20	7	2	14	0.142857
1	900056	2019-05-20	8	0	14	0.000000
2	900056	2019-05-20	9	0	14	0.000000
3	900056	2019-05-20	10	0	14	0.000000
4	900056	2019-05-20	11	2	14	0.142857
5	900056	2019-05-20	12	0	14	0.000000
6	900056	2019-05-20	13	0	14	0.000000
7	900056	2019-05-20	14	2	14	0.142857
8	900056	2019-05-20	15	0	14	0.000000
9	900056	2019-05-20	16	1	14	0.071429
10	900056	2019-05-20	17	5	14	0.357143
11	900056	2019-05-20	18	2	14	0.142857

Figure 9.24   Raw data used to verify calculations of hourly cycling traffic percentages

From this raw data, we can notice that adding up the `Pedal_cycles` column matches the total, and the percentages in the `hourly_pct` column are also correct. To summarize, we found that around a third of cycling traffic at this location is seen between 5 p.m. and 6 p.m., and the rest is scattered throughout the day. We can use this data across all location IDs to identify what percentage of cycling traffic is seen at different hours of the day in the box plot we imagined earlier. The following code creates the box plot shown in figure 9.25:

```
fig, axis = plt.subplots()

cycling_daily_hourly.boxplot(
    column="hourly_pct",
    by="hour",
    ax=axis)

axis.set(
    xlabel="Hour",
    ylabel= "% of cycling traffic in an hour",
    title="What times of the day does most cycling traffic occur?"
)
```

```
plt.suptitle(None)
```

```
plt.show()
```

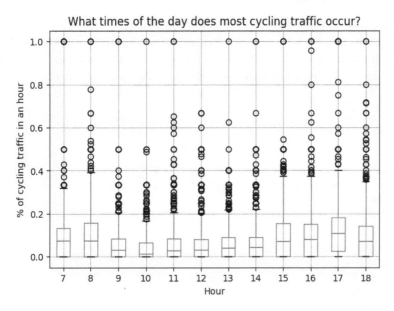

Figure 9.25   **Box plots showing how cycling traffic is distributed throughout the hours of the day**

There is a lot of noise and outliers in these box plots, but if we focus on the median lines, the middles of the boxes, we notice that there is a rise in traffic approaching 5 p.m. as well as a peak at 8 a.m. followed by a sharp drop. This tells us that there is a commuting pattern in the data as a higher percentage of cycling traffic occurs between 8 a.m. and 9 a.m., as well as between 5 p.m. and 6 p.m. The closeness of the medians between 3 p.m. and 6 p.m. also suggests that while people generally commute *to work* at the same time, the times at which people commute *from work* vary more.

Equipped with this knowledge, we can now find locations where the highest percentage of cycling traffic occurs during commuting hours. We can think of these as "commuting hotspots"—areas where a significant proportion of cycling traffic is commute driven. We already have data aggregated at the hourly level, shown in figure 9.23, so from that, we can find the hour with the highest cycling traffic for each cycling location. There are a couple of edge cases to make decisions on first:

- What happens if all cycling traffic is zero? We should probably output a missing value to show that this particular operation doesn't make sense for that location.
- What if there are multiple hours with the same amount of cycling traffic? We could either take the first or last hour we encounter the maximum value or

average the results somehow. Averaging two different hours of the day doesn't sound meaningful, so we will make the decision to use the first hour where we encounter the maximum value. That is, if the highest cycling traffic is at 8 a.m. and 1 p.m., we output 8 a.m.

The following code defines a function to calculate the highest hour for a given group, that is, a single location ID, then uses it to create a dataset with one row per location ID containing the hour in which cycling traffic was highest in the last recorded measurement year. A snapshot of this aggregated data is shown in figure 9.26:

```python
def get_highest_hour(rows):
    if rows["Pedal_cycles"].min() == rows["Pedal_cycles"].max():
        return np.nan

    return (
        rows
        .sort_values(by=["Pedal_cycles", "hour"], ascending=[False, True])
        .head(1)
        ["hour"]
        .values[0]
    )

highest_hours = (
    cycling_daily_hourly
    .groupby("Count_point_id")
    .apply(get_highest_hour)
)

highest_hours.head()
```

```
Count_point_id
900056    17.0
919150    17.0
930188    18.0
931832    16.0
931837     8.0
dtype: float64
```

Figure 9.26   Highest hour of cycling traffic per location ID

We may find a few instances of missing values where the lowest and highest cycling volume was the same, including when it was zero throughout. In figure 9.26, however, we see examples of an actual highest hour being output. One scenario we need to account for is cases where we need a tiebreak because the highest cycling traffic occurred in multiple hours. The following code retrieves raw data for such an example, which is shown in figure 9.27:

```python
cycling_daily_hourly[cycling_daily_hourly["Count_point_id"] == 941463]
```

	Count_point_id	Count_date	hour	Pedal_cycles	TotalDailyCount	hourly_pct
1476	941463	2019-09-10	7	8	53	0.150943
1477	941463	2019-09-10	8	10	53	0.188679
1478	941463	2019-09-10	9	3	53	0.056604
1479	941463	2019-09-10	10	4	53	0.075472
1480	941463	2019-09-10	11	1	53	0.018868
1481	941463	2019-09-10	12	1	53	0.018868
1482	941463	2019-09-10	13	2	53	0.037736
1483	941463	2019-09-10	14	2	53	0.037736
1484	941463	2019-09-10	15	3	53	0.056604
1485	941463	2019-09-10	16	10	53	0.188679
1486	941463	2019-09-10	17	7	53	0.132075
1487	941463	2019-09-10	18	2	53	0.037736

Figure 9.27 Hourly data for location 941463 showing that both hour values 8 and 16 had the highest cycling traffic

Because, inside our function, we sorted our data in ascending order of cycling traffic, and in ascending order by hour, we returned the earliest instance of encountering the highest traffic. We may choose to do something about this explicitly or accept that there may be a slight bias toward earlier times when calculating which hour is the busiest by location. We will do the latter in this instance because the occurrence of a tie is likely not that common.

If we look at the distribution of the busiest hours, we will be able to see at what time most locations have their cycling traffic peaks. The following code creates the histogram shown in figure 9.28:

```
fig, axis = plt.subplots()

highest_hours.hist(bins=20, ax=axis)

axis.set(
    xlabel="Hour of peak cycling traffic",
    ylabel="Frequency",
    title="Distribution of peak cycling traffic hours across locations"
)

plt.show()
```

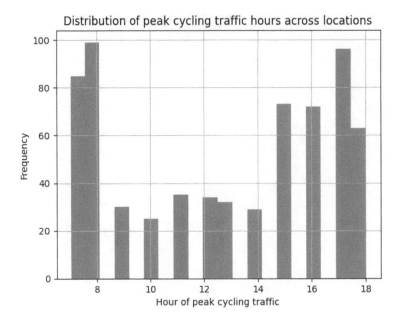

Figure 9.28   Distribution of peak cycling hours across locations

This plot reinforces the idea that most locations have their peak cycling traffic during commuter hours. Let's summarize what we've learned so far about cycling patterns:

- There is variation in cycling trends, but most importantly, there are multiple locations with increased cycling traffic over time.
- There is also variation in what percentage of traffic is cycling, but crucially, there are locations where cycling is the majority of traffic.
- There is also variation in when people cycle, but there are locations with commuting patterns of cycling traffic.
- Following on from that, there are locations where commuting hours are the busiest for cycling.

Each of these criteria could be used to find places of interest with respect to cycling. How do we decide which criterion makes sense?

> **NOTE**   If you're interested in examples of where "deciding what is best" is the primary goal, see chapter 4, which is all about choosing the right metrics.

We would need to use domain knowledge and talk to stakeholders to get a true sense of this, but for now, there doesn't seem to be a good reason not to use all these criteria. Because we are trying to filter our locations down to the ones of most interest, let's try finding locations that match all those criteria, specifically,

- Locations where the percentage of cycling traffic is high, that is, at least X%, where we have to define X
- Locations where there has been an increase in cycling traffic, that is, an increase of at least Y% where we have to define Y
- Locations where cycling is used for commuting, that is, peak cycling traffic is either 8 a.m.–9 a.m. or 5 p.m.–6 p.m.

If applying all these criteria yields too few results, we can always broaden them by looking for afternoon commuting times between 4 p.m. and 7 p.m., for example. Before combining our results to find cycling locations of interest, let's recap the process. Figure 9.29 shows the latest state of the analysis.

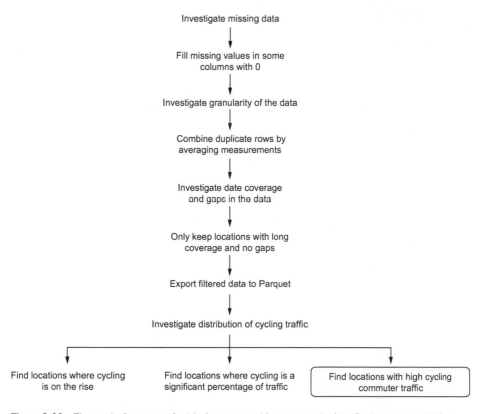

Figure 9.29 The analysis process just before we combine our results into final recommendations

Let's apply the different criteria we determined we would use to select locations of interest and see if we find anything.

COMBINING CRITERIA TO IDENTIFY TIME SERIES OF INTEREST

To find locations that match multiple criteria, we could either perform a single, large query with multiple filters or create filtered versions of each criterion and combine them at the end. We will prefer the latter approach because it allows us to investigate each subset separately. This might be useful if we find nothing is returned and want to investigate which criterion is too strict and yields no results.

Let's first filter the locations to keep only those with a significant percentage of traffic being cycling. How do we know what percentage to use as a cutoff? We haven't actually looked at the distribution of this percentage yet, so we'll start there, and the resulting histogram will show us where the majority of the data lies. The following code creates the histogram in figure 9.30, which we will use to make this decision. We will use a DataFrame we have already created, which we called `annual_bike_traffic`, that contains the percentage of traffic attributed to cycling in the latest year:

```
fig, axis = plt.subplots()

annual_bike_traffic["pct_cycles"].hist(bins=10, ax=axis)

axis.set(
    xlabel="Percentage of traffic that is cycling",
    ylabel="Frequency",
    title="Distribution of cycling traffic percentages"
)

plt.show()
```

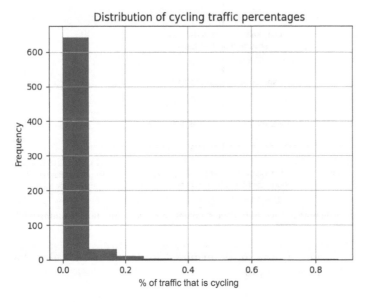

Figure 9.30   Distribution of the percentage of traffic due to cycling at each location

This histogram shows that most locations have under 10% of their traffic due to cycling. That feels like a good cutoff to distinguish areas of significant cycling traffic. The following code implements this filter and creates a filtered list of location IDs, a snapshot of which is shown in figure 9.31:

```
BIKE_PERCENTAGE_CUTOFF = 0.1

highest_cycling = (
    annual_bike_traffic
    [annual_bike_traffic["pct_cycles"] >= BIKE_PERCENTAGE_CUTOFF]
    .reset_index()
    ["Count_point_id"]
    .to_list()
)

print(len(highest_cycling))

highest_cycling[:10]
```

```
38
[942489, 945923, 941061, 945955, 944077, 945393, 931932, 941045, 946765, 942487]
```

Figure 9.31 Location IDs with significant cycling traffic

This shows there are 38 locations with at least 10% of traffic due to cycling. Now, we want to create a similar list of locations, but this time, locations that had at least a Y% increase in cycling between the first and last dates we measured. The value for Y will be somewhat arbitrary, and we may decide to tweak it if we want to return more locations. We will start with 50% and see what that gets us. The following code creates this filtered list, which yields a list of numbers similar to that shown in figure 9.31. Again, we already have the underlying values calculated from a previous DataFrame, `cycling_diffs`:

```
DIFF_CUTOFF = 0.5

biggest_increases = (
    cycling_diffs
    [(cycling_diffs["diff_pct"] >= DIFF_CUTOFF)
    & (np.isinf(cycling_diffs["diff_pct"]) == False)]    ◁──┐  We need to
    .index                                                    exclude infinity
    .to_list()                                                values, so they
)                                                             don't show up in
                                                              calculations.
print(len(biggest_increases))

print(biggest_increases[:10])
```

The result of this code tells us there are 230 such locations. Finally, we will create a third list of locations, which will be locations where the highest commuting time is either

8 a.m.–9 a.m. or 5 p.m.–6 p.m. The following code does this using the `highest_hours` DataFrame created earlier:

```
highest_commuting = (
    highest_hours
    .loc[lambda x: x.isin([8, 17])]
    .index
    .to_list()
)

print(len(highest_commuting))

print(highest_commuting[:10])
```

The output is a list of 195 locations. We now have three lists of locations to combine. What we want to know is which location IDs appear in all three lists. In Python, we can do this quite easily using set theory. In this case, a *set* is the specific mathematical concept of a collection of unique elements.

> **TIP** If you're a Python user, whenever you encounter problems with unique values, consider whether using sets is appropriate. They're often a fast and simple way to get a complex result, such as finding values that appear in two or more collections.

By converting our lists into sets, we can calculate the *intersection* of the sets, that is, elements that appear in both sets. You can think of this as finding the center of a Venn diagram of three circles, as illustrated in figure 9.32.

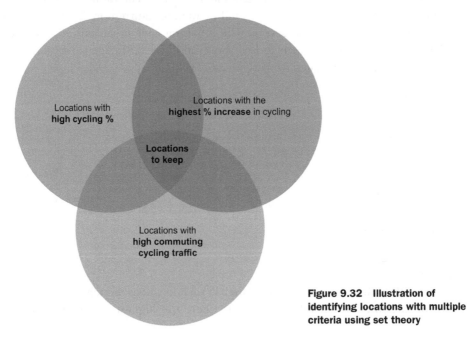

Figure 9.32 Illustration of identifying locations with multiple criteria using set theory

The following code converts our lists to sets and performs the intersection of all three to discover whether there are any overlaps. The result is shown in figure 9.33:

```
top_cycling_locations = (
    set(highest_cycling)
    .intersection(set(biggest_increases))
    .intersection(set(highest_commuting))
)

print(len(top_cycling_locations))

print(top_cycling_locations)
```

Converts the first list to a set

Finds the intersection between two of the sets

Finds the intersection between this result and the third set

```
11
{945955, 941061, 944713, 943405, 942957, 942735, 943471, 942739, 942899, 967549, 946751}
```

Figure 9.33   The list of the final locations of interest

It looks like our criteria weren't too restrictive, and we have some results—11, to be precise. These locations all have a significant percentage of traffic due to cycling, at least a 50% increase in cycling volume over time, and they have peaks at commuting times. It's time to dig into these results and understand what locations they relate to. Let's look these location IDs up in the raw traffic data, extract only location information, and limit each location to a single row. We will also sort the results by region and local authority to better see where these top locations are geographically. The following code does all this and produces the table in figure 9.34:

```
LOCATION_COLUMNS = ['Count_point_id', 'Region_name',
                    'Region_ons_code', 'Local_authority_id',
                    'Local_authority_name', 'Local_authority_code',
                    'Road_name', 'Road_category', 'Road_type']

(
    traffic[traffic["Count_point_id"].isin(top_cycling_locations)]
    .drop_duplicates(subset=["Count_point_id"])
    [LOCATION_COLUMNS]
    .sort_values(["Region_name", "Local_authority_name"])
)
```

There are locations scattered throughout the country. Unsurprisingly, perhaps, there are quite a few in London, but results stretch from Bristol in the southwest all the way to Edinburgh up north in Scotland. Once we go through and verify these locations to make sure none of them are just artifacts in the data, we are ready to present our preliminary findings to our stakeholders. However, before we summarize our findings, let's take a detour into forecasting since that is one of the ways in which time series data can be powerful.

	Count_point_id	Region_name	Region_ons_code	Local_authority_id
91927	941061	East of England	E12000006	97
74939	942899	London	E12000007	178
76690	942739	London	E12000007	107
85920	942735	London	E12000007	107
81137	942957	London	E12000007	93

(continued)

	Local_authority_name	Local_authority_code	Road_name	Road_category	Road_type
91927	Cambridgeshire	E10000003	U	MCU	Minor
74939	Kingston upon Thames	E09000021	U	MCU	Minor
76690	Lambeth	E09000022	U	MCU	Minor
85920	Lambeth	E09000022	C	MCU	Minor
81137	Tower Hamlets	E09000030	C	MCU	Minor

Figure 9.34 Information about the top cycling locations

FORECASTING TIME SERIES

We have enough to show stakeholders and start thinking about further work, but in the spirit of this being a time series problem, we should consider how well we can forecast cycling trends based on the available data. This would help us identify locations where we expect cycling to increase significantly soon, as well as open up other opportunities, such as proactive traffic management.

To successfully forecast a time series, we typically need it to obey some properties:

- *The time series should be at consistent intervals.* We've already achieved this by creating an annual time series and removing the specific date component because measurements were not usually taken on the same day each year.
- *The time series should have no gaps.* We filtered down our time series to ensure this was the case.
- *There should be as many full cycles of data as possible.* In the case of annual data, we don't necessarily have cycles, so in our case, this just means the more data we have, the better.
- *There are other properties, such as stationarity, that some models require the time series to exhibit.* This is not exhaustive, though, since other models can account for this automatically.

To see whether our time series can be successfully forecasted, let's examine one of them in more detail. Let's choose a time series that exhibits a trend, that is, one of the time series from our "biggest increases" list that has the greatest possible coverage. The following code calculates the coverage of these time series and produces the table in figure 9.35, from which we will choose our sample:

```
(
    traffic
    .query("Count_point_id in @biggest_increases")
    .groupby("Count_point_id")
    ["Year"]
    .agg(["min", "max"])
    .assign(diff=lambda df_: df_["max"] - df_["min"])
    .sort_values("diff", ascending=False)
    .head()
)
```

Count_point_id	min	max	diff
996188	2000	2019	19
983147	2000	2019	19
967547	2000	2019	19
967444	2000	2019	19
967514	2000	2018	18

Figure 9.35 Locations with the biggest increase in cycling and with their coverage calculated

Some of these locations have as much as 19 years of data, and we will pick one of those to investigate. We will arbitrarily use the first location in that list to test our ability to forecast these location-level time series. The following code takes the raw data for that location and creates a single annual time series of cycling volumes for us to use. The resulting time series is shown in figure 9.36:

```
cycling_ts = (
    traffic[traffic["Count_point_id"] == 996188]
    .groupby("Year")
    ["Pedal_cycles"]
    .sum()
)

cycling_ts
```

```
Year
2000     3
2001     0
2002     9
2003     6
2004     1
2005     9
2006     1
2007     4
2008     6
2009     6
2010     6
2011     7
2012     5
2013    16
2014     7
2015    11
2016    16
2017    10
2018    10
2019    15
Name: Pedal_cycles, dtype: int64
```

**Figure 9.36   The cycling time series
for location 996188**

One Python-specific aspect to notice is that the index of the series is an integer, whereas to make time series manipulation easier, it should be a date. The following code fixes that and allows us to plot the time series, as shown in figure 9.37:

```
cycling_ts.index = pd.to_datetime(cycling_ts.index, format='%Y')

fig, axis = plt.subplots()

cycling_ts.plot(ax=axis)

axis.set(
    xlabel="Time",
    ylabel="Number of bicycles observed",
    title="Cycling traffic over time at location 996188"
)

plt.show()
```

We have a time series of 19 annual values with an upward trend. We often want to see if a time series has seasonality, that is, patterns that repeat at the same point along the time series, but this makes less sense in the context of annual values.

To understand the individual components of a time series, we can *decompose* the series into trend, seasonal, and residual components. Trend tells us whether there is a long-term change in the average of the values, that is, whether the values are moving in a particular direction. Seasonality is the regularly occurring movements that depend

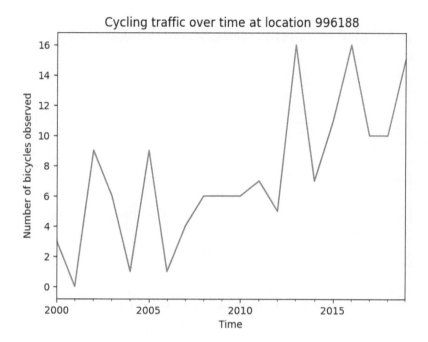

Figure 9.37 Cycling traffic time series at a specific location

on where in the time series we are. Residuals are what is left after we have taken both trend and seasonality into account. Unexpectedly high residuals mean there was something unusual about a time series at that point, which cannot be explained by its underlying trend and seasonal patterns alone.

In Python, the `statsmodels` module has various time series methods, including decomposition, which we will apply to our time series. We will implement STL (seasonal and trend decomposition using LOESS [locally estimated scatterplot smoothing]), and attempt to extract the trend, seasonal, and residual components of a time series. With a lot of these methods, we need to pick some parameter values that will alter the results. In the case of STL, we need to pick the period, how much smoothing to apply to the trend, and how many observations constitute a season.

In our case, we have annual data with no clear, regular seasonal pattern. As annual time series are a special case for some of these methods, we can turn to our AI tools for further guidance. The documentation of the library we're using may also contain hints on how to choose parameter values. In this instance, I asked ChatGPT to advise on picking these values for an annual time series with no real seasonality. A portion of its response is shown in figure 9.38.

This answer suggests that in cases where there is no clear seasonality, choosing parameter values will come down to what fits the problem best. It recommends a low value for the seasonal parameter and to favor default values where possible. We will set

) **ChatGPT**

When using LOESS (Locally Estimated Scatterplot Smoothing) for STL (Seasonal and Trend decomposition using Loess) with an annual time series, especially one that doesn't exhibit clear repeating cyclical patterns, choosing the right parameters can be a bit challenging. The key parameters in question are **"period"**, **"seasonal"**, and **"trend"**. Here's how you can approach setting these values:

1. **Period ("period"):**
   * This parameter is crucial for datasets with clear seasonality. However, for an annual time series with no obvious seasonality, its relevance diminishes.
   * If you suspect there's hidden or weak seasonality, you might experiment with different period values that could potentially capture underlying cycles (like a period that matches economic or business cycles).
   * If there's no seasonality at all, the concept of a period becomes less meaningful, and you might focus more on the trend component.

2. **Seasonal Smoothing ("seasonal"):**
   * This parameter controls the smoothing of the seasonal component.
   * For an annual series without clear seasonality, you would typically set this value low to avoid overfitting a seasonal pattern where there isn't one.
   * If you're unsure about the presence of seasonality, you could start with a minimal value and gradually increase it to see if it captures any meaningful pattern.

3. **Trend Smoothing ("trend"):**
   * This is arguably the most important parameter for an annual series without clear seasonality.
   * The **"trend"** parameter controls how smooth the trend component is. A higher value results in a smoother trend line.
   * For annual data, you might start with a moderate value and adjust based on how well it captures the long-term movements in your data. A too low value might capture noise as part of the trend, while a too high value might oversmooth important features.

Figure 9.38   ChatGPT's response regarding the parameters in the STL decomposition method

the period to 2 and seasonal to 3 and examine the output. The code is as follows and produces the decomposition plot shown in figure 9.39:

```
from statsmodels.tsa.seasonal import STL

stl = STL(cycling_ts, period=2, seasonal=3)
result = stl.fit()

result.plot();
```

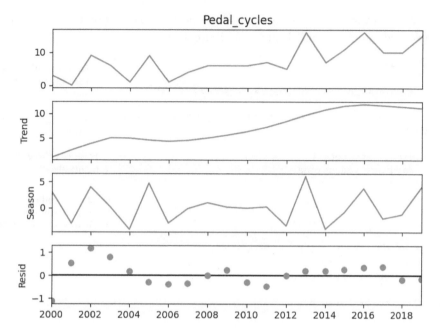

Figure 9.39   Seasonal decomposition of a single time series

This plot shows us (from top to bottom) the raw data, the trend component, the seasonal patterns, and the residuals. In the trend component, we find a smoothed version of the time series, which looks like a fairly steady rise throughout, perhaps leveling out at the end. Because we set a low smoothing value, the seasonal component mimics the peaks seen in the raw data. This is to reinforce the idea that there might not be a repeated seasonal variation, but there are distinct peaks to investigate. The residuals start off larger at the beginning and seem consistently centered around zero afterward. The peak we encounter around 2002 is unexpected if we were to simply model the series using the trend and seasonal variation, which tells us there are external factors that make the start of this series less predictable.

All in all, we have learned that the time series seems mostly predictable, apart from perhaps around 2002. Our next step is to build a forecasting model. If we had domain expertise, we could investigate possible reasons behind the higher residuals around 2002 and build those reasons in as additional variables. For now, we will use a standard forecasting method, ARIMA, to predict cycling traffic in the next couple of years.

Auto-regressive integrated moving average, or ARIMA, is another method that requires the user to choose certain parameters. Ideally, this is done automatically based on what combination of parameters produces the most accurate model. If you are an R user, you might have used R's `auto.arima` method. There are equivalents in Python, such as the one in the `pmdarima` module, which we will use here. The following code calculates

the best ARIMA model on the available data and then plots its predicted values against
the observed values. The plot is shown in figure 9.40:

```
import pmdarima as pm                                        Automatically finds the
                                                             best ARIMA model
model = pm.auto_arima(cycling_ts, seasonal=False)

training_predictions = model.predict_in_sample()            Calculates predictions
forecast = model.predict(3)                                  on the training data

predictions = pd.concat(                                     Forecasts three time
    [training_predictions,                                   points ahead
     forecast]
)                                                            Combines predicted and
                                                             forecasted values into a
fig, axis = plt.subplots()                                   single time series for plotting

axis.plot(cycling_ts, label="Observed")
axis.plot(predictions,
          label="Predicted",
          marker="^",
          color="orange",
          alpha=0.8)

axis.set(
    xlabel="Time",
    ylabel="Number of bicycles observed",
    title="Actual vs. predicted cycling traffic"
)

axis.legend()

plt.show()
```

What does this plot tell us?

- The ARIMA model misses a couple of peaks and tries to correct for them, which is especially clear around 2002.
- Because the ARIMA model is somewhat self-correcting, it tries to match the observed data's shape.
- The unexpected flatline between 2008 and 2012 also takes ARIMA by surprise, as does the subsequent peak in 2013.
- Ultimately, there isn't enough future information to go on, and ARIMA reverts to predicting average behavior into the future by predicting a drop and then a peak.

This is a particularly difficult forecasting problem because we don't have a lot of data, and there are not a lot of patterns to exploit, apart from the slightly rising trend. The fact that we only have measurements from a single day each year is an added difficulty. The best that ARIMA can do for us is predict average behavior in line with the more recent data points. To improve this forecast, ideally, we would have more historical data and additional variables that could help predict changes in cycling traffic.

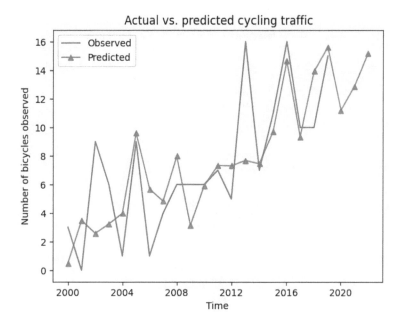

Figure 9.40 Actual vs. predicted values for a particular location's time series

That being said, we could still run this forecasting code on all our cycling time series, and for those that have recent data, we could look at the forecast for the next time point. If these forecasts remain high compared to previous values, we could use that to identify time series with an upward trend. This might be a more sophisticated way to find locations with increased cycling because locations where cycling is in decline after a mid-series peak might be filtered out more successfully. However, as it stands, it doesn't look like we would gain much for our recommendations, so it's finally time to draw some conclusions and think about next steps.

Before proceeding to the conclusion, let's look at the final diagram that documents the analysis. There were three parallel investigations into how we could narrow down the data to locations of interest. Each of them came with a decision about cut-offs (e.g., what percentage increase we treat as significant). These decision points are combined into one on the diagram because we made them together at the final stage, but they represent three separate decisions we needed to make. Figure 9.41 shows the final path we took during our analysis.

Let's now take our findings and summarize them into conclusions and recommendations.

9.2.2 *Project conclusions and recommendations*

Let's remind ourselves of our initial aims. The first phase of the project we are supporting is to identify the most suitable places around the country to improve infrastructure for cyclists. This meant finding places with already significant or increasing

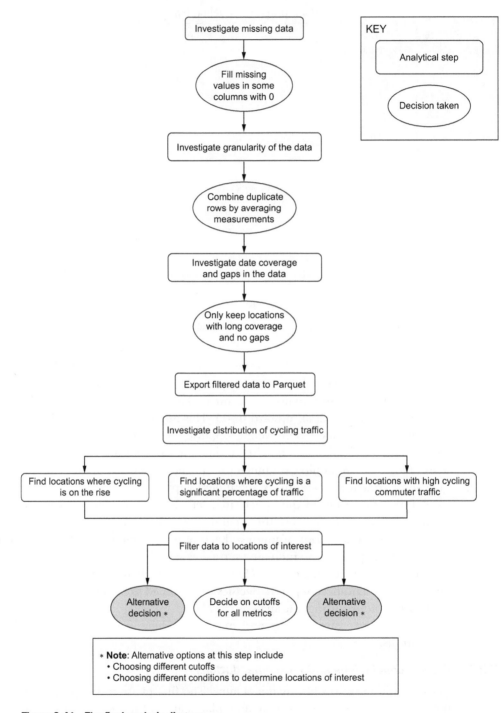

Figure 9.41   The final analysis diagram

cycling traffic. Let's also remind ourselves about what we ended up doing and the decisions we decided to make along the way.

The output of our analysis would be the 11 locations identified as meeting multiple criteria for being relevant to our aims. We could present these as a list or even as points on a map. In fact, map visualizations would be a great way to bring the data story to life here. The important thing would be to discuss these findings with our domain experts.

As for further work, this would be informed by our stakeholder conversations, but some directions we could go from here include

- *Revisiting some of our choices and assumptions*—One decision we made was to remove the time series that did not have enough coverage. However, we ended up not making use of forecasting, so if we relax this coverage criterion and allow shorter time series, we might find additional locations of interest.
- *Including additional datasets in the analysis*—Cross-referencing our findings with data about special events, road closures, or even weather would give us a better picture of locations with organically increasing cycling traffic and which locations have increases that are likely caused by external factors.
- *Visualizing data geographically*—This could also help pinpoint places where there are multiple locations of interest in close proximity. For example, three of our recommended locations of interest were in the borough of Lambeth. This sort of insight would be even easier to arrive at if locations were plotted on a map.

Activity: Further project ideas with this data

Consider some other research questions you could answer with this data that are unrelated to the project in this chapter. Here are some ideas to get you started:

- What happens when you compare traffic patterns at different levels of geography, such as regional or local authority level?
- How are traffic patterns different for different types of vehicles? Where are the hotspots for, say, cars versus buses versus heavy-goods vehicles (HGVs)?
- Based on the available data, which part of the country is most in need of additional road infrastructure?
- If you've ever been interested in geospatial data analysis, this is an opportunity to experiment with it. The Department for Transport website contains shape files, which contain locations for the major road network and can be used for geospatial analysis and visualization. You can find them at https://roadtraffic .dft.gov.uk/downloads.

9.3 Closing thoughts: Time series

There are two aspects of time series data you could target if you want to learn more. The first is getting familiar with the time series tools in your chosen toolbox. In

Python, this might be understanding the various date and time-related data types in the `pandas` library or exploring some of the statistical methods in `statsmodels`. Understanding how dates and times are represented in your toolbox is vital to successfully manipulate this kind of data. For example, at some point, you will encounter time data across multiple time zones. This is a complex and frustrating aspect of working with time data and one that it is handy to be prepared for.

The other angle you could take for further learning is to dive deeper into forecasting. There are many complex algorithms now to do accurate forecasting, but my recommendation is usually to start simple. Methods for time series forecasting have been around for decades in domains such as econometrics, long before the phrase "data science" even existed. To this end, I usually recommend the book *Forecasting: Principles and Practice* by Hyndman and Athanasopoulos (2021), available for free at https://otexts.com/fpp3. It is an excellent resource to walk you through the basics of forecasting, with code samples in R. Python translations are also available, such as https://github.com/zgana/fpp3-python-readalong.

Only after this sort of introductory material do I recommend diving into a more complex, deeper tool, such as Facebook's Prophet library (https://facebook.github.io/prophet). In the end, this is the sort of tool you would turn to in practice when attempting to forecast a time series, but knowing the fundamentals makes it easier to tailor your methods to your specific problem and understand why your forecasts might go wrong from time to time.

9.3.1 *Skills for working with time series data for any project*

Let's recap the skills required to explore, manipulate, and analyze time series data. These skills, which are applicable to any time series data project, include

- Investigating time series data for completeness (e.g., are time series measured at different locations, or do all locations have the same amount of data?)
- Establishing the granularity of the time series (i.e., is it hourly, daily, or weekly? Are there, in fact, multiple time series in the data, e.g., at different locations?)
- Understanding the coverage of the data (i.e., what period does the data cover?)
- Investigating whether the time series has gaps
- Reshaping time series data to be at a different level of granularity (e.g., summarizing hourly data at a daily level)
- Visualizing time series with appropriate charts (i.e., most often, line charts)
- Calculating the distribution of the repeated measurement (e.g., for "Number of bikes seen in an hour," what are the typical hourly counts?)
- Diving down to the individual data point level to investigate anomalies
- Decomposing a time series to identify whether it has a trend or seasonality
- Identifying temporal patterns within time series (e.g., cycling locations with a high level of traffic in the morning)

- Finding time series of interest based on multiple criteria
- Forecasting a time series into the future to predict future trends

Summary

- Time series analysis can reveal temporal patterns, such as peak times of activity or areas of growth.
- Time series can be decomposed to investigate trends and seasonal behaviors separately.
- Forecasting time series relies on having enough past data points with no gaps.
- You can determine whether a time series can be forecasted successfully by building and evaluating a forecasting model.

Rapid prototyping: Data analysis 10

This chapter covers
- Prototyping ideas quickly to support a business case
- Exploring a dataset to build a proof of concept

Sometimes, data analysis is about investigating whether an idea is viable. For example, is the available data good enough for the business to build a data-driven app? We can answer questions like this one by analyzing the data, but it would be even more powerful if we could build a working *proof of concept*. By doing this, we make the idea come to life for our stakeholders. Crucially, we also discover any obstacles to using the data for this purpose.

In this project, spanning this chapter and the next, we practice the skill of *rapid prototyping* by exploring a new dataset and building a proof of concept.

> **Real business case: Building a proof of concept**
>
> This chapter was inspired by one of the first projects I delivered as a data scientist. The data team was tasked with creating a revenue-generating product. The idea was an app that lets someone enter a vehicle's registration and display the current market conditions for that vehicle and vehicles similar to it. Defining what made a vehicle similar enough was the hard part, and that was the data-driven secret sauce behind the product. Once we'd established some rules, I built a quick proof of concept to show stakeholders that the idea worked. Building this proof of concept also meant I could communicate the specific challenges of building the product for real, which I knew because I had actually tried to make it work with the available data and systems.

10.1 The rapid prototyping process

Data teams often sit in an R&D function or are expected to do R&D as part of their job. This means they don't just analyze data to answer questions but sometimes build things that don't currently exist in the company. A valuable and often overlooked skill for an analyst is to be able to put something functional together to investigate the feasibility of an idea. This something is often called a *proof of concept* (POC), a *prototype*, or a *minimum viable product* (MVP), although an MVP is often even further along than a prototype.

> **NOTE** Terminology in this area tends to vary. In this chapter, I will be using specific definitions of "proof of concept" and "prototype." The project task will be to build a proof of concept, but in the chapter title, the more general process of building something to test an idea is called "rapid prototyping."

Although these terms tend to be used interchangeably, they are subtly different:

- A proof of concept is something that tests an idea. It doesn't have to be a polished product; it just needs to be complex enough to see whether an idea is feasible.
- A prototype evolves from a proof of concept. Once an idea has been tested, we can build a small, usable product based on the proof of concept with real data. It won't be finished, it can live in a development environment like someone's laptop, and it won't have the features of fully functioning software, but it is in a state that mimics a finished product.
- Once a prototype exists and has been presented to stakeholders, there might be a step where an MVP is created. An MVP is a pilot launch to get the product out into the hands of real users as soon as possible. It might be missing some features, but it's in a production environment, and rigor has been applied to ensure it works correctly.
- Whether we are talking about an app, a website, or a machine learning model, there will be a notion of putting it into production. Production means it is working and people are using it, whether they are internal users or external customers. Reaching the MVP stage counts as putting something into production.

Figure 10.1 shows an example of this process, including the fact that an idea can be abandoned at any of the stages from initial ideation to after a working prototype is built.

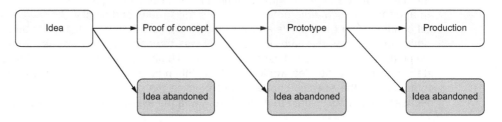

Figure 10.1   The path from an idea to production and the steps in between

Let's see a concrete example.

10.1.1 Rapid prototyping example

Suppose your stakeholders want to know which customers are likely to churn from their e-commerce platform. In other words, which customers are likely to stop using the service? They want to see a list of at-risk customers in some kind of tool or dashboard, like an "early warning system," so they can take action and prevent those users from churning.

As an analyst, you might build a model to predict users who are at risk of churning and then incorporate that into such an interactive tool. Table 10.1 shows the three stages of this product's lifecycle.

Table 10.1   An example walkthrough of the three stages

Stage	Task	Success criteria	Possible reasons to abandon at this stage
1) Proof of concept	Build a basic predictive model.	■ Basic model built to an acceptable level of accuracy. ■ Available data is sufficient to build a model.	■ Available data is insufficient for even a basic churn model.
2) Prototype	Build a working interactive tool.	■ Users can use the tool to take preventative measures to keep at-risk customers. ■ Predictions can be made in a timely manner.	■ Data required for predictions not available at prediction time. ■ No market for the product.
3) Production	Build the tool as fully functioning software with a working data pipeline.	■ Preventative measures have a tangible financial effect.	■ Insufficient return on investment. ■ Low usage of the tool.

Why is a proof of concept so important at the start? We want to understand the following as quickly as possible:

- Do we have the data to answer the question, build the predictive model, and create our app?
- Will we have the data when we need it once the product goes live? Plenty of machine learning projects have failed because, while historical data was available to train the model, new data wasn't available for the model to make a prediction at a useful time.
- What are the challenges in building this product? These might be related to data availability, but they might be any number of other technical challenges. The key is that you don't know all the challenges of building something until you actually try to build it.

What distinguishes the prototype phase from the proof of concept is that we have different questions now:

- *Is anyone interested in this product?* The product doesn't have to exist to answer this question—a prototype is sufficient. Even a dashboard or a machine learning model deployed internally within a company needs to have product market fit.
- *How would real users use this?* With a prototype, you can test your assumptions about how a real user of the product would use it without having to build the whole product. It is still early enough in the process that it shouldn't be too costly to scrap the project at this phase.

These concepts are familiar to software developers and product managers, but they also have merit for analysts. The ability to put together a proof of concept and a subsequent prototype helps analysts identify what is valuable to work on and iterate ideas faster, which in turn means a more results-oriented way of working.

Let's now put these ideas into practice. The project brief is only partly about analyzing data to answer a question. It is also about building something to evaluate whether the data could support a paying product.

10.2 Project 7: Build a proof of concept to investigate Welsh property prices

Let's look at the project, in which we will not only analyze some data, but also build a proof-of-concept data product to show to stakeholders. We will start by looking at the problem statement, the data dictionary, the outputs we are aiming for, and what tools we need to tackle the problem. We will spend more time than usual thinking about the output since we're going beyond analysis and into creating products. We can then formulate a results-oriented action plan and dive into the example solution.

10.2.1 *Problem statement*

You're working for CymruHomes Connect, a property company specializing in homes in Wales. They're looking to expand their business with the help of data; they want to provide insights about the Welsh property market to customers in the form of a new app. This app would use historic property sales data to allow users to explore property prices in their area of interest.

They have discovered that the UK government's Land Registry has a dataset called "Price Paid," which contains publicly available historical sales data. They have extracted and made available a few years' worth of this data.

> **NOTE**   Original data come from https://mng.bz/yWvB. It contains HM Land Registry data © Crown copyright and database right 2021. This data is licensed under the Open Government Licence v3.0. Thank you both to the Land Registry and Royal Mail for permission to use the house price and address data, respectively.

They have asked you to look into whether this data is indeed suitable for powering their new app. This is quite vague, but they have some ideas they'd like to incorporate:

- They are particularly interested in the analysis of property types, for example, whether a house is terraced or detached, because they believe it strongly influences their customers when choosing a property, so they'd like the analysis to include breakdowns by this dimension.
- They also believe users will be interested in comparing properties at the lowest level of granularity, so the ability to see street-level data is important.

They have only asked you to explore the data and see what questions can be answered with it, focusing on the angles they mentioned previously. However, we will go beyond their request and build a proof of concept to showcase what the final app might look like and do.

An important lesson I've learned from working in data science is that stakeholders often cannot articulate exactly what they want because they lack understanding of what is possible. Creating proofs of concept is a way to help bridge this gap and provide additional value as a data professional.

Before we discuss what our steps might be in the process, let's review the available data, the desired outcomes, and the tools we will need.

10.2.2 *Data dictionary*

As always, a key initial step is to take a look at the available data. Table 10.2 shows the data dictionary as provided by the Land Registry. Part of the data dictionary comes from Kaggle (https://mng.bz/QDWG), and the address columns are detailed here: https://mng.bz/XxWv. The definitions from the original data dictionaries are provided as is.

Table 10.2   Data dictionary of the Price Paid data

Column	Definition
Transaction unique identifier	A reference number generated automatically, recording each published sale. The number is unique and will change each time a sale is recorded.
Price	Sale price stated on the transfer deed.
Date of transfer	Date when the sale was completed, as stated on the transfer deed.
Postcode	Postal code of the address.
Property type	D = Detached, S = Semi-detached, T = Terraced, F = Flats/Maisonettes, O = Other
Old/New	Indicates the age of the property and applies to all Price Paid transactions, residential and nonresidential. Y = A newly built property, N = An established residential building
Duration	Relates to the tenure: F = Freehold, L= Leasehold
Primary addressable object name (PAON)	Typically house number/name (e.g., 42 or "Oak Cottage").
Second addressable object name (SAON)	If there is a sub-building, for example, the building is divided into flats, there will be a SAON.
Street	The street part of the address.
Locality	Additional detail about the location (e.g., a district in a city).
Town/City	The town/city part of the address.
District	The district part of the address.
County	The county part of the address.
Category type	Indicates the type of Price Paid transaction. A = Standard Price Paid entry; includes single residential property sold for full market value. B = Additional Price Paid entry; includes transfers under a power of sale/repossessions, buy-to-lets (where they can be identified by a mortgage) and transfers to nonprivate individuals.
Record status	Relevant to monthly files only. Indicates additions, changes, and deletions to the records. Yearly files contain latest versions of all records.

Now that we have seen what's available, let's look at the outcomes of this project.

10.2.3 Desired outcomes

Our stakeholders initially want recommendations about what kind of analyses we could include in a potential app with the available data. Recommendations about additional data sources to incorporate would also be useful. Finally, we have decided to build a proof of concept, partly to show the stakeholders what their potential app might look like, but also to test whether the data is sufficient to build a useful product.

10.2.4 *Required tools*

What constitutes a proof of concept will depend on your preferred tools. It might be a working web application, such as the one built with the Python library `streamlit` in the example solution. However, it could be a dashboard, such as one built with the R language's package Shiny, or with a business intelligence tool such as Tableau or Power BI.

In the example solution, I use Python and the `pandas` library for data exploration, and `matplotlib`, `seaborn`, and `ridgeplot` for visualization. I also introduce the `stream-lit` library to build the interactive, web-based proof of concept. Your tools may differ, especially for the proof-of-concept stage. The checklist for this project is that your tool can

- Load and combine large datasets from CSV files containing millions of rows
- Perform basic data manipulation tasks, such as filtering, sorting, grouping, and reshaping data
- Create data visualizations
- Create an interactive application, whether a dashboard or a web application, where different artifacts, such as charts or other visualizations, are displayed based on user input

TIP   You might find it easier to use two different tools for this project: one for the data analysis and another for building a proof of concept. If you use a programming language that contains libraries or packages for building applications, such as Shiny for R or `streamlit` for Python, you may want to use this project to try them out.

10.3 Applying the results-driven method to investigating Welsh property data

Let's now address this problem with our results-driven framework and formulate our action plan.

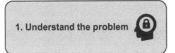

We have an idea of what our stakeholders want to see. Their interest is in whether the data is suitable to support the app idea they have. They have stated that they are particularly interested in property types and whether street-level data can be incorporated into their app. We also understand that building a proof of concept will allow us to identify possible problems with using this data, which is why we will spend the time doing so.

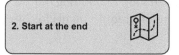

Starting at the end means thinking about the app first and foremost. We cannot know exactly what will go in the app until we analyze the data, but keeping an eye on the app during the analysis phase will help us focus on getting results sooner. Whenever we create charts during the analysis phase, we should consider whether they would be useful in the proof of concept. Therefore, our analysis won't just consider our stakeholders' requests, but also the possible preferences of future users of the app. Our minimum viable answer in this project will look more like a minimum viable product would if we were designing software, which we are to an extent.

In this instance, the data has been identified for us. However, while building our proof of concept, we may identify gaps in the data or aspects of the property market that it doesn't cover. We should consider additional data sources that would improve the quality of the app and recommend them when communicating our results to the stakeholders.

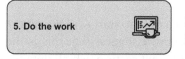

The data has been downloaded for us in its raw form from the Land Registry. However, we will need to combine the different yearly files before we start exploring the data. We may also wish to spend some time looking at the source of the data, that is, the Land Registry website, to learn more about how it was collected and what its possible limitations may be.

We will work on the project in two phases. The first phase is analyzing the available data, so our high-level steps might be

- Investigate the completeness of the data, such as identifying missing data.
- Understand the geographic breakdown of the data, such as the different address levels, like locality and district.
- Once we understand the geographic breakdown, we can extract Welsh properties to use in our app.
- We also want to investigate property types as per our stakeholders' request. Questions we may be interested in are the following: How does the sale price vary by property type? Which property types are more popular? Do these price and popularity patterns vary geographically?
- Finally, we want to identify visualizations that can be recreated in our proof-of-concept app.

Once we have completed our initial analysis, we can look to building our proof of concept. Our considerations for this phase, and therefore requirements for our proof-of-concept app, are the following:

- Any data and visualizations displayed in the app should change based on user input.
- The app should use all the real, available Welsh property data.
- Options that users can change should come from the data (e.g., a list of counties they can select from).

The proof of concept does not need to be a web application; it just needs to contain interactive elements based on real data that you can show your stakeholders. A dashboard built in a BI tool would meet these criteria. If you're a Python and Jupyter user, even having interactive widgets inside a Jupyter notebook would suffice.

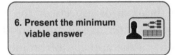

The presentation of the output would consist of communicating the results of the analysis phase, as well as allowing stakeholders to see and even try the interactive proof of concept. The two complement each other because any limitations of the proof of concept will be discovered in the analysis phase and can be communicated while demonstrating the proof of concept itself.

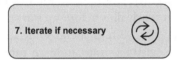

Iteration is key when rapidly prototyping ideas. Whatever tool we use to build our proof of concept should make it easy to quickly make wholesale changes to its functionality. At this stage, we are not bound by production considerations such as user authentication, permissions, or managing servers and databases. We should be able to make changes quickly based on feedback both at the proof-of-concept and prototype stages.

Now that we have an action plan outlined, it's time to start working on the project. If you are reading this chapter from start to end, I suggest that this is the time to attempt the project yourself before reading the next section, which details an example solution.

10.4 An example solution: Building a prototype to explore using house price data

Now, let's walk through an example solution. As ever, I strongly recommend attempting the project yourself first, as our solutions will differ, particularly for this project.

As for the action plan, we will combine the separate yearly files first. Then, we will explore the combined dataset, paying particular attention to property types and the geographical hierarchy of the data, as per our stakeholders' request. We will decide which visualizations will go into our app before identifying an appropriate tool with which to build our proof of concept. Finally, we will build a proof of concept using the data, where the user can change the visualizations that are displayed based on their input.

10.4.1 Analyzing data before prototyping

The first step in our process is to merge the different yearly files that our stakeholders provided. They cover the period from 2021 to 2023 inclusive. Initially, we will assume they have the same format, but we are prepared for this not to be the case.

MERGING DATASETS WITHOUT HEADINGS

Let's take a look at one of the files. The following code produces the output shown in figure 10.2:

```
import pandas as pd

prices_2021 = pd.read_csv("./data/pp-2021.csv.gz", nrows=1000)
prices_2021.head()
```

	{D707E535-5720-0AD9-E053-6B04A8C067CC}	260000	2021-08-06 00:00	SO45 2HT	T	N	F	17
0	{D707E535-5721-0AD9-E053-6B04A8C067CC}	375000	2021-09-01 00:00	SO23 7FR	S	N	F	1
1	{D707E535-5723-0AD9-E053-6B04A8C067CC}	132000	2021-06-28 00:00	SP11 6RL	F	N	L	2
2	{D707E535-5724-0AD9-E053-6B04A8C067CC}	295000	2021-09-10 00:00	SP11 6TU	T	N	F	21
3	{D707E535-5725-0AD9-E053-6B04A8C067CC}	360000	2021-08-27 00:00	SO51 0AX	T	N	F	130
4	{D707E535-5726-0AD9-E053-6B04A8C067CC}	490500	2021-06-30 00:00	GU14 6JH	D	N	F	17

(continued)

	Unnamed: 8	PERRYWOOD CLOSE	HOLBURY	SOUTHAMPTON	NEW FOREST	HAMPSHIRE	A	A.1
0	NaN	BOXALL GARDENS	KINGS WORTHY	WINCHESTER	WINCHESTER	HAMPSHIRE	A	A
1	NaN	SEDGE ROAD	NaN	ANDOVER	TEST VALLEY	HAMPSHIRE	A	A
2	NaN	NAP CLOSE	NaN	ANDOVER	TEST VALLEY	HAMPSHIRE	A	A
3	NaN	FREEMANTLE ROAD	NaN	ROMSEY	TEST VALLEY	HAMPSHIRE	A	A
4	NaN	CLOSEWORTH ROAD	NaN	FARNBOROUGH	RUSHMOOR	HAMPSHIRE	A	A

Figure 10.2   A snapshot of the raw 2021 data

Upon inspection, the files contain no headers, so we need to provide column names based on the data dictionary. Apart from that, we will convert the date column to the correct type so we can verify that the data indeed covers the years it claims to. The following code reads in each of the yearly files in turn and combines them into a single `pandas` `DataFrame`. The output, a snapshot of the combined data, is shown in figure 10.3.

```
annual_dfs = []

for year in [2021, 2022, 2023]:
    print(f"Parsing {year}")
    df = pd.read_csv(
        f"./data/pp-{year}.csv.gz",
        names=["transaction_id", "sale_price", "sale_date", "postcode",
               "property_type", "old_new", "duration", "house_number_name",
               "second_addressable_object_name", "street", "locality",
               "town_city", "district", "county",
               "category_type", "record_status"],
        parse_dates=["sale_date"])
    annual_dfs.append(df)

price_paid = pd.concat(annual_dfs, axis=0, ignore_index=True)
print(price_paid.shape)
price_paid.head()
```

	transaction_id	sale_price	sale_date	postcode	property_type	old_new	duration	house_number_name
0	{D707E535-5720-0AD9-E053-6B04A8C067CC}	260000	2021-08-06	SO45 2HT	T	N	F	17
1	{D707E535-5721-0AD9-E053-6B04A8C067CC}	375000	2021-09-01	SO23 7FR	S	N	F	1
2	{D707E535-5723-0AD9-E053-6B04A8C067CC}	132000	2021-06-28	SP11 6RL	F	N	L	2
3	{D707E535-5724-0AD9-E053-6B04A8C067CC}	295000	2021-09-10	SP11 6TU	T	N	F	21
4	{D707E535-5725-0AD9-E053-6B04A8C067CC}	360000	2021-08-27	SO51 0AX	T	N	F	130

(continued)

	second_addressable_object_name	street	locality	town_city	district	county	category_type	record_status
0	Unnamed: 8	PERRYWOOD CLOSE	HOLBURY	SOUTHAMPTON	NEW FOREST	HAMPSHIRE	A	A.1
1	NaN	BOXALL GARDENS	KINGS WORTHY	WINCHESTER	WINCHESTER	HAMPSHIRE	A	A
2	NaN	SEDGE ROAD	NaN	ANDOVER	TEST VALLEY	HAMPSHIRE	A	A
3	NaN	NAP CLOSE	NaN	ANDOVER	TEST VALLEY	HAMPSHIRE	A	A
4	NaN	FREEMANTLE ROAD	NaN	ROMSEY	TEST VALLEY	HAMPSHIRE	A	A

Figure 10.3   A snapshot of the combined Price Paid data

Let's verify that this combined dataset starts at the beginning of 2021 and ends in late 2023. We will look at the smallest and largest dates to do this, as shown in the following code, the output of which presented in figure 10.4:

```
price_paid["sale_date"].agg(["min", "max"])
```

```
min    2021-01-01
max    2023-12-31
Name: sale_date, dtype: datetime64[ns]
```

Figure 10.4   Verification that the data does indeed cover the years 2021–2023

Now that we have combined our data and verified the date range, we will export it for later use. This means our analysis and proof of concept code can reference the combined data directly:

```
price_paid.to_csv("./data/price_paid.csv.gz", index=False)
```

We are now ready to move on to the analysis phase.

INVESTIGATING DATA QUALITY

Let's do some initial sanity checking of the combined data. We are interested in looking at missing data, outliers, especially in the sale price, and breakdowns of the various categories. We will start by reading the data again. If we continue from the previous code snippets, this is not strictly necessary, but because we decided it was good practice to split the merging and the analysis code, we will write the code that way. In the example code files, the merging and analysis phases happen in separate files, so we will be consistent here, too:

```
import pandas as pd
import numpy as np
import matplotlib.pyplot as plt
import seaborn as sns

pd.options.display.float_format = '{:.2f}'.format

price_paid = pd.read_csv("./data/price_paid.csv.gz",
                         parse_dates=["sale_date"])
print(price_paid.shape)
price_paid.head()
```

Here, we also set something called the "float format." This is a way to tell pandas how to display numbers. The reason we explicitly set it is that house prices will vary significantly, and it is likely that pandas will show the largest numbers using scientific notation. That is, one million would be shown as 1e6 or similar rather than displaying all the zeros. Setting the float format will avoid this problem, and as we will be working with prices that are monetary values, two decimal points makes sense.

Let's start by looking at missing data across our columns. The following code investigates this, and the output is shown in figure 10.5:

```
price_paid.isnull().sum()
```

This output tells us that all missing data is related to addresses. We have some missing postcodes, street names, and a lot of missing data for locality and the "second addressable object name" (SAON). These latter columns will be specific to different areas and properties, so they are unlikely to be a problem. The data dictionary even suggested that not all properties have a SAON.

We should examine instances where there is no street name for a property, as this may be a problem, especially considering our stakeholders asked about street-level

```
transaction_id                             0
sale_price                                 0
sale_date                                  0
postcode                                7816
property_type                              0
old_new                                    0
duration                                   0
house_number_name                          0
second_addressable_object_name       2447845
street                                 50677
locality                             1740797
town_city                                  0
district                                   0
county                                     0
category_type                              0
record_status                              0
dtype: int64
```

Figure 10.5   Number of missing values by column

data. The following code investigates some missing street names, and the output is shown in figure 10.6:

```
price_paid.loc[price_paid["street"].isnull(),
            ["house_number_name", "second_addressable_object_name",
             "street", "postcode", "locality", "town_city",
             "district", "county"]]
```

	house_number_name	second_addressable_object_name	street	postcode
122	THE BARN		NaN	NaN	GL54 2LG
123	WISTERIA		NaN	NaN	GL2 8EB
538	TOWN MILL		FLAT 20	NaN	RG25 3JE
1081	THE OLD SCHOOL		NaN	NaN	IP27 9LG
1302	ORCHARD HOUSE		NaN	NaN	SY4 1BJ

(continued)

	locality	town_city	district	county
122	CLAPTON ON THE HILL	CHELTENHAM	COTSWOLD	GLOUCESTERSHIRE
123	TIBBERTON	GLOUCESTER	FOREST OF DEAN	GLOUCESTERSHIRE
538	OVERTON	BASINGSTOKE	BASINGSTOKE AND DEANE	HAMPSHIRE
1081	SEDGE FEN	BRANDON	WEST SUFFOLK	SUFFOLK
1302	WILCOTT	SHREWSBURY	SHROPSHIRE	SHROPSHIRE

Figure 10.6   A sample of properties with no street details

While this is only a small selection of the over 50,000 rows with missing street names, it does appear that a lot of these instances are properties that have names like "The Barn" or "The Old School." This might explain why parts of the address are missing.

We could leave these missing street names intact since, in many cases, they appear to be not applicable rather than missing. However, if we are to surface street names to users in our app, we need an option to filter on properties with no street name. We could handle this in the app itself or fill in the missing data with a placeholder value. Let's opt to make the data as clean as possible and fill in the missing value. The following code achieves this:

```
STREET_PLACEHOLDER = "-- NO STREET INFORMATION --"
price_paid["street"] = price_paid["street"].fillna(STREET_PLACEHOLDER)
```

Let's take stock of what we have done so far and start building up our diagram to document our steps. Figure 10.7 shows what we have done so far, including the decision about what to do about missing street names.

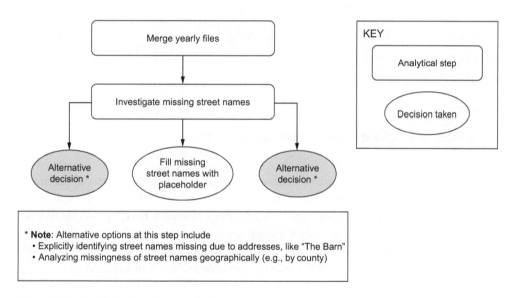

Figure 10.7   The first steps of our analysis

INVESTIGATING MISSING GEOGRAPHIC DATA

More worrying than missing street names is the fact that we have thousands of missing postcodes. Again, let's look at a selection of these. The following code finds some examples, and the output is shown in figure 10.8:

```
price_paid.loc[price_paid["postcode"].isnull(),
               ["house_number_name", "second_addressable_object_name",
                "street", "postcode", "locality", "town_city",
                "district", "county"]]
```

	house_number_name	second_addressable_object_name	street	postcode
264	6B	GROUND FLOOR FLAT	GRIMSBY ROAD	NaN
1973	GARAGE 680	NaN	EASTBROOK DRIVE	NaN
3908	KIRKBY PARK WOOD	NaN	-- NO STREET INFORMATION --	NaN
3950	CHURCH FARM	NaN	-- NO STREET INFORMATION --	NaN
4280	NORTH TOWER	NaN	DEANSGATE	NaN

(continued)

	locality	town_city	district	county
264	NaN	CLEETHORPES	NORTH EAST LINCOLNSHIRE	NORTH EAST LINCOLNSHIRE
1973	RUSH GREEN	ROMFORD	BARKING AND DAGENHAM	GREATER LONDON
3908	GRIZEBECK	KIRKBY-IN-FURNESS	SOUTH LAKELAND	CUMBRIA
3950	PENHURST	BATTLE	ROTHER	EAST SUSSEX
4280	NaN	MANCHESTER	MANCHESTER	GREATER MANCHESTER

Figure 10.8 A selection of records with missing postcode data

Looking at the house names, these also seem like properties with explicit names, as well as some references to garages. However, in this case, that does not explain why there is no postcode information since UK addresses generally have a postcode. We have a decision to make about this missing data. On the one hand, the missing records are a small percentage of the overall dataset, but on the other hand, these records still contribute to the housing market and, therefore, all contain relevant information.

We will keep records that have no postcode information, but we will be mindful of their presence while continuing our analysis. As we have reached another decision point, let's add this to our diagram in figure 10.9 to record the latest step in our analysis.

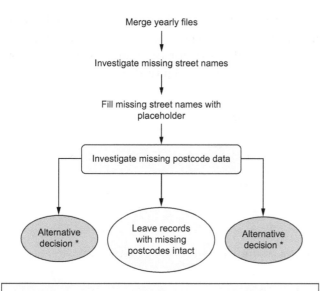

Figure 10.9 The latest diagram of our analytical steps

INVESTIGATING DISTRIBUTION AND OUTLIERS IN A PRICE COLUMN

We are also interested in the distribution of the price column as it is the key variable on which our app will be based. The following code produces a high-level statistical summary of the data, which is shown in figure 10.10:

```
price_paid["sale_price"].describe()
```

```
count      2800288.00
mean        391996.55
std        1440475.15
min              1.00
25%         173000.00
50%         270000.00
75%         420000.00
max      523000000.00
Name: sale_price, dtype: float64
```

Figure 10.10 Statistical overview of the sale_price column

There are values ranging from £1 to over £500 million, so there will be outliers to handle. The mean is also significantly higher than the median, which is shown as 50% in the diagram, suggesting that the data is right-skewed. That in itself is not worrisome because price data tends to be in that shape, but we will investigate the outliers. To start with, let's look at properties that sold for less than £1,000. The following code applies this filter, and the output is shown in figure 10.11:

```
(
    price_paid.loc[price_paid["sale_price"] < 1000,
    ["sale_price", "house_number_name",
     "street", "town_city", "postcode",
     "district", "county", "category_type"]
    ]
    .sample(10, random_state=42)
)
```

	sale_price	house_number_name		street	town_city
318226	280		15	CRAWSHAW GROVE	SHEFFIELD
552148	950		35	ST MARTINS DRIVE	BLACKBURN
1432981	950		57	NURSERY ROAD	LIVERPOOL
515898	750		26	CHANTREY ROAD	SHEFFIELD
497854	650		180	THE AVENUE	LEIGH

(continued)

	postcode	district	county	category_type
318226	S8 7EA	SHEFFIELD	SOUTH YORKSHIRE	B
552148	BB2 5HU	BLACKBURN WITH DARWEN	BLACKBURN WITH DARWEN	B
1432981	L31 4JJ	SEFTON	MERSEYSIDE	B
515898	S8 8QW	SHEFFIELD	SOUTH YORKSHIRE	B
497854	WN7 1HR	WIGAN	GREATER MANCHESTER	B

Figure 10.11   A sample of 10 properties that sold for less than £1,000

Looking at the addresses of these transactions, there does not seem to be other data errors that could explain these low sale prices. However, all these transactions are in category B, according to the `category_type` column. Consulting the data dictionary in table 8.1, we can see that category B records are nonstandard transactions, including "transfers under a power of sale/repossessions." It seems to be the case that properties categorized under B were sold for nominal amounts for reasons other than a standard property purchase. To verify this, let's look at the proportion of category A versus B in the lower-valued properties. The following code does this and produces the output in figure 10.12:

```
(
    price_paid.loc[price_paid["sale_price"] < 10_000,
                   "category_type"]
    .value_counts()
)
```

B   8372
A   25
Name: category_type, dtype: int64

Figure 10.12   Distribution of `category_type` **for low-valued properties**

This offers an explanation for the lowest values in our data. There are also properties in the range of over £500M, as evidenced by the table in figure 10.10. Let's inspect those to find out more. The following code identifies those high-value properties, and the output is shown in figure 10.13:

```
price_paid[price_paid["sale_price"] > 300_000_000]
```

	transaction_id	sale_price	sale_date	postcode	property_type
156563	{EA3278AA-FA35-2676-E053-6B04A8C015F8}	523000000	2021-09-16	NaN	O
307146	{FFA361DB-8C7C-8A03-E053-4804A8C01F61}	414108660	2021-09-30	OX4 4GB	O
497874	{E073986C-2B5A-2134-E053-6C04A8C0233B}	421364142	2021-05-28	E1 8EP	O
530132	{DBA933FA-5BCC-669D-E053-6B04A8C0AD56}	372600000	2021-03-26	EC1Y 8RQ	O
1791832	{FD226036-9858-4CB7-E053-4804A8C00430}	429000000	2022-04-22	WC1B 4JB	O

(continued)

	old_new	duration	house_number_name	second_addressable_object_name	street
156563	N	L	ONE THAMES	PHASE 1	NINE ELMS LANE
307146	N	L	OXFORD SCIENCE PARK	NaN	EDMUND HALLEY ROAD
497874	N	F	BEAGLE HOUSE, 1	NaN	BRAHAM STREET
530132	N	F	15	NaN	MALLOW STREET
1791832	N	F	VICTORIA HOUSE	NaN	SOUTHAMPTON ROW

Figure 10.13   Properties worth over £300M

Based on the names, one of these is an entire science park, and after doing some research, it appears the most expensive transaction might be something called Nine Elms Park, a large green space in a development in London, situated on Nine Elms Lane.

To conclude our analysis of the price column, lower-valued transactions are due to being a special type, category B, and the highest-valued transactions are entire developments rather than individual properties. We don't want to include those high-value transactions in our app, which is aimed at residential buyers, so we will drop the highest values. We could also consider dropping category B transactions, but perhaps users of the app might be interested if there were repossessions or other nonstandard transactions in the area they're interested in, so we'll leave that data intact. The following code keeps only the data under a high threshold, say £10M, which is a reasonable cut-off for most residential buyers. Anyone with a higher budget will be better served by more specialized real estate agencies:

```
price_paid = price_paid[price_paid["sale_price"] < 10_000_000]
```

Since we had to make a decision about outliers, let's add another step to our diagram documenting the process so far, as shown in figure 10.14.

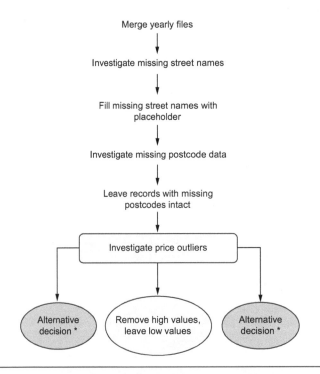

Figure 10.14   Latest diagram of the process, including the investigation of price outliers

Now, we are ready to look at other aspects of the data, namely, the various categorizations of our property transactions.

INVESTIGATING CATEGORIZATIONS IN THE DATA

There are several different ways that properties are categorized in our data. Judging by the data dictionary in table 8.1, we may want to update the names of these categories to be more descriptive. Let's look at them in turn.

Property type is of strong interest to our stakeholders. This data is labeled with individual letters (e.g., T for terraced houses). This is fine, but if we want to use the data in our app or even label charts correctly, the full names would be better. The following code remaps the property types to their full names and then creates the chart in figure 10.15, which shows the breakdown of property types in our data:

```
property_type_map = {
    "D": "Detached",
    "S": "Semi-Detached",
    "T": "Terraced",
    "F": "Flats",
    "O": "Other"
}

price_paid["property_type"] = (
    price_paid["property_type"]
    .map(property_type_map)
)

fig, axis - plt.subplots()

(
    price_paid["property_type"]
    .value_counts()
    .sort_values()
    .plot
    .barh(ax=axis)
)

axis.set(
    title="Distribution of property type",
    xlabel="Count",
    ylabel="Property type"
)

plt.show()
```

If you have seen what houses in the United Kingdom are generally like, it won't be a surprise to see that most properties are either terraced or semi-detached. Now, let's remap the other categorizing columns, starting with whether a property is a new build or not, that is, newly built at the time of purchase. The following code recategorizes

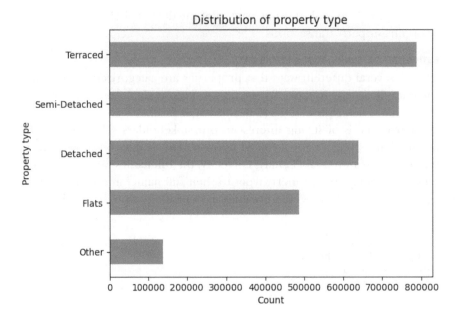

Figure 10.15   Breakdown of property types in our data

the data and produces the output in figure 10.16 to investigate the breakdown of this column:

```
price_paid["old_new"] = (
    price_paid["old_new"]
    .map(
        {
            "Y": "New build",
            "N": "Existing property"
        }
    )
)
price_paid["old_new"].value_counts()
```

```
Existing property    2588265
New build             212023
Name: old_new, dtype: int64
```
Figure 10.16   The breakdown of existing vs. newly built properties

The sanity check of this column should be that most properties were already built at the time of purchase, which is what we see in the data. Let's now update the `duration` column, which differentiates freehold from leasehold properties. Leasehold means you don't own the land your structure is on; you need to pay additional fees and renew your lease if it is expiring. The majority of properties in the United Kingdom should be freeholds. Let's verify this while also recategorizing the data. The following code does this, and the output is shown in figure 10.17:

```
price_paid["duration"] = (
    price_paid["duration"]
    .map(
        {
            "F": "Freehold",
            "L": "Leasehold"
        }
    )
)

price_paid["duration"].value_counts()
```

```
Freehold      2160470
Leasehold      639818
Name: duration, dtype: int64
```

Figure 10.17   Breakdown of freehold vs. leasehold properties

Now that we have investigated most of our property data, we should turn our attention to the aspect we haven't touched yet: geography.

10.4.2 Investigating geographic aspects of a dataset

Our stakeholders are interested only in the Welsh property market, so we need to extract only the transactions that occurred in Wales before we can build our proof of concept. This will require extracting that information somehow as we do not have an obvious country column. For more practice extracting information from addresses, see a related project in chapter 2.

Whenever we work with addresses, we have several options to extract additional information:

- Ideally, there is a column that stores the necessary information already. In this case, there isn't.
- If we have a combined address field, such as the project in chapter 2, we could extract the right address component. We also do not have that in this case.
- We could use an existing column to cross-reference against official lists, similar to what we did in the example solution of chapter 2, where we cross-referenced address data with a definitive list of cities in the United Kingdom. In the case of this project, we could also cross-reference one of the address categorizations and find the ones corresponding to Wales.

- A more complex, but possibly more accurate, method would be to use a third-party geocoding service to get a structured version of our address data. For the data in this project, we could send the service the combination of all the address columns we have and get back the same address in a standardized format, which would include the country column.

Out of these options, the third one seems to strike a balance between accuracy and effort. The last option is something to consider for a future iteration if we want to maximize accuracy, but only if we identify that the extra work is worth the effort. Let's now investigate the different address categorizations in the data and see which one could be cross-referenced against a relevant, official list.

One option is to look at the `town_city` column and cross-reference it against a list of Welsh cities. Running the following command reveals that we have 1,150 unique values for the town/city component. We will also uppercase the column just in case we have some inconsistent casing in the data:

```
price_paid["town_city"] = price_paid["town_city"].str.upper()
price_paid["town_city"].nunique()
```

Having so many values increases the possibility of errors. There could be misspellings and other duplicate values, and there are town names that exist in both England and Wales, such as Newport. Let's look at a higher level of geography instead: counties. The following code investigates the frequency of counties present in the data and also reveals the number of unique items, as shown in figure 10.18:

```
price_paid["county"] = price_paid["county"].str.upper()
price_paid["county"].value_counts()
```

```
GREATER LONDON          311630
GREATER MANCHESTER      128176
WEST YORKSHIRE          107111
WEST MIDLANDS           104199
KENT                     80920
                          ...
BLAENAU GWENT             3192
MERTHYR TYDFIL            2417
RUTLAND                   2004
NORTHAMPTONSHIRE           707
ISLES OF SCILLY             56
Name: county, Length: 115, dtype: int64
```

Figure 10.18 A breakdown of the number of records by county

From this output, we can tell there are 115 unique county values in the data, Greater London being the most common. The most frequent records tell us that the number of records per county is in the region of the tens of thousands, which makes some of the least common values suspicious. Northamptonshire is not a small county, so we would expect more than 707 records. Perhaps there are misspellings or overlapping county values. We will investigate these by looking for just the word NORTH and see what is returned. The following code does this, and the output is shown in figure 10.19:

```
(
    price_paid
    .loc[price_paid["county"].str.contains("NORTH"), "county"]
    .unique()
)
```

```
array(['NORTH EAST LINCOLNSHIRE', 'NORTH LINCOLNSHIRE',
       'NORTH NORTHAMPTONSHIRE', 'WEST NORTHAMPTONSHIRE',
       'NORTH YORKSHIRE', 'NORTH SOMERSET',
       'BATH AND NORTH EAST SOMERSET', 'NORTHUMBERLAND',
       'NORTHAMPTONSHIRE'], dtype=object)
```

Figure 10.19   All counties containing the word NORTH

We find that there are also records for both North and West Northamptonshire. If we were interested in counties in England, we may consider combining these. It is possible this data doesn't exactly match official lists, but it is easier to clean 115 county records than over 1,000 town names.

SANITY CHECKING OUR DATA FROM EXTERNAL SOURCES

For now, we want an official list of counties in Wales to cross-reference against our data. The Welsh government has this list published on their website: https://law.gov .wales/local-government-bodies.

> **NOTE**   If the website is inaccessible, a copy of its relevant content is included in the supplementary materials for this chapter. The file is called `wales-local-government-bodies.htm`. It can be found in the `data` folder and is viewable in any web browser.

The list is in bullet points about halfway down the page, as shown in figure 10.20.

From this page, we can extract the unique names of counties. Our data is in English, not Welsh, so we only need the English part of this list. We also don't need the "County Borough Council" part, as those phrases are not contained in the `county` column of our data. We will take this list of counties and assume any record

All local authorities are democratically accountable through elections held every 4 years. Local authorities have a cabinet style executive with the dominant political group or coalition making decisions under the scrutiny of the council as a whole. They employ large numbers of staff headed by a chief executive, who works with other senior officers on day-to-day business and decision-making.

The unitary authorities in Wales are:

- Blaenau Gwent County Borough Council (Cyngor Bwrdeistref Sirol Blaenau Gwent)
- Bridgend County Borough Council (Cyngor Bwrdeistref Sirol Pen-y-bont ar Ogwr)
- Caerphilly County Borough Council (Cyngor Bwrdeistref Sirol Caerffili)
- Cardiff Council (Cyngor Caerdydd)
- Carmarthenshire County Council (Cyngor Sir Gaerfyrddin)
- Ceredigion County Council (Cyngor Sir Ceredigion)
- Conwy County Borough Council (Cyngor Bwrdeistref Sirol Conwy)
- Denbighshire County Council (Cyngor Sir Ddinbych)
- Flintshire County Council (Cyngor Sir y Fflint)
- Gwynedd Council (Cyngor Sir Gwynedd)
- Isle of Anglesey County Council (Cyngor Sir Ynys Môn)
- Merthyr Tydfil County Borough Council (Cyngor Bwrdeistref Sirol Merthyr Tudful)
- Monmouthshire County Council (Cyngor Sir Fynwy)
- Neath Port Talbot County Borough Council (Cyngor Bwrdeistref Sirol Castell-nedd Port Talbot)
- Newport City Council (Cyngor Dinas Casnewydd)
- Pembrokeshire County Council (Cyngor Sir Penfro)
- Powys County Council (Cyngor Sir Powys)
- Rhondda Cynon Taf County Borough Council (Cyngor Bwrdeistref Sirol Rhondda Cynon Taf)
- City and County of Swansea (Cyngor Sir a Dinas Abertawe)
- The Vale of Glamorgan County Borough Council (Cyngor Bwrdeistref Sirol Bro Morgannwg)
- Torfaen County Borough Council (Cyngor Bwrdeistref Sirol Torfaen)
- Wrexham County Borough Council (Cyngor Bwrdeistref Sirol Wrecsam)

Figure 10.20   Official list of counties in Wales

that contains one of these counties is a Welsh property, and everything else is in England. The following code categorizes the records into England or Wales based on their county. We'll then look at the distribution of this new `country` column, which is shown in figure 10.21:

```
welsh_councils = [
    c.upper() for c in ["Blaenau Gwent", "Bridgend", "Caerphilly",
                        "Cardiff", "Carmarthenshire", "Ceredigion",
                        "Conwy", "Denbighshire", "Flintshire",
                        "Gwynedd", "Isle of Anglesey", "Merthyr Tydfil",
                        "Monmouthshire", "Neath Port Talbot", "Newport",
                        "Pembrokeshire", "Powys", "Rhondda Cynon Taf",
```

```
                              "Swansea", "The Vale of Glamorgan", "Torfaen",
                              "Wrexham"]
]

price_paid["country"] = (
    np.where(
        price_paid["county"].isin(welsh_councils),
        "WALES",
        "ENGLAND"
    )
)

price_paid["country"].value_counts(dropna=False)
```

```
ENGLAND    2663433
WALES       133800
Name: country, dtype: int64
```
Figure 10.21   The breakdown of England vs. Wales in our data

As we said earlier, it is possible that some of the values in the county column don't match the list of Welsh counties exactly. We should look at all the counties categorized as England with our method and check if any are misspellings of the Welsh counties. The following code retrieves these counties, as shown in figure 10.22:

```
print(
    sorted(
        price_paid
        .loc[price_paid["country"] == "ENGLAND", "county"]
        .unique()
    )
)
```

We could employ more sophisticated methods to find county names in this list that are almost like one of the Welsh counties, but since there aren't that many counties in total, we can do this manually. See the example solution in chapter 3 for ideas on how to do more sophisticated string matching.

At a glance, the only county that seems miscategorized is Rhondda Cynon Taf, which appears in the data with a double f at the end. Let's manually recategorize those instances as Wales to make the data more accurate:

```
price_paid.loc[price_paid["county"] == "RHONDDA CYNON TAFF", "country"]
    = "WALES"
```

```
['BATH AND NORTH EAST SOMERSET', 'BEDFORD', 'BLACKBURN WITH DARWEN', 'BLACKPOOL'
'BOURNEMOUTH, CHRISTCHURCH AND POOLE', 'BRACKNELL FOREST', 'BRIGHTON AND HOVE', 'BUCKINGHAMSHIRE'
'CAMBRIDGESHIRE', 'CENTRAL BEDFORDSHIRE', 'CHESHIRE EAST', 'CHESHIRE WEST AND CHESTER'
'CITY OF BRISTOL', 'CITY OF DERBY', 'CITY OF KINGSTON UPON HULL', 'CITY OF NOTTINGHAM'
'CITY OF PETERBOROUGH', 'CITY OF PLYMOUTH', 'CORNWALL', 'COUNTY DURHAM'
'CUMBERLAND', 'CUMBRIA', 'DARLINGTON', 'DERBYSHIRE'
'DEVON', 'DORSET', 'EAST RIDING OF YORKSHIRE', 'EAST SUSSEX'
'ESSEX', 'GLOUCESTERSHIRE', 'GREATER LONDON', 'GREATER MANCHESTER'
'HALTON', 'HAMPSHIRE', 'HARTLEPOOL', 'HEREFORDSHIRE'
'HERTFORDSHIRE', 'ISLE OF WIGHT', 'ISLES OF SCILLY', 'KENT'
'LANCASHIRE', 'LEICESTER', 'LEICESTERSHIRE', 'LINCOLNSHIRE'
'LUTON', 'MEDWAY', 'MERSEYSIDE', 'MIDDLESBROUGH'
'MILTON KEYNES', 'NORFOLK', 'NORTH EAST LINCOLNSHIRE', 'NORTH LINCOLNSHIRE'
'NORTH NORTHAMPTONSHIRE', 'NORTH SOMERSET', 'NORTH YORKSHIRE', 'NORTHAMPTONSHIRE'
'NORTHUMBERLAND', 'NOTTINGHAMSHIRE', 'OXFORDSHIRE', 'PORTSMOUTH'
'READING', 'REDCAR AND CLEVELAND', 'RHONDDA CYNON TAFF', 'RUTLAND'
'SHROPSHIRE', 'SLOUGH', 'SOMERSET', 'SOUTH GLOUCESTERSHIRE'
'SOUTH YORKSHIRE', 'SOUTHAMPTON', 'SOUTHEND-ON-SEA', 'STAFFORDSHIRE'
'STOCKTON-ON-TEES', 'STOKE-ON-TRENT', 'SUFFOLK', 'SURREY'
'SWINDON', 'THURROCK', 'TORBAY', 'TYNE AND WEAR'
'WARRINGTON', 'WARWICKSHIRE', 'WEST BERKSHIRE', 'WEST MIDLANDS'
'WEST NORTHAMPTONSHIRE', 'WEST SUSSEX', 'WEST YORKSHIRE', 'WESTMORLAND AND FURNESS'
'WILTSHIRE', 'WINDSOR AND MAIDENHEAD', 'WOKINGHAM', 'WORCESTERSHIRE'
'WREKIN', 'YORK'
]
```

Figure 10.22   A list of counties we categorized as belonging to England

As a final step in this part, we will extract only the Welsh properties into their own DataFrame so that all our analyses will be limited to Welsh properties:

```
wales = price_paid[price_paid["country"] == "WALES"].copy()
```

The next step is to explore this subset of Welsh transactions to see what aspects of the data should be included in our proof-of-concept app. But before we move on, let's review our progress so far in the form of a diagram, shown in figure 10.23. Then, we'll be ready to explore the Welsh property data to identify visualizations we want to include in our proof-of-concept app.

10.4.3   *Identifying how to present data in the prototype*

Now that we have separated the data by country, let's explore different aspects of the Welsh property market.

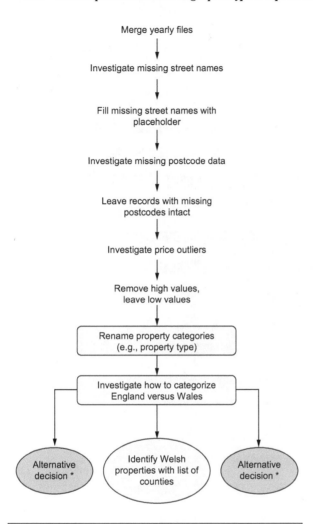

Figure 10.23   The process up until the point of identifying Welsh properties

INVESTIGATING VARIATIONS IN GEOGRAPHY

First, let's see the difference in sale price between counties. When a user wants to purchase a property, the app should help them identify what property prices look like in their desired area. The plot is shown in figure 10.24, and the code after the figure calculates and plots the median sale price by county for Welsh properties only.

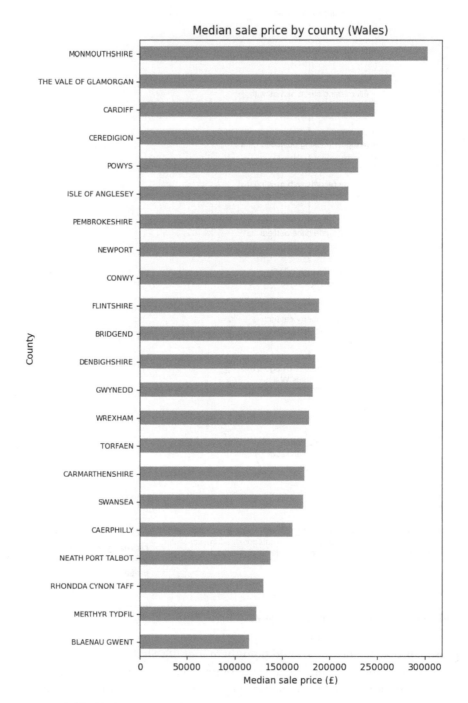

Figure 10.24   Median property price by county in Wales

```
fig, axis = plt.subplots(figsize=(6, 12))

(
    wales
    .groupby("county")
    ["sale_price"]
    .median()
    .sort_values()
    .plot
    .barh(ax=axis)
)

axis.set(
    title="Median sale price by county (Wales)",
    xlabel="Median sale price (£)",
    ylabel="County"
)

for label in axis.get_yticklabels():
    label.set_fontsize(8)

plt.show()
```

There is clear geographic disparity across counties. This data covers multiple years, so we should also investigate its temporal aspects. How has the number of transactions changed over time? The following code creates the plot in figure 10.25:

```
wales["year"] = wales["sale_date"].dt.year

fig, axis = plt.subplots()

(
    wales
    .set_index("sale_date")
    .resample("YS")
    .size()
    .plot(ax=axis, color="gray")
)

axis.set(
    title="Transactions per year",
    xlabel="Year",
    ylabel="# of transactions",
    ylim=(0, 70_000)
)

plt.show()
```

There is a definite overall downward trend in the number of transactions. Does this pattern also affect prices? We can calculate the median sale price by county and year

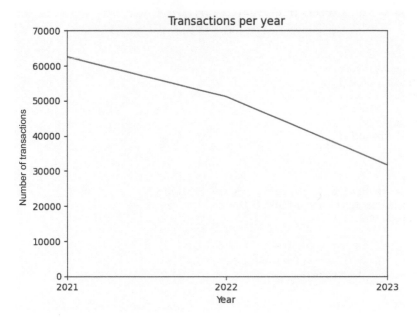

Figure 10.25   Number of annual property transactions in Wales

to investigate this. The following code calculates this and visualizes it with the heat-map shown in figure 10.26:

```
by_county_and_year = (
    wales
    .pivot_table(
        values="sale_price",
        index="county",
        columns="year",
        aggfunc="median"
    )
)

fig, axis = plt.subplots(figsize=(10, 10))

sns.heatmap(
    by_county_and_year / 1000,
    annot=True,
    cmap="Greys",
    fmt=".1f",
    ax=axis
)

axis.set(
    title="Median price by county and year (£ thousands)",
    xlabel="Year",
```

```
        ylabel="County"
)

plt.show()
```

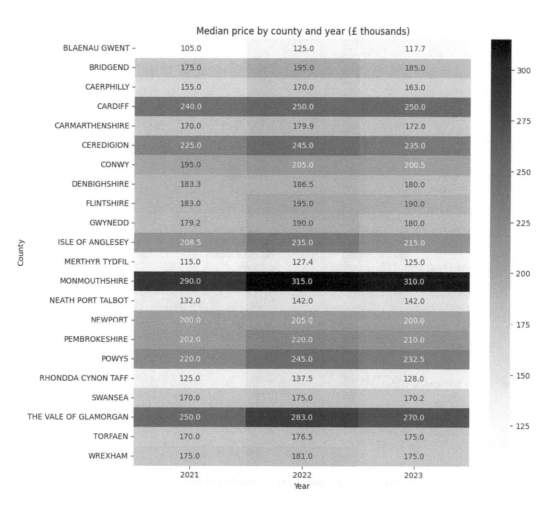

Figure 10.26   Heatmap showing property prices by county and year

In most counties, we observe an increase in the median sale price from 2021 to 2022 and then a decrease again in 2023. Although the number of transactions seems to be steadily dropping, it appears the prices have only been affected in the latest full year of data. We will want to include some aspects of this information in our final app.

Another aspect of the difference across counties might be in property type, which is something our stakeholders are specifically interested in. The code following figure 10.27 calculates the median price by county and property type and plots the heatmap in the figure.

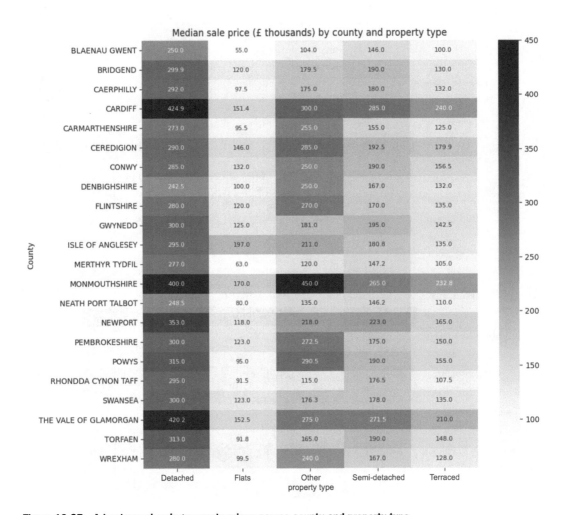

Figure 10.27   A heatmap showing property prices across county and property type

```
fig, axis = plt.subplots(figsize=(10, 10))

sns.heatmap(
    wales.pivot_table(
        index="county",
        columns="property_type",
        values="sale_price",
        aggfunc="median"
    ) / 1000,
    annot=True,
```

```
        cmap="Greys",
        fmt=".1f",                          Reduces the
        ax=axis,                            font size of the
        annot_kws={"size": 8}    ◄──────    axis labels
)

axis.set(
    title="Median sale price (£ thousands) by county and property type",
    xlabel="Property type",
    ylabel="County"
)

plt.show()
```

This heatmap tells us that detached properties have the highest value in all counties, but there is high variability in the "Other" category. This matches what is typical for the UK property market: detached properties are more desirable than semi-detached ones, which are more desirable than terraced properties. This pattern seems to exist across counties.

USING RIDGELINE PLOTS TO LOOK AT DISTRIBUTION ACROSS GROUPS

What these heatmaps don't tell us is the distribution of prices. We could use histograms or box plots to show this by county or by year. However, we might want to get a bit more adventurous to make the app stand out more visually. One option is something called a *ridgeline plots*, which looks like a smoothed histogram by category, but the histograms are stacked behind each other. To illustrate this better, the following code creates a ridgeline plot of the distribution of prices by year, as shown in figure 10.28. The data needs to be a list of prices, one list per year. Because the number of transactions is not constant for each year, we cannot use a tabular data structure, so we created three lists of prices that can be of different lengths:

```
years = sorted(wales["year"].unique())
annual_sales = []

for year in years:                  ◄─────  Creates a list of prices per year and
    prices = (                              collects this list in another list
        wales.loc[(wales["year"] == year)
                  & (wales["sale_price"] < 500_000),
        "sale_price"]
    )                                       annual_sales will be a list
    annual_sales.append([prices])   ◄─────  of pandas Series objects.

from ridgeplot import ridgeplot     ◄─────  The ridgeplot module is
                                            specialized for this kind of plot.
fig = ridgeplot(annual_sales,
                labels=[str(y) for y in years],
                colorscale="gray_r")

fig.update_layout(
    title="Welsh property sale prices over time",
    xaxis_title="Price (£)",
```

```
        yaxis_title="Year",
        showlegend=False
    )

fig.show()
```

Distribution of Welsh property sale prices over time

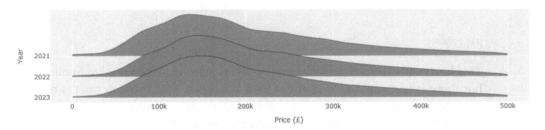

Figure 10.28   A ridgeline plot showing property prices over time

This plot shows the distribution of prices changing over time and conserves space by
having the plots overlap in a 3D effect. Let's do something similar with prices by county
to better show the spread of prices rather than simple averages. The following code collects the data for prices by county and creates the associated ridgeline plot, which is
shown in figure 10.29. This time, we will remove the temporal aspect and focus only on
properties that were sold in 2023, so our plot is as up to date and relevant as possible:

```
counties = sorted(wales["county"].unique())
sales_by_county = []

for county in counties:
    prices = (
        wales
        .loc[(wales["county"] == county)
            & (wales["sale_price"] < 500_000)
            & (wales["year"] == 2023),
        "sale_price"]
    )
    sales_by_county.append([prices])

fig = ridgeplot(sales_by_county,
                labels=counties,
                colorscale="gray",
                coloralpha=0.9,
                colormode="mean-minmax",
                spacing=0.7)

fig.update_layout(
    title="Sale prices in Wales in 2023, by county",
    height=650,
    width=950,
```

```
        font_size=12,
        plot_bgcolor="rgb(245, 245, 245)",
        xaxis_gridcolor="white",
        yaxis_gridcolor="white",
        xaxis_gridwidth=2,
        yaxis_title="County",
        xaxis_title="Sale price (£)",
        showlegend=False
    )

fig.show()
```

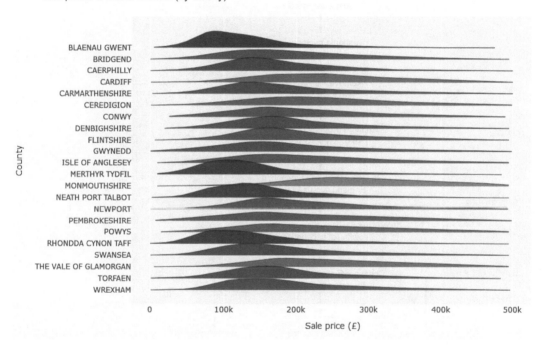

Figure 10.29   **A ridgeline plot of prices by county**

This plot is more information dense than the one in figure 10.24, which shows only median prices. We'll include this plot in the app as a reference, so users have an idea of property prices across the country. We will also include the number of transactions over time for the area a user is interested in, as well as a breakdown by property type, such as the chart in figure 10.15. These visualizations, coupled with the interactivity that we plan to add, will form our minimum viable answer for this project.

Let's revisit the entire process up until this point. Figure 10.30 shows what we have done so far, including the most recent step of deciding which visuals to include in the app.

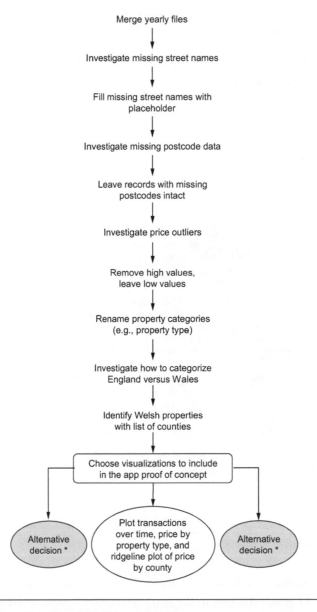

Figure 10.30   **The process until the decision of which visualizations to include in the proof of concept**

Beyond the visualizations we have chosen to include, we will want to add some interactivity to the app. We will do this in the form of filters so that the user can filter the data down to just the area they are interested in, which will update the charts accordingly. To do this, we need to understand what levels of granularity we will let users drill down to. Our stakeholders requested street-level information in the app if possible, so let's investigate whether this is possible with the available data.

INVESTIGATING GEOGRAPHIC HIERARCHY

We have several columns in the data that refer to different address components. To devise our filters for the app, we need to understand their hierarchy. Based on knowledge of address hierarchies, we would assume that the hierarchy consists of counties, districts, towns, and streets. However, the words "county" and "district" may have different meanings in different datasets, so we will verify whether this hierarchy is correct. To do this, we will count the number of distinct records in each category. The smaller the number of distinct values, the higher the level that category is in the hierarchy. The following code calculates this and produces the result in figure 10.31.

```
hierarchy = ["county", "district", "town_city", "street"]
level_counts = []

for col in hierarchy:
    num_values = wales[col].nunique()
    level_counts.append(num_values)

for z in zip(hierarchy, level_counts):
    print(z)
```

```
('county', 22)
('district', 22)
('town_city', 181)
('street', 23544)
```

Figure 10.31 Number of distinct records for each address component

Interestingly, there seems to be a one-to-one mapping between counties and districts. To verify this, we should see whether any county has more than one district mapped to it in the data or vice versa. We achieve this with the following code. Our assumption is that if both these lines of code return 0 results, then we have a perfect one-to-one mapping between counties and districts:

```
wales.groupby("county")["district"].nunique().loc[lambda x: x > 1]
wales.groupby("district")["county"].nunique().loc[lambda x: x > 1]
```

Both results return nothing, meaning there are no districts attached to more than one county, and no counties attached to more than one district. Perhaps the district column is relevant for England, but it is redundant for Wales. We can, therefore, conclude that our address hierarchy is counties, then towns and cities, and, finally, streets. These are, therefore, the three filters we will include in the app. Before we start building the app, let's export our Welsh properties as a dataset of their own, which the app can read. The app should read our cleaned and filtered data, and it should not have to manipulate it in any way. The following code exports the data to the optimized Parquet format:

```
wales.to_parquet("./data/wales.parquet", index=False)
```

That concludes the first part of the project; we prepared our data and are ready to build the proof of concept. Let's revisit what we have done so far before moving on to build the proof of concept in the next chapter.

10.4.4 *Project progress so far*

So far in the project, we

- Merged multiple years of property sales data
- Investigated the quality of the data, including missing values and outliers
- Identified geographic data of interest
- Investigated the distribution and outliers of the sale price column
- Enhanced our geographic data with external government data to separate English property transactions from Welsh ones
- Identified appropriate visualizations for our proof of concept, including a ridgeline plot
- Exported the relevant, cleaned Welsh property transactions, which our proof of concept will use

Before we move on to the final part, figure 10.32 shows our progress so far. In the next chapter, we will move on to the final part of the project, which is to build the proof-of-concept tool itself.

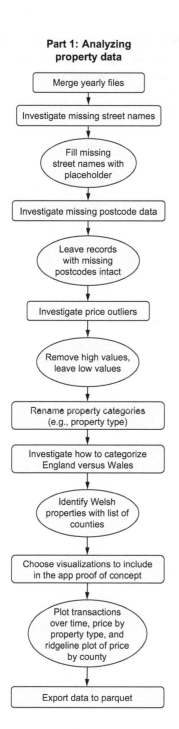

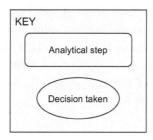

**Figure 10.32   Part 1 of the project
before building the proof of concept**

Summary

- Building a working proof of concept can be the best way to identify problems in the data that would prevent it from being used for a particular purpose.
- Exploring data with a view to building a proof of concept includes assessing whether the data is appropriate for the task.
- The output of the analysis should be a cleaned dataset that our proof of concept can use as is.

11

Rapid prototyping: Creating the proof of concept

This chapter covers
- Identifying tools to create proofs of concept
- Producing a proof of concept to showcase the reality of ideas in action

In this chapter, we will build a proof of concept using data we explored and exported in the previous chapter. In chapter 10, we identified and explored Welsh property transactions, which will need to be presented as an interactive application to end users.

The data is available for you to attempt it yourself at https://davidasboth.com/book-code. You will find the files you can use for the project, as well as the example solution in the form of a Jupyter notebook and Python scripts.

We have explored the available data, corrected issues, and identified visualizations to go into the proof of concept. In this chapter, we will build the proof of concept itself. First, let's recap the project brief.

11.1 Project 7 revisited: Building a proof of concept to investigate Welsh property prices

You're working for CymruHomes Connect, a property company specializing in homes in Wales. They're looking to expand their business with the help of data;

they want to provide insights about the Welsh property market to customers in the form of a new app. This app would use historic property sales data to allow users to explore property prices in their area of interest. The stakeholders have some ideas they'd like to incorporate:

- They are particularly interested in the analysis of property types, that is, whether a house is terraced or detached because they believe it strongly influences their customers when choosing a property.
- They also believe users will be interested in comparing properties at the lowest level of granularity, so the ability to see street-level data is important.

Let's review the data we are working with and the work done so far.

11.1.1 Data dictionary

Our stakeholders have discovered that the UK government's Land Registry has a dataset called "Price Paid," which contains publicly available historical sales data. They have extracted and made available a few years' worth of this data. Table 11.1 shows the data dictionary, not of the original data, but the dataset we exported at the end of the previous chapter, which is what our proof of concept will use.

NOTE   Original data comes from https://mng.bz/yWvB. It contains HM Land Registry data © Crown copyright and database right 2021. This data is licensed under the Open Government Licence v3.0. Thank you both to the Land Registry and Royal Mail for permission to use the house price and address data, respectively.

Table 11.1   Data dictionary of the modified Welsh property transaction data

Column	Definition
transaction_id	A reference number generated automatically, recording each published sale. The number is unique and will change each time a sale is recorded.
sale_price	Sale price stated on the transfer deed.
sale_date	Date when the sale was completed, as stated on the transfer deed.
postcode	Postal code of the address.
property_type	D = Detached, S = Semi-detached, T = Terraced, F = Flats/Maisonettes, O = Other
old_new	Indicates the age of the property and applies to all Price Paid transactions, residential and nonresidential. Y = A newly built property, N = An established residential building
duration	Relates to the tenure: F = Freehold, L= Leasehold
house_number_name	Typically house number/name (e.g., 42 or "Oak Cottage").
second_addressable_object_name	If there is a sub-building, for example, the building is divided into flats, there will be an SAON.

Table 11.1 Data dictionary of the modified Welsh property transaction data *(continued)*

Column	Definition
street	The street part of the address.
locality	Additional detail about the location (e.g., a district in a city).
town_city	The town/city part of the address.
district	The district part of the address.
county	The county part of the address.
category_type	Indicates the type of Price Paid transaction. A = Standard Price Paid entry; includes single residential property sold for full market value. B = Additional Price Paid entry; includes transfers under a power of sale/repossessions, buy-to-lets (where they can be identified by a mortgage) and transfers to nonprivate individuals.
record_status	Relevant to monthly files only. Indicates additions, changes, and deletions to the records. Yearly files contain latest versions of all records.
country	The country of the transaction. It can be England or Wales, but will all be Wales for the exported subset of data.
year	The year of the transaction.

11.1.2 Desired outcomes

Our stakeholders initially want recommendations about what kind of analyses we could include in a potential app with the available data. Recommendations about additional data sources to incorporate would also be useful. Finally, we have decided to build a proof of concept, partly to show the stakeholders what their potential app might look like but also to test whether the data is sufficient to build a useful product.

Let's review our progress in the previous chapter before continuing.

11.1.3 Project summary so far

In the previous chapter, we

- Merged multiple years of property sales data
- Investigated the quality of the data, including missing values and outliers
- Identified geographic data of interest
- Investigated the distribution and outliers of the sale price column
- Enhanced our geographic data with external government data to separate English property transactions from Welsh ones
- Identified appropriate visualizations for our proof of concept, including a ridgeplot
- Exported the relevant, cleaned Welsh property transactions, which our proof of concept will use

Figure 11.1 shows the analysis process so far.

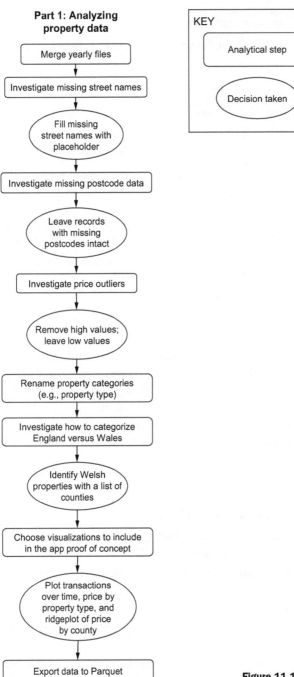

Figure 11.1   The project progress so far

We can now take the exported dataset of Welsh property transactions and use it to build our proof of concept in this chapter.

11.2 Building a proof of concept

So far, we have investigated the available data, extracted the relevant part, and explored it to understand what aspects to include in our proof of concept. Our action plan for building the proof of concept is as follows:

1 *Choose a rapid prototyping tool*—This choice will depend on what we are familiar with and what is available in our usual toolkit.

2 *Design the app layout*—We need to plan what the app is going to look like and how it will work before we start writing the code. Focusing on the end result means we minimize the amount of experimentation we need to do in building the proof of concept.

3 *Write helper functions that extract and filter our data*—Abstracting away the data from the interactive part of the app will make it easier to change the frontend of the app if we need to, without having to rewrite the data access part.

4 *Build the proof of concept*—By this point, we will have the functionality to read and filter the data, as well as a plan for what the app will look like. The final step is to build the proof of concept with the tool we decided on in step 1.

The first three steps are preparation for the final step of building the proof of concept.

11.2.1 Preparing to build a proof of concept

Let's tackle the first step, which is choosing a prototyping tool. If you have not built a working proof of concept or prototype before, this is a good point at which to explore some of the options in your existing toolkit.

DECIDING ON A RAPID PROTOTYPING TOOL

If you are an R user, for example, you might explore Shiny's capabilities. As a Python user, you also have a plethora of options available. This is another good opportunity to make use of a large language model to help you investigate the landscape. In this instance, I used Claude 3 Sonnet by Anthropic to show different options and not just ChatGPT. Here is the prompt I gave it:

> *I want to build an interactive proof of concept for a data-driven app in Python. Please suggest libraries that could help me build a web-based interactive proof of concept with the following features:*
>
> *– The ability to display visualizations, ideally using existing code that produces matplotlib charts.*
>
> *– Interactivity, i.e., dropdowns to filter the data, which will then refresh the page and all its visualizations.*
>
> *– The app needs to be web based so that users do not need to install any software to get it working.*

I will use the pandas library for data manipulation and matplotlib to create the charts, but ideally all the other features should be covered by a single additional library. Please provide a bulleted list of possible options and 1–2 sentences explaining each option.

Claude listed several options as the response, as shown in figure 11.2.

Here are some libraries that you can consider for building an interactive web-based proof of concept with the desired features:

- **Bokeh:** Bokeh is a Python library for creating interactive, web-based visualizations. It provides a high-level interface for creating plots, dashboards, and data applications. Bokeh can seamlessly integrate with Matplotlib and Pandas, making it a suitable choice for your requirements.

- **Plotly Dash:** Dash is a Python framework built on top of Plotly.js, React.js, and Flask. It allows you to create interactive, reactive web applications with minimal code. Dash supports interactivity through callbacks, making it easy to create interactive visualizations and user interfaces with dropdowns, sliders, and other UI elements.

- **Panel:** Panel is a Python library that provides a high-level interface for creating analytical applications and dashboards. It integrates well with Bokeh and other Python data analysis libraries, allowing you to build interactive web-based applications with visualizations, widgets, and layouts.

- **Streamlit:** Streamlit is a Python library that allows you to create interactive web applications with minimal code. It provides a simple and intuitive interface for building data-driven applications, including support for interactive widgets, data visualizations, and file uploads.

- **Voilà:** Voilà is a Python library that allows you to convert Jupyter Notebooks into interactive web applications. It can be useful if you prefer working in a notebook environment and want to create a shareable, interactive version of your analysis or proof of concept.

Figure 11.2   Claude 3 Sonnet's suggestions for rapid prototyping tools in Python

These are all solid options within the Python ecosystem, and all of them would be suitable for our proof of concept. I chose `streamlit`, mostly because I was already familiar with it. Otherwise, I would have spent some time reading the documentation of each library and evaluating the example code snippets to see which library would allow me to build the proof of concept the quickest.

Let's start tracking the progress of this part of the project. Figure 11.3 shows the first step that we have just taken.

Now that we have chosen our tool, let's think about the app's layout. If we know exactly what elements we want to add and where, then we can work in a results-driven way. We will only read the necessary part of the tool's documentation and only work with elements we're actually going to use.

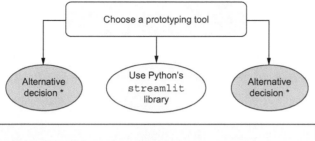

Figure 11.3   The first step toward building the proof of concept

DESIGNING AN APP LAYOUT

In this part, we need to do two things: decide on what elements will go on the page and where they will go. We have more or less already decided on this, so let's recap:

- There will be a ridgeplot showing price distribution by county for 2023.
- There will be user filters for county, town, and street.
- We will show a line chart of transactions over time.
- There will be two bar charts showing frequency and median sale price by property type, respectively.
- Depending on the target audience, we might also want to show the raw data that powers the various charts and calculations. For internal tools, I would always consider doing this for two reasons: to build trust that the calculations are correct and allow stakeholders to export the underlying data to Excel, which they invariably end up wanting to do. For a customer-facing tool, this is perhaps not necessary, but since this is a proof of concept that will be evaluated by internal users, we'll display the raw data as well.
- We might also decide to display some summary metrics about the subset of properties the user has selected.

The exact placement of these elements is mostly a personal choice, but we should at least order them logically from top to bottom. First, the user should see components they cannot change, such as the ridgeplot. Then, any subsequent elements will depend on user inputs, so the next item down the page should be the county, town, and street dropdowns. After that, we will display the summary metrics and the charts, finishing off with the raw data table at the bottom. Apart from some explanatory text, this is all we need for our proof of concept. Figure 11.4 shows a basic wireframe mockup of what we want to build.

Because this mockup includes some specific decisions we made, let's add that to the diagram of this part of the project. The latest version is shown in figure 11.5.

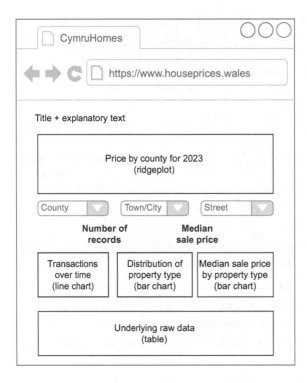

Figure 11.4   A mockup of a possible app layout

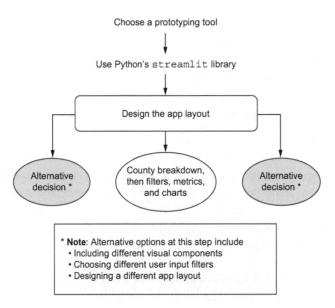

Figure 11.5   The latest progress of part 2 of the project

Now that we have our tool and an idea for the layout, let's write the data access part of our code. This is the code that the app will use to read our data and get its filtered versions based on user input.

WRITING REUSABLE HELPER FUNCTIONS

In software development, it is generally a good idea to separate data access components from the presentation layer. It is good practice to do this even for simple proofs of concept because if they develop into prototypes and working applications, we will have a reusable data access layer to use at all stages.

> ### Software development skills for analysts
>
> If you work with code, you will benefit from learning about software best practices. Analysts don't need to be software developers, but there are elements of writing good software that are relevant to data professionals.
>
> Good software development practice means readability and reusability, first and foremost. Once you get into the habit of writing clean, reusable code, which is easy to change when the requirements inevitably change, you will find a marked improvement in productivity.
>
> If you want to find out more about software skills for data people, one excellent resource is Laszlo Sragner's "Code Quality for Data Science," a Discord community dedicated to teaching all data scientists, regardless of skill level, to write better code, available at https://cq4ds.com.

In our specific app, we will require functions for the following:

- Reading in our property data as a DataFrame.
- Getting a list of counties, towns, and street names to populate the dropdowns from which the user will make their selections. These dropdowns should also depend on each other, meaning that, for example, when a user selects a county, the town/city dropdown should update to reflect only towns within that county.
- Creating all necessary visualizations based on a filtered version of the data. These functions will return actual chart objects for the app to display.

Let's walk through each of the functions in the example solution, which can be found in a file called `helpers.py`. First, here is a simple function to read the data we prepared and exported earlier:

```
import pandas as pd
import matplotlib.pyplot as plt
import seaborn as sns

from ridgeplot import ridgeplot

def load_price_data():
    return pd.read_parquet("./data/wales.parquet")
```

This is what the app will run when it first starts. Then, we need functions to populate each dropdown. Here is a function to return all possible counties in the data:

```
def get_counties(df):
    return sorted(df["county"].unique())
```

Notice how this function doesn't reference the Welsh properties directly; it simply returns all county values from any DataFrame it is given. That is because different components of the app should not depend on the specific implementation of the others. For example, the functionality to return a list of counties does not need to know where the underlying data came from. What follows is a list of towns based on a given county:

```
def get_towns(df, county, null_value):
    if (not county) or (county == null_value):
        return []

    return (
        [null_value]
        + sorted(
            df.loc[df["county"] == county, "town_city"]
            .unique()
        )
    )
```

This function takes in a null value as an additional parameter, which is a special value for when a dropdown is deselected. If a user has selected a county and then a town but wants to go back to viewing data at the entire county level, they can select this null value in the town dropdown to clear it. This null value will read something like "no town selected," so it is obvious to the user that they have cleared the town dropdown.

The final dropdown will be a list of street names, which depend on both the county and the town/city:

```
def get_streets(df, county, town, null_value):
    if (not (county and town)) or (town == null_value):
        return []

    return (
        [null_value] +
        sorted(
            df.loc[(df["county"] == county)
                    & (df["town_city"] == town),
            "street"]
            .unique()
        )
    )
```

Now we need some functions to draw our charts. First, here is the number of transactions per year, which will be similar to the chart in figure 10.25:

```
def transactions_per_year(df):
    fig, axis = plt.subplots()

    (
        df
        .set_index("sale_date")
        .resample("YS")
        .size()
        .plot(ax=axis, color="gray", marker="x")
    )

    axis.set(
        ylabel="# of transactions"
    )

    return fig
```

> **Calculates number of records per year, where "YS" means "start of year"**

Next, we want to show the breakdown of property type. We want to show both the distribution of property types and the median price by property type. We could combine this information in a single chart, for example, by representing number of transactions as the length of a bar in bar chart and the median price by a color value. However, we want the app to be as easily understood as possible, so we will separate this information into two bar charts with the following two functions:

```
def distribution_of_property_type(df):
    fig, axis = plt.subplots()

    (
        df["property_type"]
        .value_counts()
        .sort_values()
        .plot
        .barh(ax=axis, color="gray")
    )

    axis.set(
        xlabel="# of transactions"
    )

    return fig

def median_price_by_property_type(df):
    fig, axis = plt.subplots()

    (
        df
        .groupby("property_type")
        ["sale_price"]
        .median()
        .sort_values()
        .plot
        .barh(ax=axis, color="gray")
    )
```

```
axis.set(
    xlabel="Median price (£)",
    ylabel=None
)

return fig
```

Finally, we will include the ridgeplot we created in the previous chapter, so we need a helper function to create that as well. As we discovered, the ridgeplot requires data in a specific format, so we need a function to create that data and another to create the plot:

```
def get_county_ridgeplot_data(df, counties):
    sales_by_county = []

    for county in counties:
        prices = (
            df
            .loc[(df["county"] == county)
                & (df["sale_price"] < 500_000)
                & (df["year"] == 2023),
            "sale_price"]
        )
        sales_by_county.append([prices])

    return sales_by_county

def county_ridgeplot(sales_by_county, counties):
    fig = ridgeplot(sales_by_county,
                    labels=counties,
                    colorscale="gray",
                    coloralpha=0.9,
                    colormode="mean-minmax",
                    spacing=0.7)

    fig.update_layout(
        title="Distribution of house sale prices in Wales in 2023, by county",
        height=650,
        width=950,
        font_size=12,
        plot_bgcolor="rgb(245, 245, 245)",
        xaxis_gridcolor="white",
        yaxis_gridcolor="white",
        xaxis_gridwidth=2,
        yaxis_title="County",
        xaxis_title="Sale price (£)",
        showlegend=False
    )

    return fig
```

These functions will then be imported into the app, which can use them to filter our data, populate the dropdowns, and display the correct visualization based on user input. Let's add the creation of helper functions to our diagram to document our progress. This is shown in figure 11.6.

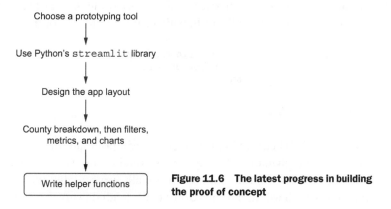

Choose a prototyping tool

Use Python's `streamlit` library

Design the app layout

County breakdown, then filters, metrics, and charts

Write helper functions

Figure 11.6   The latest progress in building the proof of concept

Now, it's finally time to build the app itself, using our chosen tool and the app layout and helper functions we created earlier.

11.2.2 *Using streamlit to build a proof of concept*

We have our tool of choice, `streamlit`, a desired layout, and helper functions to manage data access, filtering, and charts so we can build our proof of concept in a very targeted way. We need to figure out the basics of `streamlit` and only how to display text, dropdowns, charts, and tables. This means we will not be lost in a sea of tutorials and code samples—we will only take what we need.

We will now walk through the individual components of the final app, the code for which can be found in the file called house_price_app.py. To see the example solution's final app in action, open a terminal or command prompt, activate the poetry environment with the command `poetry shell`, and then run the `streamlit run house_ price_app.py` command, which should look like the example in figure 11.7. For more information on setting up your Python environment to reproduce the example solutions, see the appendix.

```
(base) c:\git\book-code\chapter-11>poetry shell
Spawning shell within C:\Users\david\AppData\Local\pypoetry\Cache\virtualenvs\the-well-grounded-data-analys
t-4Rz7GTVT-py3.11

(the-well-grounded-data-analyst-py3.11) (base) c:\git\book-code\chapter-11>streamlit run house_price_app.py

You can now view your Streamlit app in your browser.

  Local URL: http://localhost:8501
  Network URL: http://192.168.1.251:8501
```

Figure 11.7   A command prompt window showing how to run the app in the example solution

To build the app, we first set up some `streamlit` options and read in our data.

READING DATA INTO STREAMLIT

First, we will import the necessary libraries and set up some `streamlit` options, namely, that we want the page to be full width, which isn't the default option:

```
import streamlit as st
import pandas as pd
import helpers
```

> helpers in this context is the
> code in helpers.py that we
> wrote earlier.

```
st.set_page_config(layout="wide")
```

Next, we read the property data as well as the data that will populate the county drop-down as that will not change dynamically. We can also read in the data that will power the ridgeplot since, again, that will not change. Optionally, we can also get `streamlit` to cache these datasets, which will mean they don't get reloaded every time a user performs an action, such as changing a dropdown. We do this by wrapping the helper functions in small functions and annotating them with the `st.cache_data` decorator. The following is the code responsible for loading and caching the data:

```
@st.cache_data
def get_price_data():
    return helpers.load_price_data()

wales = get_price_data()

@st.cache_data
def get_counties(wales):
    return helpers.get_counties()

counties = get_counties(wales)

@st.cache_data
def get_county_data(wales, counties):
    return helpers.get_county_ridgeplot_data(wales, counties)

sales_by_county = get_county_data(wales, counties)
```

Next, we define the layout of the app.

DEFINING THE APP LAYOUT IN STREAMLIT

The apps will simply be `streamlit` elements defined in the order that we'd like the app to look from top to bottom—first, the title, brief explanation, and the ridgeplot. The following code builds these elements, and the relevant portion of the final app is shown in figure 11.8. The full explanation is omitted from the code snippet for space reasons but is shown in the figure:

```
st.title("House price explorer - Wales")
st.markdown("""This tool lets you explore...""")

st.plotly_chart(helpers.county_ridgeplot(sales_by_county, counties))
```

House price explorer - Wales

This tool lets you explore historic house price data in Wales.

You can drill down as far as the *individual street level*.

The chart below shows the distribution of house prices in different counties in 2023. The dropdowns below it let you drill down to a county, town, and street level.

Distribution of house sale prices in Wales in 2023, by county

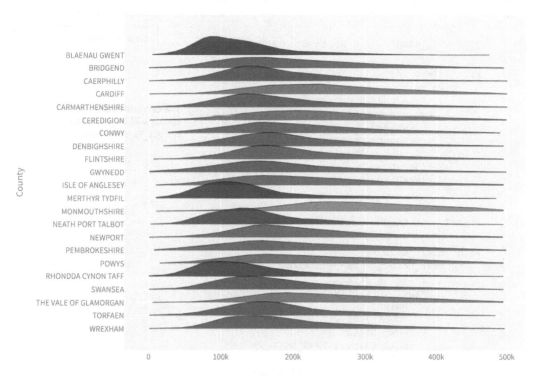

Figure 11.8   The first elements in the house price app proof of concept

Next, we will add interactivity consisting of the three dropdowns that drill into specific geographic areas. By default, adding elements to `streamlit` will add them below the previous one. Since we want the dropdowns to be on the same row, we can create some columns and add the dropdowns to them to avoid this. Each dropdown will be a `streamlit selectbox` that will be populated using our helper functions. The dropdowns that depend on others will reference the value of the other dropdowns. That is, selecting a list of towns will depend on the value selected in the county dropdown, and that value will be passed to the `get_towns` helper function. The following code creates the three dropdowns in a three-column format, and the relevant section of the app is shown in figure 11.9:

```
st.header("Explore house prices at different levels")

select_col1, select_col2, select_col3 = st.columns(3)

with select_col1:
    county_select = st.selectbox(
        'Select a county:',
        helpers.get_counties(wales),
        index=None,
        placeholder="-- Select a county --"
    )

TOWN_NULL_VALUE = "-- No town selected --"

with select_col2:
    town_select = st.selectbox(
        'Select a town:',
        helpers.get_towns(
            wales,
            county_select,
            null_value=TOWN_NULL_VALUE),
        index=None,
        placeholder=TOWN_NULL_VALUE
    )

STREET_NULL_VALUE = "-- No street selected --"

with select_col3:
    street_select = st.selectbox(
        'Select a street:',
        helpers.get_streets(
            wales,
            county_select,
            town_select,
            null_value=STREET_NULL_VALUE),
        index=None,
        placeholder=STREET_NULL_VALUE
    )
```

An example of the value the user selects if they want to clear a dropdown ⟵

The currently selected county will be passed to the get_towns function. ⟵

Figure 11.9 shows the initial state of the dropdowns. The town and street are light grey, meaning they are currently disabled until the user selects a county. Figure 11.10

Explore house prices at different levels

Select a county:

-- Select a county -- ∨

Select a town:

-- No town selected -- ∨

Select a street:

-- No street selected -- ∨

Figure 11.9   The initial state of the geographic dropdowns

shows the state of the dropdowns when some values are selected, as well as the options for the street.

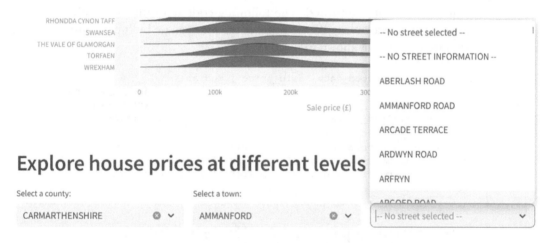

Figure 11.10   The geographic dropdowns with some values selected and the available values shown for the street

Next, we need some code that will filter the raw data down to the correct geographic level based on the user's selection.

INTERACTIVELY FILTERING DATA IN STREAMLIT

Depending on your tool, this will look different, but here, we will utilize the `query` method in `pandas`, which lets us specify the filter to apply to our data as a single string. We can build up this query string based on how many dropdowns have a value selected. The more dropdowns the user has used, the longer the query string, the more specific the query, and the less data we will retrieve. The following code builds up this query string and applies it to the data. We also build up a message that will reflect the user's choices:

```
house_filter_query = "county == @county_select"
filter_message = f"Results for {county_select}"
```

```
if town_select and town_select != TOWN_NULL_VALUE:
    house_filter_query += " and town_city == @town_select"
    filter_message += f", {town_select}"

if street_select and street_select != STREET_NULL_VALUE:
    house_filter_query += " and street == @street_select"
    filter_message += f", {street_select}"

selected_data = wales.query(house_filter_query)
```

Next, based on this filtered data, we can start calculating the summary metrics and create the charts as per our wireframe in figure 11.4. To calculate the summary metrics, we need to work out the median sale price in the filtered data, as well as count the number of records returned. The following code does this, and only if the user has selected at least a county. An example of the message we built previously, as well as the summary metrics, is shown in figure 11.11:

```
median_price = selected_data["sale_price"].median()
                                                          Selecting a county is
if county_select:                                    ←   enough to trigger
    st.header(filter_message)                             the widgets.

    metric_col1, metric_col2 = st.columns(2)
    metric_col1.metric("Number of records", f"{len(selected_data):,.0f}")
    metric_col2.metric("Median sale price", f"£{median_price:,.0f}")
```

Explore house prices at different levels

Select a county: Select a town: Select a street:

CEREDIGION   ⊗ ⌄   ABERYSTWYTH   ⊗ ⌄   ALEXANDRA ROAD ⊗ ⌄

Results for CEREDIGION, ABERYSTWYTH, ALEXANDRA ROAD

Number of records   Median sale price

5   £247,500

Figure 11.11   A message showing geographic filters the user has applied and associated summary metrics

Now, we can use our helper methods to create the relevant charts.

CREATING CHARTS IN STREAMLIT

The charts will be alongside each other, so they need to be in `streamlit` columns again. Finally, we display the filtered data as a table at the bottom of the page. The following code finishes off our app. Because the entire bottom section depends on the user having selected at least a county, I have included the entire code block, which contains the summary metrics seen previously:

```
if county_select:
    st.header(filter_message)

    metric_col1, metric_col2 = st.columns(2)
    metric_col1.metric("Number of records", f"{len(selected_data):,.0f}")
    metric_col2.metric("Median sale price", f"£{median_price:,.0f}")

    chart_col1, chart_col2, chart_col3 = st.columns(3)

    with chart_col1:
        st.subheader("Transactions over time")
        st.pyplot(helpers.transactions_per_year(selected_data))

    with chart_col2:
        st.subheader("Distribution of property type")
        st.pyplot(helpers.distribution_of_property_type(selected_data))

    with chart_col3:
        st.subheader("Median sale price by property type")
        st.pyplot(helpers.median_price_by_property_type(selected_data))

    st.header("Raw data")
    st.write(selected_data)
```

Finally, let's see the final part of the app, which contains the summary metrics, charts, and underlying data. The raw data is truncated on the figure but is shown in full in the app. This is illustrated in figure 11.12.

Before we communicate our conclusions, let's review everything we've done in this project. Figure 11.13 shows the process of exploring and cleaning the data, leading to the design and development of the proof of concept app.

We have successfully delivered our minimum viable answer. It's time to reflect on what we found and what the next steps are from here.

11.2.3 *Project outcomes and next steps*

We fulfilled the brief by investigating property types, where we found a disparity between what different property types sell for, and by investigating street-level data. We can confidently tell our stakeholders that the data is suitable for looking at both of those aspects. We then went above and beyond the brief by building a proof of concept to illustrate what their planned app might look like and whether it's even feasible to build with the available data.

Explore house prices at different levels

Select a county: Select a town: Select a street:

CEREDIGION   ✕ ⌄   ABERYSTWYTH   ✕ ⌄   ALEXANDRA ROAD   ✕ ⌄

Results for CEREDIGION, ABERYSTWYTH, ALEXANDRA ROAD

Number of records   Median sale price

5   £247,500

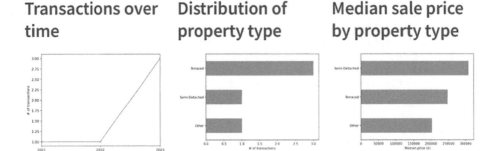

Transactions over time

Distribution of property type

Median sale price by property type

Raw data

	transaction_id	sale_price	sale_date	postcode	property_typ
3,450	{D4D42646-8177-27F6-E053-6C04A8C0A572}	270,000	2021-09-16 00:00:00	SY23 1LN	Terraced
85,259	{EED73E76-8893-6AF3-E053-6C04A8C08ABA}	202,400	2022-03-17 00:00:00	None	Other
117,193	{1061746E-9398-3C34-E063-4804A8C0F9E7}	308,000	2023-12-21 00:00:00	SY23 1LN	Semi-Detach

Figure 11.12   The bottom part of the finished proof of concept app with the raw data table truncated

There are a few points to address about our proof of concept:

- First, there are missing values in relevant address fields. To launch and possibly charge money for an app like this, the data would need to be complete. To that end, we would need to clean the data and fill in the missing address details, perhaps using a third-party geocoding service such as the Google Maps API.
- Second, the app shows the charts associated with a user's choices, even if there are only a few available records, as illustrated by figure 11.12. Depending on

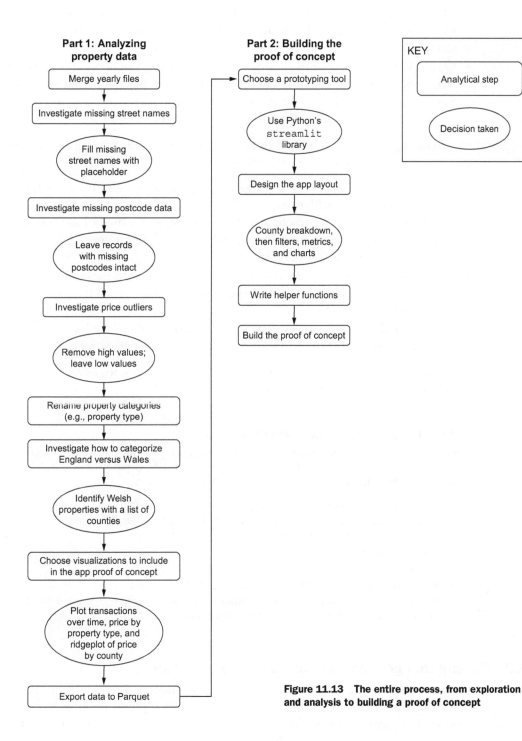

Figure 11.13 The entire process, from exploration and analysis to building a proof of concept

what we believe the user will use the summary metrics and charts for, we may wish to issue a disclaimer in the app if the sample size of properties returned is too small.

- Finally, if we iron some of these problems out and the proof of concept makes it to the prototype stage, we would need to user test it to make sure that users can find the relevant addresses. In this case, that would mean ensuring the values for county, town, and street are correctly categorized.

When presenting this app to our stakeholders, we may also want to suggest improvements for a final version. Here are some ideas:

- Users would probably want to investigate a property after seeing it on a property listing website, such as Rightmove or Zoopla. It might be useful to establish a link between those sites and our app. For example, a user might paste a link to a property on Rightmove into our app, which could then filter the data automatically based on that property's address.
- Other options for filtering the results automatically might be to simply enter an address or select it on an interactive map. This would save users time and make their experience smoother.
- We could enhance our address data with information about the local area that might affect property prices, such as crime rates or availability of utilities.

Whatever we choose to do next, it would start with a presentation to our stakeholders and a discussion about whether to take this project further into the prototype phase.

Activity: Further project ideas with this data

Think about other analyses you could do with this house price dataset. In particular, you might want to practice different approaches to building a proof of concept to develop your skills in this area. Here are some directions you may wish to go:

- Geographic data like this is perfect for map-based visualizations. You could create an application to identify transaction hotspots, areas of the country where there is a lot of "turnover" of properties.
- Are there any seasonal patterns in property sales? Do these differ across different geographic areas?
- By enhancing the data with demographic information (e.g., population data), you could see if there are places around the country where there are more property sales than is typical for an area of that size.

11.3   Closing thoughts on the rapid prototyping of ideas

As we saw in this project, it can be useful to extend an analysis by building a proof of concept from the available data. This is also true for building predictive models; rather than presenting accuracy metrics, these models can come alive if we can demonstrate how they would work in practice. Having a proof of concept and then a prototype also lets us identify problems with the data that would affect the building of a fully working product.

To hone your skills specifically in this area, there are a number of approaches:

- The obvious one is to get familiar with a rapid prototyping tool. This could be building dashboards with a BI tool, such as Power BI or Tableau. It could be learning a library for your programming language, such as Shiny for R or `streamlit` for Python. Or, it could be learning about a "no code" platform, where you can make working applications without explicitly writing code.
- Another skill that could help here, especially if you want to build working prototypes, is to learn about building for the web. Specifically, learning a bit of HTML, CSS, and JavaScript is useful to help craft bespoke web-based applications. Platforms such as the Web Design Playground (https://www.manning .com/books/web-design-playground-second-edition) are great for learning the basics.
- Learning design principles is also useful if you will be building proofs of concept and prototypes as part of your job. Knowing the fundamentals of UI and UX design principles, user flows, and storyboarding will help you build better prototypes.

Of course, the best way to learn this skill is by practicing it. Look for opportunities to build small, interactive applications to complement your analysis. They'll be useful learning experiences both for you and the stakeholders you show them to.

11.3.1 Skills for rapid prototyping for any project

To build an interactive proof of concept based on available data, the key skills, which can be applied to any similar project, include

- Focusing on the features of the prototype when exploring the available data
- Verifying the quality of our data since it will be exposed to external customers
- Enhancing the data from reputable sources (e.g., using official city names)
- Exploring interesting variations in our data to identify what to focus on in the proof of concept
- Identifying visualizations appropriate for the prototype and the intended audience
- Choosing an appropriate rapid prototyping tool with which to build a proof of concept
- Designing the layout of the app as a wireframe before writing any code
- Writing helper functions that the app can use but are not tightly coupled with the app code
- Setting up a rapid prototyping tool such as `streamlit`
- Implementing the desired layout in a prototyping tool

- Displaying data and charts in your prototyping tool
- Providing for user interaction with the presented data and visualizations

Summary

- The journey from idea to working product should include the creation of proofs of concept and prototypes, both of which are areas where analysts can participate and are a useful addition to an analyst's toolkit.
- Proofs of concept and prototypes are an effective way to bring an analysis to life for stakeholders.
- Choosing a tool for creating proofs of concept should depend on the existing tools available, how the audience will interact with the end product, and the speed at which a proof of concept can be created with the chosen tool.
- Rapid prototyping also requires a results-driven approach to ensure only necessary functionality is built in initial versions.

Iterating on someone else's work: Data preparation

Every analyst will need to continue someone else's work at some point. This "someone" might be a past version of you from months ago. The process for working on the second version of a project is the same as starting from scratch.

Because we will own this new version, we still need to understand the problem, look at the available data, and so on, even if someone else has already done it. In this project, you will get the opportunity to practice taking over from someone else. Another analyst has prepared the minimum viable answer to a stakeholder question, on which you will iterate.

The specific topic of this chapter is one that is also common in the real world: segmentation. Most businesses have questions in the form of "How are some things similar to other things?" where the thing in question could be anything from a product to a customer to an entire geographic area.

Real business case: Segmenting customers based on buying activity

The specific methods required to segment customers will come in handy for segmenting anything. For example, one project I worked on was identifying customers who bought similar used cars at auction. Having a notion of buyer similarity meant we could find more buyers to whom we could proactively recommend upcoming auctions. Being able to invite buyers to an auction because we know they buy similar stock led to more productive conversations and more eyes on our auctioned cars.

The process for finding similar entities, what we refer to here as "segmentation," is the same regardless of the type of entity. In this chapter specifically, you will practice segmenting mobile users into groups based on their app usage activity. You will work with event-level data and continue the work of another analyst who has already completed an iteration of the project.

12.1   *Finding similar entities*

The problem of segmentation appears in many places. The typical use case is finding customers who are similar to each other based on characteristics such as demographics or behavior. A business may also want to apply segmentation to its product catalog to categorize and simplify its offering.

In each case, the outcome is that different actions will be taken for different segments. Users in different financial segments will be targeted with different banking products. Products that are grouped into a segment may be recommended alongside each other to the end user. Recommendation engines make heavy use of the notion of user and product similarity.

In machine learning, segmentation, or clustering, is an example of unsupervised learning. This means that, unlike supervised prediction problems, we don't have examples of the "truth," that is, actual customer segments against which to compare our results. Our ability to measure how good our segments are is, therefore, limited. The evaluation of these segments is usually done subjectively by human experts instead.

Supervised vs. unsupervised learning

In machine learning, the difference between supervised and unsupervised learning is whether we have historical examples of correct predictions against which to compare our model's predictions.

If we are predicting the price of a house based on its properties, we need training data that includes both the properties of the houses and the prices they sold for. This is *supervised* learning because we can compare our model's predictions to actual values, thus supervising our prediction model.

In *unsupervised* learning, we do not have such past examples. There are no correct answers to compare against. Instead, we are trying to find patterns of some sort in our data, which we then evaluate more subjectively. Customer segmentation falls neatly into this latter category.

In any similarity problem, there are certain factors to consider when deciding on our approach:

- What action will we take when we have our groups? This is the most important question to ask since it motivates the entire project.
- What features are important when determining similarity? Do we care about users who live in the same area or who have similar purchasing patterns?
- On a related note, do we have redundant features? If we're segmenting cars, we don't want to include their top speed in both kilometers and miles per hour. One variable to measure a particular concept is enough.
- How many groups do we believe we will find? We may not have an exact number, but even a ballpark will help.
- How will we evaluate the outcome of the segmentation? Usually, this is done with the help of domain experts.

In this project, in addition to these factors, we will also want a checklist of actions for how to continue the previous analyst's work.

12.2   Continuing someone else's work

In a situation where we are continuing someone else's work, the first step should be to replicate their findings whether or not the original source code is available. The reasons for this are

- Having our own version of the previous pipeline means we can more easily make changes to it.
- Recreating someone else's work checks for mistakes, not with the purpose of blaming anyone, but to verify that their steps did what they said they did.
- We also want to verify the assumptions present in the previous analyst's work. It's possible they made incorrect assumptions or even just different assumptions to the ones we'd make. Being explicit about these assumptions gives everyone clarity.
- Replicating the work puts us in a better position to understand the details of the project, the limitations, and what further steps are possible. Looking at someone else's work briefly is not the same as getting into the weeds ourselves.

If we consider these factors before we start work, then, combined with our results-driven approach, we will be well equipped for the project to succeed.

Let's now take a look at this chapter's project.

> **Collaborating with others**
>
> In this project, you are indirectly collaborating with another analyst by continuing their work. You won't always be the only analyst on a project; there will be times when you share the work with other analysts. Being an effective collaborator means
>
> - Communicating your work to other technical colleagues
> - Applying best practices to your work to make your code easier to work with
> - Consistently looking for ways to improve and learn from others
>
> To hone these skills, you can contribute to open source projects or spend time looking at other people's work.

12.3 Project 8: Finding customer segments from mobile activity

In this project, we will look at mobile phone activity to identify groups of similar customers. We will examine the problem statement, the available data, the project deliverables, and the tools you will need to attempt the project.

The data is available for you to attempt the project yourself at https://davidasboth .com/book-code. You will find the files that you can use for the project, including the previous analyst's work on which we will build, as well as the example solution in the form of a Jupyter notebook.

12.3.1 Problem statement

You're working for AppEcho Insights, an analytics company focused on mobile user behavior. They analyze data on how users use their phones and provide insights to mobile phone manufacturers and app developers. Their latest initiative is customer segmentation. They want to understand whether there are groups of users who behave in a similar way. Knowing these user segments would be useful as their clients could target entire user bases with different initiatives. For example, they could market productivity tips to casual users or insights on extending battery life to heavy users.

A previous analyst already performed a basic segmentation of the user base and presented their findings to the stakeholders. Unfortunately, they left the company after that, and their code was lost. Your manager has asked you to work on a second version of the analysis, using the results of the first as a starting point.

The conclusion of the first version was that it is possible to segment customers based on the number of apps they use and the average length of their browsing sessions. The analyst proposed six unique customer categories and assigned them personas, such as "casual users" and "power users." Your stakeholders want the second version of the segmentation to be more complex and include more features. They'd like to focus on the following:

- The types of apps that people use. For example, do some customers use their phones more for social media than others?

- Look at temporal patterns. Do users prefer to browse their phones at different times of the day?
- Potentially use a more suitable segmentation method (e.g., an algorithm that can handle grouping users based on multiple dimensions).

They have provided you with the dataset of mobile events and the presentation the initial analyst delivered. The dataset consists of individual mobile events, such as a user opening or closing a mobile app. There are only a few columns, but it is possible to extract rich behavioral information. The events are timestamped, so the temporal element can also be analyzed. See chapters 8 and 9 for more details about working with time data.

NOTE The data was originally taken from https://github.com/aliannejadi/ LSApp. Thank you to Mohammad Aliannejadi for permission to use the data.

Both the data and presentation files are in the supplementary materials. Your task will be to review the analyst's work and continue the project to answer your stakeholders' questions.

12.3.2 Data dictionary

As always, a key initial step is to take a look at the available data. Table 12.1 shows the data dictionary.

Table 12.1 Data dictionary

Column	Definition
User ID	A user's unique identifier.
Session ID	Uniquely identifies a user's activity session.
Timestamp	Date and time of an individual event.
App name	The name of the app in use.
Event type	The type of the event that took place. Values are one of the following: "Opened," "Closed," "User Interaction," or "Broken."

Now that we have seen what's available, let's look at the outcomes of this project.

12.3.3 Desired outcomes

Our stakeholders want a more in-depth analysis and customer segments based on more dimensions. Our solution should consist of a recreation of the initial analysis followed by our own improvements. The final output is the definition of our user segments, meaning what factors describe each segment and which users belong to which group.

12.3.4 *Required tools*

In the example solution, I use Python and the `pandas` library for data exploration, `matplotlib` for visualization, and `scikit-learn` for clustering. To complete this project, you will need a tool that can

- Load a dataset from a CSV or similar
- Perform basic data manipulation tasks, such as sorting, grouping, and reshaping data
- Create data visualizations
- Perform segmentation (e.g., with a clustering algorithm)

You can decide to perform the segmentation "by hand," meaning decide on what values of your dimensions make up the groups. However, this becomes increasingly difficult to do manually after two to three dimensions, which is why I recommend choosing a tool that can apply a relevant algorithm.

Let's now see how we might approach this problem step by step using our results-driven framework.

12.4 Applying the results-driven method to creating the second iteration of a customer segmentation

Let's look at a results-driven approach to this problem and formulate our action plan.

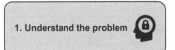

The problem statement is clear: allocate users to distinct segments. Beyond this, what we also need to understand is the work the previous analyst has already done. Only then can we understand exactly what our task is. Recreating the analyst's work is also crucial. First, we need to ensure we can replicate their results and verify their assumptions, but in this case, we also need to have the code available as the original was lost.

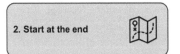

Starting at the end, in this case, means answering the questions posed in section 12.1. How many groups should there be? What kind of groups make sense in light of what our stakeholders want to do with the output? They want to be able to target different user groups with different offerings, so our evaluation of the user groups should be made with that in mind.

In this instance, the data has been identified for us. However, we should also think about ways to enhance this data. Can we extract more information from the data, or are there external sources we could join on?

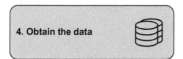

The data has been downloaded for us in its raw form. Again, however, we could enhance it. We will review some ideas for enhancement in the example solution.

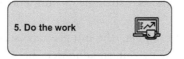

The segmentation process resembles any data analysis problem, for the most part:

- We will start by exploring the data, looking for missing and incorrect values, outliers, and so on.
- Next, we will investigate which features our records vary along. That is, do some features have more variance than others? If all customers live in the same geographic area, there is no need to include geography as one of the dimensions on which to segment them.
- We also want to visualize our data along the different dimensions in the hope of discovering obvious groups. In large, complex datasets, this is unlikely, but we might find outlier groups, such as a few customers who spend a lot more than the others.
- The final two steps are unique to the segmentation problem. First, we will choose which dimensions to segment on and apply a clustering algorithm. Different algorithms exist for different use cases, some of which are discussed in the example solution.
- Then, we will evaluate the results. We will do this by analyzing the groups to see if they meaningfully differ from one another. One way to do this is to assign group labels or personas to each group. If we can give each group a unique description, the results will be more useful than if we have created multiple segments with the same characteristics.

This step will be done once we have an allocation for each user, that is, know which of our newly created groups they belong to.

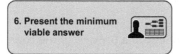

The presentation from the previous iteration was a short slide deck. We could consider creating a similar presentation as an output. At the very least, we should have all the same ingredients to hand: a list of the final groups, the number of users in each group, and what characteristics describe each group.

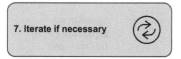

Since this will be the second iteration of the project, we should make recommendations to our stakeholders about additional steps that could be taken after our version is finished. Clearly, this is an important company initiative, which we can support by providing suggestions for further work if our stakeholders decide to allocate more resources.

12.5 An example solution: Creating customer segments

Now, let's walk through an example solution. As always, I strongly recommend attempting the project yourself first.

As for the action plan, first, we will attempt to recreate the initial analysis. Next, we will investigate the additional features requested by our stakeholders before finally grouping our customers into new segments and analyzing these groups.

12.5.1 Recreating someone else's analysis

In this first part, we will review the slides presented by the previous analyst and attempt to replicate their findings. Slide 4 contains some summary metrics, which is where we should start. Figure 12.1 shows the slide in question.

Dataset at a glance

292
users

87
apps

Most popular apps:

- Facebook

- Google Chrome

- Facebook Messenger

8
months of
events

3
event types

Figure 12.1   Slide 4 from the original presentation, showing summary metrics

Our first task is to verify that we can recreate these metrics.

VERIFYING REPORTED METRICS

First, we'll read in the data with the following code, and a preview of the rows is shown in figure 12.2. Note that the data is in the .tsv format, meaning values are separated by a tab character, not a comma:

```
import pandas as pd
import matplotlib.pyplot as plt

app_data = pd.read_csv(
    "./data/lsapp.tsv.gz",
    sep="\t",
    names=["user_id", "session_id", "timestamp",
```

Specifies the separator as the tab character

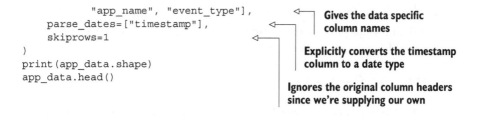

```
            "app_name", "event_type"],
        parse_dates=["timestamp"],
        skiprows=1
)
print(app_data.shape)
app_data.head()
```

Gives the data specific
column names

Explicitly converts the timestamp
column to a date type

Ignores the original column headers
since we're supplying our own

(3658590, 5)

	user_id	session_id	timestamp	app_name	event_type
0	0.0	1.0	2018-01-16 06:01:05	Minesweeper Classic (Mines)	Opened
1	0.0	1.0	2018-01-16 06:01:05	Minesweeper Classic (Mines)	Closed
2	0.0	1.0	2018-01-16 06:01:07	Minesweeper Classic (Mines)	Opened
3	0.0	1.0	2018-01-16 06:01:07	Minesweeper Classic (Mines)	Closed
4	0.0	1.0	2018-01-16 06:01:08	Minesweeper Classic (Mines)	Opened

Figure 12.2   A snapshot of the raw data

The output of the code tells us that there are over three million rows of data, and the snapshot tells us that we have one row per app event, which is when the user opens or closes an app. Let's now investigate the claims on the appendix slide, which say that missing data and events tagged as broken were dropped. The slide in question is shown in figure 12.3.

Appendix

- Rows with missing data were removed.

- Events tagged as "Broken" were removed.

Figure 12.3   The relevant part of the appendix from the slides, showing additional data cleaning steps

To investigate these additional data cleaning steps, the following code investigates missing data and produces the output in figure 12.4:

```
app_data.isnull().sum()
```

```
user_id        1
session_id     1
timestamp      1
app_name       1
event_type     1
dtype: int64
```

Figure 12.4   The result of investigating missing data

This figure shows there is one missing value in each column. Regardless of whether those missing values are in the same record, it's safe to drop missing data as it makes up a negligible percentage of our dataset:

```
app_data = app_data.dropna()
```

Figure 12.2 also shows that user ID and session ID, which should typically be integers, are treated as decimal values. This is because the version of the pandas library I'm using does not have a nullable integer type. It is not crucial to convert this column to an integer, but we will do it to be explicit and avoid any confusion. Figure 12.5 verifies that all the columns have the correct data type:

```
app_data["user_id"] = app_data["user_id"].astype(int)
app_data["session_id"] = app_data["session_id"].astype(int)

app_data.dtypes
```

```
user_id              int32
session_id           int32
timestamp       datetime64[ns]
app_name             object
event_type           object
dtype: object
```

Figure 12.5 **The corrected data types in our dataset**

Before verifying the summary metrics on the slides, let's investigate the "Broken" event type that, according to the appendix, was dropped. The following code looks at the distribution of event type as a percentage of the entire data, and the result is shown in figure 12.6:

```
app_data["event_type"].value_counts(normalize=True)
```

```
Opened            0.457351
Closed            0.455644
User Interaction  0.085779
Broken            0.001226
Name: event_type, dtype: float64
```

Figure 12.6 **Percentage breakdown of each event type**

This figure tells us that only 0.1% of our data is a "Broken" event. We don't have a lot of context about what this means, so we will agree with the initial analysis and drop these records using the following code.

```
app_data = app_data[app_data["event_type"] != "Broken"]
```

Before we go further, let's start building up our diagram of the process we are following. Figure 12.7 shows what we have done so far and where the analysis might have diverged.

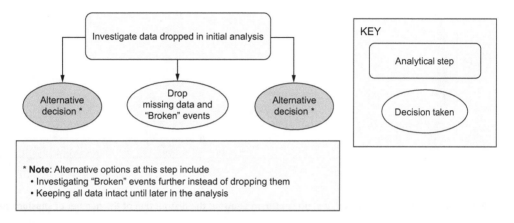

Figure 12.7 The first step in recreating the initial analysis

Let's now verify that, as per the "Dataset at a glance" slide in figure 12.1, we have 292 users, 87 unique apps, events spanning eight months, and three distinct event types. First, we verify the number of users:

```
app_data["user_id"].nunique()
```

This code returns 292, as expected. Now, we verify the number of distinct apps:

```
app_data["app_name"].nunique()
```

Again, we get the expected value of 87. Let's now look at the date range in our data:

```
app_data["timestamp"].agg(["min", "max"])
```

The output tells us the data spans September 2017 to May 2018, which is approximately eight months, as stated on the slides. We also know there are three event types since there were four when we first investigated them, and we dropped one of them entirely. The next step is to recreate some of the underlying data behind the charts in the slides.

First, there is a slide showing the number of sessions per user, as shown in figure 12.8.

Number of sessions per user seems like a useful metric to calculate as it is a proxy for how active a user is. To do this, we'll create a DataFrame where, for each user, we count how many unique sessions they have in the data. We will then explore the distribution

Most people have few sessions recorded, with outliers

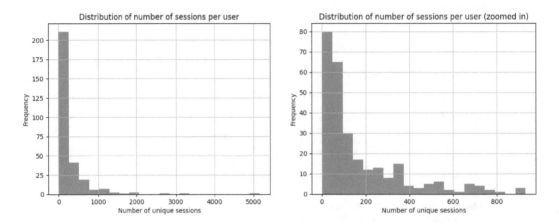

Figure 12.8   **A slide from the original presentation showing the distribution of the number of sessions per user**

of this measure. The following code creates this DataFrame, and the output showing its descriptive statistics is presented in figure 12.9:

```
sessions_per_user = (
    app_data
    .groupby("user_id")
    ["session_id"]
    .nunique()
)

sessions_per_user.describe()
```

```
count      292.000000
mean       261.113014
std        484.984555
min          1.000000
25%         45.750000
50%         95.500000
75%        289.000000
max       5153.000000
Name: session_id, dtype: float64
```

Figure 12.9   **Descriptive statistics of the number of sessions per user**

This tells us that the median number of sessions per user is 95, but there were users with a single session all the way to a user with over 5,000. Let's see this distribution visually to better understand both the spread and where the data is concentrated. The following code creates the histogram shown in figure 12.10:

```
fig, axis = plt.subplots()

sessions_per_user.hist(bins=20, ax=axis)

axis.set(
    title="Sessions per user",
    xlabel="Number of sessions",
    ylabel="Frequency"
)

plt.show()
```

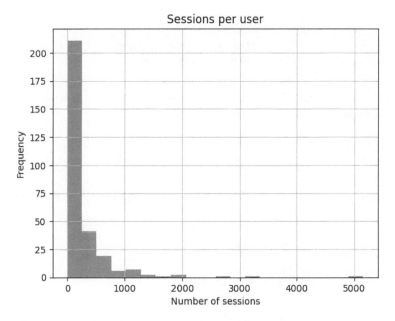

Figure 12.10   Distribution of number of sessions per user

As we might have expected from the descriptive statistics, the distribution tells us most users have few sessions, with a long tail stretching to users with thousands. The initial analysis didn't mention what the profiles of those prolific users look like, so let's investigate them. Before we do that, let's update our diagram to document the process so far. Figure 12.11 shows the latest version.

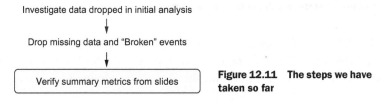

Figure 12.11   The steps we have taken so far

From this point, we will go beyond the results presented in the slides and into our own analysis. Let's now look at the data for the user with the highest number of sessions. The following code finds the users with the most sessions, and the output is shown in figure 12.12:

```
sessions_per_user.sort_values(ascending=False).head(5)
```

```
user_id
138     5153
290     3284
192     2763
31      1885
204     1851
Name: session_id, dtype: int64
```

Figure 12.12   The users with the most unique sessions

The following code extracts the raw data for the user with the most sessions: user 138. A snapshot of their data is shown in figure 12.13:

```
app_data[app_data["user_id"] == 138].head(10)
```

	user_id	session_id	timestamp	app_name	event_type
1782158	138	28802	2018-01-04 05:21:59	Phone	Opened
1782159	138	28802	2018-01-04 05:21:59	Phone	Closed
1782160	138	28802	2018-01-04 05:21:59	Phone	Opened
1782161	138	28802	2018-01-04 05:22:25	Phone	Closed
1782162	138	28802	2018-01-04 05:22:26	Telegram	User Interaction
1782163	138	28802	2018-01-04 05:24:54	Telegram	User Interaction
1782164	138	28802	2018-01-04 05:28:53	Telegram	User Interaction
1782165	138	28802	2018-01-04 05:29:02	Facebook Messenger	Opened
1782166	138	28802	2018-01-04 05:30:02	Facebook Messenger	Closed
1782167	138	28803	2018-01-04 05:35:04	Twitter	User Interaction

Figure 12.13   A snapshot of the activity of the user with the most sessions

It looks like the data for this user starts with them using various apps at around 5:30 a.m. One noticeable aspect of this data is that it starts with an "Opened" event followed immediately by a "Closed" event and then another "Opened" event, all for the same app. Is this information relevant or redundant? In the example in figure 12.13, we have some exact duplicates, namely, the first and third rows. Let's see how big this problem is.

INVESTIGATING DUPLICATE EVENT RECORDS

The following code calculates the proportion of records that are exact duplicates:

```
app_data.duplicated().sum() / len(app_data)
```

The output is 0.597, meaning nearly 60% of our data is an exact duplicate of another row. That means a record with the same user ID, same session ID, and the same event type occurring for the same app at the same time.

This result could potentially require a lot of work to investigate and clear up, so before we do anything, let's consider whether duplicates are a problem for the specific analysis we want to conduct. We are interested in

- What types of apps do people use? If we are counting things like the number of unique apps per user, duplicates won't be a problem.
- When do people use their phones? Unfortunately, having duplicate records would skew the results because we may accidentally inflate some parts of the day versus others if there happen to be more duplicates at different times of the day.

We, therefore, can't ignore the fact there are duplicates. We need to take stock of our possible options instead:

- We could simply drop duplicate records. What would happen if we did this for the example in figure 12.13? We would end up with an "Opened" event followed by two "Closed" events. The "Closed" events wouldn't be duplicates as they occurred at different times. Dropping exact duplicates is too basic and would cause additional problems.
- Another option is to drop pairs of "Opened" and "Closed" events that occurred at the same time. However, this assumes that an "Opened" event always has a corresponding "Closed" event, which may not hold in practice.
- We could also think about the problem differently. As it stands, we are not interested in the single-event level but in summarizing behavior at the user level. This means that we could say that "Closed" events are less informative. If a user opens five apps in a browsing session, we would know that even without the presence of "Closed" events.

The idea that "Closed" events are informationally redundant is quite appealing, so let's go with that approach. The following code drops events that are "Closed" and calculates the percentage of records we dropped, as well as the percentage of exact duplicates in the remaining data:

```
closed_dropped = app_data.loc[app_data["event_type"] != "Closed", :]
```

```
print(len(closed_dropped))
print(len(closed_dropped) / len(app_data))
print(closed_dropped.duplicated().sum() / len(closed_dropped))
```

The outputs of these three commands are 1,987,090, 0.54, and 0.599. This means we have just under 2 million records remaining out of an initial 3.7 million, which is about half our original data. It also tells us that we still have nearly 60% exact duplicates. Now, an exact duplicate is entirely redundant for our purposes, so we can drop those, too. The following code does this and calculates how much data we have left:

```
app_data_reduced = closed_dropped.drop_duplicates()
len(app_data_reduced)
```

We are left with just under 800,000 records. It is unusual to drop so much data as part of an analysis, but in this case, it was justified. Figure 12.14 shows the process so far, including the choices we have just made.

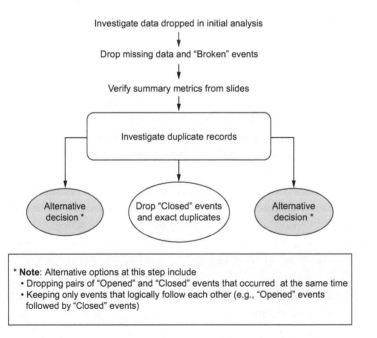

Figure 12.14   The process so far, including choices about handling duplicate data

Having cleaned up a lot of duplication, let's reexamine our data. The following code examines the first few rows, which are shown in figure 12.15:

```
app_data_reduced.head(10)
```

	user_id	session_id	timestamp	app_name	event_type
0	0	1	2018-01-16 06:01:05	Minesweeper Classic (Mines)	Opened
2	0	1	2018-01-16 06:01:07	Minesweeper Classic (Mines)	Opened
4	0	1	2018-01-16 06:01:08	Minesweeper Classic (Mines)	Opened
8	0	1	2018-01-16 06:01:09	Minesweeper Classic (Mines)	Opened
10	0	1	2018-01-16 06:03:44	Minesweeper Classic (Mines)	Opened
12	0	1	2018-01-16 06:03:45	Minesweeper Classic (Mines)	Opened
14	0	1	2018-01-16 06:03:47	Minesweeper Classic (Mines)	Opened
16	0	1	2018-01-16 06:03:49	Minesweeper Classic (Mines)	Opened
20	0	1	2018-01-16 06:03:51	Minesweeper Classic (Mines)	Opened
22	0	1	2018-01-16 06:03:52	Minesweeper Classic (Mines)	Opened

Figure 12.15   Example events after duplicate records were removed

This latest figure shows a new challenge. There are sequential instances of a user opening Minesweeper, sometimes only a few seconds apart. What could this mean?

- Was the user constantly changing their mind about whether they wanted to play?
- Was the user trying to open the app, but it kept crashing?
- Are these artifacts of how the data was collected/collated?

We would need more information to know for sure.

HANDLING RELATED PAIRS OF EVENT RECORDS

As it stands, we must make a choice about what, if anything, to do about this kind of repetition:

- We could assume that multiple repeated events related to an app are actually a single instance of the user using that app. In the case of someone opening Minesweeper 10 times in the data followed by opening another app, we could treat that as 2 events instead of 11.
- We could look at the time difference between interactions of the same app and remove interactions that are too short. This requires us to strictly define "too short," which is a strong built-in assumption.

- We could also ignore this problem entirely. Again, we are interested in user-level and session-level metrics, not individual event-level ones. If we define the length of a user session by the difference between when it started and ended, it doesn't matter what happened in between as the user was interacting with their phone one way or another.

Thinking about this in a results-driven way, we can answer our stakeholders' questions about app types and user browsing times without explicitly handling these instances of users opening and closing apps in quick succession. Since we're making another choice, we'll add that to our diagram, the latest version of which is shown in figure 12.16.

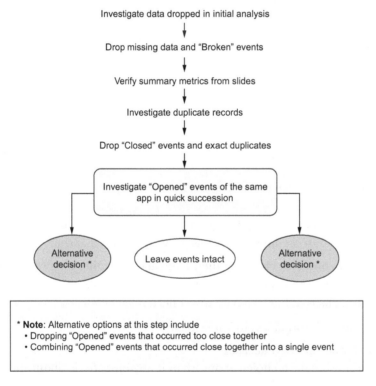

Figure 12.16   Our latest progress after investigating various types of duplicate event

Now that we've handled the duplication issue, we can recreate the chart from the slides relating to the average session length of each user. This is shown in figure 12.17.

To recreate this, we need to create a DataFrame of individual sessions and their length. First, we need to establish whether a session ID is unique to a user. If session

Most sessions last under 2 minutes.

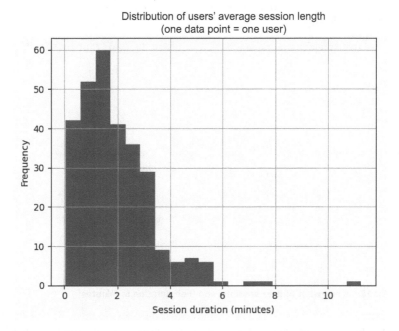

Figure 12.17 A slide from the original presentation showing the distribution of users' average session length

1 can only ever relate to user 0, we can simply group by the session ID; otherwise, we must include the user ID to distinguish between two different users' sessions, both with an ID of 1. The following code looks for session IDs that belong to more than one user:

```
(
    app_data_reduced
    .groupby("session_id")
    ["user_id"]
    .nunique()
    .loc[lambda x: x > 1]
)
```

The output of this code is an empty `pandas` `Series`, meaning there are no session IDs across multiple users. Therefore, the session ID is unique to a user. Now, we can create the DataFrame of sessions that we need. The following code does this and produces the DataFrame, which is previewed in figure 12.18:

```
sessions = (
    app_data_reduced
```

```
        .groupby(["user_id", "session_id"])
        .agg(start=("timestamp", "min"),
             end=("timestamp", "max"))
        .reset_index()
        .assign(
            duration_mins=lambda _df: (_df["end"] - _df["start"]).dt.seconds/60
        )
)

sessions.head()
```

	user_id	session_id	start	end	duration_mins
0	0	1	2018-01-16 06:01:05	2018-01-16 06:04:17	3.200000
1	0	2	2018-01-16 06:25:54	2018-01-16 06:26:26	0.533333
2	0	3	2018-01-16 06:35:35	2018-01-16 06:35:35	0.000000
3	0	4	2018-01-16 07:15:56	2018-01-16 07:21:44	5.800000
4	0	5	2018-01-16 08:02:05	2018-01-16 08:04:11	2.100000

Figure 12.18   A snapshot of user sessions and their duration in minutes

This DataFrame contains one row per user session, so grouping by user ID and averaging the session duration gives us the data we need to produce the chart from the slides. The following code does this and produces the chart in figure 12.19:

```
fig, axis = plt.subplots()

avg_session_by_user = (
    sessions
    .groupby("user_id")
    ["duration_mins"]
    .median()
)

(
    avg_session_by_user
    .hist(bins=20, ax=axis)
)

axis.set(
    title="Distribution of users' average session length \
(one data point = 1 user)",
    xlabel="Session duration (minutes)",
    ylabel="Frequency"
)

plt.show()
```

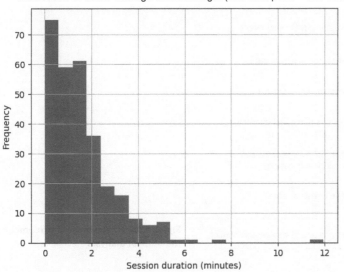

Figure 12.19   The distribution of users' average session lengths

This result tells us that most users' sessions last less than 2 minutes but with a long tail. There are sessions that are even over 10 minutes in duration. You might notice that this chart doesn't exactly match the one in the slides, as shown by the difference between figures 12.17 and 12.19. That is because we have chosen to drop "Closed" events and have therefore already diverged from the initial analysis. That's fine because we are making different assumptions and thus coming to different conclusions.

Our particular approach might skew results slightly if there are sessions that end in a "Closed" event because we'd underestimate how long those sessions are. However, since our primary goal is to look at what kinds of apps people use in a session and what time those sessions occur, the initial "Opened" event is sufficient.

We have recreated the relevant parts of the original analysis, but before moving on to our stakeholders' questions, let's recap the process. The latest diagram is shown in figure 12.20.

Let's move on to the next part of the analysis, answering our stakeholders' new questions about the users.

12.5.2 Analyzing event data to learn about customer behavior

Now that we have verified the findings of the original analysis, we can move on to our stakeholders' new questions. The first one was about what time people use their phones and whether this would be a useful dimension for clustering.

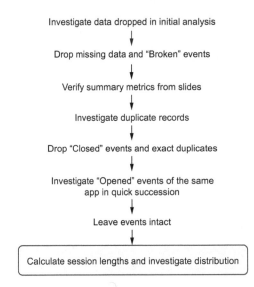

Investigate data dropped in initial analysis

Drop missing data and "Broken" events

Verify summary metrics from slides

Investigate duplicate records

Drop "Closed" events and exact duplicates

Investigate "Opened" events of the same
app in quick succession

Leave events intact

Calculate session lengths and investigate distribution

**Figure 12.20   The process of reproducing
the original analysis**

ANALYZING TIMESTAMPS TO LEARN ABOUT BROWSING BEHAVIOR

To investigate when people use their phones, we need a definition of what counts as "usage time." That is, do we care about the times that every single data point occurred? Probably not because a group of "Opened" and "Closed" events close together in time should count as one example of a user using their phone around that time.

That means we could use the start time from the session-level DataFrame created earlier. The following code creates a column to extract the hour component of the dates so we can isolate just the hour in which browsing began. Then, we plot the distribution of these "start hours," the result of which is shown in figure 12.21:

```
sessions["hour"] = sessions["start"].dt.hour

(
    sessions["hour"]
    .value_counts()
    .sort_index()
    .plot(kind="bar")
)
```

This chart tells us that most browsing sessions start in the late afternoon/early evening, with a dip in the early hours of the day. What it doesn't tell us is whether there are users who behave differently to this general trend. For that, we need to calculate what the most common starting hour, or part of the day, is for each user.

> **NOTE**   In this section, we will explore the temporal aspect of this data. If you're interested in more examples of working with time series data, see chapters 8 and 9.

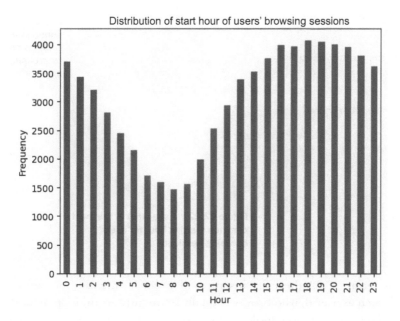

Figure 12.21   The distribution of when users start their browsing sessions

Let's now calculate the most common starting hour for each user. We can use the statistical mode for this, which simply returns the most common value. However, we need to decide what happens if there is a tie. What if someone's most common browsing time is both 8 a.m. and 5 p.m.? There is no reason to prefer one or the other, so we will leave both values in. Therefore, that user will be represented twice, which may skew the results by overrepresenting some users, but it will also retain valuable information.

The following code defines a function to return possibly multiple values of the mode for each user and then applies it to the DataFrame. A snapshot of the resulting DataFrame is shown in figure 12.22:

```
def get_modes(group):
    mode_hours = group['hour'].mode()        ◁—| Calculates the mode, possibly
    return pd.DataFrame(                          returning multiple values
        {
            'user_id': group['user_id'].iloc[0],
            'most_frequent_hour': mode_hours
        }
    )

most_frequent_hours = (
    sessions
    .groupby("user_id")                       ┐ Applies this function
    .apply(get_modes)                         │ and extracts all the most
    .rename(columns={"user_id": "duplicate_user_id"})  ◁—┘ common starting hours
    .reset_index()
)
```

```
    .drop(columns=["level_1", "duplicate_user_id"])
)

most_frequent_hours.head()
```

Cleans up
unnecessary
columns created
by grouping and
aggregating

	user_id	most_frequent_hour
0	0	16
1	0	22
2	1	17
3	2	6
4	3	18

Figure 12.22   A snapshot of the most common starting hour for users' browsing sessions

As shown in figure 12.22, there are instances of a user having multiple most frequent start times, such as user 0, who browses equally frequently around 4 p.m. and 10 p.m. From this data, we can now look at the distribution of the newly created most_ frequent_hour column to understand whether there are users who prefer different times in the day for using their phones. The following code investigates this and produces the chart in figure 12.23:

```
fig, axis = plt.subplots()

(
    most_frequent_hours
    ["most_frequent_hour"]
    .value_counts()
    .sort_index()
    .plot
    .bar(ax=axis)
)

axis.set(
    title="Distribution of most common starting time
⇨ for users' browsing sessions",
    xlabel="Hour",
    ylabel="Frequency"
)

plt.show()
```

What this chart tells us is that there are distinct groups of users who prefer to browse in the morning around 6 a.m., at lunchtime around 1 p.m., or at 5 p.m. in the evening, with another peak starting at midnight.

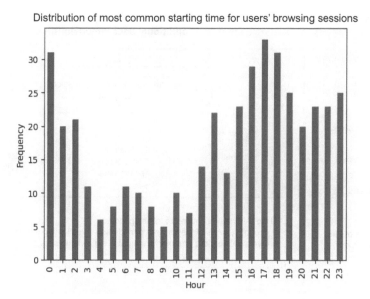

Figure 12.23   Distribution of users' most common browsing times

Before we move on to decide how to use this information in our user segments, let's add this to our growing diagram of our analysis, which is shown in figure 12.24.

We could use the data shown in figure 12.22 as a dimension in our segments, that is, the actual most common start hour for a user. However, there would be two problems:

- Some users would have multiple rows, which will not work for a segmentation problem.
- Some hours of the day are very similar, that is, it doesn't matter if a user started their browsing at 4 p.m. or 5 p.m.

We want to find distinct user groups so we can group these similar times together instead. We could have done this up front, that is, grouped different parts of the day together into "morning," "midday," and so on, and investigated the distribution of those categories. However, we would have made assumptions about which hours are similar in terms of mobile usage. By looking at the distribution of individual hours first, we can create groups that closely match what we find in the data.

CREATING CUSTOMER LABELS BASED ON BROWSING PATTERNS

Looking at the chart in figure 12.23, we could conclude there are anywhere between two and five "peaks," which could act as different parts of the day. The choice of how many categories to use will be somewhat subjective. Let's go with four categories, as

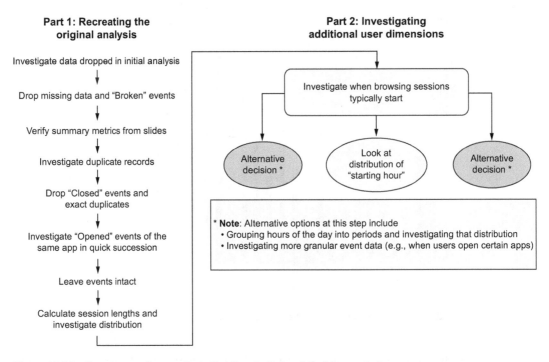

Figure 12.24   The process diagram, including the start of part 2 of the analysis

this might fit the data best without creating too many user segments down the line. Our groups will be

- Night owls, who tend to browse between 9 p.m. and 3 a.m. (inclusive)
- Early morning users, who tend to browse between 4 a.m. and 9 a.m. (inclusive)
- Midday users, who tend to browse between 10 a.m. and 2 p.m. (inclusive)
- Late-day users, who tend to browse between 3 p.m. and 8 p.m. (inclusive)

Let's create these groups and investigate how many users are in each group. The following code does the categorization and produces the output in figure 12.25:

```
bins = [-1, 3, 9, 14, 20]
labels = ['night_owl', 'early_morning_browser',
          'midday_browser', 'late_day_browser']

most_frequent_hours["category"] = (
    pd.cut(
        most_frequent_hours["most_frequent_hour"],
        bins=bins,
        labels=labels,
        ordered=True
    )
)
```

```
most_frequent_hours.loc[
    most_frequent_hours["most_frequent_hour"].isin([21, 22, 23]),
    "category"] = "night_owl"

most_frequent_hours.head()
```

Fixes additional night owl values

	user_id	most_frequent_hour	category
0	0	16	late_day_browser
1	0	22	night_owl
2	1	17	late_day_browser
3	2	6	early_morning_browser
4	3	18	late_day_browser

Figure 12.25   Users' most common browsing hours grouped into four categories

Now, we can investigate the membership in these groups. The following code calculates the distribution and produces the output shown in figure 12.26.

```
(
    most_frequent_hours["category"]
    .value_counts()
    .sort_index()
)
```

```
night_owl                154
early_morning_browser     48
midday_browser            66
late_day_browser         161
Name: category, dtype: int64
```

Figure 12.26   Distribution of the categories of users' browsing sessions

Let's now use this dataset to create a one-hot encoded representation of these categories, that is, one binary column to indicate membership in each category. Crucially, a user can be in multiple categories, as shown in figure 12.25. See chapter 6 for more examples of this in practice. The following code creates the one-hot encoding and produces the start of a user-level dataset, which we will use for segmentation. A snapshot of this new dataset is shown in figure 12.27:

```
users = (
    pd.get_dummies(
        most_frequent_hours.drop(columns=["most_frequent_hour"]),
        columns=["category"],
        prefix="time"
    )
```

get_dummies created the one-hot encoded columns.

```
        .groupby("user_id")
        .max()
        .reset_index()
)

users.head()
```

	user_id	time_night_owl	time_early_morning_browser	time_midday_browser	time_late_day_browser
0	0	1	0	0	1
1	1	0	0	0	1
2	2	0	1	0	0
3	3	0	0	0	1
4	4	1	0	0	0

Figure 12.27   A snapshot of user-level data showing which browsing time categories users belong to

We have now created a dataset that we can add additional columns to and run the segmentation algorithm on. Before we move on to the next stakeholder question, which is about what types of apps people use, let's update our diagram of the work done so far. The latest version is shown in figure 12.28.

We can now move on to our next stakeholder question about what types of apps people use.

USING AI TO LABEL DATA

Our stakeholders want us to investigate what types of apps people use and potentially use that information in the segmentation. However, we do not have data on app type directly, just a list of app names. This is a clear example of more information being contained in the raw data than we might think at first. A domain expert could easily categorize each app name into some broader category. This is a perfect use case for AI to augment our work.

There are over 80 distinct app names to categorize. It's doable but repetitive to do by hand, so let's ask an AI to do it. We can use the following code snippet to get the app names as a list to pass to the AI tool:

```
print(app_data_reduced["app_name"].unique())
```

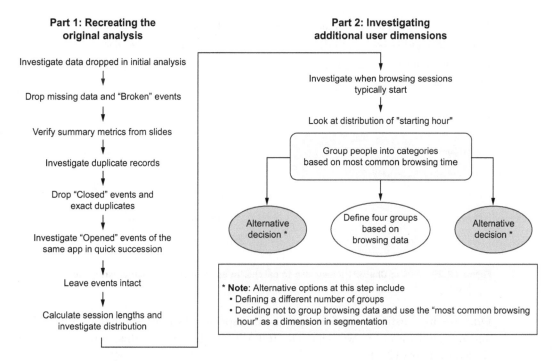

Figure 12.28 The process so far, including grouping people into categories based on when they browse

The following prompt, asking ChatGPT to categorize the app names for us, generates the output shown in figure 12.29.

> *I will provide a list of mobile application names. To the best of your ability, group them into logical categories, e.g., email, social media, web browser, mobile games, etc. I'd like the response as a table with columns* `'app_name'` *and* `'category'`. *If you are unsure what category an app belongs to, put "Unknown." Here is the list of app names: <app names follow>.*

NOTE It is important to note that these tools don't always produce the same output for the same prompt. They are also evolving all the time, so you will almost certainly get a different output than I do for the same prompt. This is a feature of the analytics process, not a bug.

To categorize these apps into logical groups such as email, social media, web browsers, mobile games, and more, I've organized them into a table. This categorization is based on the common functionalities and purposes of these apps. If I'm unsure of the category for a specific app, I've labeled it as "Unknown".

Here's the table:

App Name	Category
Minesweeper Classic (Mines)	Mobile Games
Gmail	Email
Google	Web Browser/Search Engine
Instagram	Social Media

Figure 12.29   Part of ChatGPT's response to categorize app names into broader categories

Once we are satisfied with the output, we can specifically request the data as a CSV file and merge it into our own data. The following code achieves this, and a snapshot is shown in figure 12.30:

```
categories = pd.read_csv("./data/App_Categories.csv",
                         skiprows=1,
                         names=["app_name", "app_category"])
print(categories.shape)
categories.head()
```

	app_name	app_category
0	Minesweeper Classic (Mines)	Mobile Games
1	Gmail	Email
2	Google	Web Browser/Search Engine
3	Instagram	Social Media
4	Google Chrome	Web Browser

Figure 12.30   A snapshot of the categorization data produced by ChatGPT

Let's add this latest step to our process diagram, the latest version of which is shown in figure 12.31.

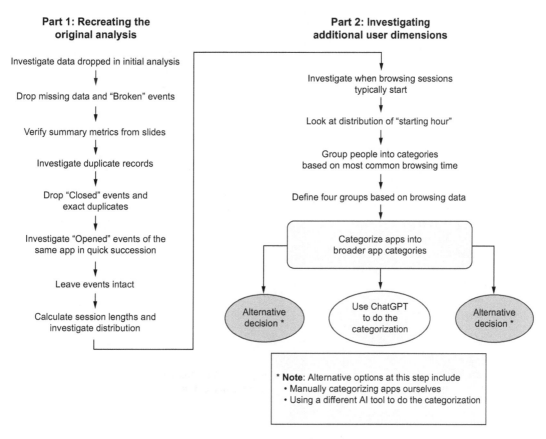

Figure 12.31 The latest diagram of our steps, including ChatGPT's categorization of apps

Let's now see the distribution of this category data. The following code calculates this and produces the output in figure 12.32:

```
categories["app_category"].value_counts()
```

There are a couple of things to notice here. One is that there are a few "Unknown" values, which we should investigate and manually categorize. The second is that there are quite a lot of categories, probably too many to be useful. First, let's resolve the "Unknown" values. The following code investigates these values, and they are shown in figure 12.33:

```
categories[categories["app_category"] == "Unknown"]
```

```
Messaging                       12
Utility                          9
Social Media                     8
Mobile Games                     5
Unknown                          5
Advertising                      5
Email                            5
Finance                          5
Video Streaming                  4
Online Shopping                  4
Music Streaming                  3
Web Browser                      3
Communication                    3
Photo Management                 3
Photo Editing                    2
Web Browser/Search Engine        2
Cloud Storage                    1
Social Media/Messaging           1
Productivity                     1
Note Taking                      1
News                             1
Navigation                       1
Health                           1
Podcasts                         1
App Marketplace                  1
Name: app_category, dtype: int64
```

Figure 12.32   Distribution of newly created app categories

	app_name	app_category
45	MUIQ Survey App	Unknown
54	Reward Stash	Unknown
68	Movie Play Box	Unknown
70	SurveyCow	Unknown
76	MetroZone	Unknown

Figure 12.33   App names that ChatGPT could not categorize

We can manually categorize these with a bit of research and some code snippets. The following code updates the category of these specific app names:

```
categories.loc[categories["app_name"]=="MUIQ Survey App", "app_category"]
 ➥ = "Survey"
categories.loc[categories["app_name"]=="SurveyCow", "app_category"]
 ➥ = "Survey"
categories.loc[categories["app_name"]=="Reward Stash", "app_category"]
 ➥ = "Rewards"
categories.loc[categories["app_name"]=="Movie Play Box", "app_category"]
 ➥ = "Video Streaming"
```

```
categories.loc[categories["app_name"]=="MetroZone", "app_category"]
➥ = "Utility"
```

Now, let's handle the second problem, which is that ChatGPT created too many categories. We can choose to ask ChatGPT to revise its categorization and ask for fewer columns, or we could use ChatGPT's categories as subcategories and define main categories ourselves. It's a personal choice, but it shouldn't take too long to do this ourselves, and that way, we have the categorization code ready if we decide to change the categories later.

REVIEWING AI-CREATED DATA LABELS

One `pandas` trick is to use the `map` method to map categories to new ones based on a dictionary. We don't want to type this dictionary out ourselves, but we can write a bit of code to print the categories in the required format, which we copy and paste into our main mapping code. The following code prints the existing categories in the right format, leaving space for the new category alongside. The output is shown in figure 12.34, so you can see how it would be pasted to create the code snippet that follows later:

```
for category in sorted(categories["app_category"].unique()):
    print(f"'{category}': '',")
```

```
'Advertising': '',
'App Marketplace': '',
'Cloud Storage': '',
'Communication': '',
'Email': '',
'Finance': '',
'Health': '',
'Messaging': '',
'Mobile Games': '',
'Music Streaming': '',
'Navigation': '',
'News': '',
'Note Taking': '',
'Online Shopping': '',
'Photo Editing': '',
'Photo Management': '',
'Podcasts': '',
'Productivity': '',
'Rewards': '',
'Social Media': '',
'Social Media/Messaging': '',
'Survey': '',
'Utility': '',
'Video Streaming': '',
'Web Browser': '',
'Web Browser/Search Engine': '',
```

Figure 12.34 Our categories in a format required by a Python dictionary

Now, we can use this output to create the following code, which updates each existing category with its new categorization. We will keep the existing category column as a subcategory, so we have two levels of app category hierarchy. Figure 12.35 shows a snapshot of the categories dataset after these updates:

```
categories = categories.rename(columns={"app_category": "app_subcategory"})

category_map = {
    'Advertising': 'Money',
    'App Marketplace': 'Entertainment',
    'Cloud Storage': 'Utility',
    'Communication': 'Social',
    'Email': 'Social',
    'Finance': 'Money',
    'Health': 'Social',
    'Messaging': 'Social',
    'Mobile Games': 'Entertainment',
    'Music Streaming': 'Entertainment',
    'Navigation': 'Utility',
    'News': 'Social',
    'Note Taking': 'Utility',
    'Online Shopping': 'Money',
    'Photo Editing': 'Utility',
    'Photo Management': 'Utility',
    'Podcasts': 'Entertainment',
    'Productivity': 'Utility',
    'Rewards': 'Money',
    'Social Media': 'Social',
    'Social Media/Messaging': 'Social',
    'Survey': 'Money',
    'Utility': 'Utility',
    'Video Streaming': 'Entertainment',
    'Web Browser': 'Browsing',
    'Web Browser/Search Engine': 'Browsing'
}

categories["app_category"]
➥ = categories["app_subcategory"].map(category_map)
categories.head()
```

	app_name	app_subcategory	app_category
0	Minesweeper Classic (Mines)	Mobile Games	Entertainment
1	Gmail	Email	Social
2	Google	Web Browser/Search Engine	Browsing
3	Instagram	Social Media	Social
4	Google Chrome	Web Browser	Browsing

Figure 12.35   A snapshot of the categories data after applying our new categorization

Before we merge this back into the main app data, let's review our process by updating our diagram. The latest version is shown in figure 12.36.

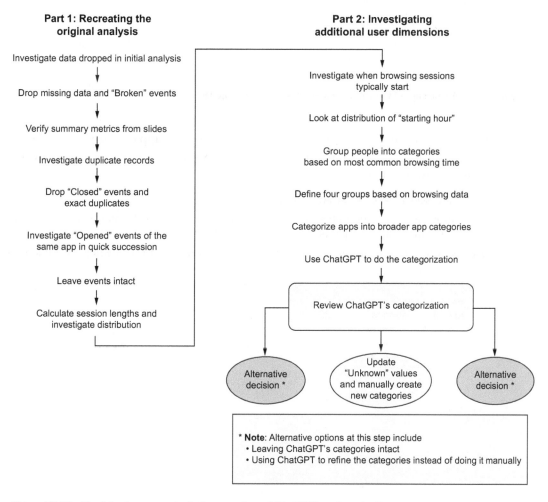

Figure 12.36   The latest process, including a review of ChatGPT's categorization

Now, it's time to merge these categories back to our original data and see how people use these various app types. The following code joins the event-level app data to the app categories, creating merged data, a snapshot of which is shown in figure 12.37.

```
app_data_merged = app_data_reduced.merge(
    categories,
    on="app_name")
assert len(app_data_reduced) == len(app_data_merged)
app_data_merged.head()
```

Raises an error message if we don't have the same number of rows after the merge

	user_id	session_id	timestamp	app_name	event_type	app_subcategory	app_category
0	0	1	2018-01-16 06:01:05	Minesweeper Classic (Mines)	Opened	Mobile Games	Entertainment
1	0	1	2018-01-16 06:01:07	Minesweeper Classic (Mines)	Opened	Mobile Games	Entertainment
2	0	1	2018-01-16 06:01:08	Minesweeper Classic (Mines)	Opened	Mobile Games	Entertainment
3	0	1	2018-01-16 06:01:09	Minesweeper Classic (Mines)	Opened	Mobile Games	Entertainment
4	0	1	2018-01-16 06:03:44	Minesweeper Classic (Mines)	Opened	Mobile Games	Entertainment

Figure 12.37   A snapshot of the app data merged with app categories

From this data, we want to find each user's most common app category. After that, we will investigate whether there are ties, that is, users who have more than one category as their most common.

ANALYZING NEWLY CREATED CATEGORY LABELS

The following code calculates the top categories per user, and a snapshot of the output is shown in figure 12.38. Note that pandas creates a column called level_1 because the mode function could return multiple values, as it did when we looked at app usage times:

```
top_categories = (
    app_data_merged
    .groupby("user_id")
    ["app_category"]
    .apply(pd.Series.mode)
    .reset_index()
)

top_categories.head()
```

	user_id	level_1	app_category
0	0	0	Entertainment
1	1	0	Social
2	2	0	Social
3	3	0	Money
4	4	0	Social

Figure 12.38   A snapshot of the "most common category per user" dataset

From this data, we can investigate whether there are users with multiple categories as their most common. We can use this level_1 column that pandas created to filter our data. Anything with a value of zero means the user's top category, so values greater than zero mean a user has multiple top categories. The following code investigates this and produces the output in figure 12.39:

```
top_categories[top_categories["level_1"] > 0]
```

	user_id	level_1	app_category
36	35	1	Utility
134	132	1	Utility
226	223	1	Social

Figure 12.39   Users with more than one top app category

Let's examine these users in more detail and see if we can decide how to proceed. The following code retrieves all records for these users and produces the output in figure 12.40:

```
top_categories[top_categories["user_id"].isin([35, 223, 132])]
```

	user_id	level_1	app_category
35	35	0	Social
36	35	1	Utility
133	132	0	Social
134	132	1	Utility
225	223	0	Browsing
226	223	1	Social

Figure 12.40   All category data for users with more than one top category

We can either remove one of those categories per user or record our data the same way we did with app times, that is, users would be allowed more than one top category. As there are only three affected users in this case, we will investigate whether we could drop one of their top categories. How do we decide which of the two categories to drop? Let's first look at the underlying data for the user with ID 35. The following code retrieves the data for that user at an individual app level, which is then shown in figure 12.41:

```
(
    app_data_merged[app_data_merged["user_id"] == 35]
    .groupby(["app_category", "app_name"])
    .size()
)
```

```
app_category     app_name
Browsing         Google Chrome              21
                 Samsung Internet Browser    1
Entertainment    Google Play Store           6
Social           Gmail                      17
                 Telegram                    7
Utility          Camera                      4
                 Samsung Gallery             5
                 Samsung Notes               1
                 Settings                   14
dtype: int64
```

Figure 12.41   User 35's app usage by category and app name

This user used the Settings app quite heavily, which contributed to the "Utility" category being joint top for them. We don't have more detailed information about why this user kept opening their phone settings. We can use what we have to decide if it's more relevant that the user uses the "Social" apps most frequently. We will drop the necessary record for this user to have "Social" as their only top category. User 132 also had "Utility" as their joint top category, so for the same reason, we'll drop that record as well. The following code cleans up the data for these two users:

```
top_categories = (
    top_categories
    .drop(
        index=top_categories[
            (top_categories["user_id"].isin([35, 132]))
            & (top_categories["app_category"] == "Utility")
            ].index
    )
)
```

Finally, let's look at user 223 and decide whether they better fit a "Social" or "Browsing" category. The following code looks at their data at an app level and produces the output shown in figure 12.42:

```
(
    app_data_merged[app_data_merged["user_id"] == 223]
    .groupby(["app_category", "app_name"])
    .size()
)
```

```
app_category     app_name
Browsing         Google                     19
                 Google Chrome               3
Entertainment    Google Play Store           9
Social           Facebook                    8
                 Facebook Messenger          7
                 Gmail                       1
                 TextNow                     6
Utility          Settings                    5
dtype: int64
```

Figure 12.42   App-level usage data for user 223

This one is trickier to categorize because they make heavy use of social apps but also frequently use the Google app. However, that could mean multiple things, some of which might not fit under "Browsing," so we'll decide that this user better fits the "Social" label. The following code removes the necessary record. We then retest the data to verify there are no users with multiple "top app category" records:

```
top_categories = (
    top_categories
    .drop(
        index=top_categories[
            (top_categories["user_id"] == 223)
            & (top_categories["app_category"] == "Browsing")
            ].index
    )
)
top_categories["user_id"].value_counts().loc[lambda x: x > 1]
```

The output of that latest snippet is an empty list, meaning we no longer have users with multiple top app categories. We can now create the indicator variables required for our clustering algorithm. The following code creates these indicator variables and produces the output in figure 12.43:

```
top_categories = (
    pd.get_dummies(
        top_categories,
        columns=["app_category"]
    ).drop(
        columns=["level_1"]
    )
)

top_categories.head()
```

	user_id	app_category_Browsing	app_category_Entertainment	app_category_Money	app_category_Social	app_category_Utility
0	0	0	1	0	0	0
1	1	0	0	0	1	0
2	2	0	0	0	1	0
3	3	0	0	1	0	0
4	4	0	0	0	1	0

Figure 12.43   The one-hot encoded version of our "top app category by user" data

The data in this format is ready to be joined to the user-level data that we created in figure 12.27. Before merging the two datasets, let's review our progress so far. The latest diagram of our analysis is shown in figure 12.44.

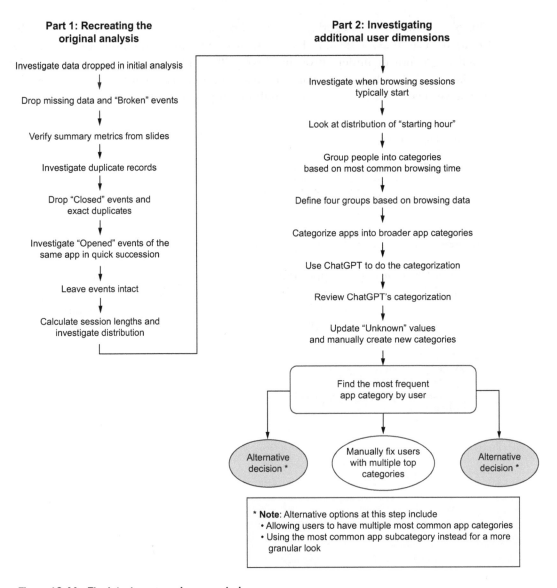

Figure 12.44   The latest progress in our analysis

We have investigated the data relating to our stakeholder questions. Now, we will merge the most frequent app category data and the most frequent browsing time data to build up our user-level dataset. We will also create and include columns from the initial analysis and have a user-level dataset ready for segmentation.

CREATING A USER-LEVEL DATASET FOR SEGMENTATION

So far, we have one user-level dataset of what times people tend to use their phones the most and another that contains the most frequent app category per user. We'll join these together and then add other metrics. The following code merges the two datasets, and a snapshot of the merged data is shown in figure 12.45:

```
size_before = len(users)
users = users.merge(top_categories, on="user_id")
size_after = len(users)
assert size_before == size_after
users.head()
```

	user_id	time_night_owl	time_early_morning_browser	time_midday_browser	time_late_day_browser
0	0	1	0	0	1
1	1	0	0	0	1
2	2	0	1	0	0
3	3	0	0	0	1
4	4	1	0	0	0

(continued)

	app_category_Browsing	app_category_Entertainment	app_category_Money	app_category_Social	app_category_Utility
0	0	1	0	0	0
1	0	0	0	1	0
2	0	0	0	1	0
3	0	0	1	0	0
4	0	0	0	1	0

Figure 12.45   A snapshot of the user-level data so far

The initial analysis involved the number of unique apps used per user and the average length of their browsing sessions to segment the users. There is no reason not to keep these metrics in there, so let's recreate them and join them to our current dataset. We will also add "number of sessions" as a proxy for how heavily a user uses their phone since, otherwise, that aspect of usage is not captured in any of our variables.

First, we can add columns relating to the number of apps and sessions straight from the raw app data. The following code counts the number of unique apps and sessions per user and produces a dataset, a snapshot of which is shown in figure 12.46:

```
user_metrics = (
    app_data_merged
    .groupby(["user_id"])
    .agg(
        number_of_apps=("app_name", "nunique"),
```

```
        number_of_sessions=("session_id", "nunique")
    )
    .reset_index()
)

user_metrics.head()
```

	user_id	number_of_apps	number_of_sessions
0	0	19	238
1	1	18	88
2	2	16	61
3	3	15	70
4	4	8	45

Figure 12.46   A user-level dataset counting the number of unique apps and sessions per user

Let's now join this table to the dataset we created in figure 12.45. The following code achieves this:

```
size_before = len(users)
users = users.merge(user_metrics, on="user_id")
size_after = len(users)
assert size_before == size_after
```

To add the average session length, we need to turn to the session-level data we created earlier in section 12.5.1. We will group it by user ID and calculate the median duration of each session per user. The following code does this and produces a dataset, a snapshot of which is shown in figure 12.47:

```
avg_sessions = (
    sessions
    .groupby("user_id")
    .agg(avg_session_length=("duration_mins", "median"))
    .reset_index()
)

avg_sessions.head()
```

	user_id	avg_session_length
0	0	0.658333
1	1	1.483333
2	2	0.533333
3	3	0.116667
4	4	0.233333

Figure 12.47   Average session duration per user

Our final step before segmentation is to merge this table into the main user-level data. The following code does this, and figure 12.48 shows all the columns in the data we will use for segmentation:

```
size_before = len(users)
users = users.merge(avg_sessions, on="user_id")
size_after = len(users)
assert size_before == size_after

users.columns
```

```
Index(['user_id', 'time_night_owl', 'time_early_morning_browser',
       'time_midday_browser', 'time_late_day_browser', 'app_category_Browsing',
       'app_category_Entertainment', 'app_category_Money',
       'app_category_Social', 'app_category_Utility', 'number_of_apps',
       'number_of_sessions', 'duration_mins'],
      dtype='object')
```

Figure 12.48   All the columns we will use to segment users

Let's export this user-level data directly to the next chapter's folder so we can start the segmentation process directly from this dataset:

```
users.to_parquet("../chapter-13/data/users.parquet", index=False)
```

Before moving on to the segmentation part in the next chapter, let's review everything we've done so far.

12.5.3 *Project progress so far*

Let's recap the progress on this project:

- We started by investigating the work behind the initial presentation and verified the summary statistics that were presented.
- We continued the analysis by diving deeper into user behavior and concluded that there are distinct groups of people who use their phones at different times.
- We used generative AI to categorize app names into broader app categories.
- We used these app categories to identify different user behaviors based on what apps a user uses the most.
- Finally, we exported a user-level dataset ready for segmentation in the next phase.

Figure 12.49 shows the entire process up to this point.

In the following chapter, we will use the exported user-level data to segment users into distinct groups to answer our stakeholders' questions.

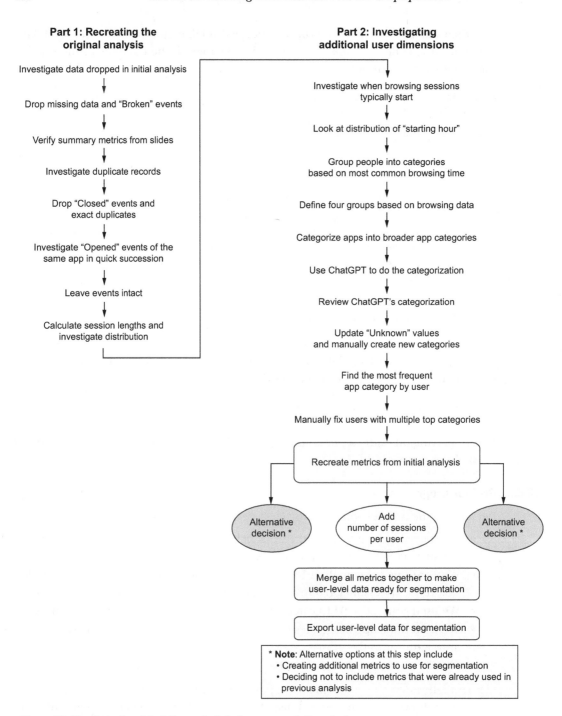

Figure 12.49   Parts 1 and 2 of the analysis before segmentation starts

Summary

- Continuing someone else's work starts with retracing their steps.
- Recreating the initial analysis helps us understand the problem and find any errors.
- When continuing someone else's work, their assumptions and decisions should be checked and verified.

13

Iterating on someone else's work: Customer segmentation

> ### This chapter covers
> - Segmenting users based on behavioral data
> - Evaluating the output of a clustering algorithm

In this chapter, we will use the dataset created in the previous chapter to segment users into groups based on their mobile browsing behavior. In chapter 12, we took over another analyst's work, verified their findings, and continued analyzing our customers' behavior. We turned an event-level dataset into a user-level one, and in this chapter, we will apply a clustering algorithm to create distinct user segments. We will evaluate these segments and address our stakeholders' questions. Let's recap the project before continuing.

13.1 Project 8 revisited: Finding customer segments from mobile activity

To recap, we're working for AppEcho Insights, an analytics company focused on mobile user behavior. They analyze data on how users use their phones and provide insights to mobile phone manufacturers and app developers.

They want to understand whether there are groups of users who use their phones in a similar way. Knowing these user segments would be useful as their

418

clients could target entire user bases with different initiatives. They'd like to focus on the following:

- The types of apps that people use. For example, do some customers use their phones more for social media than others?
- Temporal patterns. Do users prefer to browse their phones at different times of the day?
- The use of a more suitable segmentation method (e.g., an algorithm that can handle grouping users based on multiple dimensions).

We have answered their first two questions in chapter 12, where we looked at both temporal patterns and differences in app usage.

The data is available for you to attempt the project yourself at https://davidasboth .com/book-code. You will find the files that you can use for the project, including the first analyst's slides, as well as the example solution in the form of a Jupyter notebook.

We are now ready to apply a clustering algorithm to address AppEcho's final point and create more sophisticated customer groups.

13.1.1 Data dictionary

As a reminder, they have provided a dataset of mobile events and the presentation the initial analyst delivered. The dataset consists of individual mobile events, such as a user opening or closing a mobile app. There are only a few columns, but it is possible to extract rich behavioral information. The events are timestamped, so the temporal element can also be analyzed. See chapters 8 and 9 for more details about working with time data.

> **NOTE** The data was originally taken from https://github.com/aliannejadi/ LSApp. Thank you to Mohammad Aliannejadi for permission to use the data.

A key initial step is to take a look at the available data. Table 13.1 shows the data dictionary.

Table 13.1 Data dictionary

Column	Definition
User ID	A user's unique identifier.
Session ID	Uniquely identifies a user's activity session.
Timestamp	Date and time of an individual event.
App name	The name of the app in use.
Event type	The type of the event that took place. Values are one of the following: "Opened," "Closed," "User Interaction," or "Broken."

Let's also revisit what the outcomes of this project should be.

13.1.2 *Desired outcomes*

Our stakeholders want a more in-depth analysis, which we have completed, and customer segments based on more dimensions, which is the focus of this chapter. The final output is the definition of our user segments, meaning what factors describe each segment and which users belong to which group.

Before continuing the analysis, let's revisit the work done so far.

13.1.3 *Project summary so far*

In the previous chapter

- We investigated the work behind the initial presentation and verified the summary statistics presented by the previous analyst.
- We continued the analysis by diving deeper into user behavior and concluded that there are distinct groups of people who use their phones at different times.
- We used generative AI to categorize app names into broader app categories.
- We used these app categories to identify different user behaviors based on what apps a user uses the most.
- Finally, we exported a user-level dataset ready for segmentation in the next phase.

Figure 13.1 shows the work done so far.

We can now use the user-level dataset exported from the previous chapter to create user segments. In this chapter, we will choose a clustering method, apply it, and evaluate the results before identifying our conclusions and next steps.

13.1.4 *Segmentation of mobile users using clustering*

To recap, in our version of the analysis, we'll segment users on the following dimensions:

- Number of unique apps used (as a proxy for how varied their usage is)
- Number of unique usage sessions (as a proxy for frequency of use)
- Average duration of a user session
- What time of day most of their usage occurs
- What type of app they use most frequently

These dimensions make up 12 columns in total in our data. The dataset has 13 columns, but one is the user ID, which is an arbitrary integer and won't be used for clustering. The steps we will take to segment the users are as follows:

1 Transform our data so all columns are on the same scale
2 Choose a clustering algorithm
3 Apply the clustering algorithm to allocate each data point to a cluster
4 Evaluate the output

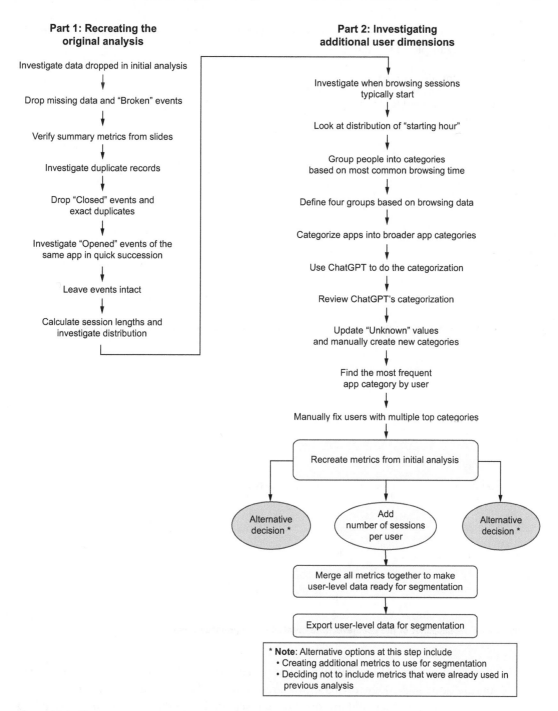

Figure 13.1   The work done on the project in the previous chapter

Let's read in this user-level data that we created in the previous chapter. Figure 13.2 shows a sample of the data:

```python
import pandas as pd
import matplotlib.pyplot as plt
users = pd.read_parquet("./data/users.parquet")
users.head()
```

	user_id	time_night_owl	time_early_morning_browser	time_midday_browser	time_late_day_browser
0	0	1	0	0	1
1	1	0	0	0	1
2	2	0	1	0	0
3	3	0	0	0	1
4	4	1	0	0	0

(continued)

	app_category_Browsing	app_category_Entertainment	app_category_Money	app_category_Social
0	0	1	0	0
1	0	0	0	1
2	0	0	0	1
3	0	0	1	0
4	0	0	0	1

(continued)

	app_category_Utility	number_of_apps	number_of_sessions	avg_session_length
0	0	19	238	0.658333
1	0	18	88	1.483333
2	0	16	61	0.533333
3	0	15	70	0.116667
4	0	8	45	0.233333

Figure 13.2   A snapshot of the user-level data created in the previous chapter

Before applying a clustering algorithm to data, we need to check whether our data is on the same scale. Figure 13.3 shows a reminder of the columns in our user-level data.

We have variables that are on different scales. The indicator columns can only be zero or one, whereas columns like the number of sessions could potentially be in the thousands. This poses a problem for distance-based clustering methods.

```
Index(['user_id', 'time_night_owl', 'time_early_morning_browser',
       'time_midday_browser', 'time_late_day_browser', 'app_category_Browsing',
       'app_category_Entertainment', 'app_category_Money',
       'app_category_Social', 'app_category_Utility', 'number_of_apps',
       'number_of_sessions', 'duration_mins'],
      dtype='object')
```

Figure 13.3   The columns available in our user-level data

TRANSFORMING VARIABLES TO BE ON THE SAME SCALE

Clustering means finding data points that are close together. The definition of "close together" requires a numeric measurement of distance. If one of our columns is on a larger scale than the others, then that column will dominate our clusters. In our case, if we use the data as is, it is most likely that users will be segmented only by the number of sessions because that is the column with the largest variation. If all columns are within approximately the same range, they will contribute equally to the clusters.

There are different scaling methods we could use. One typical approach is to transform data points into z-scores, meaning they will be measured by the distance, in standard deviations, to the mean value of that column. All data scaled this way will be approximately in the range from –5 to 5, regardless of the underlying units. If a user has a "number of sessions" value of 1 after transformation, it means their value of the number of sessions is one standard deviation above the mean number of sessions for a user. This is then directly comparable against a value of 1 for the number of apps, even though the two measures might be on different scales.

Whichever method we choose for scaling, we will only apply it to our continuous data and not the indicator columns because those are already on a comparable scale. The following code transforms our raw data into a scaled version, and figure 13.4 shows the first few rows. Notice that the data in the figure is transposed to make it easier to see values for all 12 columns:

```
from sklearn.preprocessing import StandardScaler

scaler = StandardScaler()                      ⟵── Creates a scaler object

X = users.drop(columns=["user_id"])

continuous_features = ['number_of_apps',
                       'number_of_sessions',
                       'avg_session_length']

X_scaled = X.copy()                                      Transforms only
X_scaled.loc[:,continuous_features]                      continuous columns and
  = scaler.fit_transform(X[continuous_features])   ⟵──  overwrites their values

X_scaled.head().transpose()        ⟵─┐ Shows a transposed version of the
                                     │ top five rows for readability
```

	0	1	2	3	4
time_night_owl	1.000000	0.000000	0.000000	0.000000	1.000000
time_early_morning_browser	0.000000	0.000000	1.000000	0.000000	0.000000
time_midday_browser	0.000000	0.000000	0.000000	0.000000	0.000000
time_late_day_browser	1.000000	1.000000	0.000000	1.000000	0.000000
app_category_Browsing	0.000000	0.000000	0.000000	0.000000	0.000000
app_category_Entertainment	1.000000	0.000000	0.000000	0.000000	0.000000
app_category_Money	0.000000	0.000000	0.000000	1.000000	0.000000
app_category_Social	0.000000	1.000000	1.000000	0.000000	1.000000
app_category_Utility	0.000000	0.000000	0.000000	0.000000	0.000000
number_of_apps	0.442882	0.286854	-0.025200	-0.181228	-1.273419
number_of_sessions	-0.031621	-0.349435	-0.406641	-0.387573	-0.440542
avg_session_length	-0.644248	-0.071086	-0.731091	-1.020566	-0.939513

Figure 13.4   **The first few rows of the transformed data ready for clustering**

Notice how the indicator columns still contain binary values; only the final three continuous columns have had their values scaled. Before choosing and applying a clustering algorithm, let's review the process so far and add the scaling step. Figure 13.5 shows the latest diagram.

We are now ready to choose and apply a clustering algorithm to segment our users.

CHOOSING AND APPLYING A CLUSTERING ALGORITHM

Choosing a clustering algorithm depends on the available data. Some clustering methods work with large datasets better than others, while others perform better when there are many dimensions. Some require choosing the number of clusters up front, whereas some will settle on a number by themselves based on the data. As with most data analysis methods, there are pros and cons to different approaches. See the scikit-learn documentation for more information on these pros and cons: https://mng.bz/MD5W.

For this solution, we'll keep it simple and use the most popular k-means algorithm. It's a distance-based method that groups points into the same cluster if they are close together in data space. It tries to find a solution where points within a cluster are as close together as possible, but clusters are as far away from each other as possible. That means groups should be as homogeneous as possible internally but otherwise differ from each other. Let's add this decision to our growing diagram, the latest version of which is shown in figure 13.6.

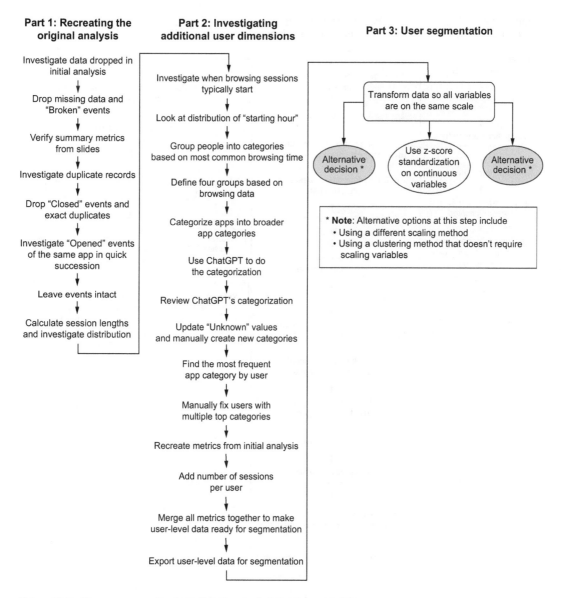

Figure 13.5 The process so far, including the start of the segmentation

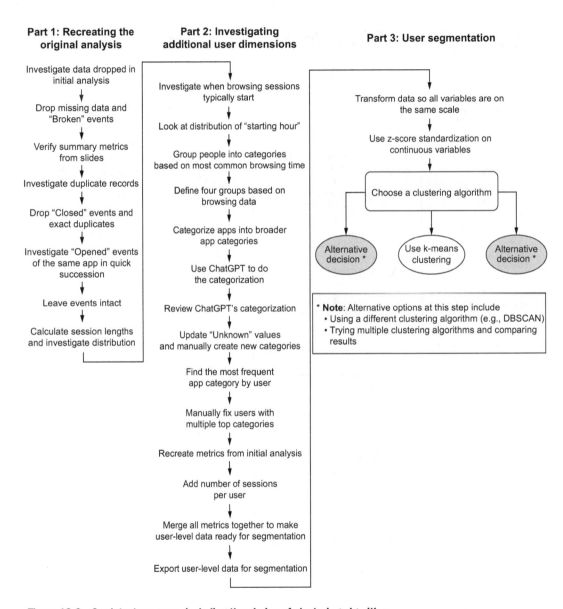

Part 1: Recreating the original analysis

Investigate data dropped in initial analysis

↓

Drop missing data and "Broken" events

↓

Verify summary metrics from slides

↓

Investigate duplicate records

↓

Drop "Closed" events and exact duplicates

↓

Investigate "Opened" events of the same app in quick succession

↓

Leave events intact

↓

Calculate session lengths and investigate distribution

Part 2: Investigating additional user dimensions

Investigate when browsing sessions typically start

↓

Look at distribution of "starting hour"

↓

Group people into categories based on most common browsing time

↓

Define four groups based on browsing data

↓

Categorize apps into broader app categories

↓

Use ChatGPT to do the categorization

↓

Review ChatGPT's categorization

↓

Update "Unknown" values and manually create new categories

↓

Find the most frequent app category by user

↓

Manually fix users with multiple top categories

↓

Recreate metrics from initial analysis

↓

Add number of sessions per user

↓

Merge all metrics together to make user-level data ready for segmentation

↓

Export user-level data for segmentation

Part 3: User segmentation

Transform data so all variables are on the same scale

↓

Use z-score standardization on continuous variables

↓

Choose a clustering algorithm

Alternative decision *   Use k-means clustering   Alternative decision *

* **Note**: Alternative options at this step include
• Using a different clustering algorithm (e.g., DBSCAN)
• Trying multiple clustering algorithms and comparing results

Figure 13.6 Our latest progress, including the choice of clustering algorithm

One important component of clustering algorithms like k-means is that we need to choose the number of groups up front. This is not straightforward, as we might not have any intuition about what number makes sense for our current case. One method for finding the right ballpark for the number of clusters is referred to as the "elbow method." This means empirically trying different numbers of groups and seeing where the benefits of adding another group start to tail off.

We will run a k-means clustering algorithm with different numbers of groups and measure something called the "inertia," which measures how closely points are to their cluster centers. A low inertia value means a better clustering structure. Bear in mind, however, that adding more groups *always lowers* the inertia because having more cluster centers means points are more likely to be close to one. Typically, we find the point where adding another cluster does not significantly lower the inertia score.

> **NOTE** In reality, unsupervised methods such as clustering are evaluated subjectively. It is more important to ask whether the clusters make sense for our use case than it is to optimize numeric metrics, such as inertia.

The "elbow method" concept is best illustrated visually. The following code runs the k-means algorithm from 3 up to 15 groups and plots the associated inertia scores, shown in figure 13.7:

```python
from sklearn.cluster import KMeans

k_values = range(3, 15)
inertia_values = []

for k in k_values:
    kmeans = KMeans(n_clusters=k, random_state=42)
    kmeans.fit(X_scaled)
    inertia_values.append(kmeans.inertia_)

fig, axis = plt.subplots()

axis.plot(k_values, inertia_values)

_ = axis.set(
    title="'Inertia' values for different values of k",
    xlabel="Number of clusters (the 'k' in k-means)",
    ylabel="Inertia"
)

axis.set_ybound(0, 900)

plt.show()
```

This shows a typical scenario where adding a cluster when there are few clusters significantly decreases the inertia value, but this pattern does not continue. In figure 13.7,

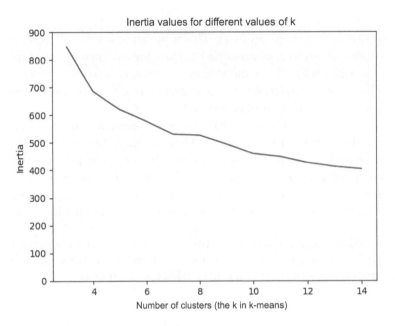

Figure 13.7   The result of clustering with a different number of groups

going from seven to eight clusters barely reduces the inertia score. Most of the time, these plots look like arms, and we're looking for the elbow, the inflection point, after which the slope of the line flatlines. In the case of figure 13.7, we will use seven as the inflection point and, therefore, start with seven clusters. Figure 13.8 shows the process with this latest decision added.

Let's apply k-means clustering to our data, choosing seven clusters to create. We'll use scikit-learn for this, the popular Python library for machine learning. We will create a k-means clustering object, apply it to the data, and create a new column in our user table, recording which of the seven clusters each user belongs to. The following code does this, and figure 13.9 shows a snapshot of the enhanced user table. Again, the data is transposed so we can see values for all columns:

```
kmeans = KMeans(n_clusters=7, random_state=42)
clusters = kmeans.fit_predict(X_scaled)
users["cluster"] = clusters

users.head().transpose()
```

Figure 13.9 shows the initial user data with all the dimensions as well as a new cluster assignment. It tells us that user 0 was assigned to cluster 3, users 1–3 were assigned to cluster 6, and so on. We will use this new column to evaluate the results.

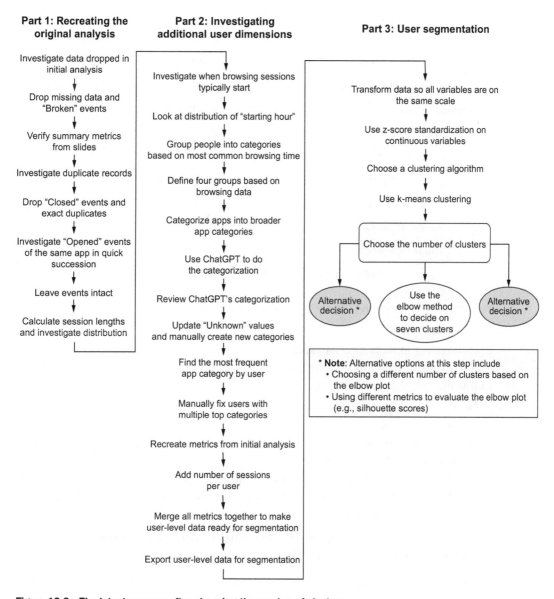

Part 1: Recreating the original analysis

Investigate data dropped in initial analysis
↓
Drop missing data and "Broken" events
↓
Verify summary metrics from slides
↓
Investigate duplicate records
↓
Drop "Closed" events and exact duplicates
↓
Investigate "Opened" events of the same app in quick succession
↓
Leave events intact
↓
Calculate session lengths and investigate distribution

Part 2: Investigating additional user dimensions

Investigate when browsing sessions typically start
↓
Look at distribution of "starting hour"
↓
Group people into categories based on most common browsing time
↓
Define four groups based on browsing data
↓
Categorize apps into broader app categories
↓
Use ChatGPT to do the categorization
↓
Review ChatGPT's categorization
↓
Update "Unknown" values and manually create new categories
↓
Find the most frequent app category by user
↓
Manually fix users with multiple top categories
↓
Recreate metrics from initial analysis
↓
Add number of sessions per user
↓
Merge all metrics together to make user-level data ready for segmentation
↓
Export user-level data for segmentation

Part 3: User segmentation

Transform data so all variables are on the same scale
↓
Use z-score standardization on continuous variables
↓
Choose a clustering algorithm
↓
Use k-means clustering
↓
Choose the number of clusters

Alternative decision *   Use the elbow method to decide on seven clusters   Alternative decision *

* Note: Alternative options at this step include
• Choosing a different number of clusters based on the elbow plot
• Using different metrics to evaluate the elbow plot (e.g., silhouette scores)

Figure 13.8   The latest process after choosing the number of clusters

	0	1	2	3	4
user_id	0.000000	1.000000	2.000000	3.000000	4.000000
time_night_owl	1.000000	0.000000	0.000000	0.000000	1.000000
time_early_morning_browser	0.000000	0.000000	1.000000	0.000000	0.000000
time_midday_browser	0.000000	0.000000	0.000000	0.000000	0.000000
time_late_day_browser	1.000000	1.000000	0.000000	1.000000	0.000000
app_category_Browsing	0.000000	0.000000	0.000000	0.000000	0.000000
app_category_Entertainment	1.000000	0.000000	0.000000	0.000000	0.000000
app_category_Money	0.000000	0.000000	0.000000	1.000000	0.000000
app_category_Social	0.000000	1.000000	1.000000	0.000000	1.000000
app_category_Utility	0.000000	0.000000	0.000000	0.000000	0.000000
number_of_apps	19.000000	18.000000	16.000000	15.000000	8.000000
number_of_sessions	238.000000	88.000000	61.000000	70.000000	45.000000
avg_session_length	0.658333	1.483333	0.533333	0.116667	0.233333
cluster	3.000000	6.000000	6.000000	6.000000	2.000000

Figure 13.9   Five rows of user data with added cluster assignments

EVALUATING THE RESULTS OF CLUSTERING

Once the clustering has finished, we want to evaluate our results, which means the following:

- Investigating the center of each cluster (i.e., what does a typical user in each group look like?).
- Looking at the spread of values for each cluster (i.e., what are typical characteristics for all users in a group?).
- Understanding whether clusters are distinct from each other. We don't want a situation where we create two clusters that are similar. We want each group to be distinctive somehow.

First, let's see how many users are in each cluster. The following code does this and produces the output in figure 13.10:

```
users["cluster"].value_counts().sort_index()
```

One thing we immediately notice is that there are two clusters with only two or three users in each. This either means those users are truly different from the others or that we need fewer clusters. One downside of a method like k-means is that asking it to create seven clusters will create seven clusters, whether or not that's warranted. Let's look

```
0     42
1     31
2     60
3     78
4      3
5      2
6     75
Name: cluster, dtype: int64
```

Figure 13.10   Number of users per cluster

at the clusters' centers, which tell us the average of each group, which we can use as a proxy for what a typical user looks like in each segment.

One thing we need to remember to do is *reverse* the transformation we did earlier to our continuous columns so that the cluster centers are on the same scale as our input data. Otherwise, the number of apps, number of sessions, and average session length would all be approximately between –3 and 3..

The following code does this reverse transformation and prints out the center values for each cluster, which is shown in figure 13.11:

```
import numpy as np

original_cluster_centers
⇒ = np.copy(kmeans.cluster_centers_)
```

Makes a copy of the cluster centers so we don't modify them by accident

```
cluster_centers = pd.DataFrame(
    data=original_cluster_centers,
    columns=X_scaled.columns
)
```

Reverses the transformation only for the continuous columns, leaving the binary ones intact

```
cluster_centers.loc[:,continuous_features]
⇒ = scaler.inverse_transform(original_cluster_centers[:,-3:])

cluster_centers.transpose().round(2)
```

What this shows us is that, for example, reading down the first column, in cluster 0, 48% of the users are night owls, 76% of them mostly use their phones for social purposes, and they average 107 unique sessions.

Clusters 4 and 5 only had two to three users. It looks like one reason why cluster 4 is a cluster of its own is that it is where the most extreme users are in terms of the number of sessions as the average is over 3,000. Cluster 5 looks like it represents users who have the longest session lengths, an average of 9.79 minutes. Based on these findings, we will decide to keep all seven clusters as they seem to represent different kinds of users.

The next step is to give each group a persona to describe them. For example, cluster 1 contains users with a lot of sessions and a high number of apps; they mostly use their phones for social media and are either late-day or night browsers. This seems

	0	1	2	3	4	5	6
time_night_owl	0.48	0.45	0.33	1.00	0.00	0.00	0.00
time_early_morning_browser	0.24	0.06	0.17	0.05	0.00	0.00	0.19
time_midday_browser	0.17	0.03	0.32	0.04	0.67	0.00	0.36
time_late_day_browser	0.36	0.48	0.53	0.22	0.33	1.00	0.60
app_category_Browsing	0.10	0.00	0.43	0.05	0.00	0.00	0.05
app_category_Entertainment	0.05	-0.00	0.13	0.05	0.00	0.00	0.03
app_category_Money	0.05	0.00	-0.00	0.05	0.00	0.00	0.08
app_category_Social	0.76	0.97	0.28	0.79	1.00	1.00	0.83
app_category_Utility	0.05	0.03	0.15	0.05	0.00	0.00	0.01
number_of_apps	15.64	24.35	7.18	18.18	27.33	19.50	17.61
number_of_sessions	107.00	893.48	39.70	185.08	3646.33	180.50	177.21
avg_session_length	3.59	2.47	0.62	1.21	1.70	9.79	1.03

Figure 13.11   Cluster centers and their associated properties

like a distinctive persona: someone who comes home from work and spends their phone time mostly socializing.

Another clear persona would be cluster 2, which contains more casual users. They have a low number of total sessions, which are generally short; they use their phones mostly for browsing and only use seven different apps on average. Users in cluster 6 browse more during the day but average shorter sessions. Perhaps they're people who use social media apps during their lunch break at work. Let's summarize the possible personas. This summary is shown in table 13.2.

Table 13.2   Summary of user personas

Group	Persona name	Persona characteristics
0	Typical social users	Average number of sessions, mostly social media, mostly late in the day and at night
1	Heavy users	High number of sessions and apps used, mostly social media, mostly late in the day and at night
2	Casual users	Low number of sessions and apps, short usage sessions, mostly for browsing
3	Night owls	All night owls, mostly social media use
4	Usage outliers	Averaging over 3,600 sessions in total over the period

Table 13.2   Summary of user personas *(continued)*

Group	Persona name	Persona characteristics
5	Session length outliers	Averaging almost 10 minutes per usage session
6	Evening social users	Average number of sessions, short usage sessions, mostly for social media, mostly late in the day

From this table, we can give each group a persona based on their statistics, but we may think there are groups that are similar and could be merged. For example, clusters 0 and 6 are not that different. You might do some of that additional merging before presenting to your stakeholders, or it might be done with their input. Either way, these kinds of subjective evaluations are how we would determine whether seven clusters was a good fit in this case.

Before summarizing our findings and discussing the next steps, let's revisit our entire process. We completed several steps from recreating the initial analysis to performing our own, and finally creating new customer segments. Figure 13.12 shows the entire process visualized.

Let's now summarize our findings and decide on the next steps.

13.1.5   *Conclusions and next steps*

In the end, adding the dimensions our stakeholders were interested in allowed us to create increasingly complex user segments. These formed our minimum viable answer. The important question is whether our findings will lead to actions. What can the business do with these customer segments? Because the company's business model is to sell these insights to mobile manufacturers and app developers, we can imagine some ways in which they could use this information:

- Having a more precise way of defining "heavy users" could help create interventions for those who use their phones too much.
- Understanding who the "casual" users are means better targeting of intermediate content (e.g., how to get the best out of your mobile).
- Having separate user segments for those who primarily use their phones for social media could lead to better targeting of other social media apps.

An important aspect of this project to realize is that our clusters were driven entirely based on our decisions. Our data manipulation choices, the choice of variables, and the choice of clustering algorithm all contributed to the final solution. A change in any of those decisions would have created different groupings. This is why collaboration with stakeholders is so important. They are the ones who can help make the decisions that create the most relevant outcomes.

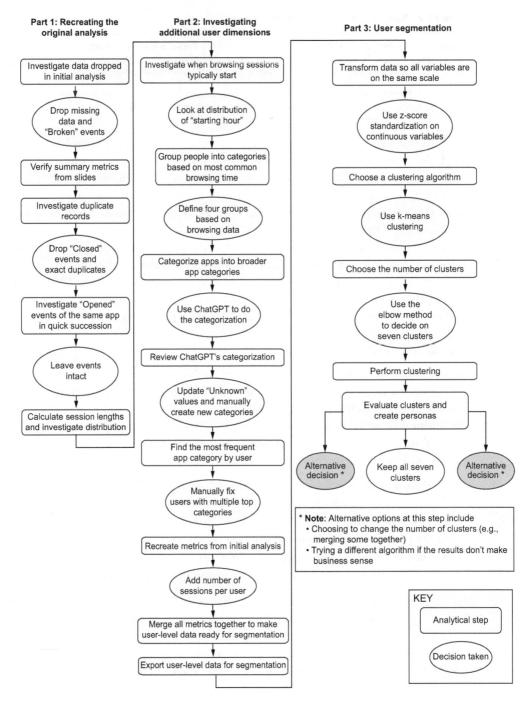

Figure 13.12   Diagram of the entire process

Presentation skills

Presenting your results as an analyst is something that comes with practice. It requires many interactions with people in a real context (i.e., in the context of an analysis they care about). The skills necessary to do this well include the ability to

- Understand your audience, their motivations, their existing understanding, and so forth
- Empathize with your audience and tailor your message
- Summarize your findings in a relevant way
- Tell the story of your analysis

This last point broadly comes under something called "data storytelling," which contains a collection of related skills. For more information, see *The Data Storyteller's Handbook* by Kat Greenbrook (Rogue Korora, 2023).

The best way to hone these skills is to present your results to a relevant audience. Getting real-time feedback from an audience is extremely valuable for improving as a presenter. Another related way is to give talks at meetups and conferences. This will help you practice communicating your expertise in a topic with confidence. Finally, building a project portfolio can be valuable in discussions with hiring managers.

What about additional work? Although there are few columns, the data is rich enough for further iterations. One idea might be to infer a user's mobile operating system. If they used the Google app, they're likely on an Android device, whereas using Apple apps would mean they're on iOS. This distinction might change the makeup of our user segments.

We also didn't make full use of the individual event-level aspect of the data. We could look at time spent on individual apps, number of times apps are opened and closed, whether there is variation in how often people switch apps, and so on. All of these considerations could give us richer user segments to explore.

One caveat of the data, which we somewhat sidestepped, is that sessions don't start and end cleanly. Sometimes, a session ends with an "Opened" event, and another starts just a few minutes later. If we wanted to explore sessions and events in more detail, we would want to clean up those sessions in more depth.

Activity: Further project ideas with this data

Think about other analyses you could do with this dataset. Here are some directions you may want to consider:

- What does app-level behavior look like for different people? Do people use different apps differently?
- What are the most popular apps in each category?
- What does the adoption rate look like in our user base for new apps? Are there any ways to enhance your data with external sources to better answer this question?

13.2 Closing thoughts: Segmentation and clustering

The skills you practiced in this project to segment users are relevant to all kinds of real-world scenarios. Segmentation comes up in many domains. Whether you want to find similar customers, microwaves, or crops, the underlying ideas are the same.

To be prepared for any clustering project in the future, it is useful to be acquainted with

- Some of the different clustering algorithms and in what scenario each is more useful
- Preprocessing techniques for unsupervised machine learning, such as the standardization we performed in this project
- Evaluation metrics, such as the inertia score we measured earlier, or more advanced concepts such as silhouette scores
- The subjective evaluation process whereby we decide whether a set of clusters is appropriate for the given business case

Having at least a surface-level familiarity with these concepts means that when you encounter a relevant project in real life, you will be able to identify clustering as an appropriate method as well as research more deeply the aspects you need to produce a minimum viable answer.

As always, the best way to hone these skills is by practicing them, so if you encounter a problem in real life where clustering is a relevant approach, use it as an opportunity to put your skills to the test.

13.2.1 Skills learned to use for any project

Let's recap the various aspects of this latest project and the skills required to complete it. To successfully continue someone else's existing analysis, the key skills that can be applied to any similar project include

- Verifying existing calculations (e.g., for reported summary metrics such as averages)
- Rerunning the existing analysis code, if available, to verify the findings
- Documenting assumptions and decisions made by previous analysts on the project

To segment records, such as customers, into distinct groups, the key skills, which apply to any such project, include

- Creating a dataset at the right level of granularity (e.g., a user-level dataset if segmenting users)
- Transforming data that is input to a clustering algorithm to all be on the same scale
- Choosing an appropriate clustering algorithm
- Using an appropriate tool to run the chosen clustering algorithm on the data
- Evaluating the results both numerically (e.g., by looking at inertia scores, and subjectively by seeing if clusters make sense from a domain expertise perspective)

Summary

- Segmentation/clustering algorithms have a wide applicability for data problems.
- Decisions we make, such as the number of clusters or what variables to include to determine them, will radically alter the outcome of a clustering algorithm.
- Tasks such as user segmentation require subjective human evaluation.
- Giving clusters personas helps identify their key characteristics.

appendix
Python installation instructions

The projects in the book are technology agnostic, and the example solutions are mostly about the process, not the specifics of Python, which is my technology of choice. However, if you are a Python user like me, you might want to recreate my results on your machine and take my example solution as a starting point. This appendix explains how to install Python and set it up in a way that mimics the setup I used for the example solutions.

Usually, the Python libraries required for a project are listed in the accompanying Jupyter notebooks and can be inferred from the `import` statements. That is, if the code in a solution imports `pandas`, you will need to have installed the `pandas` library. However, to recreate my examples exactly, you need to have the same version of each library as functionality changes across versions. There are many ways to ensure your Python environment is set up the same as mine, but generally, this is done using virtual environments.

> **NOTE** It is not necessary to have exactly the same setup to recreate the solutions in the book. You can likely use a newer Python version and newer versions of libraries such as `pandas` and get the same results. However, the virtual environments are explicitly pinned to older versions of both Python and the necessary libraries to ensure compatibility with each other. An example is the `recordlinkage` library used in chapter 3, which at time of writing is incompatible with `pandas` version 2.0.

Virtual environments let you have multiple combinations of Python libraries, even different versions of Python, on the same machine, usually one per project. I recommend creating a virtual environment in which you can run the accompanying code examples and ensure your libraries have the same versions as mine. Again, there are many ways to set up virtual environments. You may already have your favorite way to do this, or you may have never encountered virtual environments before. In this book, I use the `poetry` library, and the following sections include instructions to recreate my environment.

A.1 Installing Python

Specifically, the projects in the book use Python 3.11, but that is only a requirement if you want to recreate the example solutions exactly. If you have a different version of Python already installed, but want to recreate my environment, you can install Python 3.11 anyway as it will be separate from other Python installations.

You can either install Python directly from Python.org (https://www.python.org/downloads/) or through a bundled version, such as Anaconda (https://www.anaconda.com/download). You can also install Python through a minimal version of Anaconda, such as Miniconda (https://docs.conda.io/en/latest/miniconda.html) or Miniforge (https://github.com/conda-forge/miniforge).

I personally use Miniforge, but as long as the end result is that you have Python 3.11 installed on your machine, it doesn't matter where you got it from.

A.2 Installing poetry

`poetry` is the package and dependency management system I chose to manage my virtual environments. You can install it with your Python installation using whichever in-built package manager you have (usually `pip` or `conda`). An example command, which should be run in a terminal or command prompt, is `pip install poetry`.

> **NOTE** If you use a different method for managing virtual environments, such as `virtualenv`, I have also included a `requirements.txt` file, which contains the same information as the `poetry` files, but it is the format required for these other tools. This will still require that you use Python 3.11.

More information about `poetry` is available at https://python-poetry.org/.

A.3 Creating your virtual environment

In the materials for the book, I have supplied two files, `poetry.lock` and `pyproject.toml`, both of which you need to recreate my virtual environment with the same versions of all necessary libraries. At the time of writing, you simply need to have those two files in the root folder where you have downloaded the code for the book.

First, navigate to your code folder where these files reside and run the following command to ensure `poetry` uses Python 3.11, regardless of what other versions exist on your machine. An example of a command prompt is shown in figure A.1:

```
poetry env use /path/to/your/python3.11/python.exe
```

```
(base) c:\git\book-code>poetry env use C:\Users\david\AppData\Local\Programs\Python\Python311\python.exe
Creating virtualenv the-well-grounded-data-analyst-4Rz7GTVT-py3.11 in C:\Users\david\AppData\Local\pypoe
try\Cache\virtualenvs
Using virtualenv: C:\Users\david\AppData\Local\pypoetry\Cache\virtualenvs\the-well-grounded-data-analyst
-4Rz7GTVT-py3.11
```

Figure A.1   Command to tell `poetry` where Python 3.11 is installed

Next, run the command `poetry install` to create your virtual environment. The correct versions of the necessary libraries will be installed. Figure A.2 shows what the output might look like.

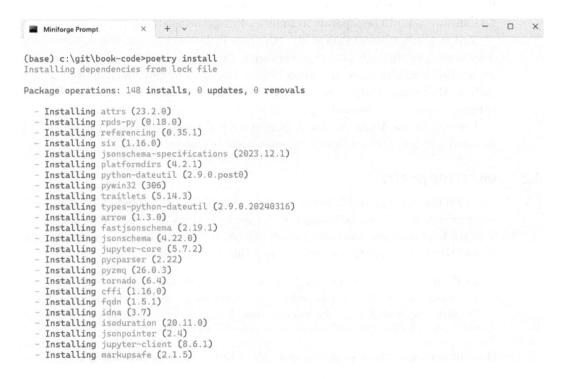

Figure A.2   Installing the `poetry` environment and associated libraries

At this point, you have a virtual environment that is set up the same as mine. You can activate it by running the command `poetry shell`.

This will activate the environment, and any subsequent Python commands will run in this environment instead of the base one. From here, you can launch Jupyter using the command `jupyter notebook`. This will launch Jupyter, and you can interact with the code using the correct versions of Python and its libraries. Figure A.3 shows the final `poetry` commands before launching Jupyter.

```
(base) c:\git\book-code>poetry shell
Spawning shell within C:\Users\david\AppData\Local\pypoetry\Cache\virtualenvs\the
-well-grounded-data-analyst-4Rz7GTVT-py3.11

(the-well-grounded-data-analyst-py3.11) (base) c:\git\book-code>jupyter notebook
[I 2024-12-16 17:19:30.070 ServerApp] Extension package jupyter_lsp took 0.3439s
to import
[I 2024-12-16 17:19:30.290 ServerApp] Extension package jupyter_server_terminals
took 0.2189s to import
[I 2024-12-16 17:19:30.536 ServerApp] jupyter_lsp | extension was successfully li
nked.
[I 2024-12-16 17:19:30.547 ServerApp] jupyter_server_terminals | extension was su
ccessfully linked.
[I 2024-12-16 17:19:30.553 ServerApp] jupyterlab | extension was successfully lin
ked.
[I 2024-12-16 17:19:30.553 ServerApp] notebook | extension was successfully linke
d.
[I 2024-12-16 17:19:35.020 ServerApp] notebook_shim | extension was successfully
linked.
[I 2024-12-16 17:19:35.158 ServerApp] notebook_shim | extension was successfully
loaded.
[I 2024-12-16 17:19:35.166 ServerApp] jupyter_lsp | extension was successfully lo
aded.
[I 2024-12-16 17:19:35.166 ServerApp] jupyter_server_terminals | extension was su
ccessfully loaded.
```

Figure A.3   Launching Jupyter from the `poetry` **environment**

index